HOW TO WATCH THE OLYMPICS

Scores and laws, heroes and zeros –
an instant initiation into every sport

DAVID GOLDBLATT and JOHNNY ACTON

with PAUL SIMPSON

Diagrams by Belinda Evans

P

PROFILE BOOKS

This new expanded and updated edition
published in 2016 by

PROFILE BOOKS LTD
3 Holford Yard
Bevin Way
London WC1X 9HD
www.profilebooks.com

A CIP catalogue record for this book is available from the British Library.

ISBN 978-1781251034

Printed and bound in Great Britain by
Clays, St Ives plc

CONTENTS

INTRODUCTION

For two and a half weeks every fourth summer, the planet reliably goes sports crazy. The most watched event in history wasn't the 1969 moon landing, the episode of *Dallas* which revealed who shot JR, or Charles and Di's wedding. It was the opening ceremony of the Beijing Summer Olympic Games. Over a billion people tuned in to at least part of the extravaganza. In 2012, with much of Asia asleep when the London Olympics kicked off, that figure slipped slightly, to 900 million. But 4.8 billion of us – some 70 per cent of the world's population – tuned in to watch the sports at some point over the next seventeen days.

In August 2016, we will all be at it again. Yet if we're honest, there's a gaping hole at the heart of the Olympic experience: most of us know remarkably little about most of the sports we've suddenly gone nuts about. Of course, you could just plonk yourself down on a sofa and keep your eyes open. No harm in any of that, but to get the most out of the Olympics it really helps to know HOW TO WATCH the proceedings. Which is where this book comes in: a training programme for the Olympics, or, to be precise, a five-point-plan of crucial need-to-know information for each sport.

The first, overarching question is WHY WATCH any given sport? Why exactly do South Koreans turn out in their tens of thousands to watch the nation's leading archers? Why do Turks venerate a 4ft 11in weightlifter? Are they all mad? Sometimes, the thrill is straightforward. Other times, you need to know the STORY OF A SPORT – why it has mattered and to whom. Only then will you grasp why Denmark comes to a standstill during the women's handball or why it seems so terribly important to the Hungarians to beat the Russians in that water polo match.

Next, you need a grasp of the BASICS. To make sense of what is going on, you have to know the object of the exercise and understand the constraints the participants are operating under. How does one win, lose and score ... and how long will it all go on for? In other words, you've got to know THE RULES. Once you've cleared this hurdle, you are ready to take on board some of the FINER POINTS. This will enhance your enjoyment immeasurably. Understanding the different spins, for example, will improve your experience of table tennis no end. Appreciating the tactical stratagems of basketball will turn the blur of bodies into a sharply focused and thrilling encounter. At this point, you will be in good enough shape to move on to the OLYMPIC HISTORY of the sport. This section provides historical context and introduces you to the legends, scandals and rivalries, showing how the sport's trajectory at the Games has reflected and occasionally shaped our times.

Finally, there are some Olympic topics that are so interesting, controversial or otherwise important that they merit sections of their own. You will find the main text sprinkled with features devoted to everything from the history of drugs in weightlifting to the peculiar antics of the man who popularised recreational canoeing and the Brazilian nation's perplexing inability to win the Olympic football tournament. Oh – and there's a useful appendix at the end of the book listing the 27 PREVIOUS OLYMPIC GAMES, with details of their host cities, their key events ... and, naturally, their mascots.

We hope you will treat this book as an amusing, knowledgeable and bizarrely passionate friend – on hand to help you get the most out of the Games. We realise you're not an expert on the finer points of dressage; we won't laugh at you if you confuse a kayak with a canoe; and we know there's something faintly ridiculous about competitive walking, or a cycling race in which the competitors can sit still on their bikes for half an hour. But we have the greatest respect for what THE GAMES are about – a cosmopolitan celebration of humanity, a demonstration of the universal power of sport and play, a showcase for the wonders of the human body and spirit – and we want to help you to enjoy them.

ps: the IOC

Olympic sports are littered with JARGON and ACRONYMS. You don't need to know the half of it to enjoy the sports, though where you do, you'll find the low-down under the relevant section of this book. The one key acronym, which crops up in any discussion of the Olympics, is the IOC. This is the INTERNATIONAL OLYMPIC COMMITTEE, created by BARON PIERRE DE COUBERTIN in 1894 to oversee what we know as the 'modern Olympics'. The IOC is made up of senior figures from international sports federations (Sebastian Coe from the IAAF, for example), prominent former Olympians, and the great and the good (it helps to have a royal connection). The IOC runs both the Summer and Winter Games, selects the host cities and approves the inclusion of new and existing sports (each of which are governed by their own international federations).

There are also 206 NATIONAL OLYMPIC COMMITTEES, which organise their countries' teams and officials. Their number is rather more than the 193 states represented at the UN, as it includes such 'nations' as Aruba, Guam and Cook Islands. Palestine is also recognised as an Olympic nation. At Rio, for the first time, refugees will compete in the Games under the IOC's own flag.

THE OPENING CEREMONY

5 AUGUST 2016

MARACANÃ STADIUM, RIO DE JANEIRO

Athletes: 12,000 (if they all show up)

-------------------------------- **OLYMPIC PRESENCE** --------------------------------

THE 1896 GAMES OPENED WITH SPEECHES AND HYMNS. PARIS failed to put on an opening ceremony in 1900 and ST LOUIS wasn't much better in 1904. But since LONDON 1908 the ceremony has been a permanent fixture.

-------------------------------- **OLYMPIC FORMAT** --------------------------------

LIKE SYNCHRONISED SWIMMING AND DIVING, THE OPENING ceremony has a fixed and a free programme. The fixed programme is set by Olympic protocol and includes a parade of athletes, flames, torches, flags and oaths. The free section is open to artistic interpretation by the host city.

-------------------------------- **PAST CHAMPIONS** --------------------------------

LONDON: 3 | PARIS, ATHENS, LOS ANGELES: 2 EACH.

WHY WATCH THE OPENING CEREMONY?

WHAT EVENT GETS THE BIGGEST TV AUDIENCE AT EVERY Olympics? Which tickets are the most oversubscribed? The OPENING CEREMONY of course. It is the moment at which after four years and more of relentless hype, cynicism, argument, scandal and uncertainty the curtain finally goes up. And it's a show that has changed out of all recognition since its first appearance at the 1896 Games, becoming along the way a strange amalgam of global ritual, military march-past, TV spectacular, Broadway musical and circus.

The ARTISTIC PROGRAMME, with which an Olympic opening ceremony begins, can be seen as a costumed folly or as a projection of the host nation's self-image – or both. And after that, there are the old favourites of the COMPULSORY PROGRAMME to look forward to – the PARADE OF NATIONS, the ARRIVAL OF THE OLYMPIC FLAG, the LIGHTING OF THE CAULDRON. The pleasures here are many: the extraordinary national costumes of the athletes, the partisan response of crowds to a nation's foes, friends and favourites … and, not least, the possibility that something might go a bit wrong.

OPENING CEREMONY BASICS

IF THE OPENING CEREMONY FOR RIO 2016 IS TO BEDAZZLE the world, it will be a triumph of creativity, originality and making do on a budget of around $4 million, roughly a tenth of what was spent at London 2012. This means that China will surely retain the dubious record of staging the most expensive Olympic opening ceremony ever: the Beijing 2008 event featured over 15,000 performers and cost around $100 million. In Rio, the creative responsibility is shared by three of Brazil's most famous film directors: FERNANDO MEIRELLES (*City Of God*, *The Constant Gardener*), DANIELA THOMAS (who had a hand in Rio's bit of the 2012 closing ceremony) and ANDRUCHA WADDINGTON, who is best known for his 2005 drama *House of Sand*. Little has leaked as to what will be on show in Rio. There is talk of street culture and a Rio carnival vibe but the organisers insist there will be no clichés. Here's a taste of the main ingredients …

THE ARTISTIC PROGRAMME

IN THE ERA OF THE GIGANTIC STADIUM SCREEN AND GLOBAL television coverage the opening ceremony of the Olympic Games is choreographed down to the last detail. This even applies to the

THE BRITISH MAKE A BID FOR PILLOW FIGHTING AS AN OLYMPIC SPORT (AND WAVE A FLAG FOR THE NHS) IN DANNY BOYLE'S LONDON 2012 SPECTACULAR

COUNTDOWN to the start of the show. At BEIJING 2008 LED-embedded drums not only beat out the seconds in the countdown to the Games but spelled out the numbers themselves in Chinese and Arabic numerals.

Once we reach zero it really is anyone's guess what's coming next. Since MOSCOW 1980 raised the stakes with a gigantic, apparently endless, array of formation dancing, marching and gymnastics and a cast of many thousands, the artistic programme has run riot. LOS ANGELES 1984 opened with the entire stadium holding up coloured squares to form the flags of each participating nation; SEOUL 1988 started in the middle of a river; and LONDON 2012 appeared to feature THE QUEEN sky-diving from a helicopter with a little help from Daniel Craig as James Bond. Thematically, the ambition has often been overweening – the story of humanity, five millennia of Chinese history, a treatise on balance and entropy in the universe.

THE COMPULSORY PROGRAMME

············· **ATHLETES ON PARADE** ·············

THE ARTISTIC PROGRAMME IS FINALLY DONE. THE LAST MIME artistes and creatures from the black lagoon have gone. It's time for the athletes. The form now is for each team to be led out by a STANDARD-BEARER provided by the hosts plus a team member who carries the national flag. The GREEKS always open proceedings and the HOSTS bring up the rear. In between, countries go in alphabetical order according to the host language. It's once around the track and then the teams line up in the centre of the stadium. The costumes worn by the (usually female) standard-bearers have often proved divertingly kitsch, as at SEOUL 1988, where they were decked out in white leather boots and peaked caps.

The response of the crowd to the teams is always interesting. ATHENS 2004 proved particularly partisan, with Turks, Israelis and Macedonians all getting the silent treatment while the Palestinians and the Serbs received very positive vibes. The biggest cheers were reserved for Greece, countries with big Greek populations like Cyprus and Australia, and war-torn Afghanistan and Iraq. The marathon of athletes from more than two hundred nations can be wearying – at LONDON 2012, the Queen looked to have dozed off by the time Great Britain's team closed the parade to the tune of David Bowie's '"Heroes"'.

············· **THE SPEECHES** ·············

NOW FOR THE SPEECHES: THREE OF THEM! PRESUMABLY THEY are scheduled at this point to give the audience a chance to get a drink or go to the toilet after the parade. There'll be something anodyne from the head of the local organising committee and something in a similar vein from the PRESIDENT OF THE IOC – it is their Olympics after all. Finally, the host's head of state or their representative declares the Games open. Mercifully, there is strict protocol on what the head of state can say, and it isn't much.

···································· **THE OLYMPIC ANTHEM** ····································

SOMETIMES THEY PLAY THE OLYMPIC ANTHEM NEXT, SOMETIMES they play it while the flag is raised or immediately afterwards. Either way they are going to make damn sure that it gets a hearing. The anthem was composed for the first modern Games in 1896 with music by SPIROS SAMARAS and words by the poet KOSTIS PALAMAS, but it didn't become a fixed feature of the ceremony until 1960. Some hosts, like the Chinese in 2008, go with the original Greek version; others get it translated into their own language, like the Italians at ROME 1960 or the Japanese version sung at TOKYO 1964. Language politics being a complicated thing in Spain, at BARCELONA 1992 the anthem was sung in a combination of Catalan, Spanish and French. In 2012, the London Symphony Orchestra and the Grimethorpe Colliery Band collaborated on an instrumental version, following a precedent set at MUNICH 1972. In Anglophone countries an English version has been sung, with various attempts to put old-school Greek poesy into some kind of plausible modern English. It does go on rather, with a lot of choral work, but the first two stanzas should give you the drift of things:

Immortal spirit of antiquity
Father of the true, beautiful and good
Descend, appear, shed over us thy light
Upon this ground and under this sky
Which has first witnessed thy unperishable fame

Give life and animation to these noble games!
Throw wreaths of fadeless flowers to the victors
In the race and in the strife
Create in our breasts, hearts of steel!

···································· **FLY THE FLAG** ····································

THE FLAG IS UP NEXT AND IT IS INVARIABLY CARRIED BY A selection of the host nation's great Olympians (eight seems to be the preferred number for ease of manoeuvre). Outfits vary, but all-white has been the look most organising committees have gone for. At 2012, the diverse cast of flag-bearers encompassed Muhammad Ali, UN secretary general Ban Ki-moon and Doreen Lawrence, the mother of murdered black teenager Stephen Lawrence.

FLAME ON

IN THE ANCIENT OLYMPICS, FIRE – STOLEN BY PROMETHEUS for humankind, or so the myth goes – burned throughout the Games at a sanctuary dedicated to the goddess Hestia. And it is from the site of her temple that the flame is ignited for the modern Games and carried by relay to each host city. In keeping with tradition, the torch continues to be lit by the final torchbearer, but there has been a turn towards novelty acts. In 1992 BARCELONA's flame was lit by the flight of a flaming arrow. At SYDNEY 2000 the cauldron was ignited by a flame that passed through water. In BEIJING a gymnast was flown by wire around the stadium before lighting a long fuse that initiated the conflagration. In LONDON, the torch first came into a view on a boat piloted down the Thames

FORTUNATELY, LIVE PIGEON SHOOTING WAS NO LONGER A SPORT AT LA 1932

by DAVID BECKHAM looking as if he was auditioning to succeed Craig as 007.

Whatever the method, the lighting of the cauldron is a peak moment of the ceremony. Over the years, the criteria used to decide who should be the final torchbearer have varied wildly. GIANCARLO PERIS lit the flame in ROME in 1960 having won a junior cross-country race to secure the honour. In TOKYO in 1964 YOSHINORI SAKAI was chosen as he was born on the day the Hiroshima bomb was exploded. MONTREAL 1976 opted for two teenage torchbearers representing French and English speaking Canada – a symbolic point that did not go unnoticed among First Nation Canadians. Leading Olympians have made obvious choices, like PAAVO NURMI at HELSINKI in 1952. The selection of the aboriginal Australian runner CATHY FREEMAN at SYDNEY 2000 and MUHAMMAD ALI in 1996 at ATLANTA were acknowledgements of the contested ethnic and national identities of the hosts.

############## **CATCH THE DOVES** ##############

THE TIME-HONOURED TRADITION OF DOVES BEING RELEASED before the lighting of the Olympic flame came to a grisly end in SEOUL 1988 when many of the birds came to rest on the rim of the Olympic cauldron and were incinerated when it was lit. The dove moment now follows the lighting of the flame. At BEIJING, the Chinese dispensed with the birds altogether, and symbolically substituted them with yellow fireworks. At London 2012, DANNY BOYLE, the opening ceremony's impresario, preferred 75 'dove bikes', ascending into the air on high wires, a spectacle inspired by American naturalist Louis Helle who once declared: 'Bicycling is the nearest approximation I know to the flight of birds.'

############## **NO CHEATIN', PROMISE!** ##############

NEXT UP ARE THE ATHLETE'S AND OFFICIAL'S OLYMPIC OATHS. They are taken by one person on behalf of everyone, sometimes while holding a corner of the Olympic flag. The athlete's oath was first said at the 1920 Games, while 1972 saw the introduction of the official's oath. Time has not been kind to the language of the Olympic oath. The first version, taken by the Belgian swimmer, water polo player and fencer VICTOR BOIN, had a certain old-fashioned grace:

> We swear, we will take part in the Olympic Games in a spirit of
> chivalry, for the honour of our country and for the glory of sport.

The most recent version has been amended by committee:

> In the name of all the competitors I promise that we shall take
> part in these Olympic Games, respecting and abiding by the rules
> which govern them, committing ourselves to a sport without
> doping and without drugs, in the true spirit of sportsmanship, for
> the glory of sport and the honour of our teams.

At LA 1984 hurdler EDWIN MOSES stalled midway through the oath and was forced to repeat the same sentence three times before he finally remembered the rest of the oath. Today's autocues make a repeat of the incident unlikely.

·································· **FIREWORKS AND MIMING** ··································

IT'S BECOME STANDARD FOR EACH OLYMPIC OPENING CEREMONY to culminate in a FIREWORK DISPLAY. These have grown progressively long, loud, large and expensive – though it is hard to imagine how any display could surpass the gigantic cascades of colour coming from the roof of the Bird's Nest stadium at BEIJING 2008. That said, most of the world saw a computer-generated version of the display on TV, the organisers having panicked that weather conditions might adversely affect the real one. And as stupendous as the LONDON 2012 fireworks were, they were slightly upstaged by a glimpse of a green, saucer-shaped UFO in the Stratford sky (check the photos online if you're curious) bringing aliens to the Games for the first time.

The obsessive control freakery exhibited in Beijing had been foreshadowed at SYDNEY 2000, where the SYDNEY SYMPHONY ORCHESTRA mimed its way through the ceremony. Eight years later, the singer LIN MIAOKE mimed as the Chinese flag entered the stadium. The real singer – a seven-year-old girl with buck teeth – was not considered suitable for display.

THE OPENING CEREMONY STORY

CEREMONIALLY, THE MODERN OLYMPICS GOT UNDERWAY WITH the unveiling of a statue of Georgios Averoff, the Greek tycoon who footed the bill for the 1896 ATHENS GAMES. Dues paid, a few days later the focus moved on to the Olympic stadium, where 80,000 spectators endured a series of speeches before the massed bands of the Greek army, navy, Athenian municipalities and far-flung provinces struck up the newly composed OLYMPIC HYMN. A quick blast from the trumpet followed, the athletes arrived and the Games began.

In PARIS in 1900, there was no opening ceremony of any kind. The Olympics had been reduced to a small athletic sideshow – a lost and chaotic component of the much grander WORLD FAIR that was running concurrently. Things barely improved at ST LOUIS in 1904. This time the Games were subsumed within the LOUISIANA PUR-CHASE CENTENARY EXHIBITION. David Rowland Francis, president of the show's organising committee, came along to the first day of athletics with a few local worthies and conducted a brief inspection of the competitors lined up on the field. The athletes then dispersed, warmed up and got on with the sport.

Flushed with success by their inaugural 1896 Games, the Greeks had agitated to host the Olympics every four years, but the IOC wanted the event to travel the world. As a compromise, Greece was permitted to hold the 1906 ATHENS OLYMPIC INTERNATIONAL EXHIBITION, an event the IOC has never officially recognised. These 'INTERCALCATED GAMES' are largely forgotten for their sporting action, but they did introduce an ATHLETES' PARADE in which teams were preceded by national flags.

The LONDON OLYMPICS of 1908 picked up on this and in the dark drizzle Edward VII and Queen Alexandra took the salute from the flags of every competing nation except the US. As shot-putter Ralph Rose, carrying the Stars and Stripes, remarked, perhaps apocryphically, 'this flag dips to no earthly king'. At STOCKHOLM 1912 the Swedes added standard-bearers with countries' names to the parade, but that was the only flourish. The rest of the ceremony was a sermon, a hymn and a few words from King Gustav V.

THE ANCIENT SPORT OF MINOAN BULL-JUMPING RE-ENACTED IN THE ATHENS 2004 OPENING CEREMONY

Baron de Coubertin had been beavering away at the Olympic logo for years and in June 1914 his FIVE INTERLOCKING RINGS device was approved by the IOC congress. Six years and one world war later, the logo made its sporting debut at the 1920 ANTWERP GAMES on a plain white flag. Since then this emblem of amateurism and internationalism has become one of the most fiercely guarded trademarks on earth. (We're not allowed to reproduce it – nor any image of the Olympic torch – in this book.)

PIGEONS made their first appearance at the Olympics in 1900 when the Belgian Léon de Lunden led the carnage in the LIVE PIGEON SHOOT contest. De Lunden killed 21 birds and was entitled to a 20,000 francs prize but in a magnanimous and Olympian spirit the top four finishers agreed to split the winnings. The event was discontinued, which was just as well as the PARIS GAMES of 1924 saw the first mass release of doves as part of the opening ceremony – a gesture of peace rather than slaughter.

The 1928 AMSTERDAM GAMES retained all these elements of the ceremony but, oddly, decided to stage the athletes' parade separately from the rest of the show – a running order that has not been repeated since. More significant was the ARRIVAL OF FIRE. Given the ancient Greek love of symbolic and sacred flame it was only a matter of time and technology before the modern Olympics got in on the act. A FLAME was first lit inside the Olympic stadium in Amsterdam in 1928, though without great ceremony, by an employee of a local utility company. LA in 1932 brought a little staging to the torch and flame, but it took BERLIN 1936 to make its ignition the big finale that the ceremony needed.

CARL DIEM, one of the leading organisers of the Berlin Games, tapped into the Nazis' obsession with classical Greece and arranged for a fire to be kindled and a torch to be lit using a parabolic mirror in Olympia. The flame was then carried by a relay of runners to Berlin through the Balkans, on a route uncannily similar (if in reverse) to the movement of German armies southwards just a few years later. No one was doing this stuff at the ancient Olympics, but Diem was tapping into a wider vein of Hellenic fire imagery: there were torch races in Greece, Prometheus's theft of fire from the gods was a resonant myth, and the sacred Olympic truce was communicated by runners across Greece. By the time the final torchbearer reached the stadium a real sense of drama had been created.

As one would expect of the austerity Games, the LONDON 1948 opening ceremony was pretty low-key. Boy scouts served as stewards. The crowd, still living on rations, brought their own picnics and British women athletes had to supply their own blouses for the parade: a 21-gun salute prior to the arrival of the torchbearer was the chief theatrical flourish. HELSINKI 1952 was just as sober, enlivened mainly by German peace activist BARBARA ROTRAUT PLEYER who, clad all in white, ran across the track and on to a podium in an effort to speak.

MELBOURNE's 1956 ceremony broke little new ground, though the equestrians, who had to compete in Stockholm due to the prohibitive expense of shipping horses to Australia, conducted their opening ceremony entirely on horseback. Over the next decade the stadiums would become larger but ROME 1960 and TOKYO 1964 retained the same format. Tokyo's release of 10,000 balloons was the only notable change.

Weeks before MEXICO 1968, widespread political protest and vicious repression had spilled across the streets of Mexico City. The ceremony was both chaotic and bombastic. With just half an hour to go, the audience was treated to screaming military music over the PA and last-minute lawn mowing. Drum rolls and chants of 'Viva Mexico' accompanied almost everything, while uniformed marines carried in the Olympic flag. Pleasingly, the athletes broke ranks at the end, spreading across the track and forcing the final torchbearer to push her way through a scrum. Many of the 10,000 doves slated for release after this were too hot and ill to fly.

MUNICH 1972 reacted strongly to this display of nationalism and militarism. The organisers were also determined to atone for the hysteria and hubris of Berlin 1936. While the Berlin Games had used a great Teutonic bell to call athletes to the stadium, Munich chose a Dutch glockenspiel playing easy listening classics like 'Jingle Bells'. The athletes' parade was accompanied by cheesy tunes specially selected for each team: the Turks got 'Turkish Delight', the Hungarians 'Gypsy Love' and the Cubans 'Habana Alegre'. Brightly clad schoolchildren danced in circles and handed out flowers to the athletes.

The game changers in the history of the Olympic opening ceremony were MOSCOW 1980 and LOS ANGELES 1984, in which the two Cold War superpowers refused to go to each other's parties and, in the other's absence, tried to put on the biggest and best show yet. Moscow drew on the traditions of both the Red Square military parade and the gigantic COLLECTIVE GYMNASTIC DISPLAYS beloved of communist officialdom. The ace in the pack was the very low-tech use of colour-square cards, held by the audience above their heads. Choreographed with precision, one segment of the stadium provided a constant and changing visual commentary on events. The opening parade was a kitsch fest of Greek imagery and Russian style. Chariots, gods, and goddesses carrying the flag of Moscow rolled by. Later on there would be conversation with cosmonauts, mass displays of rhythmic gymnastics, dancing from all fifteen Soviet republics, and a stadium full of Mishas – the Games' ursine mascot.

LA countered with high-tech razzamatazz and Americana in the sun, in a ceremony that included mass marching bands in candyfloss colours and toy soldier uniforms, an 84-strong piano ensemble bashing out out Gershwin's "Rhapsody in Blue", the musicians all

BEIJING 2008 PRESENTS FIVE MILLENNIA OF CHINESE HISTORY, WITH A CAST OF THOUSANDS

dressed in powder-blue tuxedos, and a SPACEMAN with operational jetpack flying into the stadium.

While Moscow and LA had been statements of established power, SEOUL 1988 was a great big coming-out party for South Korea. A country in ruins at the end of the Korean War, it had transformed itself into a major industrial power in three decades. The opening ceremony was suitably enormous and the dance sequence – which purported to tell the story of balance and discord in the universe – marked a step change in the narrative ambition of this element of the ceremony.

In the twenty-first century, the soaring ambitions of Olympic hosts, allied to new staging and lighting technologies, led to a series of increasingly spectacular and expensive opening ceremonies. SYDNEY 2000 opened with 130 horses riding in formations (including the Olympic rings), used nearly 13,000 performers, had a band of 2000 musicians orchestrated by six conductors, and offered a tableau that went from the life of the ocean floor to the notion of eternity by way of Australia's aboriginal and colonial histories.

ATHENS 2004 threw the kitchen sink at the opening ceremony, Eros flew, a giant helix of DNA spun round, massed ranks of bouzouki players were assembled and everyone from Alexander the Great to the goddess Hera got a walk-on part. The stadium floor was filled with over two million litres of water, all of which had to be drained away in minutes to provide a hard surface for the parade of nations that followed.

All of this was to pale in comparison with the blow-out in BEIJING 2008. Four hours long, and with over 15,000 performers, it trumped everything that had gone before. Its centrepiece was a visual retelling of Chinese history, emphasising the nation's great technological innovations – movable type, paper, gunpowder – while managing to gloss over most of the twentieth century. It concluded with the rising of a phoenix and a celebration of the burgeoning Chinese space programme. The world got the message. China is big, it's back – and it means business.

At LONDON 2012, the ceremony celebrated the host nation with such aplomb, wit and verve that one American journalist even suggested that it put the 'Great' back into 'Britain'. Almost every aspect of British popular culture – from the National Health Service to Dizzee Rascal and *Gregory's Girl* – was alluded to in Boyle's extravaganza. Yet not every Brit was enthralled. Dismissing the entire spectacle as 'leftie multi-cultural crap', Tory MP Aidan Burley declared: 'Bring back the Red Arrows, Shakespeare and the Rolling Stones.' He must have missed the bit where Kenneth Branagh, dressed as Isambard Kingdom Brunel, recited from *The Tempest*.

ARCHERY

6–12 AUGUST 2016

SAMBÓDROME MARQUÊS DE SAPUCAÍ,

MARACANÃ, RIO DE JANEIRO

Athletes: 128 | **Golds up for grabs:** 4

---------------------------------- **OLYMPIC PRESENCE** ----------------------------------

1900–20, 1972–PRESENT.

---------------------------------- **OLYMPIC FORMAT** ----------------------------------

THERE ARE FOUR ARCHERY GOLDS AT STAKE, IN INDIVIDUAL and team competitions for men and women.

---------------------------------- **CURRENT CONTENDERS** ----------------------------------

THE SOUTH KOREANS' HAVE WON ELEVEN OUT OF SIXTEEN GOLDS since the 1996 Olympics and are clear favourites. Yet they face serious challenges in the men's event from Italy (champions in 2012), Japan, China and the US and, in the women's event, Russia (who won the 2015 World Cup), China and Mexico.

---------------------------------- **PAST CHAMPIONS** ----------------------------------

SOUTH KOREA: 19 | USA: 14 | BELGIUM: 11

WHY WATCH ARCHERY?

WITH THE OLYMPIC STADIUM ON MONTJUIC PLUNGED INTO darkness, the climax of the opening ceremony of the BARCELONA 1992 Games was approaching. The Olympic torch made its final journey into the stadium, where Spanish paralympic archer Antonio Rebollo lit his arrow from it. Turning to face the high metal tower

DOUBLE OLYMPIC CHAMPION IM DONG HUYN. REMARKABLY, HE IS LEGALLY BLIND IN HIS NATIVE SOUTH KOREA

on which the Olympic flame was due to burn, he launched his burning arrow towards the top of the structure, igniting a column of fire that soared into the night sky. Not even a stadium-full rendition of Freddie Mercury and Montserrat Caballé's *Barcelona*, specially written for the Olympics, could compete.

Target archery competitions may not pack quite the same spectacular punch, but each shot offers a sequence of excitement: the tension as the archer draws back the bowstring; the snap of the arrow's release; the swish of its 150mph flight; the split-second of impact. The sport often produces exceptional sustained drama, like the nail-biting final of the men's team event at LONDON 2012, in which Italy beat the USA 219-218 with Michele Frangilli scoring the ten points required to win with the final arrow. Requiring composure under pressure, perfect balance and focus, Olympic archery is like competitive meditation with lethal weapons.

The sport is now much more spectator- and TV-friendly. Simultaneous competition with dozens of archers firing together is out, allowing viewers to savour the drama of head-to-head contests. Very long rounds of arrows have been replaced by short sets that make errors more costly and upsets more likely. Split screens, big screens and electronic scoring have been introduced. In South Korea, the leading archery nation, this has produced huge TV audiences and very large, noisy crowds. In China last year, in a spectacle worthy of the 1970s British TV show *Superstars*, former Olympic champion Zhang Juanjuan was one of seven top archers to fire arrows into falling rings. In front of a TV audience of 250 million, she and Austria's Peter Stecher each found the mark seven times (out of fifteen) to tie the contest. The sport has even received Papal blessing, though officials leading Rome's Olympic bid, keen to avoid any religious controversy, have dashed Pope Francis's hopes of staging archery in the Vatican in 2024.

In 2016, archery will be held at the Sambódromo, the stadium built to judge Rio's vast carnival schools and parades. Will the atmosphere inspire Brazil's best hope, 18-year-old MARCUS D'ALMEIDA, reductively dubbed 'archery's Neymar', to build on the silver he won at the 2014 Youth Olympics?

THE STORY OF ARCHERY

SKILL WITH A BOW AND ARROW HAS BEEN CRUCIAL TO THE development of humanity. Cave paintings in France and Spain, created around 25,000 years ago, depict archers in hunting scenes, while stone arrowheads litter Neolithic archaeological sites. The first great civilisations may have relied on agriculture for subsistence, but archery was essential to hunting and organised warfare – bowmen were a central component of the armies of ancient China, Persia, Egypt, Greece and Rome.

Alongside hunting and warfare, archery had a ritual and competitive aspect: in Homer's *Iliad*, the GREEKS hold a shooting contest at Patroclus's funeral games. Fourteenth-century records show that archers in the OTTOMAN EMPIRE competed to see who could fire an arrow the furthest, while in JAPAN the Oyakazu archery contest began in 1606. In the only known form of MARATHON ARCHERY, competitors were required to fire as many arrows as they could in 24 hours through a hole in a wall. The record, set in 1686, was 8133 scores from 13,053 attempts.

In all of these cultures, gunpowder radically altered the status of archery. By the end of the sixteenth century, most European armies had abandoned the longbow and crossbow, and the rest of the world would soon follow. In Britain, archery endured in high society as a quasi-militaristic recreation, but by the middle of the eighteenth century it was a dying art. Its revival was primarily instigated by antiquarian and collector Sir Ashton Lever, who, in 1781, founded the Toxophilite Society, which combined target archery with an enormous amount of eating and drinking. Joseph Strutt, in his survey of Georgian sport, observed: 'I have seen the gentlemen who practise archery in the vicinity of London, repeatedly shoot from end to end, and not touch the target with an arrow.'

Although the sport was already attracting a rather select crowd, the patronage in 1787 of George, the Prince of Wales, was a boon for the Toxophilite Society. Aristocratic archery clubs sprang up across England, providing a space for conviviality and flirtation for the next thirty years. Flirtation was encouraged when, in the early nineteenth century, the Royal British Bowmen permitted women to join. The decorum of archery was such that, as one contemporary wrote, 'it is the only field diversion they can enjoy without incurring the censure of being thought masculine'. Indeed, the *1829 Young Lady's Book: A Manual of Elegant Recreations, Exercises and Pursuits* suggested that 'the moment of the bending of the bow is particularly graceful'.

In the 1820s British archery peaked as a lordly pastime, with great gatherings of archery clubs on heaths and parks in huge tented enclosures. Competition was definitely secondary to feasting, merry-making, and the display of the extraordinary costumes invented by archery societies, many inspired by the era's cult of medievalism.

Although Queen Victoria was a patron of the Royal St Leonards Archers, archery never quite returned to the heady days of

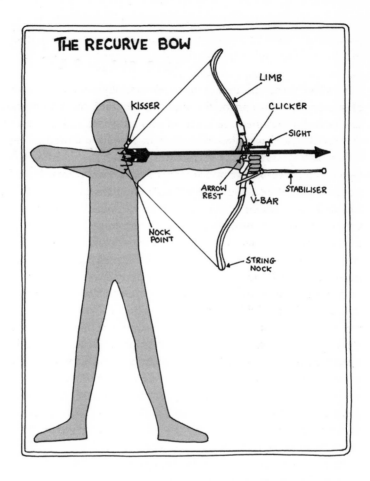

THE RECURVE BOW

LIMB

KISSER

CLICKER

SIGHT

ARROW REST

V-BAR

STABILISER

NOCK POINT

STRING NOCK

Georgian England. Over the next eighty years the sport lost much of its society glamour and settled down to a quieter life in garden parties and national meets. It did, however, evolve as a sport, with issues of format, scoring, technique and etiquette becoming standardised. It was this more sober culture that spread to countries with a strong tradition of hunting – notably AMERICA, FRANCE and the LOW COUNTRIES – and in turn led to archery's arrival at the 1900 OLYMPICS.

Game On: Archery Basics

THE 1.2M DIAMETER TARGET IS DIVIDED INTO TEN CONCENTRIC rings, with one point awarded for hitting the outermost ring and ten points for hitting the bullseye, which is just 12.2cm across. Arrows that land on a line are awarded the higher of the two scores. If an arrow splits another arrow – known as the 'Robin Hood shot' after the outlaw's legendary contest-winning feat – the points earned by the first arrow are awarded. Within the bullseye is a smaller ring called the x10. There are no additional points for hitting this, but if two contestants have the same score in the ranking round (see below), the archer with the most x10s wins. In all Olympic events, the archer stands 70m from the target, which from that range appears to competitors to be the size of the head of a carpet tack held at arm's length. They have up to twenty seconds to fire each arrow.

IN ESSENCE, ARCHERY IS ONE OF THE SIMPLEST SPORTS IN THE world – yet the way the Olympic archery events are structured is quite complicated.

Sixty-four archers take part in the INDIVIDUAL competitions, which begin with the RANKING ROUND, in which contestants shoot 72 arrows (in SIX ENDS of twelve arrows), after which they are ranked by score from 1 to 64. In the head-to-head ELIMINA-TION ROUNDS, the 1st-ranked archer competes against the 64th, the 2nd against the 63rd, and so on. Matches are decided in sets, which consist of three arrows for each archer. The highest scorer is awarded two points. If scores are level, each contestant gets a point each. The first archer to SIX SET POINTS wins. If the match is drawn 5-5, each athlete shoots one arrow and the one closest to the middle wins. If no arrow is closer, they shoot again until the outcome is resolved.

The TEAM event is a variation on that theme. Each team consists of three archers who have competed in the individual compe-tition. Their scores in the individual ranking round are added together to seed the teams, who play off in a series of knock-out matches. These games are also played in sets, with each archer having two shots. The points for winning or drawing sets are the same as in the individual competition but a team only needs FIVE SET POINTS to win. If the match is drawn 4-4, each archer in both teams fires one shot and the arrow closest to the centre wins. If no arrow is closer, the second and then the third closest are compared. In the unlikely event of there still being no winner, the teams shoot again.

ETIQUETTE

AS ONE WOULD HOPE IN A SPORT THAT USES LETHAL WEAPONRY, etiquette and safety are high on archery's agenda. Competitors must wait for the command to start and are not allowed to collect arrows while others are shooting.

If you hear someone shouting 'Fast!' it is not an attempt to increase the pace of shooting but to stop it. The call requires everyone to stop shooting immediately and return any unshot arrows to their quivers. Rather quaintly, archers are expected to offer to pay for any damage caused to a competitor's equipment.

53-YEAR-OLD SYBIL 'QUEENIE' NEWALL AT LONDON 1908

THE RECURVE BOW

THE DEFINING FEATURE OF THE MODERN OLYMPIC BOW HAS been in existence for more than three millennia. Called the recurve bow, it has tips that curve away from the archer when the bow is unstrung. This allows the bow, when tense, to store more energy than a straight-limbed bow of the same size. Today's bows are made of complex layers of fibreglass, carbon and wood, with detachable limbs and all manner of additions and contraptions to aid stability and thus increase accuracy.

BOW PARTS

THUMB RING A twanging bow string and flying arrow can be hard on the fingers. Archers use these small leather flaps as protection.

CLICKER Archers try to achieve the same strength of draw every time they fire. The clicker is a small wire attached to the central part of the bow to help them with this. The clicker sits on the arrow as it is drawn back and drops off it when it has been pulled back the correct distance.

KISSER Consistency is everything in archery. To ensure they get into the correct positions when drawing, competitors touch these little buttons placed on the strings to their faces or lips.

STABILISER Archers like their bows evenly balanced to suit their styles and postures. Stabilisers – rods of varying length and weight – are attached to bows to absorb vibration.

THE FINER POINTS

FOR THE SPECTATOR, MUCH OF ARCHERY'S PLEASURE COMES from watching how an individual athlete or a team performs over a series of contests, as the tension escalates. Most Olympic archers hit the bullseye most of the time, so the difference between winning and losing comes down to fractions of a centimetre, and tiny wobbles and movements when firing. Fussing with the equipment may signify that an archer is cracking under pressure. Competing at Olympic level requires all-round composure, meditative poise and balance.

IN THE ZONE DUDE! JUSTIN HUISH SHOOTS FOR GOLD AT ATLANTA 1996

Archers liken using the bow to a golf swing. It can be broken down into tiny component parts, from the stance, to the raising of the bow, to the pattern of breathing. Each of these must be perfected and all of them combined in a smooth automatic set of movements that can be executed faultlessly under the highest competitive pressure.

ARCHERY GOES TO THE OLYMPICS

ARCHERY APPEARED AT EVERY OLYMPICS BUT ONE BETWEEN 1900 and 1920 and took a different format every time. Unlike most other early Olympic sports, the archery event was open to women from the start: British archer Queenie Newall won a gold in 1908 at the age of 53, still the record for the oldest female champion in any Olympic sport. Archery's embrace of diversity has extended to disabled athletes: in 1984, in Los Angeles, New Zealand archer Neroli Fairhall became the first paraplegic athlete to compete at an Olympics.

The star of the early Games was HUBERT VAN INNIS of Belgium, winner of six golds and three silvers between 1900 and 1920.

However, archery was then ditched from the Olympics due to its failure to create an international federation, which was made a condition of a sports participation at the games by the IOC. :

That was perhaps unsurprising, as only France, Belgium, the USA, the Netherlands and Great Britain had ever taken part. And although archery established an international federation for itself in 1931, the sport was sustained for the next half-century mainly by the USA. In the mid-1950s *Sports Illustrated* reported that there were more than four million amateur archers in the country. FRED BEAR (his real name) and his TV descendants drew on backwoods nostalgia and the mystique of big-game hunting to promote archery, while in Hollywood HOWARD HILL – the self-styled 'world's greatest archer' – advised ERROL FLYNN for his role as Robin Hood and offered dazzling bow-work and trickery in his own films. More recently, enthusiasts like actress GEENA DAVIS (who just missed out on inclusion in the 2000 US Olympic team), *Jurassic World* star CHRIS PRATT and WILLIAM SHATNER (AKA Captain James T Kirk) have sprinkled some stardust on the sport.

When archery returned to the Olympics, the Americans swept the board in 1972 and 1976. Only America's boycott of the 1980 Games prevented them from making it three in a row. American dominance continued in the men's events through the 1980s and 1990s. At Los Angeles, DARRELL PACE was so far ahead of his rivals that he held a press conference mid-event on the final day. In 1996 the gold was won by 20-year-old JUSTIN HUISH, who had learned the sport by firing arrows through his parents' garage from a neighbour's lawn. He turned up at the Olympics looking like a classic California slacker, with his beard, pony-tail and reversed baseball cap. First impressions weren't entirely deceptive. In the run up to the 2000 Games, Huish was busted for possession of marijuana; he quit the team and has since retired.

American archery has never been as dominant since and at ATHENS 2004 the US team didn't win any medals at all. The new masters of the sport are the SOUTH KOREANS. An Olympic gold secures a South Korean a generous life-long pension and huge public acclaim. The nation's women, who hold six Olympic records and share the other with Ukraine, have dominated every team event since 1988. KIM SOO-NYUNG, the most successful archer of the modern era, has taken four golds, a silver and a bronze at three different Olympics. The men's team has won gold at three of the past six Games.

Four years ago, competing at Lord's cricket ground, the South Koreans took three out of four golds and, although they only won bronze in the men's team event, set a new Olympic record with 2087 points in the 216 arrow ranking round. That record was inspired by Im Dong-hyun, a two-time Olympic champion who shot a WORLD RECORD 699 in a 72-arrow round before being knocked out in the last 16 of the men's individual competition. His achievement is all the more remarkable because he is legally blind – when asked how he sees the target, he replied that it looks as if 'different colour paints have been dropped in water'. At RIO 2016, South Korea's hegemony in the women's competition faces a strong challenge from two MEXICANS: Aída Román and Mariana Avitia, who picked up silver and bronze in 2012, their country's first medals in this sport.

ATHLETICS

12–21 AUGUST 2016

ESTÁDIO OLÍMPICO JOÃO HAVELANGE,
MARACANÁ (Track, field and combined events)

FLAMENGO PARK, COPACABANA (Race walk)

SAMBÓDROMO, MARACANÁ (Marathon)

Athletes: 2200 | Golds up for grabs: 47

OLYMPIC PRESENCE

MEN 1896–PRESENT; WOMEN 1928–PRESENT.

OLYMPIC FORMAT

24 TRACK EVENTS, 16 FIELD EVENTS (FOUR JUMPING AND four throwing for each gender), five road events (men's and women's marathons and 20km walks, men's 50km walk), and two combined events (men's decathlon and women's heptathlon).

CONTENDERS

AMERICA HAS TOPPED THE ATHLETICS MEDALS TABLE IN ALL but three of the 27 modern Olympic Games and may do so again in Rio. In London, their strongest challengers were RUSSIA but many of that country's athletes have been implicated in a doping scandal. The only other nations to win more than one gold in 2012 were JAMAICA (4), GREAT BRITAIN (4), ETHIOPIA (3) and KENYA (2). The 2016 hosts BRAZIL missed out on a medal completely in London. The last Brazilian to secure gold in an athletics event was Maurren Magi, winner of the women's long jump in Beijing.

PAST CHAMPIONS

USA: 320 | USSR/RUSSIA/UNIFIED: 97 | GREAT BRITAIN: 53 | FINLAND: 48

WHY WATCH ATHLETICS?

ATHLETICS, BOXING AND WRESTLING ARE THE SPORTS THAT connect the ancient Games to the modern Olympics, and whether the yardstick is worldwide television audience or iconic historical moments, athletics is the biggest of the three. Does anyone not have an indelible image in their head of Fosbury flopping, Mo Farah's 'Mobot celebration' after he stormed to victory in the 10,000m at London 2012, or Usain Bolt annihilating his opponents in Beijing? And that's before you consider the politics – from Jesse Owens' defiance at Berlin to the Black Power salutes at Mexico 1968.

The hold Olympic athletics exercises on the global imagination has a lot to do with the SIMPLICITY of the constituent disciplines. We can all relate to running, jumping and throwing, and there is an extraordinary thrill in watching individuals who can do these things better than anyone else on the planet. And while all sports are to some extent dramatic, the starkness of athletics magnifies the drama: little can compare with the despondency of the relay runner who lets down his team by dropping his baton, or the elation of the javelin thrower who produces a medal-winning personal best after a sequence of no-throws.

Another fascinating aspect of Olympic athletics is the POLITICAL dimension. The glory attendant on athletic success has always been co-opted by the powers that be, from the rulers of ancient Greek city states to the Third Reich and beyond. The stadium is an arena in which a nation can demonstrate its supremacy to its own citizens and to the rest of the world. The stakes may not now be quite as high as during the Cold War, when Olympic athletics morphed into a blatantly symbolic battle between opposing regimes, but there are still plenty of engrossing nationalistic and ideological subplots. China, for example, has still not fulfilled its ambition of properly challenging the US, winning only one gold in the past two Games.

Although athletics is self-evidently elitist, it is also remarkably democratic. There are events tailored to short and nippy people (STEEPLECHASE), human stick insects (HIGH JUMP), and the super-sized (HAMMER and SHOT PUT). This diversity, and the universality of athletics, means that everyone can find something with which to identify, while at the more recherché end of the spectrum, some of the minority sports can make one marvel at the oddity of the competitors' excellence. How exactly does one go about becoming a champion at the POLE VAULT, for example, and what can possibly induce someone to commit their youth to Olympic WALKING?

THE STORY OF ATHLETICS

THE ACTIVITIES AT THE HEART OF ATHLETICS ARE SO fundamental that providing dates for their origins is virtually meaningless. Walking is an Olympic discipline, for example, and hominids are thought to have been at it for four million years. As for the javelin, even wild chimpanzees wield spears.

We are on slightly firmer ground when we trace the roots of what might be termed organised athletic events. The oldest known example was the bizarre SED FESTIVAL, conducted in Egypt from the First Dynasty (3100–2890 BC) onwards. After thirty years on

PHARAOH DEN (c.2945 BC) SHOWS HE STILL HAS THE LEGS FOR THE JOB AT THE SED FESTIVAL

the throne, pharaohs were expected to prove their continued vigour by running between points representing the borders of their kingdom. They did this in public, with jackals' tails tied to their waists.

A related practice in many ancient societies was the use of athletic challenges for INITIATION. Young men of the Hamer tribe in south-western Ethiopia jump cattle to prove their virility (a man must leap over a bullock four times before he can get married), and have doubtless been doing it since their ancestors took to pastoralism back in the mists of time. Bull-leaping (in which girls and boys took part) was similarly important to the Minoans of Crete (2700–1450 BC).

The next stage in the evolution of athletics was the introduction of the crucial ingredient of COMPETITION. The emerging empires and city states of the Bronze Age naturally wanted their soldiers to be fit and proficient at throwing spears and so forth, and used track and field events to develop useful skills for the battlefield. At the same time, athletics worked in the other direction, by channelling aggressive impulses that might otherwise have led to fighting. To borrow George Orwell's phrase about football, it was 'war minus the shooting'. Rulers sponsored athletic competitions because this allowed them to demonstrate their power while diffusing the combative energies of their subjects, or of rival cities.

Many of the earliest recorded athletic meetings were held as part of FUNERAL CELEBRATIONS. According to legend, the Irish Tailteann Games, which included pole jumping, high jumping and spear throwing, were initiated by King Lugh (1829–1600 BC) to commemorate the death of his mother. Funeral games also play a prominent role in the *Iliad*, Homer's account of the Trojan Wars. Achilles, the hero of the Greek armies frequently referred to as 'the fast runner', responds to the death of his beloved friend Patroclus by holding commemorative games which feature a foot race, boxing, wrestling and a spear-throwing contest. The competitions had a triple purpose: they established a basis for the distribution of the fallen warrior's possessions; they allowed his comrades to get his death out of their systems by asserting their strength and fitness; and they provided opportunities for 'immortal fame'.

GREECE was the seedbed of modern athletics. The great quadrennial meeting at OLYMPIA (see below), and the other pan-Hellenic sporting festivals at Corinth, Nemea and Delphi, served many of the same functions as the modern Games. They fostered a sense of cultural unity, helped rival states assess their relative strengths, and satisfied the perpetual quest for glory.

ATHLETICS AT THE
ANCIENT OLYMPICS

The ancient Olympic Games were part of a religious festival dedicated to Zeus, the king of the Greek gods. Conventionally dated to 776 BC, they took place every four years at OLYMPIA in south-western Greece, and endured until around the end of the fourth century AD, when they were suppressed by the Christian Byzantine emperors. The festival was initially a local affair but by the fifth century BC it had expanded to receive competitors from the Black Sea to the western Mediterranean. A few months ahead of each Games, heralds would travel throughout the Greek-speaking world to invite athletes and spectators to travel to Olympia, declaring a sacred truce which guaranteed their safe passage. That this was generally observed during a period of almost perpetual warfare between city states illustrates the religious significance of the Games.

The ZEUS link was emphasised throughout the festival. On arrival at Olympia, the athletes had to swear in front of a fearsome image of the god that they were free Greek men who had been in training for at least ten months. A hundred oxen were sacrificed to Zeus during the gathering, and in around 432 BC a colossal gold and ivory statue of the god, by Phidias, was unveiled in his temple on the site. Standing thirteen metres high, it was one of the Seven Wonders of the ancient world.

In its early days, the sporting aspect of the festival consisted of nothing but athletics. Indeed, for the first fifty years or so there was only one event: the STADE, a 192-metre sprint along the length of the *stadion* or stadium. It was run bare-footed on a course of rolled sand. The winner of the first recorded race, in 776 BC, was Koroibos, a cook from the nearby city of Elis.

AND THEY'RE OFF ... GREEK RUNNERS ON A VASE, 6TH CENTURY BC

Other events were gradually added to the schedule. In 724 BC the authorities introduced the DIAULOS, a race to the end of the stadium and back, which was roughly equivalent to the 400m. The DOLICHOS or 'long race', which consisted of between 20 and 24 lengths of the *stadion*, made its debut four years later. In 708 BC the first non-athletics event, WRESTLING, was added to the programme. Later additions included CHARIOT RACING, BOXING, a nasty form of no-holds-barred combat called the PANKRATION (which, alarmingly, has recently been revived), and the HOPLITODROMOS, a race of two lengths of the stadium run in armour.

More interesting from an athletics perspective was the PENTATHLON, which was introduced at the same time as wrestling. It consisted of a stade foot race, a jumping event, discus and javelin throwing, plus wrestling. On the evidence of a fifth-century BC poem composed in honour of a pentathlete named Phallyos, which claims he leapt over sixteen metres in the course of winning the competition, the JUMPING event must have involved multiple bounds, like today's triple jump. The DISCUS, in contrast to modern practice, was launched from a platform with the feet in fixed position. Its weight and dimensions were not standardised: instead, competitors had to use the biggest projectile that any of them produced for the occasion. The JAVELIN was also thrown in a way that's unfamiliar to us now. It was wrapped in cord, one end of which was tied to the thrower's fingers. At the moment of release, the cord would unwind at terrific speed, imparting a stabilising rotation to the javelin that allowed it to sail well over 100 metres.

Athletes initially competed clothed but in 720 BC a sprinter called Orsippos became separated from his loincloth during the stade race and went on to win it. A Spartan named Akanthos figured this was no coincidence, and promptly won the double-stade in a similar state of undress. Thereafter, NUDITY became standard. It is tempting to think this is why unmarried women were not allowed to attend the Games but the real reason is likely to have been religious. Zeus was a macho god who wouldn't have taken kindly to any dilution of the testosterone-charged atmosphere.

Then as now, there were no financial rewards for the winners. They had to make do with OLIVE WREATHS, plus the right to have their statues installed at Olympia. But the spin-off benefits were considerable. Promising athletes were generously sponsored by their native city states and victors could expect to be showered with gifts, pecuniary and otherwise. Indeed, the kudos attached to having an Olympic champion became so great that athletes were frequently poached. Sotades, for instance, won the long race at the 99th festival as a Cretan and contested the subsequent Games as an Ephesian. An early example of the big money transfer.

The main perk of victory, however, was IMMORTALITY. This wasn't entirely illusory: athletes like LEONIDAS of Rhodes, who won all three running events at four consecutive Games between 164 and 152 BC, are still remembered today.

The ROMANS inherited the Greek taste for organised games, which they often linked to religious festivals. But they liked their sports bloody, preferring gladiatorial contests and chariot races to purely athletic disciplines. In PRE-COLONIAL AMERICA, by contrast, tribes like the Jicarilla Apache and Osage built running tracks to keep their warriors fit, while in remote parts of Europe throwing contests served as tests of manhood. The VIKINGS used hammer-throwing as a method of divvying up newly conquered land – the further a warrior threw the implement, the more territory he could claim.

The most glamorous sporting competitions in MIDDLE AGES and RENAISSANCE EUROPE were the jousting tournaments, held to hone the fighting skills of the knights. But it was the activities of regular soldiers that fed more directly into the evolution of modern athletics. SHOT-PUTTING, for instance, grew out of the practice of hurling cannon-balls.

By the seventeenth and eighteenth centuries, the main sponsors of athletic competition were the ruling classes of the British Isles. Aristocrats were much given to organising foot races between their employees, and gambling on the results. The Earl Bishop of Cloyne in County Cork famously held a curate's race to determine the winner of an ecclesiastical post in his gift, forcing the competitors to run across the sands for his amusement. It was the near worship of the classical world by the same British elite that provided the spur for the first pan-athletic meeting of the (reasonably) modern era. In 1612, a lawyer named Robert Dover established the annual COTSWOLD OLYMPICK GAMES near Chipping Campden in Gloucestershire, with King James I's blessing. The programme included running, jumping and sledgehammer throwing.

The classical revival also underpinned the OLYMPIADE DE LA RÉPUBLIQUE that was held in revolutionary France, as well as the attempts by the Greeks to revive the ancient Games in 1859, 1870 and 1875, the WENLOCK OLYMPIC GAMES (first held in 1850, they featured running and hurdles) and the GRAND OLYMPIC FESTIVAL held annually at Liverpool from 1862–7, which had a programme startlingly like that of the 1896 Games in Athens. Another symptom of admiration for the ways of ancient Greece was the incorporation of physical exercise into the curriculum of schools and colleges in Europe and the USA. This played a vital role in the development of modern athletics. The meetings held at Shrewsbury School in 1840 and Exeter College, Oxford in 1850, for example, were among the first pan-athletic competitions of the modern era.

Outside the academies, a two-man gravel running track was built around the perimeter of Lord's Cricket Ground in LONDON in 1837 and in 1863 the first known indoor athletics meeting was held at Ashburnham Hall in the same city, featuring four races and a triple jump competition. The next stage was the establishment of national associations and championships. The ENGLISH AMATEUR ATHLETICS ASSOCIATION kicked off the process in 1880 and was soon followed by the American Athletic Union (1888) and the Union des Sociétés Françaises de Sports Athlétiques (1889). The world governing body, the IAAF (International Amateur Athletics Federation) was founded in 1912, and continues to govern the disciplines, having relaxed its 'Amateur' rules in 1982. It finally changed the tag from 'Amateur Athletics' to 'Athletics Associations' in 2001.

Under new president Sebastian Coe, the IAAF must confront the greatest doping scandal to afflict the sport since the 1970s, when East Germany dominated track and field thanks to 'state plan theme 14-25' in which athletes were systematically administered hormones and steroids. The programme helped secure 11 golds at Montreal in 1976. The current scandal, which has led to Russia being banned for systematic doping and credible charges that corrupt elements within the IAAF were complicit, overshadows the future of the entire sport.

Game On: Athletics Basics

The diverse disciplines that constitute athletics fall into five categories: running, jumping, throwing, walking and combined events. Unless stated otherwise, the events below are contested – separately – by both sexes.

The excitement of athletics events tends to be proportionate to the simplicity of the challenge. 'Jump as far as you can' is a clearer proposition than 'do as big a hop and skip as you can, leaving something in reserve for one last huge jump'. Consequently, the long jump enjoys a higher status than the triple jump, except where the viewer's priorities are twisted by patriotism (as with the British triple jumper Jonathan Edwards). Similarly, being the fastest man on earth is more liable to impress than being the best at negotiating various obstacles over 3km. But it would be wrong to dismiss the minority disciplines. It may not be easy to think your way into the mind of a hammer thrower, but the skill and dedication of such competitors can be breathtaking.

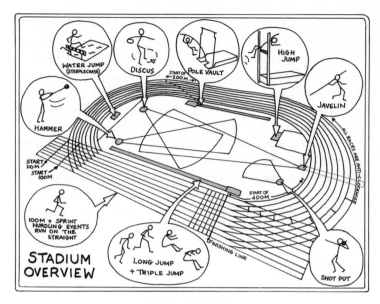

STADIUM OVERVIEW

RUNNING

ALTITUDE MAKES A SIGNIFICANT DIFFERENCE TO PERFORMANCE. Runners at the 1968 Games at Mexico City (2240m above sea level) benefited from a reduction in air resistance that had a similar effect to a tailwind of 1.5m/sec. This was great for the sprinters, but runners over longer distances suffered, as there was approximately 3 per cent less oxygen available to them than at sea level. Athletes who live and train at altitude, such as those from Africa's RIFT VALLEY, have a definite advantage in distance events as their bodies grow accustomed to using oxygen more efficiently. When they come down to sea level, their lungs are supercharged with the gas.

Races up to 400 metres are run in LANES, as is the first 100m of the 800m, after which the athletes 'BREAK' – they are allowed to leave their starting lanes and move to the inside of the track, which offers the shortest and quickest route. In the longer races, athletes break from the start. The race time of an athlete is determined by the moment at which their torso breaks the finishing line.

SPRINTING

IN EVENTS OF 400M OR LESS, ATHLETES BEGIN IN STARTING blocks. Explosiveness is the name of the game as they aim to spring out of their blocks and reach top speed as soon as possible. A FALSE START is registered if a runner leaves their blocks less than a tenth of a second after the starting gun is fired (the time it takes for the information to be relayed from the ears to the brain and muscles). It used to be that athletes were each allowed one false start but the rules were amended to allow just one false start by anyone in a race – and instant elimination thereafter. Then in 2010 they were further tightened so that just one false start led to disqualification: an absurd rule that soon had major repercussions, when Usain Bolt false started at the 2011 World Championships in Korea and was unable to defend his 100m title.

A GOOD START is vital in the sprints, though perhaps not as vital as people tend to think. A bad start is only about five-hundredths of a second slower than a good one and a top runner may be able to make up the difference during the race. But the psychological advantage of getting away quickly is invaluable. Mental condition is one of the key determinants of sprinting performance. Watch how the athletes PSYCH THEMSELVES UP before their races, posturing, blocking out crowd noises and indulging in 'hundred metre stares'.

USAIN BOLT CASUALLY SHATTERS THE 100M RECORD AT BEIJING

Note that RECORDS do not count in the 100m and 200m (and the sprint hurdle events, long and triple jump) if a TAILWIND of 2.1m/second or more is recorded at any point during the race.

·· **100M** ··

THE ULTIMATE EXPRESSION OF HUMAN SPEED IS RUN OVER A straight course. To save surveyors and building contractors from going nuts, international 100m courses are allowed to deviate by up to 2cm in length and to rise or fall up to 10cm between start and finish.

At Olympic level, men usually complete the course in 43 to 46 strides – USAIN BOLT took 41 at London 2012 – and women in 47 to 52. A top male sprinter typically reaches a maximum speed of around 12 METRES PER SECOND (26.8mph) between 60 and 70m into a race. The equivalent figures for women are about 11m/s (24.6mph) at 50–60 metres. During the acceleration phase, both sexes run about 4.6 strides per second.

100M OLYMPIC RECORDS
MEN: 9.63, USAIN BOLT (JAMAICA), LONDON 2012.
WOMEN: 10.62, FLORENCE GRIFFITH JOYNER (USA), SEOUL 1988.

·· **200M** ··

THE 200M IS SIMILAR IN DISTANCE TO THE ANCIENT STADE but is actually derived from the furlong (220 yards, one-eighth of a mile). Throughout modern Olympic history, the event has been run on a 400m track with athletes going round a full bend, but prior to 1960 Americans competing in domestic competitions ran the 200m on straight tracks. Evidence accumulated before that date suggests that the technical demands of running around a bend add about one-third of a second to race times.

The athletes are still going flat out – Bolt's world record time is almost exactly twice his equivalent in the 100M – but there is a noticeable decline in speed in the second half of the race.

200M OLYMPIC RECORDS
Men: 19.30, Usain Bolt (Jamaica), Beijing 2008.
Women: 21.34, Florence Griffith Joyner (USA) Seoul 1988.

RACING AND RACE

There are two elephants in the locker room of international athletics. One is the role of drugs in the sport, the other the relationship between race and athletic performance. Almost everyone agrees about the former (the use of artificial chemicals as contrary to the competitive spirit), at least in theory. The second subject is highly controversial.

What are the facts? As of 2015, the world record for every Olympic men's running discipline was held by an athlete of AFRICAN DESCENT. Indeed, the 800m, 1500m, 3000m steeplechase, 5000m, 10,000m and the marathon record were all held by Africans. The comparable statistics for women are less clear-cut but both sprint records currently belong to black athletes. There are lies, damned lies and statistics, but are black people simply better runners than everyone else?

The answer is 'yes and no': yes, in that it clearly helps to have African ancestry; no, because the notion that people in that category form a single ethnic group couldn't be more erroneous. Africa is, by a distance, the most genetically diverse continent, and Zulus and Berbers, for example, have about as much in common physically as the Scandinavians and the Chinese.

What is incontrovertibly true is that two ethnic groups overwhelmingly boss Olympic running. The best SPRINTERS have WEST AFRICAN ancestry and the top LONG-DISTANCE RUNNERS are almost invariably EAST AFRICAN. Remarkably, a huge proportion of them come from just one area – the Kalenjin region of the Upper Rift Valley in Kenya. Scientists point to the typical physiologies of the ethnic groups concerned. West Africans and their American, Caribbean and European descendants tend to have narrow hips, well-developed musculature and an unusually high proportion of fast-twitch muscle fibres – all qualities that are advantageous to sprinting. Kalenjins, on the other hand, are usually small and light, with muscles packed with slow-twitch fibres. They also come from a high-altitude region, so their bodies use oxygen more efficiently, making them ideally equipped for endurance running.

Interestingly, the Chinese openly embrace the concept of racial differences in athletic ability. In 2004, the *People's Daily* reported that the CHINESE have 'congenital shortcomings' and 'genetic differences' that mitigate against track and field success. This might be seen as a case of getting the excuses in early. The doctrine usefully allows the success of the

THE EAST AFRICAN EXPRESS: KENENISA BEKELE OF ETHIOPIA SHOWING THE WAY
HOME TO KENYAN ELIUD KIPCHOGE AT BEIJING 2008

likes of Liu Xiang, winner of the 110m HURDLES in Athens, to be attributed
to stereotypical Chinese virtues like discipline, hard work and clever
technique. It's intriguing to note that the JAPANESE have always produced
strong MARATHON runners – their trainers often put their success down
to a combination of low body fat and their willingness to endure pain.

One thing is certain: only a fool would bet on a non-East African winning the men's 10,000m, or a white man winning the 100m. But a Jamaican
winning the former or an Ethiopian the latter is just as unlikely.

400M

THE 400M MAKES DEMANDS ON COMPETITORS THAT HAVE
led the IAAF to describe the event as an 'endurance sprint'. Even
the fittest athletes are incapable of running at top speed for more

than 30–35 seconds before they start to suffer the effects of oxygen depletion. At this stage the body begins to respire anaerobically to make up the deficit, and the consequence is a build-up of lactic acid in the muscles. As anyone who has experienced a 'stitch' can testify, this is decidedly uncomfortable. Successful 400m runners therefore need to be cussed individuals with an ability to ignore pain – and be extremely quick.

Once upon a time, top 400m runners could be divided into 200/400m and 400/800m specialists, the latter including the great Cuban ALBERTO JUANTORENA, who won both events at Montreal 1976, and the former MICHAEL JOHNSON, who won both 200m and 400m at Atlanta 1996. It seemed inconceivable that either feat would be repeated, until USAIN BOLT started winning 400m races.

400M OLYMPIC RECORDS
MEN: 43.49, MICHAEL JOHNSON (USA), ATLANTA 1996.
WOMEN: 48.25, MARIE-JOSÉ PÉREC (FRANCE) ATLANTA 1996.

MIDDLE DISTANCE

MIDDLE-DISTANCE RUNNING IS MUCH MORE TACTICAL THAN sprinting, because athletes cannot go flat out all the way through their races. They must conserve as much energy as possible until the final bend, while constantly monitoring what their opponents are doing.

This is what's fun to try to assess. Do the athletes look as though they have something left in the tank for a sprint finish? Or are they feeling the strain? If an athlete BREAKS AWAY from the main pack before the end, have they gone too soon or timed it to perfection? You can expect to see the best runners cruise up from mid-pack to second or third as they pass the bell – unless they are oddballs like Kenya's 1970s star HENRY RONO, who used to accelerate every second lap or so, to break other athletes' resistance well in advance of the last lap.

800M

THE SHORTEST OF THE MIDDLE-DISTANCE RACES CONSISTS OF two laps of the stadium. Competitors start off in lanes but 'break' after 100 metres. A bell is rung at the beginning of the final lap, as it is in all multi-lap races. At this point the pace picks up via a para-Pavlovian reaction which adds considerably to the drama.

800M OLYMPIC RECORDS
MEN: 1:40.91, DAVID RUDISHA (KENYA) LONDON 2012.
WOMEN: 1:53.43, NADEZHDA OLIZARENKO (USSR) MOSCOW 1980.

1500M

THE 'METRIC MILE' IS THE BLUE RIBAND EVENT OF MIDDLE-distance running. It demands greater stamina than the 800m but almost as much leg-speed – to compete at this level a male competitor needs to run consecutive laps in an average time of 55 seconds – plus an ability to gauge the precise moment to break out of the pack and hit the front. The 1500m and, to a lesser extent, the 800m are often rough races, with plenty of jostling and barging. Britain's Steve Ovett used to create space for himself by shoving the runner in front with a straight arm. Competitors in big 1500m races have sometimes come to blows.

1500M OLYMPIC RECORDS
MEN: 3:32.07, NOAH NGENY (KENYA), SYDNEY 2000.
WOMEN: 3:53.96, PAULA IVAN (ROMANIA) SEOUL 1988.

STEEPLECHASE

THE STEEPLECHASE – WHICH BEGAN AS A FORM OF IRISH cross-country in which participants raced between churches – is a muscle-sapping 3000m race with 28 hurdles and 7 water jumps. The obstacles are 36in high in men's steeplechasing and 30in in women's; they don't collapse if you crash in to them, so some competitors deliberately land on the top of the fences to help themselves get over them. The water jump consists of a hurdle followed by an upward sloping pit of water 12 feet long. The further the athletes jump, the less wet they get, but they nearly always land with one foot in the water, on the upper part of the slope, to reduce the jarring.

STEEPLECHASE OLYMPIC RECORDS
MEN: 8:05.51 JULIUS KARIUKI (KENYA) SEOUL 1988.
WOMEN: 8:58.81, GULNARA GALKINA (RUSSIA) BEIJING 2008.

LONG DISTANCE

THE OLYMPICS HOST 5000M, 10,000M AND MARATHON events. In earlier times there was also CROSS-COUNTRY but this was dropped after the catastrophic Paris 1924 event, in which the competitors were poisoned by fumes from a power plant.

5000M & 10,000M

LONG-DISTANCE RUNNING IS LIKE MIDDLE-DISTANCE RUNNING, only more so. It is extremely tactical, with the athletes either trying to break their opponents by building up unassailable leads or making damned sure they have something left in reserve for the last lap. Despite the energy-sapping earlier stages of these races, the last few hundred metres can be thrillingly fast.

5,000M OLYMPIC RECORDS
MEN: 12:57.82, KENENISA BEKELE (ETHIOPIA) BEIJING 2008.
WOMEN: 14:40.79, GABRIELA SZABO (ROMANIA) SYDNEY 2000.

10,000M OLYMPIC RECORDS
MEN: 27:01.17, KENENISA BEKLE (ETHIOPIA) BEIJING 2008.
WOMEN: 29:54.66 TIRUNESH DIBABA (ETHIOPIA) BEIJING 2008.

MARATHON

THE MARATHON WAS DEVISED AS A HEADLINE-GRABBING centrepiece for the Athens Olympics in 1896. It was inspired by the legend of PHEIDIPPIDES, a Greek soldier who in 490BC supposedly ran 26 miles to Athens to deliver news of the Greek victory over the Persians at the Battle of Marathon, only to drop dead of exhaustion. The standard distance was extended at the London Games in 1908 at the behest of the British royal family, who wanted the race to begin beneath the windows of the nursery at Windsor Castle and to finish opposite the royal box in White City Stadium, 26 miles and 385 yards away.

Marathon runners obviously need great STAMINA. They also have to SHIFT. The men's world record time of 2:03:59 and the women's 2:15:25 equate to 26 sub-five-minute miles in a row. Until the 1970s you could be a top-class male marathon runner on stamina alone, but it has since become the domain of men who can do a sub-four-minute mile, not just sub-five – and sprint at the finish. Likewise for women's marathon racing. In the light of which, it's no surprise that 10,000M RUNNERS often double up in the marathon, or move on to the marathon when they've finished with the 10k – notably the sublime HAILE GEBRSELASSIE.

MARATHON OLYMPIC RECORDS
MEN: 2:06:32, SAMUEL WANJIRU (KENYA) BEIJING 2008.
WOMEN: 2:23:07 TIKI GELANA (ETHIOPIA) LONDON 2012.

HURDLING

RHYTHM AND TECHNIQUE ARE EVERYTHING IN HURDLING. The best performers seem to float over the barriers, expending the minimum of energy and barely disrupting their step patterns. The world record times for the women's and men's 400m hurdles are less than five seconds slower than those for regular races over that distance. Maintaining a consistent STRIDE PATTERN is extremely difficult. The standard way of clearing a hurdle, with the leading leg extended and the other one bent either sideways or underneath the body, is also very demanding.

The HURDLES are designed to collapse if they are hit sufficiently hard and there are no penalties for doing this, provided the contestants make reasonable attempts to jump them. They often are hit, although this is something hurdlers seek to avoid. A collision disrupts RHYTHM and slows progress in proportion to its severity. In extreme cases it can cause a highly unpleasant fall. But hurdlers learn to cope with knocking a few over in the course of a race if that's what it takes.

When watching the hurdling events, attempt to get an early fix on who is running with the best rhythm. The smoothness or otherwise of their LEADING LEG movements is the key – if a runner has to stutter to correct their STRIDE PATTERN, they're finished.

········ **110M (MEN), 100M (WOMEN), 400M (MEN AND WOMEN)** ········

ALL OLYMPIC HURDLES RACES CONSIST OF TEN JUMPS. THE women's sprint is 100m, the men's 110m. There are differences too in the height of the hurdles (1.067m in the men's race, 0.8m in the women's) and the distances from starting line to the first hurdle, one hurdle to another, and the last hurdle to the finish. The hurdles used in the 400m races are lower – 0.914m and 0.762m for men and women respectively – but this time the course is laid out in the same way for both sexes: a 45m dash to the first obstacle, 35m between subsequent hurdles and a 40m sprint at the end.

110M/100M HURDLES OLYMPIC RECORDS
MEN: 12.91, XIANG LIU (CHINA) ATHENS 2004.
WOMEN: 12.35, SALLY PEARSON (AUSTRALIA) LONDON 2012.
400M HURDLES OLYMPIC RECORDS
MEN: 46.78, KEVIN YOUNG (USA) BARCELONA 1992.
WOMEN: 52.64, MELANIE WALKER (JAMAICA) BEIJING 2008.

································ **RELAYS: 4 × 100M, 4 × 400M** ································

OLYMPIC TEAMS ARE COMPOSED OF EACH NATION'S FASTEST runners, but speed alone is not enough: smooth HANDOVERS are the secret of success. Exchanging a baton with a colleague without substantially reducing the speed of its progress is an art, and teams often come to grief under pressure. Batons must be passed within a transition zone which extends ten metres each side of the nominal distance of each leg. The recipient must start on the inside of the first line and time their start so as to be going as fast as possible when the baton is handed over. They mustn't go too fast however, or they will have to slow down dramatically to ensure that the handover occurs before they cross the front of the zone.

The 4 × 100m is run in lanes staggered as for a regular 400m race. The first leg of the 4 × 400m is also run in lanes, which continue through the transition zone to a point 100 metres into the second leg. At this stage the runners BREAK, seeking a good position on the inside of the track. The transition zones thereafter can look extremely chaotic, with teams jostling for position along the nearside line of the zone and several athletes often taking off from much the same point at much the same time.

Traditionally, the FIRST LEG of a relay is run by the second-fastest member of a team, the SECOND by the third fastest, the PENULTI-MATE by the slowest and the final leg – the ANCHOR LEG – by the quickest.

4 × 100M Relay Olympic Records
MEN: 36.84, JAMAICA, LONDON 2012.
WOMEN: 40.82, USA, LONDON 2012.

4 × 400M Relay Olympic Records
MEN: 2:55.39, USA, BEIJING 2008
WOMEN: 3:15.17, SOVIET UNION, SEOUL 1988.

JUMPING

SPEED OF APPROACH IS THE KEY TO LONG- AND TRIPLE-JUMPING success. Pay careful attention to the consistency of the competitors' TAKE-OFF POINTS. If they are erratic, or repeatedly take off too early, it is likely to prey on their minds during the run-up. For HIGH JUMPERS it is a question of getting in the zone, bouncing jauntily and smoothly on the approach and gauging the optimum launching point. For all of them, it's vital to make a good start. A jumper rarely recovers from a series of bad jumps in the early rounds.

As with sprinters, jumpers' PRE-PERFORMANCE RITUALS are worthy of attention. Long jumpers in particular are known for their strange psyching techniques, acting out a complete jump in their minds, with accompanying jerks and twitches, before setting off.

DICK FOSBURY DEBUTS HIS FLOP AT MEXICO CITY, 1968

Jumpers also often encourage the crowd to clap a rhythm to which they can match their stride – runners tend to shut out the noise, whereas jumpers feed on it.

Rather sadly, contests for STANDING JUMPS were abandoned in 1912, depriving us of such exponents as RAY EWRY, aka 'THE HUMAN FROG', who made a clean sweep of the standing jump events at three consecutive Games between 1900 and 1908. Paradoxically, the key to his success was a bout of childhood polio. The young Ewry exercised his way out of his wheelchair, developing legs so powerful that he could leap more than nine feet backwards.

HIGH JUMP

EACH CONTESTANT HAS A MAXIMUM OF THREE ATTEMPTS AT every height, after which the BAR IS RAISED until only one jumper is left in the competition. In the case of a TIE, the jumper with the fewest failures at the last cleared height prevails. If these are identical, the number of failures in the whole competition is taken into account and if all else fails there is a JUMP–OFF.

TAKE–OFF POINT is crucial in the high jump. Too close to the bar and the jumper will clip it as they rise. Too far and they will hit it as they fall. The angle of approach is equally critical. Most top high jumpers arrive at an angle of 30–40 degrees. The aim is for the body to reach its highest point just as it reaches bar level, which is easier said than done.

Until 1968, high jumpers typically crossed the bar facing downwards. After DICK FOSBURY won the Mexico City event with his face pointing skywards, his revolutionary 'FLOP' technique became standard almost overnight.

HIGH JUMP OLYMPIC RECORDS
MEN: 2.39M, CHARLES AUSTIN (USA) ATLANTA 1996.
WOMEN: 2.06M, ELENA SLESARENKO (RUSSIA) ATHENS 2004.

LONG JUMP

SUCCESS HINGES ON SPEED ON THE RUNWAY AND TRANSLATING it into forward motion through the air. This explains why many top sprinters – notably CARL LEWIS and MARION JONES – have adapted easily to long jump.

TAKE-OFF POINT is again critical. Competitors must take off from a point on or before a 20cm-wide board laid flush with the running track – ideally, the front foot leaves the ground a few millimetres from the forward edge. FOUL JUMPS frequently occur and are verified by a slab of putty in front of the take-off board, which takes on an imprint of the foot of any jumper who goes over the line.

Each jumper gets THREE ATTEMPTS, then the eight with the longest jumps to date go through to the final, where they get another three goes. The longest jump of the day wins the competition.

LONG JUMP OLYMPIC RECORDS
MEN: 8.90M, BOB BEAMON (USA) MEXICO CITY 1968.
WOMEN: 7.40M, JACKIE JOYNER-KERSEE (USA) SEOUL 1988.

TRIPLE JUMP

THE RULES AND STRUCTURE OF THE TRIPLE JUMP ARE MUCH the same as those for the long jump. Smooth transitions between the HOP, SKIP AND JUMP are vital. In the hop phase, competitors must land on the foot with which they took off. They then take a giant step, landing on the opposite foot, before jumping in such a way as to land on two feet. As in long jumping, the distance of a jump is taken from the mark in the sand nearest to the launching board.

TRIPLE JUMP OLYMPIC RECORDS

MEN: 18.09M, KENNY HARRISON (USA) ATLANTA 1996.
WOMEN: 15.39M, FRANÇOISE MBANGO ETONE (CAMEROON) BEIJING 2008.

······································ **POLE VAULT** ·······································

THE POLE VAULT INVOLVES RUNNING DOWN A TRACK WHILE holding one end of a long, flexible pole, planting the other end in a small box and using the energy of the unbending pole to climb as high as possible. Skilful exponents push themselves upwards from the top of the pole just as it reaches a vertical position, which allows them to clear heights of almost 6m. The rules are much the same as in the high jump – THREE FAILURES at a given height and you're out.

POLE VAULT OLYMPIC RECORDS

MEN: 5.97M, RENAUD LAVILLENIE (FRANCE) LONDON 2012.
WOMEN: 5.05M, ELENA ISINBAYEVA (RUSSIA) BEIJING 2008.

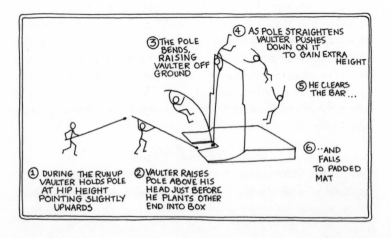

THROWING

STRENGTH IS OBVIOUSLY VITAL IN THE THROWING EVENTS, BUT speed is equally important. The distance an object is thrown is directly related to the speed of the relevant parts of the body at the instant of release. In the javelin and shot put, the VELOCITY OF THE THROWING ARM is what matters; in the discus and hammer, what matters is the rate at which the whole BODY IS SPINNING at the moment of truth. Top performers glide across the launching circles like twenty-stone ballet dancers. Getting your ANGLES RIGHT is also essential. If the trajectory of a throw is too high, its energy will be wasted on vertical climb rather than horizontal distance; too low and the projectile will come to ground prematurely. SMOOTHNESS OF DELIVERY is another imperative. The best javelin throwers make their implements slice through the air with scarcely a flutter.

Olympic athletes have THREE INITIAL ATTEMPTS in all the throwing events. The eight athletes who register the longest distances during this phase of the competition go through to the final, where they are allowed another three attempts.

·· **DISCUS** ··

MEN USE A 2KG DISCUS 22CM IN DIAMETER, WOMEN A 1KG model, which explains why the women's Olympic record is superior to the men's – uniquely in Olympic sport. Competitors skip-spin across a 2.5m throwing circle, turning one and a half times, before using their momentum and the torsion generated by rapidly twisting their bodies to hurl the discus as far as possible. The optimum ANGLE OF RELEASE is around 35 degrees. For a throw to count, the discus must land within 20 degrees of a line projecting straight forward from the throwing circle.

DISCUS OLYMPIC RECORDS
MEN: 69.89M, VIRGILIJUS ALEKNA (LITHUANIA) ATHENS 2004.
WOMEN: 72.30M, MARTINA HELLMANN (EAST GERMANY) SEOUL 1988.

NO ATHLETE, MALE OR FEMALE, HAS THROWN THE DISCUS AS FAR IN THE MODERN OLYMPICS AS EAST GERMANY'S MARTINA HELLMANN

JAVELIN

BY THE 1980s, JAVELIN THROWERS HAD BECOME SO GOOD (THE top men were hurling their weapons over 100m) that their efforts were starting to threaten athletes on the running track. The IAAF responded by changing the design specifications of competition javelins, altering their centres of gravity to make them plunge to earth sooner than they otherwise would. For a throw to count, the tip of the javelin must strike the ground before any other part of it, but it's not necessary for it to actually stick in the ground.

Men's javelins must weigh at least 800g and be 2.6–2.7m long. The comparable figures for women are 600g and 2.2–2.3m.

A fast but controlled RUN-UP is essential, as is launching the javelin at the optimum angle: it should be pointing upwards by 30–40 degrees. The throwing arm should move smoothly but rapidly and the follow-through should generate as much power as possible. Javelin throwers typically perform a little skip before braking and launching. And they often wear huge support belts to reduce the stress these movements exert on their lower backs.

JAVELIN OLYMPIC RECORDS

MEN: 90.57M, ANDREAS THORKILDSEN (NORWAY) BEIJING 2008.
WOMEN: 71.53M, OLISDEILYS MENÉNDEZ (CUBA) ATHENS 2004.

·· **SHOT PUT** ··

THE MEN'S SHOT PUT WEIGHS 7.26KG AND HAS A DIAMETER OF 110–130mm, while the women's is 4kg and 95–110m across. The aim of the exercise is to launch the projectile solely by a rapid extension of the throwing arm, which initially cradles it under the thrower's chin. Putters add OOMPH to their throws by moving rapidly across a 2.135m throwing circle and slamming the leading foot into a 10cm high stop board, thus setting up a Newtonian counter-reaction that adds energy to their puts. Some putters glide across the circle in a straight line, others spin once before releasing the metal ball.

SHOT PUT OLYMPIC RECORDS

MEN: 22.47M, ULF TIMMERMANN (EAST GERMANY) SEOUL 1988.
WOMEN: 22.41M, ILONA SLUPIANEK (EAST GERMANY) MOSCOW 1980.

·· **HAMMER** ··

THE HAMMER CONSISTS OF A METAL WEIGHT OF THE SAME mass and dimensions as the shot put attached to a wire 1.17–1.215m in length, with a grip at the far end. As with the shot, the throwing circle is 2.135m in diameter. Athletes ROTATE up to four times, using a heel-toe-heel footwork sequence, before launching the hammer. They wear gloves to prevent the handle from skinning their fingers.

Of all the throwing events, the hammer offers the highest chance of mayhem. If a competitor releases the projectile prematurely, the PROTECTIVE CAGE that surrounds much of the throwing circle is likely to be demolished.

HAMMER OLYMPIC RECORDS

MEN: 84.80, SERGEY LITVINOV (USSR) SEOUL 1988.
WOMEN: 78.18, TATYANA LUSENKO (RUSSIA) LONDON 2012.

WALKING

RACE WALKING GREW OUT OF A CRAZE FOR COMPETITIVE 'pedestrianism' in the UK and USA in the eighteenth and nineteenth centuries. Huge wagers were staked on how long it would take selected individuals to walk between specified points. Celebrity walkers ranged from mutton-chop whiskered men to elderly women. In 1749, an 18-month-old girl walked the half a mile length of Pall Mall in 23 minutes, to the delight of her backers.

······ **20KM WALK (MEN & WOMEN), 50KM WALK (MEN)** ······

COMPETITORS MUST HAVE ONE FOOT IN CONTACT WITH THE ground at all times and the ADVANCING LEG must be straight from the moment it touches the ground to the point where it is in a vertical position. Several judges are on hand along the course to monitor the walkers and issue RED CARDS if they infringe the rules. If a competitor receives three such cards (each judge can only issue one per athlete), he or she is disqualified.

20KM WALK OLYMPIC RECORDS
MEN: 1:18:46, CHEN DING (CHINA) LONDON 2012.
WOMEN: 1:25:02, ELENA LASHMANOVA (RUSSIA) LONDON 2012.
50KM WALK OLYMPIC RECORDS
MEN: 3:35:59, SERGEY KIRDYAPIN (RUSSIA) LONDON 2012.

COMBINED EVENTS

'IS THE WORLD'S SECOND GREATEST ATHLETE GAY?' ASKED Daley Thompson's T-shirt at a press conference following his victory in the DECATHLON at LA in 1984. Clearly aimed at Carl Lewis, the jibe wasn't the most charming moment of the Games, but beneath the yobbishness lay a valid question. Was Lewis, who had just won golds in the 100m, 200m, long jump and 4 × 100m relay, really the best male athlete in the world or did that title properly belong to the man who had outdone all-comers over ten different events? A similar question could be asked of women heptathletes with reference to their specialist sisters.

·········· **DECATHLON (MEN), HEPTATHLON (WOMEN)** ··········

THE MEN'S DECATHLON IS HELD OVER TWO DAYS. ON DAY one the 100M, LONG JUMP, SHOT PUT, HIGH JUMP and 400M are contested, while the 110M HURDLES, DISCUS, POLE VAULT, JAVELIN and 1500M take place on day two, in that order.

The WOMEN'S HEPTATHLON also takes two days to complete. The order of events is 100M HURDLES, HIGH JUMP, SHOT PUT, and 200M on the first day; LONG JUMP, JAVELIN and 800M on the second.

Competitors in both disciplines must pace themselves carefully. It's no good exhausting yourself in the 110m hurdles if you have to compete in the discus, pole vault, javelin and 1500m later in the day. As a consequence of the punishing schedules, performances tend to be more pedestrian than they would be if the events were more

BRITAIN'S JESSICA ENNIS MADE THE HEPTATHLON HER OWN AT LONDON 2012. NOT THAT SHE COULD QUITE BELIEVE THE GOLD MEDAL WAS FOR REAL

spread out. The top athletes aim for CONSISTENCY and keeping the leader in their sights. POINTS are awarded for distances thrown and times registered, and the decathlete/heptathlete who accumulates most points over the course of the competition is the winner.

DECATHLON OLYMPIC RECORD
MEN: 8893 POINTS, ROMAN ŠEBRLE (CZECH REPUBLIC) ATHENS 2004.
HEPTATHLON OLYMPIC RECORD
WOMEN: 7291 POINTS, JACKIE JOYNER-KERSEE (USA) SEOUL 1988.

ATHLETICS GOES TO THE OLYMPICS

ATHLETICS HAVE BEEN AT THE HEART OF EVERY OLYMPIC Games. Here's a summary of some of the highlights.

.... 1896 ....

THE FIRST EVENT OF THE MODERN OLYMPIC ERA WAS A HEAT of the MEN'S 100M, which was won in 12.2 seconds by FRANK LANE of the USA. His compatriots went on to collect nine of the twelve winners' medals on offer (silver rather than gold). For home fans, the victory of SPYRIDON LOUIS in the MARATHON was the highlight. Some 70,000 euphoric Greek spectators cheered home the 24-year-old farmer, who was joined on the last lap by the nation's two crown princes.

.... 1900 ....

NOBODY WOULD CALL THE 1900 PARIS OLYMPICS A TRIUMPH of organisation. Most of the athletic events were held in an uneven field dotted with trees, with a grass track 500 metres long. Nevertheless, heroes managed to emerge, most of them American. RAY EWRY (the frog man – see 'Jumping') won all three standing jumps and ALVIN KRAENZLEIN became the first modern Olympic great, winning the 60m sprint, the 110m and 200m hurdles and the long jump in the space of three days. In the process, he introduced the world to the extended leg method of hurdling (athletes had previously bunny-hopped over the obstacles with both legs tucked under their bodies) and narrowly avoided being beaten up by Myer Prinstein, who he defeated in the long jump after reneging on a promise not to compete on a Sunday (Alvin turned up, the trusting Prinstein didn't).

-------------------------- **1904** --------------------------

US DOMINANCE OF ATHLETICS CONTINUED IN ST LOUIS, NOT least because 197 of the 233 competitors were American. GEORGE POAGE and JOSEPH STADLER became the first AFRICAN-AMERI-CAN medallists (Poage in the 200m and 400m hurdles; Stadler in the standing high jump and standing triple jump) and Ewry again sprang his way to a clean sweep of the standing jump titles. The apparent winner of the MARATHON, a New Yorker named FRED LORZ, was discovered to have covered eleven miles of the course in a car. The gold medal was snatched from his neck and awarded to THOMAS HICKS of Massachusetts, who completed the race forti-fied with brandy and strychnine. Black South African runner Len Tau finished ninth in the race, a creditable performance given that he had been chased nearly a mile off course by dogs.

-------------------------- **1908** --------------------------

THE MARATHON AGAIN STOLE THE HEADLINES IN LONDON IN 1908. The first runner to appear in front of the 90,000 crowd was an exhausted Italian waiter named DORANDO PIETRI. In his delirium he tried to run around the track the wrong way, collapsed five times and was eventually helped over the line by officials. Not surprisingly, the American runner-up JOHNNY HAYES lodged a complaint. It was upheld and he was awarded the gold. (Pietri was, however, given a silver cup by Queen Alexandra – oddly enough, at the suggestion of Arthur Conan Doyle.) As had become the norm, the USA won far more athletic gold medals than anyone else (sixteen) but the British and Irish team did manage to claim seven of their own.

-------------------------- **1912** --------------------------

THE 1912 OLYMPICS IN STOCKHOLM SUGGESTED THAT THE Europeans might be beginning to close the gap on the Americans. This time, the main challengers were the FINNS, who won six athletics titles compared with the USA's sixteen – a thrashing on paper but a stunning victory on a per capita basis. HANNES KOLEHMAINEN was the pick of the bunch, winning the 5,000m, 10,000m and cross-country. But the biggest story of the Games was JIM THORPE, who won both the pentathlon and decathlon, breaking the world record in the latter with a score that would still have earned him silver in 1948.

··· **1920** ···

THE ANTWERP GAMES INTRODUCED THE WORLD TO PAAVO Nurmi. The original and greatest 'FLYING FINN' won gold medals in the 10,000m and the individual and team cross-country events, helping his nation to match the USA's total of nine athletics victories. He also won a silver in the 5000m.

··· **1924** ···

NURMI COLLECTED FIVE MORE GOLDS IN THE SECOND PARIS Games, which coincided with a fierce heatwave. He would almost certainly have won a sixth had the Finnish authorities not prevented him entering the 10,000m out of concern for his health. Long jumper WILLIAM DEHART HUBBARD became the first BLACK ATHLETE to win an individual gold, although the shine was slightly tarnished by the fact that his fellow American ROBERT LEGENDRE had broken the world record for the discipline the previous day while competing in the pentathlon. This was the Olympics that inspired *Chariots of Fire* with two British athletes triumphant: Harold Abrahams won the 100m and Eric Liddell, who withdrew from the 100m because his religious beliefs prevented him from competing in a heat on Sunday, securing gold in the 400m.

··· **1928** ···

AS WELL AS NURMI WINNING HIS NINTH GOLD IN THE **10,000m,** THE AMSTERDAM Olympics threw up three significant firsts. WOMEN were finally allowed to compete in track and field events, though their programme was soon drastically cut (see opposite); Japanese triple jumper MIKIO ODA of Japan won Asia's first gold medal; and PAT O'CALLAGHAN was victorious in the hammer, giving the new Republic of Ireland its first gold medal. He would retain his title in Los Angeles four years later.

'ELEVEN WRETCHED WOMEN': THE 1928 WOMEN'S 800M

Although the IOC had graciously allowed females to compete in the relatively demure disciplines of tennis, golf and sailing since 1900, with archery added to the list in 1904 and swimming and diving in 1912, there were no Olympic WOMEN'S TRACK AND FIELD EVENTS until the 1928 GAMES IN AMSTERDAM. Even then, the decision to include them was controversial.

The prevailing view in certain circles was that women were not biologically suited to strenuous exercise, an attitude supported by spurious scientific claims that athletic activity threatened women's fertility by jiggling their internal organs around. Harold Abrahams, the winner of the 1924 100m, as immortalised in *Chariots of Fire*, spoke for many when he wrote: 'I do not consider that women are built for really violent exercise of the kind that is the essence of competition. One has only to see them practising to realise how awkward they are on the running track.' Heaven knows what he would have made of JARMILA KRATOCHVÍLOVÁ, the 1980s Czech middle-distance runner, who had pecs like Arnold Schwarzenegger. Unfortunately, the women's 800m final at Amsterdam played into the hands of the chauvinists. One old-school sports reporter wrote that, 'Below us on the cinder path were eleven wretched

AN UNDIGNIFIED SPECTACLE? LINA RADKE (GERMANY) LEADING THE FIELD HOME IN 1928'S INFAMOUS WOMEN'S 800M

women, five of whom dropped out before the finish, while five collapsed on reaching the tape.' Footage of the event shows that there were actually only nine runners, all of whom finished the event. But several of them did then collapse in exhaustion.

As more progressive observers pointed out, this would have been considered routine in a men's race, where competitors were expected to give their all. The event had also been won (by LINA RADKE of Germany) in a world record time of 2:16.8, and so might have been expected to be rather draining. But the dinosaurs seized on the 'unfeminine' sight of spent females sprawled on the ground and banned women from racing further than 200m, a ruling that was not rescinded at Olympic level for 32 years.

1932

IN LOS ANGELES, AUTOMATIC TIMING MADE ITS FIRST appearance, ditto the PHOTO FINISH, which was used to correct the result of the 110m hurdles. The bronze medal was initially awarded to Jack Keller of the USA, then to Donald Finlay of Great Britain. The great all-rounder BABE DIDRIKSON qualified for all five women's events on her home soil and won golds for the javelin and 80m hurdles, and a silver for the high jump.

1936

BERLIN 1936 IS BEST REMEMBERED FOR JESSE OWENS, WHO made a mockery of the Third Reich's theory of racial

JESSE OWENS ON HIS WAY TO A FOURTH OLYMPIC GOLD AT BERLIN

superiority with victories in the 100m, 200m, 4 × 100m relay and the long jump. The local crowds took Owens to their hearts and Germany's Luz Long publically befriended him during the long jump competition, to the dismay of the Nazi authorities. They weren't best pleased with the medals table either – Germany came second with five golds while the Americans racked up fourteen.

-- **1948** --

THE STAR OF THE SHOW AT LONDON'S SECOND GAMES WAS Dutch housewife FANNY BLANKERS-KOEN, who won golds in the 100m, 200m, 80m hurdles and 4 × 100m relay. USA's ALICE COACHMAN won the high jump to become the first BLACK FEMALE Olympic champion, while the men's decathlon title was claimed by seventeen-year-old American BOB MATHIAS, who remains the YOUNGEST MALE Olympic athletics champion. When asked how he intended to celebrate, he said 'I'll start shaving I guess.' MICHELINE OSTERMEYER, a French concert pianist, used her delicate fingers to win golds in the discus and the shot put (the latter event making its Olympic debut for women) and bronze in the high jump.

-- **1952** --

WITH THEIR FINE RECORD IN LONG-DISTANCE RUNNING, THE Finns had every reason to expect a hatful of victories on home soil. They had reckoned without Czech phenomenon EMILE ZÁTOPEK. Having collected golds in the 5000m and 10,000m, he thought it might be worth trying his hand at the marathon, a distance he had never attempted before. He won it by more than two and a half minutes.

-- **1956** --

THE HOME NATION GOT OFF TO A STORMING START IN THE athletics at Melbourne, with BETTY CUTHBERT completing a double in the women's 100m and 200m and anchoring Australia's victory in the 4 × 100m relay. America's BOBBY MORROW matched Cuthbert's feat in the men's sprint events.

1960

AFTER 64 YEARS, A RUNNER FROM A NON-ANGLOPHONE nation – Germany's ARMIN HARY – won the men's 100m in Rome. ABEBE BIKILA of Ethiopia broke the marathon record, running in his bare feet, becoming the first black African gold medallist. Women were finally allowed to run more than 200m again, with LYUDMILLA SHEVTSOVA (USSR) claiming the first WOMEN'S 800m since 1928. The athletics cold war also heated up, as the SOVIET UNION came within a whisker of matching the American haul of victories – the final tally was eleven golds to twelve.

1964

THE TOKYO GAMES PRODUCED TWO STUNNING VICTORIES from the walking wounded. BIKILA won the marathon again, in another record time, just six weeks after having his appendix removed,

TWO GLOVES, ONE STRUGGLE: TOMMIE SMITH AND JOHN CARLOS GIVE BLACK POWER SALUTES ON THE PODIUM

and American AL OERTER collected his third men's discus title while wearing a neck brace. The Soviet Union's mysterious Press sisters secured three golds – Tamara won the shot put and discus, Irina the pentathlon – but their record-breaking careers came to an abrupt end when testing to verify the gender of athletes was introduced in 1966.

1968

THE ATHLETIC EVENTS IN Mexico City were marked by the effects of high altitude. BOB BEAMON of the USA sailed through the thin air to break the WORLD

LONG JUMP RECORD by almost two feet (his record stood until 1991 and remains the Olympic record). Five of the male triple jumpers exceeded the existing record distance and there were world records in all the men's races up to and including 400m with America's JIM HINES becoming the first man to officially run the 100m in less than 10 seconds. Contrariwise, the distance races were won in slow times due to the exhaustion induced by the low-oxygen atmosphere; the great RON CLARKE was nearly killed by the 10km race. Other highlights included DICK FOSBURY introducing the world to the 'flop' method of clearing the high jump bar; KIP KEINO, first of the world-beating Kenyans, who won the 1500m by a (still unrivalled) margin of 20m; and sprinters TOMMIE SMITH and JOHN CARLOS being kicked out of the Olympic village after their infamous BLACK POWER SALUTES at the men's 200m award ceremony.

-- **1972** --

A NEW GREAT FINNISH LONG-DISTANCE RUNNER EMERGED IN Munich, when LASSE VIRÉN claimed the men's 5000m and 10,000m, a feat he would repeat in Montreal. ULRIKE MEYFARTH of West Germany became the youngest individual athletics champion by winning the women's high jump at the age of sixteen. East German WOLFGANG NORDWIG brought a sequence of sixteen US victories in the pole vault to an end and the USSR finally managed to come first in the athletics medals table, with VALERI BORZOV achieving a sprint double in the 100m and 200m, despite almost missing the 100m quarter-finals because he had fallen asleep.

-- **1976** --

ALBERTO JUANTORENA (CUBA) BECAME THE FIRST MAN TO complete the 400m/800m double (he was a newcomer to the latter event). VIKTOR SANEYEV (USSR) won his third triple jump title and Hungarian javelin thrower MIKLÓS NÉMETH became the first son of an Olympic gold medallist to win one of his own – his father Imre had won the hammer in 1948. The top nation was the GDR (EAST GERMANY), with eleven athletics golds. The GDR would enjoy stunning athletics success until its demise in 1989, much of it attributable to a systematic doping policy.

··· **1980** ···

THE USA BOYCOTTED THE MOSCOW GAMES IN PROTEST AT the Soviet invasion of Afghanistan, and the absence of American athletes gave other nations a chance to shine – among them Great Britain. STEVE OVETT and SEBASTIAN COE's battle in the middle-distance races ended with each winning the event for which the other was the favourite (Ovett the 800m, Coe the 1500m).

··· **1984** ···

THE ATHLETICS IN LA WAS COLOURED BY A TIT-FOR-TAT SOVIET-led boycott. The introduction of the WOMEN'S MARATHON was a belated slap in the face to the school of 1928 (see p.63). CARL LEWIS matched Jesse Owen's achievement in Berlin with victories in the 100m, 200m, 4 × 100m and the long jump, and ED MOSES extended his 400m hurdles winning streak to an incredible 102 races. ULRIKE MEYFARTH now became the oldest winner of the women's high jump at the age of 28, and Britain's SEBASTIAN COE retained the 1500m – some achievement in the blue riband event.

The (now discontinued) women's 3000m is remembered for the clash between MARY DECKER, darling of the LA crowd, and a shy, tiny 'British' South African named ZOLA BUDD. Seventeen hundred metres into the final, Decker bumped into Budd, who had to stretch her left leg outwards to avoid falling. The American promptly tripped over Budd's other leg, pitching off the track and out of the contest. The crowd booed Budd for the remainder of the race, which was won by Romania's MARICICA PUICA.

··· **1988** ···

THE STORY OF THE SEOUL OLYMPICS CAN BE SUMMED UP IN two words: BEN JOHNSON. The Canadian athlete astonished the planet by storming to victory in the men's 100m final in a world record time of 9.79 seconds, then plunged it into dismay by fail-ing a drug test. There was a strong shadow of suspicion, too, over FLORENCE GRIFFITH JOYNER's scarcely credible performance in the women's 100m final, winning the race in 10.54 seconds (still the Olympic record). FLO-JO had arrived at the Games having im-proved inexplicably in the course of the preceding year, and one look at her was enough for many sceptics. As the US coach Bill Dellinger had remarked at the US team trials (albeit not about Flo-Jo): 'That wasn't a sprint – that was chemical warfare.'

-- **1992** --

THE FIRST OLYMPICS SINCE THE FALL OF THE BERLIN WALL SAW Britain's LINFORD CHRISTIE become the oldest winner of the men's 100m by a margin of four years. DERARTU TULU of Ethiopia became the first black female African Olympic champion with victory in the women's 10,000m. The most emotional episode of the Games began 150 metres into the semi-final of the men's 400m, when Britain's DEREK REDMOND felt his right hamstring pop and collapsed to the ground. His father Jim raced down from the stands, put his arm around his stricken son and told him, 'we started your career togeth-er so we're going to finish this race together.' The 65,000 crowd gave the two Redmonds a standing ovation as they hobbled their way to the finishing line. The USA's EVELYN ASHFORD won a remarkable fourth gold (for the 4 × 100m relay) in three Olympic Games; she might well have won more had it not been for Flo-Jo.

-- **1996** --

ATLANTA PRODUCED TWO ASTONISHING DOUBLES: MICHAEL JOHNSON took the 200m and 400m double (the first by any male athlete in a non-boycotted Games), while MARIE-JOSÉ PÉREC of France matched him in the women's division. Men's 10,000m champion HAILE GEBRSELASSIE ran the second half of the race in 13: 11.6, a time only bettered in three Olympic 5000m finals.

-- **2000** --

WHEN MARIE-JOSÉ PÉREC CRACKED UP AND FLED SYDNEY under the weight of media scrutiny, the way was clear for Australian CATHY FREEMAN to win the women's 400m. Her victory, achieved in a hooded bodysuit in front of a record Olympic crowd of 112,524, was of huge significance to the nation's Aboriginal people. Another highlight was American athlete MARION JONES' drive for five Olympic titles. She won three of them – the 100m, 200m and 4 × 400m – but in 2007 admitted taking performance-enhancing drugs and was stripped of her medals. Her husband, the gargantuan shot putter C.J. Hunter, tested positive for nandrolone at Sydney. In winning the triple jump, Jonathan Edwards became the first British Olympic champion in that event since 1908.

·· **2004** ···

The Greek hosts had high hopes of victory for sprinters Konstantinos Kenteris and Ekaterini Thanou, but to intense local embarrassment, the pair failed to turn up for a drugs test the day before the opening ceremony, claiming they had been involved in a motorbike accident. Liu Xiang became the first male Chinese athlete to win an Olympic athletics gold with victory in the 110m hurdles. Britain's Kelly Holmes notched up a double in the 800m and 1500m. Her compatriot Paula Radcliffe had bad luck in the women's marathon, forced to withdraw 23 miles into the race due to stomach trouble. Brazilian Vanderlei de Lima had an even worse time in the men's equivalent – he was attacked by an Irish priest – though he still came third. The Moroccan Hicham El Guerrouj – perhaps the greatest ever middle distance runner – took golds in the 1500m and 5000m.

·· **2008** ···

athletics at Beijing's Games belonged unquestionably to Usain Bolt. The 6ft 5in Jamaican produced the most exciting outcome the sport can offer – a world record in an Olympic 100m final. Even more impressive in some ways was his performance in the 200m. Many witnesses of Michael Johnston's annihilation of the field in the event in Atlanta believed he had set a world record that would stand for fifty years. It lasted just eight, as Bolt justified his surname in a time of 19.30 seconds.

·· **2012** ···

Bolt broke his own olympic record in the 100m, winning in 9.63 seconds, but for the locals the highlight of the athletics was one golden hour on the evening of 4 August 2012 in which Great Britons Jessica Ennis (heptathlon), Greg Rutherford (long jump) and Mo Farah (10,000m) all became Olympic champions.

Great Britain had never won a men's long-distance Olympic gold before and Farah secured his place in history by triumphing in the 5,000m a week later. The subsequent charges of doping against several Russian athletes – including Yuliva Zaripova (winner of the women's steeplechase), Ekaterina Poistogova (who secured bronze in the same event) and Maryina Savinova (the women's 800m champion) – cannot obscure the achievements of Ennis, Rutherford and Farah.

10 ATHLETIC GREATS

TEN OF THE GREATS – IN ORDER OF APPEARANCE.

1. Jim Thorpe, USA (Gold 2)

When King Gustav of Sweden placed a gold medal around the neck of the winner of the 1912 pentathlon and decathlon, calling him the greatest athlete in the world, Thorpe replied 'Thanks, King.' This alone would have secured him immortality. The part-Native American, part-Caucasian was given a ticker-tape parade on his return to New York but things turned sour when it emerged that he had earned $25 a week in 1909 and 1910 playing minor league baseball in North Carolina. This was deemed an intolerable breach of the 'amateurs only' rules. The IOC asked Thorpe to return his gold medals and struck his name from the record books. In 1983, thirty years after his death, the decision was reversed.

....

2. Paavo Nurmi, Finland (Gold 9, Silver 3)

The Flying Finn's haul of nine gold medals ties him with Carl Lewis as the most successful male Olympic athlete. In 1924, he won the 1500m in a world record time, rested for 26 minutes and then repeated the feat in the 5000m.

....

3. Mildred 'Babe' Didrikson, USA (Gold 2, Silver 1)

At the Los Angeles Games in 1932, the Texan all-rounder won the javelin and 80m hurdles and tied for the high jump (she was relegated to silver by the judges for a style contravention). Such was

TWO OF THE GREATS: MILDRED DIDRIKSON THROWING THE JAVELIN AT LA 1932 AND THE INELEGANT BUT DEVASTATING EMIL ZÁTOPEK AT HELSINKI 1952

her versatility that she became, under her married name of Mildred Zaharias, the most successful female golf player of all time. She was pretty damned good at basketball, too.

4. Jesse Owens, USA (Gold 4)

One afternoon in May 1935, Owens set six world records in 45 minutes. But the sprinter and long jumper from Cleveland, Ohio is most celebrated for his four victories at the Berlin Olympics in 1936. Adolf Hitler actually treated him marginally better than the leader of his own country, sending him an inscribed photograph. 'It wasn't Hitler who snubbed me,' Owens later said. 'It was FDR who snubbed me. The President didn't even send me a telegram.'

5. Fanny Blankers-Koen, Netherlands (Gold 4)

The 'Flying Housewife' from the Netherlands is still the only female athlete to have won four golds at one Games, triumphing in the 100m, 200m, 80m hurdles and 4 × 100m relay in London in 1948. She wasn't even at her peak when she did it. Having competed in the 1936 Olympics as an eighteen-year-old, her best years overlapped with the

Second World War, during which she broke world records for the high and long jumps and various sprint and hurdling events. At the grand old age of 33 she registered another record, in the pentathlon.

6. Emil Zátopek, Czechoslovakia (Gold 4, Silver 1)

Known as the 'Czech Locomotive', Zátopek was the toast of the Helsinki Games of 1952, with victories in the 5000m, 10,000m and the marathon (he was carried aloft by the Jamaican relay team after this last victory). He is a rare exception to the rule that a beautiful style is the most efficient: his head rocked from side to side, his torso twisted, and he made a hell of a racket (his loud wheezing was one reason for the nickname). Zátopek was promoted to the rank of lieutenant colonel in the Czech army in recognition of his athletic exploits but was sent to do manual labour in a uranium mine after lending his support to the 1968 uprising.

7. Abebe Bikila, Ethiopia (Gold 2)

Abebe Bikila, the winner of the 1960 and 1964 Olympic marathons, only failed to win one race at the distance during his career – the 1963 Boston Marathon. A member of the Imperial Bodyguard of Haile Selassie, the great Ethiopian has a stadium named after him in Addis Ababa. Tragically, he was rendered quadriplegic in a car accident in 1969 and died four years later.

8. Carl Lewis, USA (Gold 9, Silver 1)

The only man to successfully defend Olympic titles in the 100m and long jump, Lewis is the joint most successful Olympic athlete of the modern era (with Paavo Nurmi). At the 1984 Olympics he equalled Jesse Owens' haul of four golds.

9. Michael Johnson, USA (Gold 4)

No athletics coach would encourage his charges to run like Johnson, who took extraordinarily short steps and leaned backwards. But nobody could argue with the results. Olympic 400m champion in 1996 and 2000, he also knocked an astounding third of a second off the 200m world record in the final at Atlanta. And that record – Pietro Mennea's 1979 time in Mexico – was widely regarded as the toughest in athletics

10. Usain Bolt, Jamaica (Gold 6)

The laid-back Jamaican showman has taken sprinting into a new dimension, regularly beating top class fields by margins of several metres, and with an apparently casual air. Many believe him capable of running the 100m in less than 9.5 seconds. And he may bag further records if his move up to 400m works out. He has suggested that he fancies playing 20/20 cricket when he retires from international athletics in 2017.

BADMINTON

11–20 AUGUST 2016

RIOCENTRO PAVILION 4, RIO DE JANEIRO

Athletes: 172 | **Golds up for grabs:** 5

········· **OLYMPIC PRESENCE** ·········

A DEMONSTRATION SPORT IN 1972 AND 1988, BADMINTON became a full Olympic sport in 1992.

········· **OLYMPIC FORMAT** ·········

THERE ARE FIVE EVENTS: MEN'S SINGLES AND DOUBLES, women's singles and doubles, and mixed doubles.

········· **CURRENT CONTENDERS** ·········

CHINA WON ALL FIVE GOLDS, TWO SILVERS AND A BRONZE IN 2012 and will expect to dominate in Rio. Their principal challengers will be DENMARK, INDONESIA, JAPAN, MALAYSIA and SOUTH KOREA.

········· **PAST CHAMPIONS** ·········

CHINA: 16 | SOUTH KOREA: 6 | INDONESIA: 6

WHY WATCH BADMINTON?

IN 1876, ENGLISH JOURNALIST HENRY JONES SET OUT AN EARLY version of the rules for what he called 'The Anglo-Indian Game of Badminton'. He concluded by suggesting that: 'Any garden that has a small lawn provides the suitable locus ... given a fair sky and a happy, light-hearted company, Badminton will furnish healthy enjoyable recreation and amusement for both old and young of both sexes for many an afternoon.' You might think him right. Badminton is a gentle, slow-moving, recreational affair, is it not?

Think again. The SHUTTLECOCK may be mere cork and feathers but struck correctly it can split a watermelon in two. Shuttlecocks have been recorded flying at SPEEDS in excess of 200mph. One time and motion study asserted that top-class badminton players cover twice as much ground as tennis players and are engaged in rallies for twice as long. On average, they play 2,000 strokes during a match. The speed and power of badminton is more than matched by its tactical complexity, virtuoso technique and compelling court battles.

In ASIA, where people have been playing shuttlecock games for over two thousand years, this sport really matters. When in 1992 badminton stars Susi Susanti and Alan Kusuma returned from the Barcelona Olympics with INDONESIA's first gold medals in any sport, the whole of Jakarta turned out to see the recently engaged couple parade through the city in an open-topped car, to which was fixed a gigantic shuttlecock. At the Athens and Beijing Olympics, the CHINESE love of the game gave badminton the biggest TV audiences of any single event and in 2008 the locals packed the badminton arena to see their heroes. Lin Dan, notionally a lieutenant colonel in the People's Army, celebrated his victory in the men's singles by throwing his shoes and racquet into an ecstatic crowd.

So forget the world of genteel English garden parties and take a look at Olympic badminton – 250 million Indonesians and 1.3 billion Chinese can't be entirely wrong.

THE SHUTTLECOCK

The shuttlecock is a remarkably stable device, almost always flying with the cork bottom forward, however it is struck. It is thus capable of great speed, but once the energy of a stroke has been spent the drag imparted by the feathers makes the shuttlecock decelerate very sharply. This makes lobs and lofts and dropshots possible, strokes that are enhanced by the shuttlecock's tendency to fall at a steeper angle than it rises.

Most of us make do with nylon shuttlecocks but these are far too slow and insensitive for competition play. Top-level shuttlecocks are made from sixteen feathers embedded in a rounded cork base covered with leather. Goose feathers are the best. Duck feathers are sometimes used but they tend to dry out and break. The feathers – nearly all from China, where goose is a popular dish – must come from the left wing of the bird, and each wing provides only seven or eight feathers of the requisite size. As shuttlecocks are easily bent and broken, players may get through a dozen or more during a match. They also have to be used quickly: they cannot be vacuum-packed and begin to degrade after a couple of months on the shelf.

THE STORY OF BADMINTON

THERE IS EVIDENTLY A SPECIAL PLEASURE THAT HUMANS derive from the arc of an object that appears to float through the air, as you can find versions of the shuttlecock all over the world. In New Mexico, the Native American Zuni have played with dried corn husks set with feathers since ancient times. The pre-Inca Mochi of northern Peru tossed a shuttlecock as part of their fertility rites while in Amazonia people still play *Paetec*, using a coin-weighted corn husk with feathers attached.

In ancient China *Ti Jian Zi* was the shuttlecock game, in which players used their feet to keep the sophisticated feathered shuttlecocks aloft. Crossing the social divides of imperial China, it was played by soldiers, children and ladies of the court for almost two millennia, spreading to Thailand, Vietnam, Laos and Malaysia. In medieval Japan the shuttle (known as the 'small barbaric demon') was struck with a bat or *hagoita*.

Europeans began to play shuttlecock games in the early sixteenth century. In the royal courts of France and Sweden and in the streets of London, the flight of the shuttle had the same cross-class and cross-gender appeal as in Asia. In England, the game was known as battledore and shuttlecock, and was played with racquets covered in vellum. It was a fashionable pastime at the court of James I, but was also played by children in the streets, who would sing nursery rhymes and counting games as they kept the shuttle aloft. It caught on in France, too, where as a rare example of a game played by both sexes, it was regarded as full of erotic potential. Count Rivarol, enjoying the game in Versailles, wrote with relish, 'How I'd like to be a shuttlecock to be able to stroke uncovered generous breasts and come to rest at the foot of young beauties.'

Despite their love of shuttlecock games, none of these civilisations moved beyond forms of competitive KEEPY-UPPY, transfixed by the deceleration and fall of the shuttlecock, and almost oblivious to the possibilities of speed, power and confrontation. All this changed in the mid-nineteenth century, when British army officers and imperial officials discovered the many variants of the game that were played in Madras, Bombay, Calcutta and Peshawar. Though their rules varied greatly, the Anglo-Indian hybrids that emerged all included court markings, a high net, oppositional playing and a system of scoring.

These versions were probably tentatively combined at a weekend party in the 1860s at BADMINTON HOUSE, home of the Duke of Beaufort. The association between this country house and the game became fixed in 1873, when an extensive correspondence began in the sporting journal *The Field* over the precise rules of the 'Badminton game of battledore'. In response, a Major Forbes submitted a pamphlet published in Calcutta by the Great Eastern Hotel Company that decreed an hourglass-shaped court and allowed up to three a side. Two years later in 1875 the first badminton club was opened in Folkestone, Kent. Similar clubs sprung up in other English seaside resorts and in towns populated by retired officers of the British Raj. In 1893 the Badminton Association was established in SOUTHSEA and the game's rules were codified and published.

By the eve of the First World War badminton had found new blood in the rest of the British Isles, northern France and Denmark. In the inter-war years the sport made its way down the social scale to the British lower middle classes, travelled back to India and Malaysia, where it was played by the last generation of imperial officials and the local elites, and found favour in Australia, Canada, Denmark and New Zealand.

Badminton became an enduring popular craze in the UNITED STATES in the 1930s, with leading baseball and football players taking to it with the kind of zeal they now show for golf. Enthusiasts included Hollywood stars Douglas Fairbanks Jr, Joan Crawford, James Cagney, Boris Karloff and Ginger Rogers. One New York hair salon even put a badminton court on its flat roof so customers could play while they waited.

Despite this kind of fan base, the sport never achieved the social cachet of tennis in America – badminton clubs were never exclusive enough to provide the kind of deal-making opportunities found at the country clubs.

260KM AN HOUR ... CHINA'S LIN DAN STRIKES AT BEIJING 2008

Badminton on Ice: Hugh Forgie

Badminton was big enough in the USA in the 1930s for a small number of professionals to make a living playing exhibition games. Most famous of all was Hugh Forgie, who abandoned professional ice hockey to take up the game. 'I did for badminton what the Harlem Globetrotters did for basketball,' he recalled, and for a time he even worked as the Globetrotters' half-time show.

PRE-WAR BADDERS TRICKSTER KEN DAVIDSON

Born in Ontario, Forgie began touring in 1935, challenging all-comers, before teaming up with British trick-shot artist Ken Davidson in a show so spellbinding that they sold out a 38-week run at the London Palladium, where the audience included King George and Queen Elizabeth. Forgie starred in two badminton movies – *Flying Feathers* and *Volley Oops!* – and became world pro champ in 1941, not losing a game for 11 years. After the war, as the public tired of comedy badminton, he upped the ante, putting his act on ice. In his travelling revue show of the early 1950s, *Ice Capades*, Forgie would play extraordinary rallies on skates, culminating in a frenzied one-man game in which he would serve and receive, skidding back and forth around the net. His great regret, in later life, was that so few of the 85 million people who saw him under-stood badminton, telling one journalist: 'I really had the game down cold.'

Game On: Badminton Basics

The game begins with a serve. Serves must be made from below the waist, with the racquet head below the hand and with both feet on the ground. Serves that are not touched by the receiver must land in the SERVICE AREA to win the point. If they touch the net, and land in, a LET is called and the point replayed.

RALLIES

RALLIES ARE WON WHEN THE SHUTTLE TOUCHES THE FLOOR of a demarcated area on the opponent's side of the court or if it goes out of play. Shuttles that land on the line are considered in play. Shuttles that clip the net but go over it are considered legal. Whoever wins the rally gets the next serve; points are won whether one is serving or receiving (a change from original practice).

GAMES AND MATCHES

GAMES ARE WON BY THE FIRST PLAYER TO REACH 21 POINTS. If the score is tied at 20-all the game continues until someone is two points clear. If the game reaches 29-all, then the next point decides the game.

MATCHES are the best of three games.

THE FINER POINTS

THE SERVE IS NOT KING

UNLIKE TENNIS, SERVICE DOES NOT GIVE AN OVERWHELMING advantage nor does it produce the fastest strokes. Players tend to opt for serves that go low over the net, using flicks and spin to deceive the receiver.

MAKING SPACE FOR THE SMASH

IN SINGLES, PLAYERS SPEND MUCH OF THEIR TIME TRYING TO manoeuvre their opponents around the court, hoping to open up space for a decisive winning shot – an unplayable SMASH, perhaps, or a lethal DROP SHOT.

FORCING THE LOB

IN DOUBLES, WHERE THERE IS LESS SPACE ON THE COURT, players try to force opponents into making HIGH LOBS, thereby

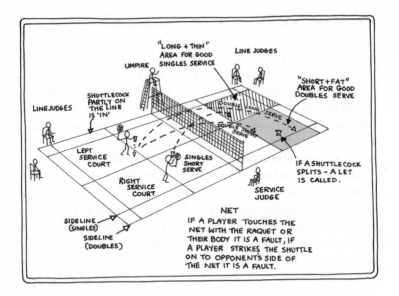

setting up SMASHING OPPORTUNITIES for themselves. They do this by playing drop shots close to the net.

FORCING ERRORS

THE TOP PLAYERS ARE SO GOOD THAT SPACE RARELY OPENS up and RETURN LOBS are brilliantly placed. Therefore, most points are won on mistakes, where a return is put into the net or out of play.

THE IMPORTANCE OF DECEPTION

GIVEN HOW HARD IT IS TO HIT A WINNER, THERE IS A premium on deceiving your opponent, gaining an advantage by disguising your shot or changing it at the last moment. A split-second shift of the angle of the racquet head produces a SLICE, dropping the shuttlecock short, a result that can also be achieved by abruptly shortening the hitting action. The best players can put a certain amount of SPIN on their shots and sometimes produce a DOUBLE MOTION SHOT, in which the stroke begins in one direction before the player suddenly snaps into a different one.

BADMINTON GOES TO THE OLYMPICS

IN 1934 AN INTERNATIONAL BADMINTON FEDERATION WAS SET up in Southsea but with just nine members its global reach was limited. In fact, it took badminton until 1972 to gain a place as a demonstration sport and another twenty years to achieve full Olympic status. What changed its standing was the surging popularity of the game in Asia, which helped support the creation of a small but sustainable world professional circuit. The shuttlecock game had gone home.

The balance of badminton power began tilting eastward in the 1960s. In post-independence Malaysia and Indonesia, badminton acquired huge public status. The game had arrived in INDONESIA in the 1920s via the gyms and games halls of the Chinese communities of Singapore and Malaya. By the 1930s rival clubs were competing in Jakarta and the game had spread throughout Java, providing a rare opportunity for Chinese, Javanese and other ethnic groups to socialise without the presence of the colonial Dutch elites. Given the long folk memory of Asian shuttlecock games, badminton did not seem like a foreign sport at all. In the years after independence this culture nurtured world-class players like RUDI HARTONO, one of Indonesia's few global sports stars.

In the 1970s the game became popular in SOUTH KOREA. As with the American craze of the 1930s, under conditions of rapid urbanisation and rising affluence, the lower middle classes, who were excluded from golf and tennis clubs, opted for badminton. The game boomed in CHINA in the 1980s and 1990s, gaining popularity as the government sports system nurtured champions.

The rising power of Asian badminton was heralded by the creation of the breakaway WORLD BADMINTON FEDERATION in 1978. In a direct challenge to the control exercised over world badminton by the four British national associations, the WBF called for the expulsion of Taiwan as a precondition of Chinese membership, the expulsion of apartheid South Africa and the introduction of one-nation one-vote decision-making. It then established the Independent World Championships and called for a boycott of the All-England tournament. Three years later the IBF blinked, signing a union with the WBF on the latter's terms.

Now a truly global game, with the weight of Asian numbers behind it, badminton was introduced as a demonstration sport at the Seoul Olympics and took its permanent place at the Games in 1992. South Korea and Indonesia shared the gold medals that year and in 1996 the Dane POUL-ERIK HØYER LARSEN became the only non-Asian to win gold in the men's singles. Nearly everything else has been won by the CHINESE, who have received nearly half of all the medals awarded at the Olympics for badminton, including sixteen golds.

Definitive proof that badminton had left the genteel world of English garden parties far behind has been provided by occasional DOPING controversies and more frequent allegations of MATCH FIXING. Rumours of players taking it easy against certain opponents – particularly compatriots – had dogged the sport for years but no one was quite prepared for the scandal that overshadowed the women's doubles triumph by ZHAO YUNLEI and TIAN QING at London 2012 when four teams – one each from China and Indonesia and two from South Korea – were expelled for trying to lose a match. All four teams had qualified for the quarter-finals before the final round of matches and knew that a defeat could ease their route to the final or improve their country's medal prospects.

If China's Wang Xiaoli and Yu Yang lost to South Korea's Jung Kyung-eun and Kim Ha-na, they could not face their compatriots Zhao Yuneli and Tian Qing before the final. Unfortunately for them, their opponents decided it was in their interests to lose too. In a loser-takes-all contest, during which no rally lasted longer than four shots and serves routinely sank into the net, the Chinese ultimately lost. It proved a Pyrrhic defeat, as both pairs – along with teams from South Korea and Indonesia who had similarly disgraced themselves – were disqualified. The scandal did prove one thing: the banned players didn't know how to lose intentionally without making their intentions painfully apparent.

Stung by charges that its format was to blame, the WBF has changed the rules for Rio: in all the doubles tournaments, second-placed teams will enter a second draw to determine their opponents in the quarter-finals and group winners will be seeded.

BASKETBALL

6–21 AUGUST 2016

CARIOCA ARENA 1, BARRA OLYMPIC PARK,
YOUTH ARENA, DEODORO OLYMPIC PARK,
RIO DE JANEIRO

Athletes: 288 | Golds up for grabs: 2

OLYMPIC PRESENCE

MEN SINCE 1936 (DEMONSTRATION SPORT 1904, 1924); WOMEN since 1976.

OLYMPIC FORMAT

IN BOTH MEN'S AND WOMEN'S TOURNAMENTS, TWELVE TEAMS play in two groups of six. The top four from each group progress to the knock-out stages.

CONTENDERS

IN THE MEN'S EVENT, THE USA REMAIN THE TEAM TO BEAT – especially if the best basketball player in the world, LEBRON JAMES, is in the squad. Yet there are many foreign players in the NBA now, and strong leagues in Europe, so expect the likes of ARGENTINA, SPAIN, SERBIA and LITHUANIA to be in contention. In the WOMEN'S COMPETITION the AMERICANS are even more dominant as they aim for their sixth straight gold medal, but AUSTRALIA, FRANCE, RUSSIA and SPAIN will be in the hunt for medals. With home advantage, BRAZIL who finished fifth in the men's competition in 2012 and won silver in the women's event in 1996 should challenge strongly.

PAST CHAMPIONS

USA: 21 | USSR/RUSSIA: 5 | ARGENTINA & YUGOSLAVIA: 1

Why Watch Basketball?

Why watch basketball? Why ever not? Those lucky enough to attend should expect something amazing. On the basketball court, human beings almost fly: the best can hang in the air, seemingly able to hit time's 'Pause' button so they can move the ball between their hands before shooting.

If the game's vertical dimension inspires awe, its horizontal axis releases adrenaline, even if you're only watching on TV. Basketball is a game of incessant flow and action that demands intricate, rapid teamwork and transcendent moments of individual genius. In the basketball court's tight spaces, INSPIRATION, SPONTANEITY and TRICKERY are constant, as players, unable to barge or push, must seek out space, throw no-look passes, steal the ball, turn and switch direction in an instant.

The rules require teams to SHOOT AT THE BASKET at least EVERY 24 SECONDS. This creates a pulsating ebb and flow of advantage and disadvantage, and huge scores too – often over 100 points on each side (the 2008 Olympic final finished 118-107). There may not be much midfield, but every game is a blizzard of action, punctuated with jump shots and the high-energy surges of players hard-driving to the net. All of this occurs in an arena where the crowd is closer to the benches and the action than in any other sport.

The Story of Basketball

By the closing years of the nineteenth century the YMCA had established a network of sports halls and gymnasiums throughout Europe and North America. In the United States, it was rapidly losing members to the great outdoor sports – American football and baseball – while its emphasis on gymnastics was proving a tad too rigorous for America's youth. It was in this context that LUTHER GULICK, head of the training school for YMCA instructors in Springfield, Massachusetts, encouraged his students and staff to develop indoor games that could bring the punters back to the YMCA's 'halls of health'.

JAMES NAISMITH, a thirty-year-old Canadian student, considered and rejected variants of American football, soccer and lacrosse, before formulating a 13-rule game that would soon become BASKETBALL. The first recorded match was played NINE-A-SIDE in December 1891, with a peach basket nailed to the rafters as the goal. The sport was an instant hit, and over the next decade Springfield's instructors did such a good promotional job it was soon second only to baseball in terms of national participation. The rules were quickly and systematically adapted – nine-a-side became FIVE-A-SIDE, the basket was replaced by a backboard and a net, regulations on fouls and free throws were introduced – but it was still essentially the same basic no-contact game of passing, dribbling and shooting that Naismith had invented.

Thereafter, the game grew through two different channels. In the USA, the school and college sport was accompanied by the emergence of a huge urban basketball culture, especially among the ethnic enclaves of America's great industrial cities, and by a growing circuit of professional leagues and exhibition matches. These somewhat chaotic leagues, which featured roughhouse play and courts surrounded by wire mesh, eventually coalesced to form what we now call the NATIONAL BASKETBALL ASSOCIATION (NBA) in 1946.

In the rest of the world, basketball was introduced by the YMCA or the American army, or both. In urban gyms and sports clubs in the Mediterranean, Eastern Europe, Australia, Japan, the Philippines and China, basketball became an immensely popular recreational game. As it never acquired elite professional status, the communist nations (300 million people play the game in China) could challenge only at American college level. Meanwhile, the NBA – the apex of global basketball – remained in a league of its own.

The readmission of professionals into the Olympics in 1992 brought these worlds back together, to an extent. While the Americans remain the dominant force in men's and women's basketball, the professionalisation of the game in Europe and China and the flow of foreign talent into the NBA have made the Olympic contest a bit less one-sided.

GAME ON: BASKETBALL BASICS

SCORING: 3-2-1

THE AIM IS TO SCORE MORE POINTS THAN THE OPPOSING team. This is done by putting the ball through the net they are defending. How many points you score depends on where the ball was released. If it was thrown from outside the 6.25m line (a LONG BASKET), it's a THREE-POINTER. More common is the TWO-POINT FIELD GOAL, scored from open play inside the line. A FREE THROW, taken unimpeded from the free throw or foul line in front of the basket, scores ONE POINT.

TIME IN, TIME OUT

THE GAME IS FIVE-A-SIDE. EACH TEAM HAS ANOTHER SEVEN players on the bench and SUBSTITUTIONS are unlimited. Though the starting five on a team are generally the strongest unit and play the most minutes, it is virtually unheard of for anyone to play an entire match. At the Olympics, basketball is played in FOUR QUARTERS, each ten minutes long, with a half-time interval of fifteen minutes. In the event of a tied score at the end of the fourth quarter five minutes of OVERTIME are played. Coaches can call a one-minute TIME OUT, during which play is suspended, twice in the first half, three times in the second half and once in overtime.

MOVING AND DRIBBLING

PLAYERS CAN THROW, BOUNCE, ROLL AND PAT THE BALL, BUT they must not kick or punch it. They can take THREE STEPS with the ball but must then shoot or pass. If they bounce the ball, one-handed, they can DRIBBLE with it an unlimited distance. If the ball goes over the sidelines, the last team to touch it loses possession. Their opponents then have five seconds to get the ball to the place where it passed out of play and five seconds to release it.

FOULING UP

IN THEORY, BASKETBALL IS A NON-CONTACT SPORT. PLAYERS are not allowed to impede an opponents' movement with their

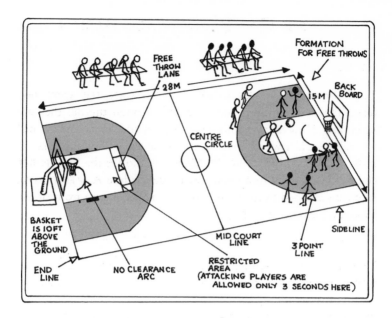

arms, elbows or hips, nor can they grab, charge, barge or trip them. That said, there is a lot of hidden contact and the quality of officiating can vary.

FOULS committed by a team concede possession to the opposition. If the foul was committed on a player in the act of shooting, a FREE THROW (see diagram above) is given. If the team has already accumulated four TEAM FOULS in a quarter then any additional foul results in TWO FREE THROWS for their opponents. Players also have fouls counted against them individually. When they reach five PERSONAL FOULS they are excluded from the game (though they can be subbed). TECHNICAL FOULS are also awarded for acts of violence and unsportsmanlike behaviour.

·············· **NO GOAL HANGING, NO GOALTENDING** ··············

BASKETBALL HAS DEVELOPED A SERIES OF RULES TO MAINTAIN the right balance between attack and defence. To prevent GOAL HANGING, the coloured rectangle in front of the basket – referred to as the PAINT or the KEY – is a restricted area. Attacking players can spend no longer than three seconds inside it. Another flaw in the old rules was that a very tall player could stand close to the basket and swat everything away. To stop this kind of GOALTENDING, players cannot block shots on the downward element of their arc nor are defensive players allowed to try to gain an offensive foul from their opponents inside the small arc drawn 1.25m in front of the basket. This prevents defenders from simply impeding players who are driving towards the basket.

THE SHOT CLOCK

ONE FAVOURITE TACTIC FOR TEAMS WAS TO PLAY KEEP-BALL, thereby wasting time and grinding down the opposition – effective but terminally dull. To cut this out, the NBA introduced the SHOT CLOCK, which is usually positioned above the backboards and on the scoreboard. Once a team takes possession they have 8 SECONDS to get the ball into the opponents' half and 24 SECONDS to shoot on goal. If they don't do either, the other side wins possession.

THE FINER POINTS

THE SHOT LOCKER: JUMP, FADE, SPIN AND LAYUP

THE BREAD AND BUTTER OF BASKETBALL IS THE JUMP SHOT. A player leaps into the air and at the high point of the jump launches the ball in an arc towards the basket, over the hands of jumping defenders. Look out for variations that create a bit more space and time for the player to make the shot. When they have their back to the basket, players often leap and SPIN through 180 degrees before shooting. This can be combined with a FADE, in which a player jumps up and drifts backwards away from the defender. Closer to the basket, players use the LAYUP. As they leap, the ball is sent vertically up towards the backboard and SPIN imparted by the fingers makes it drop directly into the net or bounce off the backboard and through the hoop.

THE DUNK

THE MOST SPECTACULAR SCORE IS THE DUNK, SOMETIMES KNOWN as the SLAM DUNK, in which the player drops or pushes the ball through the hoop from ABOVE THE RIM. Even in its most rudimentary versions, this is an extraordinary display of athletic power and strength, often completed with an emphatic flourish, leaving the player swinging from the edge of the hoop. This play wasn't envisaged by Naismith and it was banned in the American college game from 1967 to 1976. However, it's been a staple of the modern sport, especially since the game became the preserve of giants (the legendary 1992 USA Dream Team had only one player under 6ft 6in). In the women's game, where players aren't as tall, the slam dunk is rarer.

HIS AIRNESS MICHAEL JORDAN IN ACTION AT BARCELONA 1992

Most dunks come from a drive by a player towards the hoop and a massive leap, but look out for a high ball passed above the hoop, caught by a player in flight, and slammed into the net: this is the ALLY-OOP. Most spectacular of all, a leap combined with a spin produces the OVERHEAD REVERSE DUNK. Some dunks are powerful enough to break the whole structure holding up the basket or shatter the glass backboard.

················· **GIMME BACK MY BALL: THE REBOUND** ·················

AS MOST TEAMS SCORE WITH MOST ATTACKS IN BASKETBALL, getting hold of the ball is key. Occasionally defences will STEAL the ball, by intercepting a pass or capitalising on an opponent's mishandling. But more commonly – and crucially – shots bounce off the rim or the backboard and are seized as REBOUNDS.

⋯⋯⋯⋯ **THE FURIOUS FIVE: PLAYER POSITIONS** ⋯⋯⋯⋯

DIVISION OF LABOUR IN BASKETBALL IS FLUID: ALL PLAYERS participate in nearly every attacking and defensive move. That said, teams play with two back court players (the GUARDS), a CENTRE and two FORWARDS, each of whom – as the diagram below explains – has particular duties.

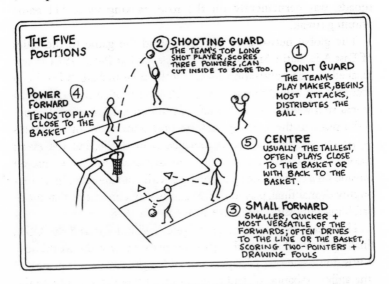

THE FIVE POSITIONS

② SHOOTING GUARD
THE TEAM'S TOP LONG SHOT PLAYER, SCORES THREE POINTERS, CAN CUT INSIDE TO SCORE TOO.

① POINT GUARD
THE TEAM'S PLAY MAKER, BEGINS MOST ATTACKS, DISTRIBUTES THE BALL.

④ POWER FORWARD
TENDS TO PLAY CLOSE TO THE BASKET

⑤ CENTRE
USUALLY THE TALLEST, OFTEN PLAYS CLOSE TO THE BASKET OR WITH BACK TO THE BASKET.

③ SMALL FORWARD
SMALLER, QUICKER + MOST VERSATILE OF THE FORWARDS; OFTEN DRIVES TO THE LINE OR THE BASKET, SCORING TWO-POINTERS + DRAWING FOULS

⋯⋯⋯⋯ **PICK AND ROLL** ⋯⋯⋯⋯

PICK AND ROLL IS THE ATTACKING PLOY EVERY OLYMPIC basketball team uses. When the ball carrier is being marked by a defender, a second member of the attacking team will move so as to put himself between the two, sometimes called SETTING A SCREEN. At this point the defender faces a dilemma: if they keep marking the ball carrier, the screen setter can pivot and roll around them into space to receive the ball; if the defender goes with the screen setter, he gives the ball carrier space to shoot or make a decisive pass – THE PICK AND POP.

BASKETBALL GOES TO THE OLYMPICS

JUST THIRTEEN YEARS AFTER ITS INVENTION, BASKETBALL appeared as a demonstration sport at the 1904 St Louis Games. There were collegiate, YMCA and schools tournaments, plus an amateur six-squad competition that was the closest thing to an Olympic contest. It was won by the BUFFALO GERMAN YMCA from upstate New York. In the years before the First World War the Buffalo team, like all the early semi-professional barnstorming squads, was permanently on the road, racking up a 111-game winning streak.

The global network of YMCAs spread the game to the cities of East Asia, Latin America and Europe, and at PARIS 1924 it was recalled as a demonstration sport. By the time basketball had been accepted as a full Olympic sport, at BERLIN 1936, it had acquired a global ruling body (FIBA), a raft of professional American leagues and a place in the sporting cultures of dozens of countries. JAMES NAISMITH himself presented the medals in Berlin, but the event hardly showed the sport in its best light: matches were played outside on a tennis court packed hard with sand and clay. In a thoroughly dismal final, played in wet and windy conditions that made dribbling impossible, the USA beat Canada 19-8.

The LONDON Games of 1948 were held indoors and the USA, finally permitted to play the game properly, showed the world how it was done. The official report noted that the Americans possessed 'the agility of bantams', and that 'as soon as these giants entered the arena, opposing teams seemed to wilt'. In the final they thrashed France 65-21.

At HELSINKI 1952, the SOVIET UNION – and Cold War politics – made their mark. The Soviets clawed their way to the final, where, in a dour and mean-spirited game, they tried to play keep-ball; the Americans beat them anyway, 36-25. The URUGUAYAN bronze medallists were more combative: in their game against France they lost so many players to personal fouls that they played the final minutes with just three on the court. When the referee called a further foul against them he was rushed by the bench; two Uruguayans were eventually banned from the Games. Things were little smoother the

PREMATURE US CELEBRATIONS IN THE CONTROVERSIAL 1972 MEN'S FINAL

next day, when the match between a four-man Uruguay and three-man Argentina culminated in a massive on-court brawl.

In MELBOURNE in 1956 the USSR team arrived with JAN KRU-MINSH, a 7ft 3in Latvian centre, but the AMERICANS, including the great BILL RUSSELL (five-time winner of the NBA Most Valuable Player Award), ran rings around them and everyone else, beating the USSR 89-55 in the final. Rome, Tokyo and Mexico City all went the same way, though the Yugoslavs and Soviets were getting closer.

In 1972, at the MUNICH Games, the gap finally closed. The USSR led the USA for almost the whole of the final game, but with three seconds to go American DOUG COLLINS was bundled out of the court and the US was awarded two free throws. Looking battered but composed, Collins sunk them both and the USA took the lead for the first time, 50-49. The Soviets restarted, a long ball went nowhere, the buzzer went and the Americans exploded with joy and relief. Then chaos erupted on the court when one of the officials claimed a time out had been called with one second left on the clock. The game was restarted and the Soviets again failed to score, only for the officials to insist that a third restart was required but, as urged by FIBA secretary general Renato Williams Jones (who had no right to intervene), with three seconds rather than one second on the clock. At the third attempt the Soviets launched a court-length pass to SASHA BELOV whose simple layup made it 51-50. The Americans ignored the medal ceremony.

Over the next four Games, the Cold War pendulum swung back and forth. In MONTREAL in 1976 the Americans were denied a full measure of revenge when the YUGOSLAVS knocked the Soviets out in the semi-final. The USSR won the inaugural women's gold medal and would dominate the Olympic tournament until 1988, when the Americans took over. The USA WOMEN are currently on an unbroken streak of six consecutive gold medals.

With the Americans boycotting the 1980 MOSCOW Games, the Soviets expected to wrap up their second men's gold, only to be knocked out again in the semi-finals by eventual champions YUGOSLAVIA. With the USSR absent at Los Angeles in 1984, the USA cruised to victory. At SEOUL, four years later, the SOVIETS outplayed the Americans to win 82-76 in the semi, before beating the Yugoslavs in the final.

Four years later, the world of Olympic basketball looked wholly different: the Soviet Union had ceased to exist; Yugoslavia, America's other chief basketball competitor, was riven by war; and the IOC had decided to allow professionals to compete in all sports. The NBA made the most of the unprecedented opportunity, assembling the greatest pool of basketball talent ever to go to the Games. Including such stellar players as MICHAEL JORDAN, MAGIC JOHNSON, LARRY BIRD and CHARLES BARKLEY, the so-called 'DREAM TEAM' won every game, by an average of 43.8 points. Their smallest margin of victory was in the final, in which they beat Croatia 117-85.

ATLANTA 1996 and SYDNEY 2000 brought more of the same, but the opposition was getting stronger and more confident while the Americans became a little complacent, almost blowing it in the semi-finals against Lithuania in 2000. The warning of Sydney was not heeded, and in ATHENS the Americans were narrowly beaten in the semi-finals by a fleet-footed ARGENTINA, led by NBA star MANU IGNOBILITY, which went on to win gold. The US team at BEIJING 2008 was termed, inevitably, the 'REDEEM TEAM'. Equipped with leading lights KOBE BRYANT, LEBRON JAMES and Dwyane Wade, they duly swept to victory. At 2012, the US broke records – beating Nigeria 156-73, the largest winning margin in Olympic history, while Carmelo Anthony scored 37 points – but were pushed all the way by Spain in the final until James, inevitably, scored five straight points – with a three-point shot and a right-handed slam dunk – to secure the gold medal.

BOXING

6–21 AUGUST 2016

RIOCENTRO PAVILION 2, RIO DE JANEIRO

Athletes: 286 | **Golds up for grabs:** 13

OLYMPIC PRESENCE

MEN 1904–1908, 1920–PRESENT; WOMEN 2012-PRESENT (though women's boxing was a demonstration sport in 1904).

OLYMPIC FORMAT

MEN COMPETE IN TEN WEIGHT DIVISIONS; WOMEN IN THREE. One boxer per nation is allowed in each weight category. Each competition is seeded and proceeds on a knock-out basis (no pun intended), culminating in a final. There is no third place fight – both losing semi-finalists receive bronze medals.

CONTENDERS

IN BOTH LONDON AND BEIJING, NINE DIFFERENT COUNTRIES shared the gold medals. In 2012, GREAT BRITAIN (3) won the most golds, followed by UKRAINE and CUBA with two apiece. The other triumphant nations were CHINA, JAPAN, KAZAKHSTAN, IRELAND, RUSSIA and the USA. The decision to open the competition in Rio to PROFESSIONAL boxers makes the outcome very hard to predict.

PAST CHAMPIONS

USA: 50 | CUBA: 34 | USSR/RUSSIA: 23

Why Watch Boxing?

It isn't a bad question. Why would you want to settle down in a comfy chair to watch a pair of adults systematically knock seven bells out of each other? But to its fans, boxing is the very essence of sport, pitting man against man (or woman against woman) with no tools at their disposal but their fists and their wits – a purity of proposition that, despite all the controversies that surround the sport, gives boxing a fundamental honesty. And if sport is about asserting dominance over other people, and people are in some sense their bodies, what could be more sporting than an activity that involves attacking and defending the body?

One thing Olympic level boxing definitely is not is crude. A thug wouldn't last eleven seconds out there. Boxing isn't just about hitting people – it's at least as important not to be hit. Achieving a winning balance requires skill, speed, guile, and courage. The sport is not so much an exercise in savagery as a recognition and containment of it. It takes the unpleasant primal urge to beat the daylights out of someone and turns it into a discipline. Boxing is essentially a Western martial art – or, as it is sometimes called, the 'sweet science'.

For all its virtues, boxing has had a chequered history. Fortunately for the Olympic watcher, most of the negatives have applied to the professional game. Tainted by associations with organised crime, pre-match stunts so corny that even the World Wrestling Federation might baulk at them and pitifully punch-drunk ex-fighters who didn't know or weren't told when to stop, it has lost its soul in pursuit of profit. Olympic boxing – historically a sport for amateurs – is different gravy. Though not always squeaky clean, it is significantly safer than the much hyped world title bouts that drive pay for TV revenues, partly because there are only three rounds (compared to ten or twelve). Olympic boxing also has a refreshing clarity – there is only one Olympic champion per weight division and competitors can't avoid facing opponents they don't fancy.

Because the stakes are so high, both in terms of the prizes on offer and the risk of getting seriously hurt, Olympic boxing can be electrifyingly tense. It can draw you in like no other sport, its visceral nature allowing you to 'feel' a smidgen of what the fighters experience. And there is a good chance of a legend emerging. Olympic boxing has consistently thrown up magnificent warriors, among them SUGAR RAY LEONARD, WLADIMIR KLITSCHKO and the incomparable MUHAMMAD ALI.

A final excellent reason to watch the boxing in Rio is the tournament for WOMEN. This competition made its full Olympic debut in London. The jury still can't decide whether this represents a triumphant achievement of equality or a demeaning folly. There's only one way to make your own mind up ...

THE STORY OF BOXING

KNOWN TO THE ANCIENT EGYPTIANS AND SUMERIANS, BOXING made its first appearance at the ANCIENT GAMES in Olympia in 688 BC, where contestants bound their hands with leather straps for protection and fought on until one of them surrendered or could not continue. The Romans invented a typically dark variant of the sport, which used a metal studded glove known as a *cestus*. Losing a fight was often fatal.

After the Roman Empire's collapse, boxing disappeared from view in much of Europe. In the absence of a powerfully policed state, carrying of arms became much more common – history suggests an inverse relationship between the popularity of boxing and the prevalence of weapons. In a nutshell, you don't want to start a public fight if everyone is armed to the teeth, and the authorities won't like it either. Even so, various forms of folk boxing survived, some pretty hard-core. In INUIT HEAD PUNCHING, the combatants took it in turn to hit each other as hard as they could, with the receiver offering no defence whatsoever. RUSSIAN FIST FIGHTING, first mentioned in the thirteenth century, also had a variant of this extreme form of the sport, as well as regular two-way boxing and organised team brawls.

The modern sport developed out of PRIZE-FIGHTING, which rose to prominence in England in the seventeenth century. The participants fought for money, with BARE KNUCKLES and minimal rules – there were no weight divisions or limits on the number or duration of rounds. The cash was often put up by aristocrats – the first recorded bout in 1681 involved the butler and the butcher of the 2nd Duke of Albemarle (the butcher won) – but prize-fighting was also popular in less illustrious circles, where it was often the subject of huge wagers.

The Englishman JACK BROUGHTON is credited with the introduction of BOXING GLOVES, or 'mufflers' as he called them, although their use was initially restricted to training and exhibition matches. BROUGHTON'S RULES, published in London in 1743, were designed to bring order to the chaos that characterised unregulated prize-fighting. Hitting a man when he was down was forbidden, as was grasping an opponent below the waist. A boxer who was floored was given 30 seconds to recover – if he failed to beat the count he lost. Canny fighters exploited this rule by dropping to one knee when they needed a breather, although this was frowned on. Manliness or 'nobility' was the emerging sport's central ideal. 'The manly stand-up fight is surely far preferable,' opined the American *Spirit of the Times* in August 1837, 'to the insidious knife, the ruffianly gang system or the cowardly and brutal practice of biting, kicking or gouging now so prominent.'

The LONDON PRIZE RING RULES, published in 1838, further gentrified proceedings, specifying a ROPED SQUARE RING and forbidding headbutting, biting and HITTING BELOW THE BELT. But the event that made boxing a modern sport was the publication, in 1867, of the MARQUESS OF QUEENSBERRY CODE. The eponymous aristocrat, later responsible for Oscar Wilde's downfall, didn't actually write the famous Rules – he published them. They were penned in 1867 by a Cambridge University athlete called JOHN GRAHAM CHAMBERS for the sport's first amateur championship, held at Lillie Bridge in London. The twelve rules, which stipulated the wearing of gloves, introduced the 10 COUNT for fallen boxers and established the system of THREE-MINUTE ROUNDS with one-minute rest periods, are the basis of the laws that govern boxing today.

Initially designed for amateur boxing, the Queensbury Rules were eventually adopted by the professional game too, a process hastened in England by an 1882 court ruling that declared bare knuckle fights to be criminal assaults, irrespective of the participants' consent, and left spectators vulnerable to the charge of aiding and abetting. The subsequent almost universal ADOPTION OF GLOVES had far reaching effects. As the huge mitts could be used to block punches, the 'forearms upright' style of the bare knuckle boxer fell out of favour. Bouts became longer and more tactical, with more emphasis on defence. From the perspective of the punch receiver, gloves were a mixed blessing. They diffused the impact but allowed the aggressor to punch harder as there was less danger of damaging the hand.

The organisers of the amateur championships at Lillie Bridge in 1867 had deliberately excluded 'riff-raff' from the sport but the British AMATEUR BOXING ASSOCIATION, founded in 1880, was happy for blue-collar workers to compete and did not bar boxers on the grounds of race. The ABA's establishment was a crucial moment in a battle for the soul of the sport between the upper and working classes. This was emphatically won by the latter but the process proved much more protracted in the USA than in Britain. Wealthy club men controlled the amateur sport in America until the *Chicago Tribune* started what became known as the GOLDEN GLOVES TOURNAMENT in 1926.

The late nineteenth and early twentieth centuries were characterised by a widening split between the amateur and professional codes. The former featured shorter rounds and an emphasis on sparring (the demonstration of skill) rather than fighting (continuing to the point of exhaustion or knock-out). Many boxers now regard Olympic boxing as the perfect grounding for the huge payday that the professional sport can deliver.

The spread of Queensbury Rules boxing was gradual – FRANCE, in the years leading up to the First World War, was the first nation other than Britain, Ireland and the United States to really warm to the sport – but ultimately comprehensive. The first global body for amateur boxing, the FÉDÉRATION INTERNATIONALE DE BOXE OLYMPIQUE founded in Paris in 1920, had only five member nations – England, France, Brazil, Belgium and the Netherlands – but by the time the AMATEUR INTERNATIONAL BOXING ASSOCIATION (AIBA) came into existence in London in 1946, the number had grown to 25. The first WORLD AMATEUR BOXING CHAMPIONSHIPS were held in 1974. The USA and, to a lesser extent, Great Britain and Ireland are still major forces in the amateur sport but they have been joined by the likes of Cuba and countries from the Eastern bloc, with boxers from Latin America and the Far East flourishing in the lighter divisions.

······································· **WOMEN'S BOXING** ·······································

ASTONISHINGLY, GIVEN THAT THE EVENT ONLY MADE ITS Olympic debut at London 2012, women's boxing was a demonstration sport at the St Louis Games in 1904. The competitors look like extras from *Upstairs Downstairs* in their knickerbockers but they could doubtless pack a punch.

Even then, women's boxing was already almost two centuries old. The earliest record of an all-female bout dates from 1722, when Elizabeth Wilkinson, billed as the 'Cockney Championess', defeated Martha Jones at an inn near Oxford Circus in London. By the second half of the nineteenth century, WOMEN'S PRIZE-FIGHTING was popular enough to be outlawed in several European

THE AFGHAN WOMEN'S BOXING TEAM TRAINING FOR LONDON 2012

nations and American states. In Britain, the sport became illegal in 1880. It never disappeared entirely, however.

In 1954, a fight involving Barbara Buttrick was broadcast on American national television, but the real breakthrough in the women's sport came in the 1970s and 1980s after a series of legal challenges to the bans in force in many countries. It still took a while for the sport's governing bodies to sanction women's boxing. In 1996, the British Amateur Boxing Association voted to allow women to fight under its auspices and five years later the first AIBA World Championships were held in Scranton, USA.

GAME ON: BOXING BASICS

OLYMPIC BOXING IS A SIMPLE SPORT AT HEART: THE FIGHTER who lands the most scoring punches tends to win. Alternatively, a bout may be won by a KNOCK-OUT, in which a floored opponent fails to get up from the canvas before the referee has counted to ten, or due to disqualification or withdrawal. Punches below the belt or to the back are forbidden, as are holding, wrestling and tripping. To count, a blow must be landed with the white portion of the glove, which denotes the knuckles and the first bone of the fingers. Thumbs should rest on the upper joints of the next two fingers.

··························· **THE RING AND THE SECONDS** ···························

BOXERS FIGHT IN AN ELEVATED RING – 20 FT SQUARE, WITH a padded post in each corner. The edge of the ring is defined by a 'fence' made of four ropes. Men fight three 3-minute rounds; women do four bursts of 2-minutes. Fighters rest for 60 seconds between each round. In 2016, in a departure from usual practice, men will not wear headguards, though women continue to do so.

Each boxer is allowed two assistants, known as SECONDS. Both are allowed to mount the apron of the ring and one can enter the ring between rounds. Their jobs include advising and encouraging their boxer, towelling them dry of sweat, attending to minor injuries and, if necessary, withdrawing them from the fight by literally THROWING IN A TOWEL.

WEIGHT DIVISIONS

THERE USED TO BE JUST EIGHT WEIGHT DIVISIONS IN BOXING BUT at the Olympics the figure has risen as high as twelve. In Rio there will be ten for men (from light-flyweight at 49kg through to super heavyweight at 91kg plus), and three for women (51kg, 60kg and 75kg).

Competitors must attend a general WEIGH-IN at the start of the tournament to register weights within the parameters of the divisions they are entered in. They are also subject to a weigh-in on the morning of every day they fight. Any boxer who fails to make the requisite weight is eliminated.

WAYS OF WINNING

THE CLASSIC MEANS TO WIN A BOUT IS A KNOCK-OUT, WHEN a fallen boxer fails to get back on his feet within a count of ten. Boxers can also win if their opponent retires, indicated by their second 'THROWING IN THE TOWEL' into the ring, or by the referee stopping a fight and eliminating a contestant. Most bouts are won on POINTS. If both boxers are still standing at the end of a bout, the one who has accumulated the most points is declared the winner.

A referee can stop a contest for a number of reasons, including: BOXER OUTCLASSED (where the referee deems one boxer to be taking excessive punishment); HEAD BLOWS (where a fighter cannot defend themself after receiving one or more blows to the head); or DISQUALIFICATION. With no protective headgear for men in 2016, there is a risk that more contestants will be eliminated because they have cuts that need stitches. Referees can also issue a WARNING, for serious or persistent fouls. If a boxer is issued with a warning, two points are awarded to the opponent. Three warnings and you're out.

SCORING

FOR THE FIRST TIME IN OLYMPIC HISTORY, FIGHTS IN RIO will be scored by five judges, using the ten-point system preferred in professional boxing. The change reflects dissatisfaction with the computer punch-count system which was introduced in 1992 to prevent such anomalies as the decision at Seoul 1988 where

America's ROY JONES JR lost a final despite landing nearly three times as many punches as his South Korean opponent Park Si Hun. Initially hailed as a step forward, the punch-count system was soon criticised for rewarding the volume of punches, instead of technique and strategy and not giving enough weight to body shots and combinations. Many US and Mexican boxers loathed the system so much that they refused to compete in amateur events. Under the new system, judges will score each round. A winner is given ten points, the loser nine. A point is deducted for each knock-out a fighter suffers. Fighters are judged on aggression, defence, clean punching and command of the ring rather than on the blow-by-blow basis used in previous Games. In the professional game, rounds can be drawn but in the Olympics, judges must pick a winner for every round.

SAFETY AND EQUIPMENT

BOXING IS POTENTIALLY DANGEROUS. YOU ONLY HAVE TO LOOK at a punch-drunk ex-pro to see the long-term effects of too many blows to the head. At amateur level, extensive measures are taken to minimise the risks. These include FEWER ROUNDS, a maximum age of 40, and, at previous Games, HEAD GUARDS for men (while women have fought with CHEST PROTECTORS). In Rio, men will fight bare-headed. The belief is that the greater visibility will help TV audiences identify with the fighters and, the AIBA insists, there is no evidence that they protected contestants against brain damage, a view that is not universally held. Scrapping the old scoring system, which effectively incentivised boxers to aim for their opponent's head, is also designed to make the sport safer.

There is extensive medical supervision for Olympic boxing events: for every bout, a boxer must be certified fit to fight by a doctor appointed by the AIBA Medical Commission, and there are complex rules about how long boxers who have suffered blows to the head of varying severity must wait before fighting again. One knock-out or RSCH (Referee Stops Contest due to Head-blows) leads to a bar on competing for thirty days; three within a twelve-month period leads to an enforced 360-day break.

The Finer Points

STANCE

Boxers typically stand sideways on to their opponents, with the left foot advanced. The fists are raised, the right one protecting the chin and the left one doing most of the work via JABBING. The active use of the right fist is largely restricted to HOOKS and UPPERCUTS. This stable position is maintained by the fighter moving around the ring with their left foot leading and right foot following without overtaking it. Fighters known as SOUTHPAWS reverse the limb positions, leading with their right feet and jabbing with their right hands.

Each boxer has a characteristic STANCE. Some fighters hold their hands at or slightly above the level of their heads. FLOYD PATTERSON was famous for using this 'Peek-a-Boo' stance. Other boxers hold their hands low. Most find a happy medium.

PUNCHES

Most punches fall into one of four categories:

The JAB is the most commonly used punch and is made with a quick, straight extension of the lead hand.

The HOOK is a curving punch delivered in a sweeping arc. Usually made with the lead hand, it begins with the fist at waist level and ends (if all goes to plan) with it striking the side of the opponent's head.

The UPPERCUT is a punch typically made with the rear hand that moves rapidly upwards from the waist towards the opponent's chin.

The CROSS is often a surprise punch. It is thrown with the rear hand, with the lead hand simultaneously taking up a defensive position. It's like an orthodox fighter momentarily turning into a southpaw (or vice-versa).

STYLE

Every boxer has a basic approach to their art, determined by body type and personality, and each has its 'structural' strengths and weaknesses. Much of the character of a bout is

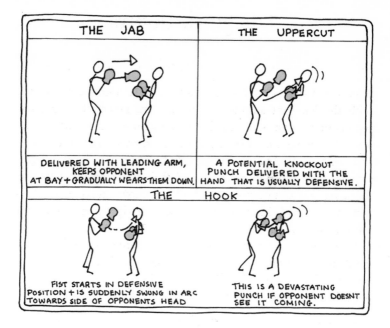

THE JAB	THE UPPERCUT
DELIVERED WITH LEADING ARM, KEEPS OPPONENT AT BAY + GRADUALLY WEARS THEM DOWN.	A POTENTIAL KNOCKOUT PUNCH DELIVERED WITH THE HAND THAT IS USUALLY DEFENSIVE.

THE HOOK

FIST STARTS IN DEFENSIVE POSITION + IS SUDDENLY SWUNG IN ARC TOWARDS SIDE OF OPPONENTS HEAD	THIS IS A DEVASTATING PUNCH IF OPPONENT DOESNT SEE IT COMING.

determined by the way the protagonists' styles mesh. Other things being equal (which they never are), a SLUGGER will do well against an IN-FIGHTER but poorly against an OUT-FIGHTER (see below).

In truth, it's not quite that simple. The best boxers change style to suit the circumstances, and not all of the common styles are mutually exclusive. You can easily be an out-fighter/counter-puncher.

IN-FIGHTERS like to get in their opponents' faces. Classic examples include JOE FRAZIER and the great Hungarian light middleweight LÁSZLÓ PAPP.

OUT-FIGHTERS do the opposite, preferring to keep their distance and wear their opponents down with long range jabs. No one could call him typical, but MUHAMMAD ALI (who made his name at the Olympics as CASSIUS CLAY) fell into this category, as does FLOYD MAYWEATHER JR, a bronze medallist at Atlanta.

SLUGGERS (the most famous of whom was probably GEORGE FOREMAN) rely on power rather than finesse. They need good chins because they tend to get hit a lot.

Punchers (take a bow, Oscar de la Hoya) stay close to their opponents, looking to catch them with uppercuts and hooks.

Counter-punchers seek to exploit momentary lapses in their adversaries' defences while they are throwing punches, rapidly launching counter-punches of their own. This 'get yours in first' policy, brilliantly exemplified in the 1990s by Roy Jones Jr, requires excellent reflexes.

Ali – The Greatest Ever Olympian?

Who is the greatest ever Olympian? There are several candidates: Usain Bolt, Fanny Blankers-Koen, Larysa Latynina, Carl Lewis, Michael Phelps. But mention one name and their advocates are liable to say 'Oh yeah…I guess so', even if it is largely on the basis of what he did thereafter.

Cassius Clay – later Muhammad Ali – didn't fight like other boxers. He kept his hands low, ducking or swerving away from punches rather than blocking them, a tactic designed to infuriate his trainers. But he trusted himself to evade the most savage hay-makers purely through the speed of his reactions. Ali also threw out the rule book when it came to punching, aiming almost all his shots at his opponents' heads. There was method in his madness. He was an 'out-fighter', who liked to keep his distance from the other boxer, evading every punch while landing stinging jabs. Some of them are so fast it's hard to spot them in slow motion.

The eighteen-year-old boxer who won the light heavyweight gold at Rome 1960 – after overcoming a fear of flying so intense he nearly didn't attend – was a long way from the finished article but all the ingredients were there. He faced a dangerous opponent in Poland's Zbigniew Pietrzykowski (known as 'Ziggy' to nervous American commentators), a tricky southpaw with a monstrous right hook, but Clay was quick, smart and sassy enough to score a comprehensive victory.

At the after-fight press conference, a Soviet journalist posed a tricky question: how did the boxer feel about the fact that there were many places he, as a black American, was barred from in his own country? Clay robustly defended the US, asserting that 'we've got qualified people

STINGING LIKE A BEE – CASSIUS CLAY AT ROME 1960

working on that problem', but on his return to Louisville, Kentucky, he was forced to recognise that the c ten ommie hack had a point. Having been refused service in a hamburger joint, despite a 'do you know who I am?' routine, he and his friend were pursued by bikers to Jefferson County Bridge on the Indiana border. The ensuing fight didn't go well for the bigots but the episode made Clay feel his Olympic victory was merely hollow tokenism. He hurled his gold medal into the Ohio River in disgust.

Thirty-six years later, visibly shaking from the effects of Parkinson's disease, Muhammad Ali was given the honour of lighting the Olympic cauldron at Atlanta. He was also awarded a gold medal to replace the one he had jettisoned. The medal itself was found in 2014 and handed over to the Ali family who rewarded the finder Robert Bradbury with a $200,000 cheque.

Boxing Goes to the Olympics

GIVEN THE PRESENCE OF THE SPORT AT THE ANCIENT GAMES AND the classical-mindedness of the organisers, it seems odd that there was no boxing tournament in Athens in 1896. The explanation is that they felt the contemporary sport was too ungentlemanly. So boxing made its modern Olympic debut at ST LOUIS in 1904. The competitors were all American, an unsatisfactory arrangement blamed on a late decision to include the sport.

At LONDON 1908, the British fielded most of the boxers and won all five weight divisions. One exception was Australia's REGINALD 'SNOWY' BAKER, who won a silver in the middleweight but felt – and this would become a recurring theme in Olympic boxing contests – he had been hampered by biased officiating. He may have had a point – the winner, JOHNNY DOUGLAS, was the referee's son. Baker lodged a complaint but to no avail.

There was no boxing at STOCKHOLM 1912, as the sport was banned in Sweden. Pugilism returned at ANTWERP 1920, with eight weight classes. The USA won three of them, GREAT BRITAIN two. These nations topped the medals table at PARIS 1924, the first Games at which each country was limited to one entrant per weight category. At this stage, bouts consisted of three rounds, the first two 3 minutes long and the final one 4 minutes.

The extra minute in the last round was dropped for the AMSTERDAM Games in 1928, a tournament marked by unruly crowds. The most shameful episode occurred at the end of the flyweight semi-final. When South Africa's HARRY ISAACS was declared the winner, supporters of the USA's JOHN DALEY surrounded the judges, intimidating them until they reversed their decision. The officials cravenly claimed they had mixed the fighters' scores up.

At LOS ANGELES 1932, boxers wore gum-shields and 'cup protectors', as groin guards are euphemistically known. At BERLIN 1936, the GERMAN hosts shared top spot in the medals table with FRANCE, as the USA had done with ARGENTINA and SOUTH AFRICA in 1932.

Changes were afoot after the Second World War. BRONZE MEDAL FIGHT-OFFS were discarded after LONDON 1948, and four years later two new weight categories (light welterweight and light middleweight) were added to the Olympic programme. American boxers dominated the HELSINKI 1952 tournament, claiming half the gold medals.

At MELBOURNE 1956 SOVIET BOXERS really made their mark, winning three gold medals (Great Britain and the USA each picked up two). But the star of the show was Hungary's LÁSZLÓ PAPP, who won the light middleweight division to become the first boxer to win three Olympic titles.

The tournament at ROME 1960 is best remembered for introducing the world to a cocky young light heavyweight called CASSIUS CLAY. As MUHAMMAD ALI, he was to secure immortality through contests with the winners of the heavyweight title at the next two Games: JOE FRAZIER (1964) and GEORGE FOREMAN (1968).

CUBA emerged as a major boxing power at the 1972 Olympics in Munich, winning three gold medals. The Communist Caribbean nation has topped the boxing table in five of the subsequent ten Games. It had to play second fiddle to the USA in 1976, when the American brothers MICHAEL AND LEON SPINKS both won golds, as did the great SUGAR RAY LEONARD in the light welterweight division. Meanwhile, bantamweight GU YONG JO won NORTH KOREA's first Olympic boxing title.

THE REVOLUTIONARY CUBANS

One of the most striking features of Olympic boxing over the last four decades has been the dominance of the Cubans. Since 1972, seven heavyweight champions have come from the island, and they have landed a stack of medals in other weights.

The secrets of Cuba's success include a state system that identifies promising boxers at a young age and nurtures them carefully thereafter, plus a ban on professional fighting that came into effect in 1962. The cycle of victory is also self-reinforcing, with former champions training and imparting their wisdom to the next generation. Yet the country's biggest advantage probably is cultural. Cubans regard Olympic boxing as their thing. Successful fighters are considered heroes of the Revolution and are feted accordingly.

The attitude that has powered so many Cuban boxers to the top of the podium was exemplified by TEÓFILO STEVENSON, heavyweight champion at three successive Games between 1972 and 1980. In the late 1970s, he was reportedly offered $5m to fight Muhammad Ali. Teófilo refused, saying 'What is one million dollars compared to the love of eight million Cubans?'

In the absence of American boxers, Cubans notched up five victories at Moscow 1980, including a third successive heavyweight crown for the awesome TEÓFILO STEVENSON. Cuba boycotted the 1984 Games, where the wearing of headguards was mandatory. The light heavyweight competition was mired in controversy when EVANDER HOLYFIELD was disqualified in the semi-final for allegedly throwing a knock-out punch after the referee had called 'break'. The eventual gold medallist, Yugoslavia's ANTON JOSIPOVIC certainly wasn't convinced – he hauled Holyfield on to his winner's podium at the medal ceremony.

SEOUL 1988 was marred by outrageous judging in the final of the light middleweight competition, which American ROY JONES JR inexplicably lost to South Korea's PARK SI HUN. The host nation hardly covered themselves in glory in the bantamweight contest either. When local boxer BYUN JONG-IL lost to Bulgaria's ALEXANDER HRISTOV after having two points deducted for head-butting, his trainer climbed into the ring and walloped the referee, New Zealander Keith Walker, on the back. In the ensuing mayhem, one of the security guards kicked Walker in the head. On a brighter note, KENYA'S ROBERT WANGILA became the first black African to win an Olympic boxing gold.

The CUBANS were back at BARCELONA in 1992, winning seven golds including the first of three from Teófilo Stevenson's heavyweight successor FELIX SAVON. Cuba topped the medals in 1996, 2000 and 2004. In 1996, the US had further cause for grievance when Floyd Mayweather Jr was mysteriously adjudged to have lost the semi-final to Bulgaria's Sefarim Todorov even though the American boxer looked such a clear winner that the referee held his hand up in victory even as the judges' baffling verdict was being announced. In 2008, CHINA entered the picture for the first time, winning two gold medals in Beijing.

Four years later, the full Olympic debut of women's boxing should have stolen the headlines but once again the focus was on some bizarre officiating. In the most egregious case, Japanese bantamweight Satoshi Shimizu was beaten by Azerbaijan's Magomed Abdulhamidov despite knocking down his opponent five times – Abdulhamidov was led back to the dressing room on wobbling legs. The decision was overturned on appeal.

GREAT BRITAIN enjoyed their best boxing Olympics since 1956, with Luke Campbell (bantamweight), Anthony Joshua (super heavyweight) and Nicola Adams (flyweight) all collecting golds in a packed Excel Arena, and Fred Evans only losing the welterweight final to the Games' most gifted boxer, Kazakhstan's SERIK SAPIYEV.

Yet even before the first punch was thrown in London, the AIBA had decided the sport required revamping. The biggest change for Rio will be the admission, for the first time in the history of the Games, of professional boxers. Too many fighters, the authorities worried, were turning pro before even attempting to win a gold medal. New rules were needed. The changes to the scoring system and headgear policy are significant enough but the decision to admit professionals – and for the AIBA to create its own league so that fighters can earn a monthly salary and win prize money but still compete in the Olympics – was a radical departure. The plan was roundly condemned by those who run the professional game – and by promoters like the inevitable DON KING – yet the AIBA is convinced such changes will safeguard the future of the sport. It is so convinced that it now prefers to be known as IBA (International Boxing Association), dropping the a-word (although it still uses its traditional title). Who knows where this will all lead? We may know better after the last punch has been thrown in Rio.

CANOEING

7–11 AUGUST 2016 (Slalom);

15–20 AUGUST 2016 (Sprint)

OLYMPIC WHITEWATER STADIUM, DEODORO

(Slalom), LAGOA RODRIGO DE FREITAS (Sprint)

Athletes: 330 | Golds up for grabs: 16

·········· **OLYMPIC PRESENCE** ··········

SPRINT CANOEING WAS A DEMONSTRATION SPORT AT THE 1924 Games, and became a full event in 1936 with the first women's events held in 1948; SLALOM arrived in 1972, missed the next four Games but returned in 1992 and has featured ever since.

·········· **OLYMPIC FORMAT** ··········

OLYMPIC CANOEING IS DIVIDED INTO SPRINT AND SLALOM. IN both, heats are followed by semi-finals and then a final. There are four slalom (three for men, one for women) and twelve sprint events (eight for men, four for women), each designated by a letter plus a number: K stands for kayak and C for canoe, and the numeral denotes the number of occupants per boat. Distances are 200m or 1000m for men and 200m or 500m for women.

·········· **CONTENDERS** ··········

GERMANY AND HUNGARY WON THE MOST GOLD MEDALS IN London, with GREAT BRITAIN and FRANCE just behind. Expect AUSTRALIA, BELARUS, the CZECH REPUBLIC, DENMARK, NEW ZEALAND, RUSSIA, SLOVAKIA and UKRAINE to be in contention. In the C2 1000m sprint, BRAZIL'S Erlon Silva and Isaquias Queiroz have realistic hopes of a podium finish. Britain's best hope is in the C2 slalom as DAVID FLORENCE and RICHARD HOUNSLOW aim to improve on the silver they achieved in 2012.

USSR/RUSSIA: 29 | GERMANY: 28 | HUNGARY: 22

WHY WATCH CANOEING?

WITH CONTESTANTS COMPETING DIRECTLY AGAINST EACH other, SPRINT CANOEING offers much the same kind of excitement as rowing – and, for that matter, all forms of racing in lanes. There is also an atavistic thrill in watching paddlers going flat out, especially teams of them working in unison. There's something satisfyingly primitive about the spectacle, doubtless reflecting the importance of simple watercraft in the lives of our ancestors.

SLALOM CANOEING, by contrast, is like watching people flung into a gigantic washing machine. How are they going to make sense of their chaotic environment and assert dominion over the teeming waters? The answer: by becoming one with their boats. This is particularly true of KAYAKERS, who are organically coupled to their vessels via their spray decks. The two effectively become one organism – an aquatic centaur, if you like. As the boats go one at a time, slalom is more about mastering the elements (albeit in contrived form) than directly competing with other contestants. Fascinating to watch, it demands strength, courage and quickness of thought.

THE STORY OF CANOEING

PREDATING THE INVENTION OF THE WHEEL BY SEVERAL MILLENNIA, the canoe is one of the most ancient forms of transport: the oldest known example, displayed in a museum in Assen in the Netherlands, dates from around 8000 BC. The first canoes were dugouts, made from hollowed-out tree trunks, but over time all manner of variations were developed, from Polynesia's outrigger canoes to North America's birch bark constructions. The word 'canoe' is believed to be derived from *kenu*, the Carib term for a dugout.

The first kayaks – the word comes from the Inuit *qayaq*, meaning 'man boat' – were constructed by the Inuit around 4000 years ago. Made by stretching seal skin over driftwood frames, they were tailored to fit their owners, with a length typically three times that of their outstretched arms.

Canoes were used by European explorers in North America as early as 1615, when Samuel de Champlain, the founder of Québec, paddled his way through the Great Lakes. It was not until the second half of the nineteenth century, however, that canoeing was adopted as a middle-class sport. Tribal gatherings aside, the earliest SPRINT RACES were held at the inaugural regatta of the English Canoe Club in 1866, organised by the redoubtable JOHN MACGREGOR (see below). The New York Canoe Club was formed in 1871, followed by the American Canoe Association in 1880, and the Canadian equivalent in 1900.

Competitive SLALOM CANOEING arrived relatively late on the scene. The first competition, held in SWITZERLAND in 1932, was a sedate flat-water affair modelled on slalom skiing. Enthusiasts soon realised that white-water racing offered far more thrills and spills. The first world slalom championship was staged, again in Switzerland, in 1949.

THE CHAPLAIN OF THE CANOE

The man who first popularised canoeing as a sport was an eccentric London barrister named JOHN MACGREGOR (1825–92). His aquatic adventures started in early infancy, when he and his parents were rescued from a burning boat en route to India. The next maritime drama came at the age of twelve, when he stowed on board a lifeboat dispatched to aid a ship in distress near Belfast.

A champion marksman as a young man, MacGregor seems to have acquired a taste for canoeing during a trip to the USA and Canada in 1858, though a journey to Siberia may have played a part. His interest remained dormant until a train accident robbed him of the ability to hold a rifle steady.

Then, in 1865, he commissioned a firm in Lambeth to build the first of his seven double-ended canoes, all named *Rob Roy*. The boat was 15 feet long, 28 inches wide and 9 inches deep, with an open cockpit and a cedar

THE CHAPLAIN IN A SPOT OF BOTHER

deck covered with rubberised canvas. Despite these canoe-like features, it was propelled kayak-style, with a double-bladed paddle.

Thus equipped, MacGregor launched the maiden voyage of the *Rob Roy* from Gravesend in Kent. He lit a cigar and, to the astonishment of local bargemen, paddled down the Thames and into the English Channel, where he was joined by a school of porpoises. Inspired by this success, he had the canoe ferried to the continent and embarked on a tour of the waterways of Belgium, France, Switzerland and Germany. His account of the journey, *A Thousand Miles in the Rob Roy Canoe*, was a publishing phenomenon in 1866. Subsequent trips to the Baltic and the Middle East inspired two more bestsellers.

MacGregor caused a sensation wherever he went, not least because he was 6ft 6in tall, and in the habit of paddling in a Norfolk jacket and straw boater. Ships would alter their courses to gawp at him. During his voyage down the River Jordan, a group of overexcited villagers plunged into the water, grabbed the *Rob Roy* and deposited it, with its occupant still in the cockpit, in the tent of the local sheikh. He was more than happy to play up to all the attention, performing magic tricks and sometimes entertaining spectators by lighting lengths of magnesium ribbon. He did have a serious side, though, notably a compulsion to distribute rabidly anti-Catholic religious tracts, hence his nickname 'The Chaplain of the Canoe'.

GAME ON: CANOEING BASICS

THE FIRST THING TO GET YOUR HEAD AROUND IS THE difference between CANOEING and KAYAKING. Not only will this help you make sense of paddle-related goings-on at the Games, it will also endear you to practitioners of both arts, who get heartily sick of people confusing the two or using the terms interchangeably (a situation not helped by Olympic nomenclature, which brackets them together as 'canoeing').

CANOES are propelled with single-ended paddles by people kneeling on one knee. KAYAKS are propelled with double-ended paddles by seated individuals. Whereas canoes are open in design, kayaks are 'closed' vessels, whose occupants seal themselves in by stretching skirt-like devices called spray decks over the rims of their cockpits. This was an essential precaution for the Inuit hunters who invented the craft, to prevent their boats filling up with icy Arctic water. They also invented an ingenious technique of righting themselves when they capsized, known as the ESKIMO ROLL.

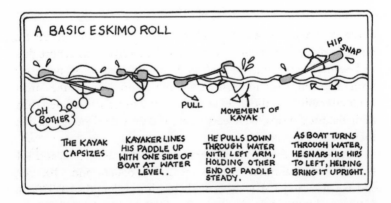

A BASIC ESKIMO ROLL

HIP SNAP

OH BOTHER

PULL

MOVEMENT OF KAYAK

THE KAYAK CAPSIZES

KAYAKER LINES HIS PADDLE UP WITH ONE SIDE OF BOAT AT WATER LEVEL.

HE PULLS DOWN THROUGH WATER WITH LEFT ARM, HOLDING OTHER END OF PADDLE STEADY.

AS BOAT TURNS THROUGH WATER, HE SNAPS HIS HIPS TO LEFT, HELPING BRING IT UPRIGHT.

The second key distinction is between SPRINT events, which take place on calm water on straight courses divided into lanes, and SLALOM events, which involve negotiating a series of gates on decidedly non-straight stretches of turbulent 'white' water. Whereas sprint canoeing and kayaking are first-past-the-post races, slalom has a time trial format.

SPRINT CANOEING

MEN'S SPRINT RACES ARE HELD OVER 200M AND 1000M (canoes and kayaks), women's over 200m and 500m (kayaks only). There are no turns, just straight, lung-bursting charges to the finishing line. It takes around 30 seconds for each kind of boat to complete a 200m course.

There can be up to eight boats in an Olympic heat, with each allocated a nine-metre wide lane. To help prevent FALSE STARTS, the boats are aligned with their noses in small cones which automatically drop away at the start signal. Any boat guilty of two false starts is disqualified.

Throughout a race, competitors must endeavour to keep their boats within the FOUR-METRE-WIDE CENTRAL AREAS. If they deviate, they must move back towards the centre. If one boat comes within five metres of another, it must take immediate remedial action or risk disqualification. If it leaves its allocated lane, this punishment is automatic; CAPSIZING also brings disqualification.

·· **EQUIPMENT** ··

SPRINT CANOES AND KAYAKS ARE COMPLEX DEVICES, typically made from a combination of Kevlar, carbon fibre, fibreglass and sometimes foam, bonded in layers by epoxy or polyester resin. The emphasis in sprint canoeing is on speed rather than manoeuvrability so the boats are longer and more streamlined than their slalom cousins, with very narrow beams. This design makes them easy to capsize.

The boats in the sprint classes are delineated as K1, K2 and K4 (kayaks with maximum lengths of 520cm, 650cm and 1100cm), and C1, C2 and C4 (canoes with maximum lengths of 520cm, 650cm and 900cm). Each also has a minimum weight.

Sprint kayaks are equipped with foot-controlled RUDDERS under their hulls, which are operated by the sole or front paddler. This removes the need for corrective strokes, allowing all the paddling energy to be channelled into forward motion. By contrast, sprint canoes are rudderless, which makes the use of corrective strokes essential.

Slalom Canoeing

The 2016 Olympic slalom course in Deodoro has (like five of the six courses in Olympic slalom history) been artificially constructed, dropping 4.5m along its 250-metre length, with a water flow of 12-13 cubic metres per second.

---------------------------------- **THE COURSE** ----------------------------------

All slalom courses must have the following features:

Length of 250 to 400 metres (generally navigable by a good single male canoeist in around 95 seconds).

Equal ease/difficulty of navigation for right- and left-handed canoe paddlers (kayakers, by definition, paddle ambidextrously).

18 to 25 gates, six or seven of which must be negotiated uphill. Green and white gates must be crossed with the boat heading downstream, red and white ones in the opposite direction.

Gates must consist of either one or two suspended poles set at least 1.2 metres apart. In the case of a one-pole gate, the other pole is placed on the bank of the course to define the gate line (the imaginary line a competitor must cross). The lower end of each pole must be about 20cm above the water line.

The distance between the last gate and the finish line must be between 15 and 25 metres.

The ideal Olympic course will have at least one gate combination which offers competitors several different options; constant changes of direction; and a gamut of daunting water features, including eddies, waves and rapids.

---------------------------------- **SCORING** ----------------------------------

Competitors get two runs in the heats, with their better times determining progression. Semi-finals and finals are single-run affairs, which leaves no margin for error.

Time penalties, which are added to the time taken to complete the course, are incurred for failing to negotiate gates correctly. For a gate to be crossed successfully, it must be tackled from the right

SLOVAKIA'S HOCHSCHORNER TWINS PADDLING TOWARDS A THIRD SUCCESSIVE GOLD IN THE C2 SLALOM, 2008

direction and in the right running order (Gate 2 comes after Gate 1 and so on); the head of each competitor must cross the gate line at the same time as at least part of the boat; and neither of the gate posts must be touched by boat, paddle or body. If either or both the poles are touched, a TWO-SECOND PENALTY is incurred.

If a gate is missed, a 50-SECOND PENALTY is incurred. A gate is deemed to be missed if any part of a competitor's head breaks the gate line in the wrong direction; part of the head breaks the gate line without part of the boat doing the same simultaneously; a competitor intentionally pushes a gate pole to aid negotiation; a competitor's head is underwater when the gate line is crossed (this isn't unheard of); or the gate is tackled out of sequence or omitted altogether.

In practice, MISSING A GATE is fatal to hopes of a medal. The same is true of CAPSIZING, which is deemed to have occurred if a competitor has left their boat altogether. Turning a boat upside down does not in itself constitute capsizing. If the occupant(s) manage(s) to execute an ESKIMO ROLL, there is no penalty and the boat can continue.

································· **EQUIPMENT** ·································

LIKE THE SPRINT EQUIVALENTS, SLALOM CANOES AND KAYAKS are typically made from permutations of Kevlar, carbon fibre, fibreglass, foam and resin. At Olympic level, they are usually tailor-made for the course they will tackle. As they are invariably designed with maximum manoeuvrability in mind they are not as stable as they could be.

The difference between slalom kayaks and canoes is less obvious than in sprint racing, as both are decked and equipped with cockpits. The canoeists, however, must still kneel rather than sit. Rudders are not permitted on either kind of boat.

The weight and length stipulations for Olympic slalom boats are delineated in three classes: K1, C1 and C2 (kayak/canoes with minimum lengths of 3.5m, 3.5m and 4.1m; minimum widths and weights are also stipulated).

LOVE AND LOSERS AMONG THE RAPIDS

The women's kayak slalom at the 1992 BARCELONA GAMES was enlivened by the (non-)performance of Costa Rica's GILDA MONTENEGRO, who accumulated a remarkable 470 penalty points on her first run. She spent most of her next attempt upside down, breaking her helmet as her head banged along the bottom of the course. It transpired that she had never even trained for the event until a month before the Games. Belatedly realising that his country had one more canoeing berth at Barcelona than he had thought, Costa Rican coach Rafael Gallo had decided to offer the place to the nice lady who had worked for him as a raft guide.

Montenegro was so traumatised by the experience that she wouldn't go near a kayak for eighteen months. She was made of stern stuff, however, and reappeared at Atlanta determined to complete the course without missing a gate. She achieved her ambition on her second run, finishing 28th of 30 competitors. Her gutsy attitude so impressed OLIVER FIX, the German winner of the men's single slalom at the 1996 Games, that the couple ended up married.

THE FINER POINTS

CANOE SLALOM IS FAR LESS NEAT THAN THE MORE FAMILIAR ski version. Unlike snow, water doesn't stay put, and contestants have to negotiate some of the gates backwards, i.e. with the canoeist heading uphill. When this involves turning around into a waterfall, nerves of steel are required.

In SLALOM CANOEING, watch how the competitors use different kinds of stroke to manoeuvre their craft. Long wide sweep strokes are used to turn around, quick short strokes to move forward and push strokes to move backwards. The very best canoeists let the water do their work for them, rather than battling against it, using it to assist in spins and to help them glide from one side of a current to the other.

CANOEING GOES TO THE OLYMPICS

SPRINT CANOEING APPEARED AS A DEMONSTRATION SPORT AT the 1924 Games in Paris, with races featuring canoes and kayaks. The medals were divided between the USA and Canada, which was no great surprise as all the competitors belonged to the Canadian Canoe Association or the Washington Canoe Club.

When canoeing became a full medal sport at Berlin in 1936, AUSTRIA and GERMANY won most of the medals, setting a pattern of Central and Eastern European success that has continued ever since. Women joined the party at the London Games in 1948.

Two individuals stand out in the history of Olympic sprint canoeing. Sweden's GERT FREDRIKSSON accumulated six men's kayak gold medals between 1948 and 1960, repeatedly devastating his opponents with sprint finishes at 1000m and the now discontinued marathon distance of 10km. Even he, however, must bow to the great BIRGIT FISCHER, who won a staggering eight sprint kayaking golds between 1980 and 2004, three for the GDR and five for the reunited Germany. Just as effective in team events as singles, she became both the youngest and oldest Olympic canoeing champion at the ages of 18 and 42 respectively. Had East

Germany not boycotted the 1984 Games, her tally would have been even greater.

Various sprint events have fallen by the wayside in the course of Olympic history, including the men's 10km, which was never much of a sprint in the first place, and men's 500m races, which were replaced by 200m equivalents at the London Games.

SLALOM CANOEING made its debut at the Munich Games of 1972. The West Germans spent 17m Deutschmarks constructing an artificial slalom course at Augsburg, only to find that the East Germans had built an exact replica in Zwickau for their practice sessions. The GDR duly won all four slalom medals.

Largely as a result of the expense involved in building consistent and spectator-friendly artificial courses, slalom was absent from the next four Olympics, but it reappeared at Barcelona and has been a permanent fixture ever since. In 2012, the Slovakian Hochschorner twins were going for their fourth consecutive gold in the C2 slalom but lost out to GREAT BRITAIN's TIM BAILLIE and ETIENNE SCOTT, who won the nation's first Olympic slalom gold. An ecstatic crowd at the Lee Valley course saw the greatest day in the history of British slalom canoeing as Baillie and Scott jumped into the water for a celebratory embrace with Florence and Hounslow.

CYCLING

Road: 6–10 AUGUST 2016, **Race:** FLAMENGO PARK,
COPACABANA; **Time Trial:** PONTAL, BARRA
Track: 11–16 AUGUST 2016: RIO OLYMPIC
VELODROME, BARRA
BMX: 17–19 AUGUST 2016: OLYMPIC BMX
CENTRE, DEODORO
Mountain Bike: 20–21 AUGUST: 2016:
MOUNTAIN BIKE CENTRE, DEODORO
Athletes: 505 | **Golds up for grabs:** 18

······················· **OLYMPIC PRESENCE** ·······················

TRACK CYCLING AND ROAD RACING FOR MEN MADE THEIR
debut in 1896 and cycling has been present at every Games since.
Women's road racing arrived in 1984 followed by track racing in
1988. Mountain biking was added to the Olympic programme in
1996 and BMX racing in 2008.

······················· **OLYMPIC FORMAT** ·······················

THERE ARE FOUR CYCLING DISCIPLINES: TRACK RACING ON A
banked indoor circuit (featuring five different events), BMX, MOUN-
TAIN BIKING and ROAD RACING. The last of these is held on public
roads and comprises two different events: individual time trialling
and straight racing. There are men's and women's events in every
category.

······················· **CONTENDERS** ·······················

GREAT BRITAIN WERE TRIUMPHANT IN 2012, WINNING EIGHT
GOLD medals. With so many champions from London retired
– notably British trio Bradley Wiggins, Chris Hoy and Victoria

Pendleton and Kazakhstan's Alexander Vinokourov – the competition for medals will be much less one-sided in Rio, with FRANCE (track and mountain biking), the NETHERLANDS (BMX), AUSTRALIA (omnium, sprint), BELARUS (time trial), NEW ZEALAND (time trial), SWITZERLAND (mountain biking) and the USA (sprint) all strong in particular events. On the road, the men's competition will feature the world's top professional cyclists, who will have contested the Tour de France only weeks before. Expect a serious challenge from SOUTH AMERICA in the BMX class.

·· **PAST CHAMPIONS** ··

FRANCE: 41 | ITALY: 32 | GREAT BRITAIN: 26

THE BOYS ARE BACK IN TOWN: GB'S GOLD-WINNING ROAD RACE TEAM LINE UP FOR LONDON 2012: FROM LEFT, IAN STANNARD, CHRIS FROOME, BRADLEY WIGGINS, DAVID MILLAR AND MARK CAVENDISH

Why Watch Cycling?

Olympic cycling offers many diverse pleasures. For techno heads, the sport showcases the latest designs and newest materials; speed freaks can enjoy the sight of teams sprinting flat-out on the high banking of the velodrome; and the more sadomasochistically inclined will relish the gruelling spectacle of the road racing. Mountain biking is good for those who like something closer to rallying, while the BMX competition combines a tricksy urban edge with manic multi-rider racing.

For its sheer variety of races, cycling offers even more than athletics: SPRINTS, MIDDLE-DISTANCE RACES and ENDURANCE events; all-against-all racing, individual TIME-TRIALLING against the clock, individual and team PURSUITS AND CHASES; 'devil take the hindmost' competitions in which the BACK MARKER is eliminated every time the pack crosses the line; and the wild gyrations of POINTS RACES, in which the cyclists score points on a one-lap sprint every ten laps. All of these formats can be seen at the Olympics.

The Story of Cycling

Some have claimed that the first bike was sketched by Leonardo da Vinci, others to have found a prototype in a stained-glass church window in Stoke Poges, Buckinghamshire, but the earliest properly documented ancestor of the bike is the two-wheeled wooden scooter designed by German engineer Baron Karl Friedrich von Drais in 1817. Sitting astride his contraption, the Baron pushed the vehicle with his feet and steered using his revolutionary pivoting front wheel and handle bars. On a good day the Baron could maintain a steady 8mph. The machine was briefly fashionable, but soon disappeared.

The key technological advance came in 1866 when the Parisian carriage manufacturers Michaux experimented with putting pedals on the front wheel of what they called the *velocipede*. It was an instant hit. Within a year or two the Michaux factory was turning out hundreds of VELOCIPEDES, while copies were soon being made in America and in Coventry, England. That said, the bikes of the 1860s and 1870s were novelties and luxuries – and riding them was a tricky business. Known as boneshakers, they lacked suspension, had hard rubber tyres and were difficult to steer. None of this deterred a large number of wealthy young men from racing their new toys.

The first CYCLE RACE on a track was held in France in 1868 at Saint-Cloud, and a year later the first race on public roads was run between Paris and Rouen. Given that the pedals were attached to the front axle of these bikes, the inevitable trajectory of technological change was to place the saddle over the top of the front wheel, which became progressively bigger to accommodate the rider's legs; the back wheel became progressively smaller. While capable of considerable speed, these 'penny-farthings' were tricky to balance and not very manoeuvrable.

In 1885 John Kemp Starley from Coventry designed his version of the safety bike, known initially as 'Rover'. This machine had equal-sized wheels, a pedal-driven chain that turned the back wheel and an early form of bike gear. Within a few years it had swept the high-wheel bike aside, a process accelerated by a flood of innovations in component design: pneumatic tyres, gears, brakes and freewheels.

These changes, combined with the mass production of cheaper machines, made the bicycle a mass mode of transport. Like bike ownership, racing was no longer the preserve of a tiny minority, and a new generation of competitive cyclists found huge audiences for their races on both public roads and specially built tracks. By 1900 there were more than 300 VELODROMES in France and people were flocking to tracks in New York, London, Brussels, Milan and St Petersburg.

Yet almost as soon as the bike had emerged it was overtaken by the motor car, the new symbol of industrial speed. In response, cycling made ENDURANCE its calling card. In America, in particular, enormously long track races were established, while the TOUR DE FRANCE – first raced in 1903 – became the keystone of continental European ROAD RACING. In Britain, road racing was all but killed off by the authorities, who considered bicycling a public menace.

The Town Police Clauses Act of 1888 made cyclists liable to arrest for 'furious pedalling'.

Both track and road events were actively supported by bike manufacturers, becoming openly professional. Consequently, the leading participants were excluded from amateur competitions like the Olympics. But the gents had to play second fiddle in the great races of the European season. This situation lasted until 1996, when the Olympic events were opened to professional cyclists.

The new classes, MOUNTAIN BIKING and BMX RACING, came of age as organised sports through their inclusion in the Games in 1996 and 2008 respectively.

GAME ON: CYCLING BASICS

·· **TRACK RACING** ··

INDIVIDUAL SPRINT IS A TWO-PERSON RACE OVER THREE LAPS of the velodrome. However, the racing rarely starts until the last lap: the previous two circuits are nearly always games of cat and mouse, with the riders staying close to each other as they seek out momentary advantage – a flicker of hesitation from an opponent is the signal to suddenly break away and sprint for the line. The FIRST LAP must be conducted at a minimum of walking pace, but after this riders may GRIND TO A HALT, balancing on the banking like a pair of samurai poised to begin a duel. At the 1964 Tokyo Games, Italy's Giovanni Pettenella and France's Pierre Trentin balanced motionless on their bikes for a record 21 mins 57 seconds.

TEAM SPRINT has two teams of three riders racing over three laps (two riders over two laps for women), starting on opposite sides of the velodrome. In contrast to individual sprints, the teams race in line, at full tilt from the start, with each team member having to take the lead on one of the laps before peeling off. Just one rider is left to complete the final lap.

TEAM PURSUIT is contested by two teams; four riders over 4km. They begin from mid-way on the velodrome's two straights, exactly opposite each other. The team whose third rider completes the distance first wins; alternatively, if a team manages to catch the opposition's third rider, it wins the race instantaneously.

Keirin was invented in Japan in the late 1940s, where it rapidly became a national betting craze. Six riders contest the eight-lap race. The first five and a half laps are led by a pace-setter on a motorcycle. The early circuits are raced at relatively leisurely 30kmh for men (25kmh for women), then the pace-setter ratchets things up to 50kmh (45kmh for women) before leaving the track with around two and a half laps to go; then the pack races for the line.

The Omnium is track cycling's pentathlon in which cyclists compete in a variety of races accumulating points from each of them towards their grand total. There are six races in all, held over two days. And they run in the following order:

The Scratch Race is a long-distance race on the track – no sprints, no points, just first over the line; 15km for men, 10km for women.

In the Individual pursuit men race for 4km, women for 3 km; the cyclists start on opposite sides of the track and chase each other.

In the Elimination race all 24 competitors start together, with the last cyclist over the line eliminated every two laps.

The Time trial has cyclists racing separately from a standing start, against the clock; 1km for men, 500m for women.

The Flying lap is a 250m time trial in which contestants race separately, but are allowed a warm-up lap to build up speed.

Lastly, the Points race is a gruelling 40km for men, 25km for women, with a 250m sprint every ten laps for which points are awarded, and big bonuses available for lapping opponents. The winner is the cyclist who accumulates the most points.

ROAD RACING

With the loss of team competitions, the Olympics' road racing programme has been reduced to just two events. In the Individual road race all competitors start together and race over approximately 256km of public roads for men, and 130km for women: first across the line wins. In the Time trial, the riders start 90 seconds apart, and the winner is the rider with the fastest time over a shorter course; around 60km for men and 30km for women.

MOUNTAIN BIKE

IN RIO, THE MOUNTAIN BIKE COMPETITION WILL BE A SCRATCH race around A semi-landscaped 5.4km course. Men will do seven laps, and women six. The race begins with a mass start, and first across the line wins. The final layout of the course will be decided at the last minute to take account of the weather but it is guaranteed to feature rough terrain, obstacles, sharp drops, jumps and a lot of mud.

BMX

BMX BIKES ARE RACED ON A PURPOSE-BUILT COURSE. THE cyclists start on a high ramp and descend into a circuit of tight corners, bumps, banking and jumps that will take around 40 seconds to complete. All riders will race the course once by themselves to determine seeding and then compete in eight-bike heats to determine the quarter-finalists. The semis and finals involve multiple races in which riders score points according to their finishing places.

THE FINER POINTS

THE MOST IMPORTANT THING TO REMEMBER ABOUT CYCLING is that most of the effort a cyclist expends goes into overcoming air resistance. You use much less energy if someone else is in front of you, moving the air before you get there and shielding you from winds. This is called DRAFTING or SLIPSTREAMING and it explains a lot about how races are conducted. It makes a huge difference to speeds and energy consumption in all races except individual time trials, which are a test of the solo rider, unaided, against the clock.

On the track, time trials aside, slipstreaming is a vital part of racing. In the INDIVIDUAL SPRINT the advantage to be gained by slipstreaming is so huge that most of the race is a battle of wits at walking speed to be the cyclist following rather than leading. The KEIRIN, which begins at a flying start, is one way of avoiding these shenanigans and forcing riders to go all out. Even so, many riders will aim to ride right behind the leader until the very last straight.

In TEAM EVENTS, staying in precise formation to create the most effective slipstream is vitally important; look out for the smoothness and regularity with which the team members change position in line, to share the workload at the front without losing speed or rhythm.

Slipstreaming is not a significant aspect of MOUNTAIN BIKING and BMX racing, because the courses are so bumpy and complex that there is barely any space to tuck in behind another rider. In these events, sharp acceleration and braking, brilliant balance and technical cornering are the skills to watch out for. In both of these disciplines, cyclists will also jump small obstacles.

On very steep, muddy mountain-biking courses, the riders may just have to PICK UP THEIR BIKES and run. Bikes are also prone to mechanical failure and tyre damage on the rough circuits. Mountain bikers – alone among Olympic cyclists – are allowed to carry tool kits, and must do their own running repairs.

Cycling Goes to the Olympics

As with most sports, cycling's early Olympic years witnessed some odd and gentlemanly events. In ATHENS in 1896, during the interminable 300-lap, 100km track race, the eventual gold medal winner, LÉON FLAMENG of France, stopped racing and waited for his Greek opponent Georgios Kolettis, who had encountered a mechanical problem. (It is still etiquette in the Tour de France for the leaders to dawdle if the Yellow Jersey has a mechanical problem.) In the road race from Athens to Marathon and back, the eventual winner, Greek cyclist ARISTIDIS KONSTANTINIDIS, fell heavily three times and needed two bikes to complete the course.

Given the legal and policing restrictions on road racing in Britain, cycling at the 1908 LONDON GAMES was a track event only. No medals were awarded in the 1000m sprint. In the final, two riders fell and withdrew, while the two who completed the course failed to do so within the minimum specified time and were disqualified. In ANTWERP in 1920 the road race course crossed six railway lines. Officials were on hand to note how much time each cyclist lost at each crossing. Initially South African HENRY KALTENBRUN seemed to have won the gold, before officials worked out that Swede HARRY STENQUIST had lost so much time to the trains that his adjusted time was faster.

Many cycling formats have fallen off the track over the last century. Departed friends include the POINTS RACE, the TEAM ROAD RACE and the TANDEM. Perhaps the saddest casualty for the purist is the TEAM TIME TRIAL, for nothing can compare with the speed and spectacle of a time trial team in perfect formation.

In the years after the Second World War, Olympic cycling remained a small, men-only, amateur affair, though the Games served as a stepping stone for some, like Italy's ERCOLE BALDINI, the sprint champion in 1956, who went on to a very successful professional road racing career. The ROME GAMES of 1960 were the first for over 30 years to be held in a country in which cycling was anything more than a curiosity. The hosts saw local sprinting favourite SANTE GAIARDONI win two golds on the track, but the cycling is now mainly remembered for the road race, held in searing 34-degree heat. Danish rider KNUD JENSEN, suffering from sunstroke, collapsed, fractured his skull and died – the first athlete to die during a competition at the Games since

FRENCH DUO SCHILLES AND AUFFAY IN THE 2000M TANDEM AT LONDON 1908

the 1912 marathon. At the autopsy, traces of amphetamines were found in his blood.

The first DOPING TEST was introduced into Olympic cycling in 1964. Eight years later in Munich, two bronze medallists were disqualified after testing positive for banned substances: the Spanish road racer Jaime Huelamo, and Aad van den Hoek, a member of the Dutch time trial team.

ENGINEERING rather than pharmacy was the key to West Germany's success at the 1976 Games, where the team sported silk jerseys (banned by the IOC) and raced on helium-filled tyres (permitted). In 1980 and 1984 MEDICINE conquered all. In Moscow, safe from any meaningful doping checks, the Soviets and the East Germans ran amok. In 1984, at Los Angeles, the US won four golds and five other medals – successes that were later tarnished by the revelation that some medallists were given BLOOD TRANSFUSIONS before racing in order to increase the concentration of red blood cells in their system and boost oxygen uptake to the muscles. The practice was not then against Olympic rules, although the medical guidelines discouraged it.

More positively, 1984 saw the Games' first WOMEN'S CYCLING EVENTS. There was a dramatic end to the road race when American cyclist CONNIE CARPENTER-PHINNEY won the gold in a photo-finish, jumping forward over the line like a street biker mounting the kerb. Change has accelerated since then. British cyclist CHRIS BOARDMAN'S AERODYNAMIC BIKE helped him win gold in the 4km pursuit at Barcelona in 1992, initiating a complete redesign of track bikes to incorporate complex modern materials. At Atlanta 1996, the professionals arrived and the great Spanish road racer MIGUEL INDURAIN, five-times winner of the Tour de France, won gold in the individual time trial; an up-and-coming American rider called LANCE ARMSTRONG finished sixth.

MOUNTAIN BIKING made its debut at Atlanta. People had experimented with off-road cycling in California during the 1970s, and the first commercially produced mountain bikes appeared in the 1980s. They had sturdier frames than road bikes, robust suspension systems, wider tyres and upright riding positions, making them far easier to ride on irregular surfaces. They were a huge sporting

WOMEN'S MOUNTAIN BIKE LEGEND, PAOLA PEZZO

and recreational hit: a World Championship was held in 1987 and within a decade mountain bikes were outselling every other type combined, though most were used on urban roads. An Olympic berth became inevitable.

The queen of mountain biking has been Italian rider PAOLA PEZZO, who won the gold medal in 1996 and 2000, staging an amazing comeback in Sydney after taking a big fall and dropping some way behind the leading pack. She also gained considerable notoriety for her appearances in fairy-tale costumes for her cycling shoe sponsor, and the Italian press's obsession with her cleavage.

BMX – short for Bike Moto Cross – completed the current quartet of cycling disciplines at Beijing in 2008. While mountain biking was the new mainstream, BMX bikes had more of a cult following. These small-wheeled, single-geared bikes – first ridden in Santa Monica, California in the late 1960s – are prized for their lightness and manoeuvrability, qualities that account for the huge BMX freestyle trick-riding scene. Latvia's Maris Strombergs – known as 'The Machine' – has lived up to his nickname, winning the men's event in 2008 and 2012.

At London 2012, Great Britain swept aside their rivals in road and track cycling, breaking Olympic records in five events: BRADLEY WIGGINS (time trial), JASON KENNY (individual sprint), CHRIS HOY and VICTORIA PENDLETON (keirin), and LAURA TROTT (omnium) all won individual golds and British teams were victorious in the men's sprint, men's pursuit and women's team pursuit. Also starring in Britain's men's sprint team, Hoy became the most decorated Olympic cyclist of all time, with six golds and one silver. Wiggins, who had become the first Briton to win the Tour de France just before the Games, now also has seven medals, including four golds. Both cyclists are now retired and knights of the realm.

DIVING

7–19 AUGUST 2016

MARIA LENK AQUATIC CENTRE, BARRA
DA TIJUCA, RIO DE JANEIRO

Athletes: 136 | **Golds up for grabs:** 8

OLYMPIC PRESENCE

MEN, 1904–PRESENT; WOMEN, 1912–PRESENT

OLYMPIC FORMAT

MEN AND WOMEN COMPETE IN SPRINGBOARD AND PLATFORM events, in both individual and synchronised competitions.

CONTENDERS

IN THE PAST TWO OLYMPICS, CHINESE DIVERS HAVE WON THIRTEEN out of sixteen gold medals. Expect more of the same in Rio. In the men's events, their toughest competition may come from RUSSIA'S Ilya Zakharov and AMERICA'S David Boudia, who both won gold in London. Britain's TOM DALEY, a bronze medallist in 2012, could do even better in the 10m competition if he avoids injury. In the women's competition, the biggest threats to China's hegemony are ITALY'S Tania Cagnotto and NORTH KOREA'S Kim Kuk-hyang.

PAST CHAMPIONS

USA: 49 | CHINA: 33 | USSR/RUSSIA: 8

WHY WATCH DIVING?

OF ALL THE SPORTS SHE COULD HAVE FOCUSED ON FOR THE climactic final sequence of *Olympia*, Leni Riefenstahl chose diving.

In the most controversial and innovative Olympic film ever made, Riefenstahl created a series of stunning images that capture the many compelling facets of the sport: the iron nerve required to maintain poise when leaping from a platform higher than a two-storey house; the grace and acrobatic brilliance of the diver's flight; the spectacular moment of entry and engulfment, as the body strikes the water at more than thirty miles an hour.

The sport hasn't changed very much since, though new technologies create micro-ripples and bubbles to soften the water, lowering its surface tension. Still, getting it a fraction wrong can be lethal. Russian diver Sergei Chalibashvili died after attempting a three-and-a-half reverse somersault in the tuck position during the World University Games in 1983; on the way down, he smashed his head on the board.

THE STORY OF DIVING

THE EARLIEST RECORD OF DIVING IS A PAINTING IN A BURIAL chamber south of Naples that dates from 480 BC, but people were probably doing it long before. As an organised sport, diving began in northern Europe in the nineteenth century. In Sweden and Germany the nationalist gymnastic movements were part of a wide cultural current that venerated nature and urged athletes to embrace wild waters and the sea. Inevitably, diving became part of the curriculum.

The sport assumed competitive form in the municipal swimming pools of Victorian Britain. In 1883 England's Amateur Swimming Association held the first PLUNGE DIVING CHAMPIONSHIPS, where competitors leapt from starting blocks into the pool and stayed underwater for as long as possible. By 1895 the British National Diving Championships boasted separate events for standing and running dives, with springboards. HIGH-BOARD DIVING was pioneered in Scandinavia by Otto Hageborge and C.F. Mauritzi, who came to London in the 1890s and put up a tower in Highgate Ponds, where they wowed the public with fancy dives and twists.

Diving arrived at the Olympics in 1904 in a state of flux. Different traditions in the Anglo-Saxon world and continental

Europe remained unreconciled; the judging and scoring of dives was problematic, and equipment and techniques were primitive. The sport has been sharply rationalised since, and the Olympics has provided a testing ground for its development. At Sydney 2000, SYNCHRONISED DIVING made its debut at the Games.

GAME ON: DIVING BASICS

OLYMPIC DIVING COMES IN TWO DISTINCT FORMATS, USING 3-METRE SPRINGBOARDS and 10-METRE PLATFORMS. There are competitions in both formats for men and women and for INDIVIDUAL and SYNCHRONISED diving. Synchronised divers perform the same dive simultaneously, or mirror-image dives (PINWHEELING), and are judged on the quality of the individual dives and their relationship to each other.

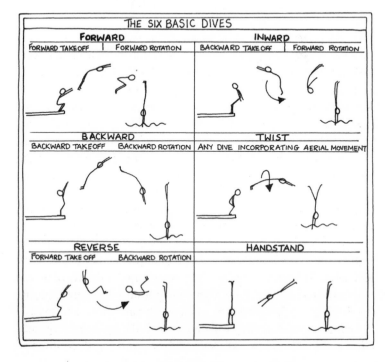

THE SIX BASIC DIVES

FORWARD
FORWARD TAKE OFF | FORWARD ROTATION

INWARD
BACKWARD TAKE OFF | FORWARD ROTATION

BACKWARD
BACKWARD TAKE OFF | BACKWARD ROTATION

TWIST
ANY DIVE INCORPORATING AERIAL MOVEMENT

REVERSE
FORWARD TAKE OFF | BACKWARD ROTATION

HANDSTAND

In all formats, there are two rounds: a COMPULSORY set of dives (chosen by the judges) and an OPTIONAL set (chosen by the athletes).

···································· **SCORING AND JUDGING** ····································

WHAT MAKES A GOOD DIVE? IT TOOK NEARLY THREE DECADES for Europeans and North Americans to agree on this. The consensus today is that, out of a possible ten, a dive scores up to three points each for the quality of TAKE-OFF from the board, FLIGHT through the air and ENTRY into the water. The remaining point can be awarded as a bonus in any one of these categories. The score is then multiplied by a degree of difficulty factor (DD) – so you get a lot more points for three twisting somersaults, for example, than for a quick half-pike. Olympic competitions have seven judges. To calculate the final score for a dive, the top and bottom scores are excluded and the remaining five averaged.

·· **BASIC DIVES** ··

THERE ARE SO MANY DIFFERENT DIVES THAT THE SPORT HAS invented a complex alphanumeric code to describe them all. That said, the basics are simple. A dive is defined by three features: the form of the TAKE-OFF, the position of the diver during FLIGHT, and the ROTATIONS – somersaults and twists – performed during the dive. There are six ways in which divers spring from the board or platform: FORWARD; BACK; REVERSE; INWARD; TWIST; AND HANDSTAND.

A diver can assume four different POSITIONS in flight: STRAIGHT; PIKE; TUCK; and FREE. And there are two kinds of rotation: SOMER-SAULTS and TWISTS.

THE FINER POINTS

IF YOU WANT TO DO YOUR OWN SCORING, LOOK OUT FOR these key points:

TAKE-OFF. Judges are looking for smoothness of approach and the steadiness of handstands.

FLIGHT. A high apex of flight is awarded extra points, while getting too close to the diving board or platform is penalised. Pointed

FOUR POSITIONS AND TWO ROTATIONS

STRAIGHT	PIKE
TUCK	FREE FLYING
SOMERSAULT	TWIST

toes score well, but divers lose marks if they let their feet drift apart.

ENTRY. The diver should enter the water at 90 degrees to the surface; the more acute the angle of entry the lower the score. Similarly, the fewer splashes a diver creates on entry, the higher the score.

Finally, BEWARE OF GREEKS IN TUTUS. The Chinese should have won one more gold in the synchronised diving competition at Athens 2004, where Bo Peng and Kenan Wang were well ahead of their rivals in the final stretch. Before they could make it on to the boards, a man in the audience dashed on to a diving board and stripped off to reveal a PINK TUTU. After a few minutes of clowning and cheering, he dived into the pool before being apprehended. The arena calmed down but the rattled Chinese scored zero for their next dive, handing gold to the Greeks.

DIVING GOES TO THE OLYMPICS

DIVING IS AN UNLIKELY AND ERRATIC BAROMETER OF GLOBAL politics, but since 1904 it has boiled down to a series of fights between the USA and its various challengers for political hegemony: first the Germans, then the Japanese in the inter-war period, followed by Cold War duels with the Eastern bloc. Today, American diving is grappling with the burgeoning power of China.

Diving made a fractious Olympic debut in ST LOUIS in 1904, where America and Germany quarrelled over the rules of almost every acquatic event. (US officials banned the Germans from the 4 × 50yd swimming relay on the grounds that they weren't all from the same club, thus clearing the path for American swimmers to monopolise the medals.) In the dive events, the PLUNGE FOR DISTANCE competition – in effect, an underwater long jump, now, sadly, discontinued at the Olympics – was unproblematic. But the FANCY DIVING proved difficult.

The Germans had brought their own diving board – a plank covered with coconut matting – that was mounted on a floating pontoon in the lake. They also wanted dives to be marked only for acrobatic content and not for the quality of the entry or finish: the Germans twisted and rolled beautifully but were happy to crash into the water belly or back first. Some Germans refused to compete and, after Alfred Braunschweiger walked off in a huff during a third-place play-off, the German delegation was so incensed that Dr Theodore Lewald, the Imperial High Commissioner to the World's Fair (of which the Games were a part), withdrew his offer of an honorary bronze statuette for the winners. The American winner, George Sheldon, refused to accept his medal at the time due to the chaos.

Over the next twenty years the format of the sport was steadily rationalised. TARIFF VALUES were introduced for different dives in 1908, and a blend of COMPULSORY AND OPTIONAL ROUTINES became the norm. WOMEN began to compete in 1912, and springboard diving was added to the platform version.

Still, the complexity of the rules and the BIAS OF JUDGES created problems. At the women's platform competition in Paris in 1924, the Swedish and Danish judges awarded first place to their compatriots and, not to be outdone, the American judge ranked all three American divers in joint first place. The British and French judges backed CAROLINE SMITH, whose consequent victory was the first of seven in a row for American female platform divers. Twelve years later in Berlin, Marjorie Gestring was an unexpected gold medallist in the 3m springboard: the American, who was just 13 years and 268 days old when she triumphed, remains the youngest ever Olympic champion in an individual event.

GREG LOUGANIS

Born to Swedish and Samoan parents, Greg Louganis was adopted by Greek-Americans in southern California. After early encounters with acrobatics and dancing, he became a teenage diving sensation, winning a silver medal at the Montreal Olympics at sixteen and winning the World Championships two years later. After missing the 1980 Moscow Games due to the US boycott, Louganis excelled in Los Angeles, winning two golds with record scores. He repeated the feat in Seoul in 1988, but in the preliminary springboard competition smashed his head on

BRIEF ENCOUNTER: GREG LOUGANIS AT SEOUL 1988

the board after attempting a reverse pike somersault. Despite the concussion and the two-inch wound in his scalp, he performed the dive later in the competition and won the gold.

In 1994, Louganis made his comeback as an announcer and star turn at the Gay Games. He was now out of the closet and, the following year, disclosed in his autobiography that he was HIV positive – causing some consternation among the diving fraternity, who panicked over the possible consequences of his blood leaking into the pool at the Seoul Olympics. He also revealed the shatteringly tough childhood he had endured – learning difficulties, bullying at school, sexual abuse at home, teen bingeing on drugs and alcohol. Diving was not merely his vocation but his salvation. Since then, Louganis has appeared in several Hollywood movies, publicly campaigned on HIV issues, taken up competitive dog agility trials and returned to diving as a coach.

During the Cold War, the sport's international tensions resurfaced. In Melbourne in 1956 Mexican JOAQUIN CAPILLA won the platform gold on his final dive, edging the American diver Gary Tobian by just 0.03 points. The US team alleged that the Soviet and Hungarian judges were biased but Capilla kept his gold. He is still Mexico's most successful Olympian, having also won two bronze medals and a silver.

Thereafter, under American pressure, the authorities began tightening up on judging. In 1960, a Soviet judge was removed after accusations of partiality. Despite all the brouhaha, the USSR never broke American hegemony, and its gold medal in the men's springboard at Moscow 1980 required both the absence of the USA and some help from officialdom. ALEKSANDR PORTNOV of the Soviet Union was allowed to repeat a dive after claiming he had been distracted by crowd noise. He went on to win gold, though three other divers protested that they had been subjected to the same noise.

America's extraordinary domination of Olympic diving peaked in the Reagan years with the arrival of GREG LOUGANIS (see above). Since his retirement the balance of power has shifted to the CHINESE, whose rise is attributable above all to their obsessive and meticulous coach XU YIMING. Working without books, equipment or facilities in the wake of the Cultural Revolution, Yiming constructed his own diving boards and trampolines with which to train his youngsters. His dedication has paid off spectacularly: since 1992 China has won thirteen men's gold medals, and seventeen women's, including four apiece for the brilliant FU MINGXIA – who in 1991 became world champion at the age of twelve, the youngest in any sport, ever – and WU MINXIA, a double Olympic champion in 2012.

EQUESTRIANISM

6–19 AUGUST 2016
OLYMPIC EQUESTRIAN CENTRE,
DEODORO, RIO DE JANEIRO

Athletes: 200 | **Golds up for grabs:** 6

OLYMPIC PRESENCE

1900, 1912–PRESENT.

OLYMPIC FORMAT

THERE ARE INDIVIDUAL AND TEAM COMPETITIONS IN DRESSAGE, show jumping and cross-country eventing. Equestrianism is one of the few Olympic sports at which men and women compete against each other on equal terms.

CONTENDERS

IN RECENT YEARS THE STRONGEST EQUESTRIAN NATIONS have been GERMANY, THE NETHERLANDS, THE US, BRITAIN and NEW ZEALAND. Yet the sport has still not entirely emerged from the doping scandals that beset it after Beijing 2008, and it is possible there could be more upsets and surprises in Rio.

PAST CHAMPIONS

GERMANY: 23 | SWEDEN: 17 | FRANCE: 12

WHY WATCH EQUESTRIANISM?

AT THE ROME GAMES IN 1960, ALL SEEMED LOST FOR AUSTRALIA in the equestrian competition. One of their riders, BILL ROYCROFT, had fallen badly during the steeplechase: his horse, OUR SOLO, had somersaulted over an obstacle, thrown him to the ground and then landed on him. Somehow, Roycroft had managed to remount and finish the course; then, after being administered oxygen and whisky, he'd been flown to hospital in a helicopter for treatment on a broken collar bone. The following day was the show jumping, the final discipline in the event, and Australia had only two fit horse-rider combinations left. They needed three, so Roycroft insisted on competing. Heavily sedated, he was hoisted on to his horse by the rest of the team, before producing a flawless round that earned him and his team a gold medal.

Olympic equestrianism is not for the faint-hearted: EVENTERS have to lead their horses over more than thirty huge fences, ditches, banks and water jumps, while SHOW JUMPERS must, under pressure of time, negotiate some terrifyingly high barriers and gallop through a complex array of obstacles. The intricate movements of the DRESSAGE, which demand the appearance of effortless control, are rigorously scrutinised, with riders penalised if the horse's head is in the wrong position. With its roots in military horsemanship and fox hunting, equestrianism was once the most exclusive Olympic sport, and it still retains an aristocratic and military cast. On the other hand, it allows men and women to compete as equals, and, increasingly, the women are coming out on top.

The Story of Equestrianism

FOR MORE THAN THREE MILLENNIA HUMAN BEINGS HAVE TRAINED horses for transport, war, work and pleasure. DRESSAGE and EVENTING have their roots in the practical needs and competitive spirits of the cavalry regiments of early modern Europe. Dressage, an adaptation of the French word for 'training', was initially a means to an end, a system that prepared horse and rider for the parade ground and the battlefield by emphasising style, control and precision. Modern dressage was first systematised by the Neapolitan nobleman FEDERICO GRISSONE, who established his riding academy in Naples in 1532 and published *Gli ordini di cavalcare*, the defining guide to horsemanship for more than three centuries. Fortunately, some of his crueller ways of motivating horses – forcing their heads under water if they showed any fear of the wet stuff and putting live hedgehogs under their tails – never really caught on.

Grissone's influence spread to German-speaking Europe, Scandinavia, Russia and Britain, but his French disciples proved the most enthusiastic. In the late eighteenth century, the court of Versailles was the centre of world dressage, with dressage master FRANÇOIS ROBICHON DE LA GUÉRINIÈRE embellishing a strictly utilitarian military discipline with something of the artistry of the modern sport. In the nineteenth century the focus shifted to GERMANY, where dressage remained integral to military horsemanship. Indeed, proponents of classical dressage were not delighted when their discipline became an organised sport at the Olympics of 1912. The schism between competitive and non-competitive dressage persists today.

EVENTING was preceded by endurance races for cavalry officers, the earliest recorded instance being a race from Vienna to Wiener Neustadt in 1687. In the late nineteenth century, endurance racing took off in the American west, with the Pony Express, cow herders and the US cavalry all providing competitors for riding marathons. German and Austrian officers tested each other in a race held in 1895 between Vienna and Berlin, a distance of more than 330 miles, while in France cross-country cavalry dashes were popular among the officer class. A combination of endurance racing, steeplechasing and all the other equine disciplines – a test of the all-round horsemanship expected of cavalry officers – was held in France in 1902. This CHAMPIONNAT DU CHEVAL DES ARMES proved a massive success with the cavalry fraternity, and the format was soon adopted across Europe. Like dressage, it made its debut at the Olympics in 1912.

SHOW JUMPING, as the name implies, has less practical origins. Equipped with the new hunter saddle for English-style riding, nineteenth-century foxhunters took great pleasure in leaping over walls, brooks and all manner of natural obstacles in pursuit of their quarry. Jumping competitions were a natural progression. The Royal Dublin Society staged contests for wide and high leaps in 1865, and in 1883 American show jumping made its debut at Madison Square Gardens in New York. Something close to this style of competition was seen in 1907 with the inaugural International Horse Show at Olympia in London. Combined with dressage and eventing, it would form the basis of the Olympic sport that debuted in 1912.

GAME ON: EQUESTRIANISM BASICS

DRESSAGE

IN THE DRESSAGE, RIDER AND HORSE HAVE TO PERFORM A series of closely defined movements, displaying mastery in the TROT, WALK and CANTER as well as more complex moves like the HALF-PASS, in which the horse moves diagonally. Points are awarded by a panel of judges.

At the Olympics, individual and team events are conducted at the same time. Riders' perform the same movements in a compulsory order in the first two rounds – the GRAND PRIX and the GRAND PRIX SPECIAL – and their scores count towards the team's total. After the team medals are awarded, the top eighteen individual riders go through to the GRAND PRIX FREESTYLE, in which they perform an original sequence of MOVES SET TO MUSIC. The scores from this freestyle round decide who wins.

The judges SCORE each individual movement from zero to ten, and factor in the degree of difficulty. They also produce a score (called a collective mark) for four key qualities of the competitor's performance: the freedom and regularity of the horse's paces; the impulsion of the horse; the submission of the horse to the rider; and the posture of the rider. In the freestyle, marks are also awarded for interpretation and artistry.

SHOW JUMPING

IN THE SHOW JUMPING, HORSE AND RIDER MUST COMPLETE A course of around FIFTEEN FENCES within a time limit, but not against the clock. PENALTY POINTS are accumulated for a variety of faults and the rider or team with the lowest number of faults wins.

At the Olympics there are five rounds of show jumping, grouped into three.

ROUND 1 This round, over a short course, is the first qualifying round of the individual event and also determines the starting order in the team event.

ROUNDS 2 AND 3 Both of these count towards individual qualification. The top 45 riders go through to the final round (though only three can qualify from any one country). Scores from round 2 also contribute to team scores; the cumulative scores after round 3 determine the team medals.

ROUNDS 4 AND 5 The slate is swept clean for the 45 riders who made it through rounds 2 and 3 and they now face further rounds to determine the individual medals. The field is whittled down to twenty for the final round and the lowest cumulative score in this last stage of the competition wins. This scoring system does throw up some anomalies – in 2012, Nick Skelton finished fifth, despite four clear rounds, because he clipped one fence in the last round, whereas Switzerland's Steve Guerdat won gold after incurring 12 penalty points over the five rounds.

FAULTS IN SHOW JUMPING
Obstacle knocked down: 4
First disobedience of horse: 4
Feet in the water jump: 4
First fall of rider: 4
Second fall of rider: 8
Second disobedience of horse: ELIMINATION
Fall of horse: ELIMINATION
Exceeding the time limit: ELIMINATION

EVENTING

FORMERLY A THREE-DAY COMPETITION, NOW SPREAD OVER four days, eventing begins with two days of dressage, followed by a day of cross-country and a day of show jumping. The DRESSAGE and SHOW JUMPING phases are very similar to the pure dressage and show jumping competitions. In the CROSS-COUNTRY, riders must complete an obstacle course which is usually 5.7km long and features up to 45 jumps. They must complete the course within a set time and accumulate as few faults as possible. Team and individual competitions run concurrently, with an additional jumping test at the end to determine the individual classifications.

SCORING is complex. DRESSAGE is marked in the same way as the stand-alone event, then mathematically converted to penalty points – riders try to accumulate as low a score as possible across the three events. In both the JUMPING and CROSS-COUNTRY an optimum and a maximum time for completing the course are set. Riders who finish outside the maximum time are eliminated and for every second they go over the optimum time further penalty points are collected. In show jumping, penalty points are acquired in the usual way. In the cross-country all falls lead to elimination, refusal and disobedience score twenty penalty points, and four instances of disobedience (or three at the same fence) lead to elimination. This is, after all, a sport rooted in military discipline.

THE FINER POINTS

SWING IS THE THING: DRESSAGE

AS DUKE ELLINGTON PUT IT, 'IT DON'T MEAN A THING IF IT ain't got that swing.' Despite its stuffy image and the ramrod straight backs of the riders, dressage is all about swing and rhythm, or as the Germans more onomatopoeically put it, the *Schwung*. Horse and rider should move with ease, grace, suppleness and precision: hesitations, imbalance and shuffling are poor form.

Much of a dressage routine involves horse and rider effortlessly moving between different stride patterns – walk, trot and canter – while displaying technical variants of each of these gaits and performing diagonal movements, like the HALF-PASS, where the horse moves forward and sideways simultaneously. Look, too, for the PIROUETTE, in which horse and rider rotate through 360 degrees.

NOT FOR THE FAINT-HEARTED: EVENTING AT MELBOURNE 1956

CROSS-COUNTRY

THOUGH THE COMPETITION IS BUILT AROUND AN OPTIMAL time for the course, riding flat out is virtually impossible: all riders need to decelerate and show caution in tackling the tougher obstacles. Look out for horses tiring towards the end of the course: clipping obstacles, skidding on landing and heaviness of movement all suggest an animal approaching its limits.

FAULTS AND FENCES: SHOW JUMPING

THE FENCES IN SHOW JUMPING ARE HIGHER AND WIDER THAN those in eventing. Don't be fooled by the TV pictures – the fences are gigantic, even if you are a horse. The riders must balance speed against accuracy of jumping – at the highest levels, even a single fault can be disastrous. The best riders prepare the horse for each jump, approaching at the right angle and speed, while adjusting the mount's stride to find the right take-off point.

EQUESTRIANISM GOES TO THE OLYMPICS

EQUESTRIAN EVENTS DEBUTED AT PARIS 1900 BUT DIDN'T return until 1912 when the modern form of the sport was defined at the STOCKHOLM OLYMPICS. The Swedish court was anxious to bring the sport back to the Games, and the campaigning work of COUNT CLARENCE VON ROSEN, Master of the Horse to the King of Sweden, paid off. Dressage, eventing and show jumping were contested at Stockholm – albeit only by serving military commissioned officers. Sweden swept the medal board.

The 1912 DRESSAGE was a simpler affair than today's version, but the very existence of a judging system was a radical development in the rarefied world of elite cavalry regiments. SHOW JUMPING had an even more complex and idiosyncratic scoring system than it does today, while the EVENTING course was extremely arduous. It became even harder: in 1932, the eventing was so difficult that only the USA and Netherlands teams finished it – the bronze was left unclaimed. As recently as 1968, in Mexico City, only three of fourteen teams completed a challenging eventing course, on which two horses died. The IOC introduced a trimmed version of the event at Athens in 2004.

ETIQUETTE was very strict too. At the 1920 Antwerp Games, the Swede GUSTAF BOLTENSTERN, winner of the dressage gold in 1912, was disqualified for practising in the ring prior to the competition. Fellow Swede BERTIL SANDSTRÖM was disqualified from the 1932 dressage event for making a clicking noise to control his horse; he insisted that the judges had heard the creaking of his saddle.

The Swedes were in trouble again in 1948 when Sergeant GEHNÄLL PERSSON was promoted to lieutenant just three weeks before the Games. As a commissioned officer he was now able to compete, and the Swedes duly won the dressage gold. Two weeks later he was demoted. The IOC and the sport's ruling body reacted by stripping the Swedes of their medal and, thankfully, abandoning the officers-only rule. (Persson – and Sweden – would return to triumph in 1952 and 1956.) Mexico's leading show jumper HUMBERTO MARILES won gold in the London Games even though his horse, Arete, was blind in one eye. In later life, Mariles shot a

THE AMAZING LIS HARTEL, HELSINKI 1952

man in a road rage incident and served five years in jail, only to be re-imprisoned for drug trafficking in France. He was found dead in his cell.

The post-war years were the final flourish for the military men. COLONEL HARRY LLEWELYN and his ride FOXHUNTER were the heroes in 1952, clinching an amazing last-minute comeback and gold medal for a British show jumping team that had looked totally beaten. At the same Games, the Danish rider LIS HARTEL, on JUBI-LEE, took silver in the dressage, becoming the first woman to win an equestrian medal at the Games – just as remarkably, she had suffered polio as a child and was paralysed below the knees.

SEND IN THE CAVALRY

Up to 1948, cavalry officers were the stars of Olympic equestrianism, and some were starrier than most. The show jumping in Los Angeles 1932 was won by Japanese cavalryman TAKEICHI NISHI on Uranus, a victory that made him such a celebrity that for a while he became a member of the Hollywood set around Mary Pickford and Douglas Fairbanks Jnr. He later served as a tank commander, and was killed in the defence of Iwo Jima in 1945. At the Berlin 1936 Games LIEUTENANT KONRAD FREIHERR VON WANGENHEIM, a member of the German eventing team, fell and broke a collar bone in the steeplechase. He clambered back on to his horse, jumped the remaining 32 obstacles, and presented himself for the following day's show jumping with his arm in a sling. Wangenheim then had another severe fall: his horse threw him and toppled on to him, but he still managed, in great pain, to complete the course and secure a gold medal for Germany in front of 100,000 spectators.

As with Nishi, the war was the ruin of him. After being captured on the Eastern front, Wangenheim was imprisoned for more than a decade and died in a Russian POW camp in 1953, just days before his planned release. He was found hanged.

In 1956 equestrianism achieved the unique feat of becoming the only Olympic event to have been held, in its entirety, in a different country from the rest of the Games. Australia's strict quarantine laws made the equestrian competitions a logistical nightmare, so Stockholm was used as the venue. Eight years later in Tokyo, German lawyer REINER KLIMKE won gold in the team dressage event, the first of six golds (he also picked up two bronzes) that he won between 1964 and 1988 – making him the most decorated Olympian in the history of dressage.

In recent years, Olympic equestrianism has been riven by DOPING SCANDALS and conflicts with animal welfare groups. In 2004 CIAN O'CONNOR and his horse WATERFORD CRYSTAL were stripped of their show jump-

CIAN O'CONNOR WINS GOLD ON THE DOPED-UP WATERFORD CRYSTAL

ing gold medal (Ireland's only gold of the Athens Games) after the horse tested positive for a banned drug. The problem of doping appeared endemic when, on the eve of the show jumping competition in BEIJING in 2008, horses from the Irish, Norwegian, Brazilian and German teams failed their drug tests and were excluded from the event. A year later, the German equine sports federation dismissed all of their Olympic teams after show jumper MARCO KUTSCHER confessed to the press that his horse had been doped at Beijing. Arguably the greatest result of LONDON 2012 was that no contestant was disqualified because their horse had failed a drug's test.

The media spotlight in London four years ago was initially on Princess Anne's daughter ZARA PHILLIPS, who picked up a silver in TEAM EVENTING – the competition in which her father, Mark, won gold in 1972. But Great Britain's CHARLOTTE DUJARDIN soon hit the headlines, securing gold in the individual dressage and the team event, with the help of CARL HESTER and LAURA BECHTOLSHEIMER. Yet the greatest equestrian feat of these Games was MICHAEL JUNG'S individual gold in the eventing, which made the German rider the first person to hold the Olympic, World and European titles at the same time.

The welfare of the horses remains a contentious issue. In the run-up to London 2012 ANIMAL RIGHTS ACTIVISTS called for a boycott of the equestrian events. Their campaign began when a video depicting the dressage training and warm-up technique *rollkur* went viral. Swedish rider PATRIK KITTEL was seen drawing his horse's neck round and down so that its nose was touching its chest. Many within the sport consider this a perfectly legitimate and cruelty-free form of training, but viewers were alarmed at the state of the horse's tongue (which turned blue) and Kittel received death threats.

FENCING

6–14 AUGUST 2016

CARIOCA ARENA 3, BARRA DA
TIJUCA, RIO DE JANEIRO

Athletes: 212 | **Golds up for grabs:** 10

OLYMPIC PRESENCE

MEN, 1896–PRESENT; WOMEN 1924–PRESENT.

OLYMPIC FORMAT

THERE ARE INDIVIDUAL CONTESTS FOR ÉPÉE, FOIL AND SABRE for men and women. In the team's events, in keeping with the FIE's rotation of events at the Olympics, men will contest foil and épée, women a team épée and a team sabre in Rio.

CONTENDERS

IN THE WOMEN'S EVENTS LOOK OUT FOR THE ITALIAN ROSSELLA FLAMINGO in the épée. In the foil, her compatriots ELISA DI FRANCISCA and ARIANNE ERRIGO will be hard to beat. In the sabre, Russia's SOFYA VELIKAVA and Ukrainian star OLGA KHARLAN have been in medal-winning form. In the MEN'S EVENTS, the favourites include France's GAUTHIER GRUMIER in the épée and South Korea's GU BONGIL in the sabre. American catwalk star former BMX rider and hip-hop fan IMODEN RACE could give the sport some pizzazz if he prevails in the foil.

PAST CHAMPIONS

ITALY: 48 | FRANCE: 41 | HUNGARY: 35

WHY WATCH FENCING?

IT IS HARD NOT TO SEE COMPETITIVE FENCING THROUGH THE lenses of literature or cinema. The DUEL has been a staple dramatic device from Shakespeare through popular historical novels such as *The Count of Monte Cristo* to the swashbuckling movies of Douglas Fairbanks Jr and Errol Flynn. Therein lies the problem: fencing's compressed and technical artistry can look colourless against the implausible flourishes of big-screen swordplay. To see the sport properly you need to recalibrate your mind. Fencing is a EUROPEAN MARTIAL ART: the stylish and refined remnant of an aristocratic code of masculine conduct – but not so refined that the dangers have been entirely eliminated, nor a code so strict as to prevent GAMESMANSHIP and cheating. Once the eye has adjusted to this extraordinary form of ritualised combat and recognised its sparse beauty, the *Three Musketeers* will look like a music-hall novelty turn.

THE FLASHING BLADE: MEN'S FOIL FINAL, TOKYO 1964

THE STORY OF FENCING

EUROPE'S MEDIEVAL NOBILITIES WERE A WARRIOR CLASS AND their wills were enforced at the point of a sword. After the arrival of gunpowder, the sword's role as a signifier of status kept it in business: who could and couldn't publicly bear arms was a matter of considerable legislation. For those who were permitted to use a sword it became, through DUELLING, a means of resolving disputes in the aristocratic theatre of honour. Fencing, the structured art of swordsmanship, developed largely to serve this often illegal cult.

The oldest European guide to swordplay is the WALPURGIS, a late thirteenth-century German manuscript in which a monk-like figure instructs a student who is armed with a sword and a small shield known as a buckler. The arrival, in the fifteenth century, of the printing press in Europe led to a proliferation of FENCING MANUALS. Printed in runs of more than a thousand, these tomes were among the bestsellers of the day, illustrated by artwork from such luminaries as Dürer and Michelangelo.

Baldassare Castiglione's *The Book of the Courtier*, published in Venice in 1538, was one of the most widely read works of the Renaissance. In this instruction manual for the social class one below Machiavelli's *Prince*, Castiglione noted that skill with a sword was central to the life of the courtier, 'for beside the use of them he shall have in war … There happen oft times enough variances between one gentleman and another, whereupon ensueth a combat.'

In the sixteenth and seventeenth centuries, demand for instruction was insatiable, and Italian masters supplied the market all over Europe. Achille Marozzo, author of *The New Text on the Art of Arms*, analysed the techniques of thrusting and parrying, while Camillo Agrippa's *Treatise on the Science of Arms* defined the stances (or guards) that are still in use today. ITALY was at that time an agglomeration of small states, each of which had its own school of swordsmanship, and it was only in the 1890s, after the creation of a unified Italian nation, that a single style and set of rules was agreed. By that time, FRANCE, a centralised nation whose nobility had proved even more enthusiastic about duelling, had eclipsed Italy.

When Louis XIII took the throne in the early seventeenth century the parkland of the Bois de Boulogne was awash with aristocratic blood. Duelling rules allowed multiple seconds to engage each other in combat, which resulted in mass fencing brawls. British ambassador Lord Herbert wrote home, 'There is scarce a Frenchman worth looking on who has not killed his man in a duel.' Even Cardinal Richelieu's edicts banning duelling could not eliminate it. Eventually, when Louis XIV gathered the French nobility under the state's watchful eye at the Palace of Versailles, some kind of control was established. In the Sun King's regimented world, FENCING was reinvented as a courtly practice. Fighters were encouraged to engage in a dialogue of blades rather than an unstructured melee. The FOIL, a lighter sword, was introduced and the legitimate areas of attack on the body were restricted. Despite these measures, injuries abounded, and after three court masters lost eyes in the early 1700s MASKS were introduced.

A EUROPEAN MARTIAL ART: FENCING AL FRESCO AT THE FIRST MODERN GAMES (ATHENS, 1896)

The process of codification was completed in the nineteenth century. The illegal but widespread underworld of duelling was given its definitive form by the Comte de Chatauvillard of the Paris Jockey Club in his compendious *Essai sur le duel*, published in 1836. The official technical text of the public world of fencing was provided by the state: in 1877 the French Ministry of War issued its biblical *Manuel d'Éscrime*, which held sway over fencing practice for over half a century. By the late nineteenth century fencing had assumed something close to its modern form, with weapons, protective clothing and rules broadly as they are today. Competitive fencing found a new home in exclusive urban clubs. Fencing masters gave lessons and fought at gala exhibition events in front of thousands of well-heeled spectators. For fencing to emerge as a sport, it required new rules and technologies to make it a non-lethal activity (and less susceptible to cheating, as well as the destruction of the military and aristocratic milieus in which it had been forged. The First World War delivered both.

GAME ON: FENCING BASICS

FENCING BOUTS CONSIST OF THREE THREE-MINUTE SEGMENTS, fought out on a PISTE – a strip that must be between 1.5m and 2m wide. Fencers score when they hit the opponent's TARGET AREAS, which vary according to the kind of sword used. The winner is the one who scores MOST HITS, and in the event of a tie one minute of OVERTIME is played. To encourage fencers to attack, lots are drawn before overtime to determine who wins in the event of another tie.

·· **PENALTIES** ··

PENALTIES CAN BE AWARDED FOR JOSTLING, DEFLECTING HITS with the hand and refusing to salute one's opponents. Referees award a YELLOW CARD and a warning for the first infringement, a RED CARD and a PENALTY POINT after this, and a BLACK CARD for a third offence, which means disqualification. It is illegal to parry a blade with the arm, but this often happens: high-level fencing is played at such speed that referees rarely catch it.

CHOSE YOUR WEAPONS

THREE TYPES OF WEAPON ARE USED IN OLYMPIC AND international fencing, and different rules apply to each.

FOIL The lightest and most flexible of the swords was developed in eighteenth-century France as a training weapon. A hit is scored only with the point of the sword and only on the torso.

ÉPÉE Closer to the classic duelling sword of the nineteenth century, the épée may strike at any part of the body, but only with its tip – a style originally devised to draw blood but not to kill.

SABRE Derived from cavalry swords and duelling weapons like the rapier, the sabre is designed for cutting and slashing as much as thrusting. Points are scored with any part of the sword anywhere from the waist up – including the mask and back.

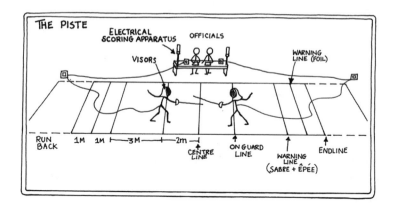

ELECTRONIC SCORING

KEEPING SCORE IS HARD IN FENCING, BECAUSE THE ACTION IS SO fast. In early Olympic contests, there were unsuccessful experiments with dye-tipped swords and points that snagged clothing to reveal hits. The ELECTRICAL ÉPÉE was first introduced into the European championships in 1935 and was considered a success. The foil equivalent arrived in 1955 and the sabre in 1988.

.... **TEAM EVENTS** ....

THREE-MEMBER TEAMS COMPETE WITH EACH FENCER FIGHTING all three opponents. The total hits from all the bouts are added up to determine the winners.

THE FINER POINTS

.... **WHO CAN HIT WHOM? RULES OF PRIORITY** ....

IF BOTH FENCERS SCORE A HIT SIMULTANEOUSLY, WHO GETS the point? To solve this problem, FOIL AND SABRE fencing have RULES OF PRIORITY: the person who attacks first has priority and normally gets the point. Defenders can gain priority and become attackers after an opponent's strike fails, but they must be quick to claim it or they will lose priority. If no priority can be determined, no one gets a hit. In ÉPÉE, which has no rules of priority, hits registered within 0.04 seconds of each other score for both fencers, unless their scores are equal and one point from victory – in which case, no one scores.

.... **GETTING TECHNICAL** ....

AFTER A HIT HAS BEEN SCORED AND THE BOUT STOPPED, THE referees will describe the winning exchange in technical terms. Commentators may use these terms too, so it's good to know them.

ATTACK: the first offensive action

PARRY: a successful defence and deflection of an attacking blade

RIPOSTE: an attack that follows a successful parry

REMISE: an attack that follows a successful parry but with no withdrawal of the fencing arm

REDOUBLE: an attack after an opponent has lost his or her chance at priority due to inaction or slowness.

.... **SWORDS AND STYLES** ....

FOIL Foil bouts are closely regulated by the rules of priority and are often technical affairs, with small and rapid movements the key to gaining advantage.

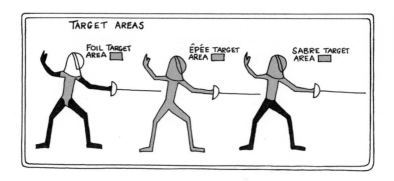

TARGET AREAS

FOIL TARGET AREA

ÉPÉE TARGET AREA

SABRE TARGET AREA

Épée The épée duel is closest in style to classical duelling: the whole body is the target, there are no rights of priority, and collisions are permitted. Counter-attacking is often the preferred style. Many fencers will try to provoke rather than launch attacks and respond when a gap opens.

Sabre As the sabre can score a hit with any part of the blade and as parries are hard to execute, defence in this discipline is usually all about footwork and positioning. Because cuts as well as thrusts are allowed, more flamboyant bladework is on display, and the flèche – a run and leap at the opponent with an outstretched sword – is also permitted.

Protect and Survive:
Kit and Injuries

Fencing has a fatal past and remains a dangerous sport. A Russian contestant was run through the chest at the 1980 Olympics. At the 1982 World Championships Vladimir Smirnov was killed when a foil pierced his mask and his eye; three years later, at the same event, a Frenchman impaled his thigh on a broken blade and was saved by a Spanish doctor who leapt from the audience to help him.

Consequently, fencing has gone to considerable lengths to design equipment that will prevent injury. Olympic athletes have to don a lot of kit. Their FENCING JACKETS are now partly made of Kevlar (used in bulletproof vests etc.). Women wear a plastic chest protector beneath this. An additional protective layer called a PLASTRON is worn under the ARMPIT (a weak point in past competitions) and regulations are so exacting that this cannot have a seam. GAUNTLETS are designed to prevent a blade running up a competitor's sleeve. FENCING MASKS have become more robust; they have to withstand 12kg punch tests, and VISORS must now be able to resist a force of 56kg. Fortunately, these days the most likely injuries for fencers are twisted ankles and lower back pain – studies show that fencers are less likely to get injured than American football players and soccer stars. More recently, the FIE has tried to make the sport more TV-friendly by introducing coloured kit and clear masks that reveal the fencers' faces.

FENCING GOES TO THE OLYMPICS

FENCING IS ONE OF FOUR SPORTS TO HAVE APPEARED AT every Olympic Games, though the rules were not settled until the foundation of the FIE (INTERNATIONAL FENCING FEDERATION) in 1913. Before then, fencing was a quirky Olympic presence. Unlike any other event, there were separate competitions for AMATEURS and FENCING MASTERS, who were deemed a special and permissible category of PROFESSIONALS. There were also competitions in which both groups took part – a kind of early pro-am fencing. Foil had been present since 1896 and épée and sabre were soon added, but there was experimentation in 1904 when a single sticks competition (fencing with wooden poles) was held, and in the non-recognised 1906 Games there were medals for the unorthodox three-pointed sabre. In 1904, CUBA'S fencers took gold in individual foil and épée but had to call in New Yorker Albertson Van Zo Post to make a trio when they won the only Olympic medal for a MIXED TEAM.

Fencing's ARISTOCRATIC AMBIENCE is best captured by the re-cord of the six-man British team at the 'Intercalated Games' of 1906, which included one knight and two peers of the realm. They sailed from England to Athens in a yacht called the *Branwen*, owned by Lord Howard de Walden. Theodore Cook, the team captain, wrote up a report of the expedition, which included the squad's favourite classical quotations in Greek and Latin. Edward VII, who like most crowned heads of Europe attended the Games, was so excited by the fencing that he agreed on his return to become a patron of the art.

Aristocratic insouciance notwithstanding, fencing was characterised by some bitter feuding – notably at STOCKHOLM 1912. In the foil event the French insisted that the upper arm be included in the target area; the Italians refused to accept this and the French stormed out. The Italians then argued for a rule change in the épée that would have extended the permissible length of the sword; the French refused and the Italians quit.

In the 1920s, fencing was still a vocation rather than a sport, typified by the NADI BROTHERS from Livorno. Taught to fence from an early age, NEDO NADI won his first gold medal in 1912 and five at the 1920 Antwerp Games, before turning professional. (His multiple haul of gold medals stood as a record for fifty years, until swimmer Mark Spitz won seven events at the 1972 Games.) With his younger brother, ALDO, Nedo formed a partnership that fought a celebrated series of exhibition bouts. He lived the life of an itinerant playboy, moving to Hollywood, where he trained movie stars and choreographed fights.

At the 1924 Olympics, a contest boiled over into a real duel for the last time. In the final rounds of the sabre competition, it was evident that the Italian fighters were going soft on team favourite ORESTE PULITI, easing his path to the medals. The tactic was denounced by the French president of judging Adrien Lajoux and Hungarian judge Gyorgy Kovacs. After making threatening remarks to both judges, Puliti was disqualified. Inevitably, Puliti and Kovacs met the following day at the Parisian cabaret, the *Folies Bergères*, where the exchange turned violent and satisfaction was demanded. The two met on the Italian–Yugoslav border in November and duelled for more than an hour, injuring each other seriously.

For much of the inter-war period fencing was favoured by the elites of Europe's FASCIST STATES, satisfying their predilection for blood sports, warrior cults and medievalism. Oswald Mosley encouraged British fascists to embrace the foil, General Franco fenced with enthusiasm, and Reinhardt Heydrich, Himmler's deputy in the SS, was so obsessed with fencing that he had the FIE's archive

CONTROVERSY AT LONDON 2012: KOREAN FENCER SHIN A-LAM GLARES AT GERMANY'S BRITTA HEIDEMANN, WHO HAS JUST 'STOLEN' HER GOLD

seized from Belgium and brought to his office in Berlin, from where he planned to run the global sport. As a journalist, MUSSOLINI had shown a penchant for duelling and, as 'Il Duce', he liked to show off by practising in front of foreign journalists. The Italian fencing team received considerable support under his rule and the dictator enlisted Nedo Nadi – despite his anti-fascist convictions – as coach. In HUNGARY, the country's mastery of the sabre (it won every gold medal between 1924 and 1960) was incubated in the *salles* and clubs of the ultranationalist army.

Since the Second World War, the pre-eminence of France and Italy has been steadily eroded. WEST GERMANY became a fencing power in the late 1970s and early 1980s, driven by their obsessive, workaholic head coach Emil Beck, but the most significant change in the world of fencing came about as a result of the crushing of the 1956 uprising in Hungary, the nation that had dominated the sabre since the 1920s. The ensuing exodus of top-class fencers led to the establishment of new schools in SWEDEN, POLAND, ROMANIA and, ironically, the SOVIET UNION – a legacy that has been bequeathed to RUSSIA, which is now among the strongest countries in the sport.

Between 1924 and 1960 individual foil was the sole WOMEN'S EVENT, though a team foil competition was introduced in Rome. In 1996, the women's épée was added, followed by the sabre in 2004. While the USA, Switzerland, Ukraine, South Korea and China have won medals in the women's events, the old fencing nations still have it their own way most of the time. Italy's VALEN-TINA VEZZALLI won six golds in individual and team events in the foil between 1996 and 2012. Yet the competition at London 2012 was more diverse than most Olympics, with Venezuela's Rubén Limardo victorious in the men's épée and South Korea winning the team sabre event.

The London Games showed that the margin of success can be thinner than a foil blade. In the women's épée event, South Korea's Shin A-lam looked set for a place in the final, with the clock set on zero, but Austrian referee Barbara Csar ruled there was still a second left, during which time Germany's Britta Heidemann scored. Distraught, the South Korean stayed on the piste for 75 minutes while arguments about the result raged but her appeal was rejected by the FIE who tried to console her with a special medal recognising her 'sporting spirit'.

FOOTBALL

3–20 AUGUST 2016

RIO DE JANEIRO (MARACANÃ)

BOTH MEN'S AND WOMEN'S FINALS

RIO DE JANEIRO (João Havelange),

BELO HORIZONTE (Mineirão),

BRASILIA (Garrincha stadium),

MANAUS (Amazônia arena),

SÃO PAULO (Corinthians)

SALVADOR (Itaipava Arena Fonte Nova)

Athletes: 504 | Golds up for grabs: 2

-------------------------------- **OLYMPIC PRESENCE** --------------------------------

MEN'S FOOTBALL 1904–1928; 1936–PRESENT; WOMEN'S 1996–PRESENT.

-------------------------------- **OLYMPIC FORMAT** --------------------------------

THERE ARE SIXTEEN TEAMS IN THE MEN'S TOURNAMENT, twelve in the women's. Aside from up to three older players, all members of a MEN'S TEAM must be UNDER 23. There are no age restrictions for the women.

-------------------------------- **CONTENDERS** --------------------------------

PLAYING ON THEIR OWN TURF, WITH THE CHANCE OF A golden triumph in the Maracanã stadium, BRAZIL will be favourites in the men's competition, an event they have, astonishingly, never won (of which more later). Neighbours ARGENTINA will be keen to spoil the party. In the women's event, USA have won four out of five gold medals – the other going to NORWAY – and are looking to win this competition for the fourth time in a row. JAPAN, who lost the 2015 Women's World Cup final to the US, and reigning European champions GERMANY look to be the biggest threats to the Americans.

•• **PAST CHAMPIONS** ••

USA: 4 | GREAT BRITAIN: 3 | HUNGARY: 3

WHY WATCH OLYMPIC FOOTBALL?

SHOULD THE WORLD'S GAME BE AT THE WORLD'S GAMES? Many think not. As with tennis, even the victors would acknowledge that the Olympic tournament is hardly the pinnacle of the sport. This is less true, however, of the WOMEN'S COMPETITION than the men's, as the former is open to footballers of any age. The MEN'S COMPETITION is a bit of a hotchpotch, being essentially an UNDER-23 TOURNAMENT. To make matters worse, as Olympics years coincide with the European Football Championships, the top European countries either don't take part or field weakened teams. And yet the event has been graced by some of the game's all-time

WHO SAYS OLYMPIC FOOTBALL ISN'T IMPORTANT? MONTEVIDEO TURNS OUT EN MASSE TO GREET THE URUGUAYAN TEAM ON ITS TRIUMPHANT RETURN FROM THE 1924 GAMES

greats – from Hungarian genius FERENC PUSKÁS to LEV YASHIN (the only goalkeeper to be chosen as European Footballer of the Year) and ROMÁRIO, the top scorer at Seoul 1988, six years before he won the World Cup with Brazil. The BEIJING TOURNAMENT featured the likes of LIONEL MESSI and RONALDINHO.

The men's competition has its merits. FIFA, the sport's governing body, organises global tournaments at under-20 and under-17 levels, but there is no under-23 equivalent, making the Olympics the closest thing to a World Cup for this age group. And for non-European nations, the men's competition is a showcase for the best rising talent in the sport, seasoned with the experience provided by a smattering of older players. So while British fans remain underwhelmed by this competition, for South American, Asian and African nations Olympic football is a very big deal indeed.

THE STORY OF FOOTBALL

THE EARLIEST RECORDED FOOTBALL-LIKE GAME, PLAYED IN CHINA in the fifth century BC, involved kicking a ball through a hole in a piece of cloth suspended from two poles. As there were no teams, it was essentially a form of target practice. The ANCIENT GREEKS introduced passing and tackling in a game called *phaininda*, which was adopted by the ROMANS and renamed *harpastum*, but the sport probably had more in common with handball or rugby than with football. Feet don't appear to have played a particularly active part in the various forms of 'football' played in Europe during the MIDDLE AGES either, except as weapons. Typically played on Shrove Tuesday, these games were semi-formalised brawls in which two teams of indeterminate size vied to convey an inflated pig's bladder to one end or other of a village or town. The one medieval game that did concentrate on footwork was *kemari*, a ritualised form of keepy-uppy practised in Japan, which was itself derived from the Chinese game of *cuju*.

Football as we know it evolved in the public schools of ENGLAND during the nineteenth century, and in 1848 a common set of rules was drawn up at Cambridge University. The key subsequent development was the restriction of the right to handle the ball to one player per team during the 1860s. By the beginning of the modern Olympic era, football had become a significant force – and a working-class passion – in Britain's industrial cities, with the first FOOTBALL LEAGUE founded in 1888. The sport soon took root in South America and continental Europe, courtesy of expat Brits and anglophile locals. And – for men's football, at least – the rest is history.

The story of WOMEN'S FOOTBALL is rather less well known. At the start, it developed very much in parallel with the men's game. The earliest recorded match was a 7-1 victory for a North of England eleven over the South in 1895. The first organised women's tournament was launched in the north-east of the country in 1917. Popularly known as the MUNITIONETTES' CUP, it was contested by workers in the region's armaments factories. The most celebrated team was DICK KERR'S LADIES, formed in a Preston munitions factory. The team toured the USA and drew a crowd of 53,000 at a Boxing Day fixture at Goodison Park in Liverpool in 1920. That same year, a French women's team toured England, with its organiser Madame Milliat declaring that 'Football is not wrong for women. Most of these girls are beautiful Grecian dancers.'

Such views cut no ice with the ENGLISH FA which, in 1921, made the less than enlightened decision to BAN WOMEN'S TEAMS from playing at its affiliated stadiums, arguing that 'the game of football is quite unsuitable for females and ought not to be encouraged'. This led to the formation of the breakaway English Ladies Football Association and the establishment of a Challenge Cup. Although the tournament attracted much attention in its early days, women's football – lacking the FA's support – gradually sank from prominence in the nation of its birth. Only when the governing body rescinded its ban in 1971 did its fortunes begin to revive. By this stage, nations in which the women's game did not face the same kind of institutional chauvinism had surged ahead, notably GERMANY, CHINA, the USA and the SCANDINAVIAN nations. The first UEFA women's Championship was won by SWEDEN in 1982 and eight years later the USA captured the inaugural FIFA women's World Cup.

Game On: Football Basics

Unless you are a Martian or truly can't stand the sport, you'll be fully aware that the object of the exercise is to get the ball into the opponents' net more often than they get it into yours. You'll also have an inkling that the players, bar the goalkeeper, are not allowed to use their hands or arms. The one rule that can give trouble is offside …

································ **THE OFFSIDE LAWS** ································

A player is in an offside position if they are in the opponents' half of the pitch, in front of the ball, and closer to the other team's goal line than the second-to-last opponent. This applies to any part of the player's body except the arms.

Crucially, however, a player will only be penalised if: they were in an offside position at the moment the ball was last touched by another player; they didn't receive the ball directly from a throw in, goal kick or corner; or they are deemed to be ACTIVELY INVOLVED IN PLAY. In 2015, FIFA tried to clarify what 'actively involved' meant, stipulating that a player in an offside position must be penalised if they 'make an obvious action which clearly impacts on the ability of an opponent to play the ball'.

Decisions relating to offside are frequently controversial for two reasons. First, it can be extremely difficult to judge whether a player is ahead of the second to last opponent at the moment the ball is played, particularly if the referee's assistant responsible for making the call isn't precisely parallel to the player at the time. Secondly, determining whether a player is active remains, despite FIFA's efforts, more a matter of judgement than of incontrovertible fact.

································ **COMPETITION FORMAT** ································

As host nation, Brazil is guaranteed a place in both the men's and women's competitions. Everyone else has to qualify via preliminary continental tournaments. In the women's tournament, France and Germany qualify as the two best performing European teams at the 2015 Women's World Cup and a third place will be decided by a play-off.

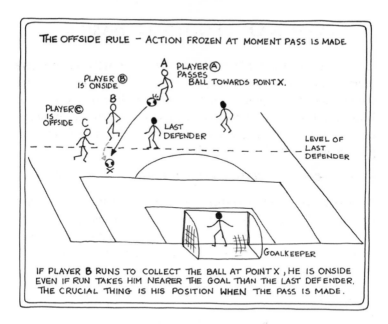

THE OFFSIDE RULE — ACTION FROZEN AT MOMENT PASS IS MADE.

A   PLAYER Ⓐ PASSES BALL TOWARDS POINT X.

PLAYER Ⓑ IS ONSIDE

PLAYER Ⓒ IS OFFSIDE C

B

LAST DEFENDER

LEVEL OF LAST DEFENDER

GOALKEEPER

IF PLAYER B RUNS TO COLLECT THE BALL AT POINT X, HE IS ONSIDE EVEN IF RUN TAKES HIM NEARER THE GOAL THAN THE LAST DEFENDER. THE CRUCIAL THING IS HIS POSITION WHEN THE PASS IS MADE.

Both tournaments will begin with a GROUP STAGE (four groups of four for the men, three groups for the women), in which each nation will play the other three teams in its group. The top two from each group will progress to a KNOCK-OUT STAGE, culminating in a final at the great Maracanã stadium.

############### **EXTRA TIME AND PENALTY SHOOT-OUTS** ###############

AS WITH THE WORLD CUP, GROUP MATCHES WILL CONSIST of two 45-minute halves with no extra time if the scores finish level. During the knock-out stages, 30 minutes of EXTRA TIME will be played if required, followed by a PENALTY SHOOT-OUT if no winner has emerged. (The 'golden goal' system, whereby the first team to score in extra time won the match there and then, was used in the Games in 1996 and 2000 but has now been dropped.)

In a PENALTY SHOOT-OUT each team takes five penalty kicks and the one that scores the most wins. If the scores are still level, the shoot-out enters 'sudden death' – the first team to find itself ahead when both sides have taken the same number of penalties wins.

The Finer Points

Should your first experience of football come at the 2016 Games, the following ought to increase your enjoyment of the spectacle.

WATCHING THE MIDFIELD BATTLES

Pay attention to how the players make and exploit space: good players are constantly moving into positions where they can receive passes while escaping the attention of opponents. Most of the time, the team that dominates the middle third of the pitch goes on to win the game. Possession isn't everything in football – what you do when you have the ball is what matters – but the ability to retain it is the hallmark of most good teams. Unless a team is drilled and organised to deny space to their opponents, chasing the ball can be dispiriting and tiring; the team that controls the ball is usually master of its own destiny.

WATCHING THE WATCHERS

Ask yourself whether it's entirely reasonable for the individuals responsible for making the decisions about key incidents to be the only people on the planet without recourse to replays. The issue of whether and how much the officials should have access to technology burns continually.

WATCHING THE WOMEN

Seasoned fans might want to take a break from the men's game until the final stages and concentrate on the female tournament. The action is slower and less athletic but the levels of skill can be high. The first player to score an Olympic goal – scoring direct from a corner – in either event at the Games is America's Megan Rapinoe, who made history in a thrilling semi-final against Canada at London 2012.

FOOTBALL GOES TO THE OLYMPICS

AFTER FEATURING AS AN EXHIBITION SPORT AT THE TWO PREVIOUS Games, football made its full Olympic debut at LONDON 1908. Only six teams took part, including two from France, and the quality was decidedly uneven. The Danes, who lost the final 2-0 to GREAT BRITAIN, scored 26 goals in their other two Games, including a 17-1 drubbing of France B, in which SOPHUS NIELSEN hit the net ten times. The number of participating nations rose to eleven in 1912, but in many respects the tournament mirrored its predecessor. Once again there was a handful of big scores, another player (GOTTFRIED FUCHS of Germany) bagged ten goals in one match, and Great Britain again beat Denmark by a two-goal margin in the final.

The BELGIUM and CZECHOSLOVAKIA final at ANTWERP 1920 was the highlight of the Games for the locals, so when some youths dug a tunnel under the perimeter fence several thousand of them squeezed in for free. Their presence put such a strain on the already full 40,000-capacity stadium that a detachment of troops was stationed around the touchline to prevent the crowd spilling on to the pitch. The Czechs saw the soldiers' deployment as deliberate intimidation. They were already disgruntled by the appointment of English referee John Lewis, whose decision-making had so outraged the home crowd during a qualifying match in Prague that they had physically attacked him. Czech morale did not improve when the Belgians quickly went two goals ahead. When Mr Lewis sent off their star player Karel Steiner in the 39th minute, the Czechoslovakian team stormed off the pitch and was disqualified.

The next two Olympic golds went to URUGUAY, inculcating this football-obsessed country in a winning habit that they maintained at the first World Cup in 1930. The arrival of the World Cup, combined with America's lack of enthusiasm for soccer, led to the sport being dropped for the Los Angeles Games in 1932, but it was back with a bang at BERLIN. Anyone who thinks BAD BEHAVIOUR in football is a modern disease should reflect on that 1936 tournament. During the opening encounter between ITALY and the USA, the Italian players prevented the German referee from sending off

Achille Piccini by pinning his arms to his sides and clamping his mouth shut. Piccini stayed on the pitch, and the Italians won 1-0 and went on to take gold.

The Azzurri's triumph was a bitter disappointment to hosts Germany and, in particular, to Adolf Hitler who saw his only football match at the Games: a 2-0 defeat to Norway. He had agreed to watch after being assured that Germany would win gold and, when Norway took the lead, Josef Goebbels noted: 'The Führer is very agitated.' When Norway made it 2-0 five minutes from time, Hitler left in disgust.

The SWEDES won in 1948 with a side that boasted three firemen, but it was to be 36 years before another non-communist nation captured gold. The rise of professionalism in Western Europe and South America deprived countries from those parts of their best players, allowing state-sponsored teams of 'AMATEURS' from Eastern Europe to clean up. In 1952, Hungary, inspired by the genius of Puskás, Nándor Hidegkuti, József Bozsik and Sándor Kocsis, won gold; a year later this legendary side would be the first foreign team to beat England at Wembley, winning 6-3, a scoreline that flattered the English. The Italians did their best to end Eastern European dominance in 1964, selecting three members of the Inter Milan team that had just won the European Cup. When it was pointed out that some of their players were not strictly amateur, they withdrew in a huff.

In 1984, the IOC relaxed the participation criteria to allow PROFESSIONAL FOOTBALLERS from Europe and South America to compete, provided that they hadn't previously played more than five times for their country. The final was duly contested by FRANCE and BRAZIL, with the French winning 2-0 in front of a 100,000 crowd. The SOVIET UNION temporarily restored the old order at SEOUL 1988 but by then the Eastern bloc was on its last legs.

The eligibility rules were changed again for the BARCELONA 1992 Games: from then on, a squad could be fully professional, as long as no more than three of its members were over 23. In Barcelona, a SPAIN side starring Pep Guardiola beat Poland 3-2 in a pulsating final.

Perhaps as a result of the absence of many of the top European players, due to their continental championships being held in the same summers as the Games, the African nations have broken through in the Olympics to a much greater extent than in the World Cup, providing three of the eight finalists and two of the four winners since the mid-1990s (NIGERIA in Atlanta and CAMEROON in Sydney). Since then, central and South America have dominated: ARGENTINA were victorious in Athens and Beijing while MEXICO were the surprise winners at London 2012.

WOMEN FOOTBALLERS finally joined the Olympic party in 1996 at ATLANTA, where the host nation collected gold, defeating China 2-1 in the final. This was a mixed blessing for American goalkeeper BRIANA SCURRY, who had unwisely promised a *Sports Illustrated* journalist that she would run naked through the streets of Athens, Georgia, if the USA triumphed. Sure enough, in the wee hours of the night following the final, Scurry ran ten metres along a deserted side street wearing nothing but her gold medal.

The 2000 women's final was won by NORWAY, who beat the USA courtesy of a 'golden goal' in extra time. The American women maintained their 100 per cent record of final appearances in Athens and Beijing, overcoming Brazil on both occasions. The second victory proved that there was life after the great MIA HAMM, who retired after the 2004 Games having scored more international goals (158) than any player of either sex, despite having been born with a club foot.

America's triumph at London 2012 was not without controversy. They prevailed 4-3 in a magnificent semi-final against Canada, for whom Christine Sinclair scored a hat-trick, with a little help from Norwegian referee Christina Pedersen who gave an indirect free kick against Canadian keeper Erin McLeod for holding the ball longer than six seconds. (Technically, the decision was correct but the rule is rarely enforced.) The ensuing free kick hit a Canadian arm and Pedersen awarded a penalty from which Abby Wambach made it 3-3. The US rode their luck in the final too, beating Japan 2-1 after German referee Bibiana Steinhaus failed to give a penalty when American midfielder Tobin Heath handled in the area.

After all the fuss about Great Britain fielding Olympic football teams for the first time since 1972, their campaigns were a bit of an anti-climax. A women's squad consisting of sixteen English players and two Scots lost 2-0 to Canada in the quarter-finals. A men's squad comprised of thirteen English players and five Welshmen exited at the same stage, losing to South Korea on penalties – an outcome that supporters of the Three Lions are all too familiar with. After the Games, FIFA announced that it would not accept another Great Britain team unless all four home nations – England, Scotland, Wales and Northern Ireland – agreed. That is exceedingly unlikely, so this strange chapter of Olympic football history must now be considered closed.

Brazil's Olympic curse

How can a nation that has won five World Cups still be chasing its first Olympic football gold? The anomaly is so great that when Brazil lost the final at London 2012, the defeat revived talk of the country's 'Olympic curse'. There would be no more fitting stage on which to break that curse than the Maracanã, the stadium where the country lost the deciding game in the 1950 World Cup to Uruguay, a defeat that so scarred the nation's psyche that one Brazilian fan committed suicide, three died of heart attacks and manager Flavio Costa is rumoured to have left the stadium disguised as a nanny. Changing their shirts from white to yellow and green, the national team eventually recovered from this trauma, winning the World Cup in 1958, 1962, 1970, 1994 and 2002. Yet in the Olympics, all the teams have to show for their efforts are five silver medals: three for the men (1984, 1988, 2012) and two for the women (2004 and 2008). It's not a great record, considering the country's Olympic footballers have included such illustrious names as Falcão, Romário, Rivaldo, Neymar and Marta, one of the greatest women footballers of all time.

To be fair, Brazil didn't make their Olympic football debut until 1952 when the rules about amateur players favoured Eastern bloc, nations, who won the men's competition for eight Games in a row between 1952 and 1980. The Seleção were never in serious contention for a medal until 1976, when they lost the play-off for bronze to the Soviet Union. Things began to perk up when the IOC relaxed the rules, allowing some professionals to compete in the 1984 Games. With future World Cup-winner Dunga bossing midfield, Brazil reached the final, losing 2-0 to France. Four years later, they

BRAZIL'S SEOUL 1988 TEAM, BEFORE LOSING THE FINAL TO RUSSIA.
BACK ROW: CRUZ, TAFFAREL, ANDRADE, ALOISIO, WINCK, JORGINHO, FERREIRA;
FRONT ROW: BEBETO, MILTON, HAMILTON, NETO, ROMÁRIO

really ought to have won with a squad that included four other future World Cup winners – goalkeeper Claudio Taffarel, defender Jorginho and forwards Bebeto and Romário. After overcoming West Germany on penalties in the semi-final, they were the better side in the final against the Soviet Union and went ahead through Romário's seventh goal of the competition. Creating chances, but not finishing them, they let the USSR back into the match and lost 2-1, undone by a quick Soviet counter-attack in extra time.

Instead of building on that, Brazil didn't even qualify for Barcelona, returning to the Games in 1996. With Mario Zagallo as coach, and RONALDO, ROBERTO CARLOS AND RIVALDO all in the squad, expectations were high. Things proceeded roughly to plan in Atlanta until Brazil met Nigeria in the semi-finals. In a stirring encounter, Brazil scored the first four goals – although one of them was an own goal from Roberto Carlos – and, 3-1 up with twelve minutes to go, looked set for victory. When Dida was beaten by Victor Ipekba's 20-yard shot, the dynamic of the game changed. Kanu capitalised on a frantic goalmouth scramble to take the match into extra time and, four minutes later, weaved past two defenders to score the decisive 'golden goal'. This turnaround was hailed, with a degree of exaggeration, as the worst sixteen minutes in the history of Brazilian football. Juninho probably summed up the national sentiment best when he said that winning the bronze – which the Seleção duly did – was 'not a big deal'. It didn't help that the Brazilian women's team imploded in similar style, losing their semi-final 3-2 to China after leading 2-1 with eight minutes to go.

Four years later in Sydney, the men's team were knocked out by another golden goal – in the quarter-final against eventual winners Cameroon. The men's team missed out on Athens but national honour was partially restored when the women's side scored fifteen goals – Marta got three of them – and secured silver, losing 2-1 in extra time to the US in the final. In Beijing, the women lost the final in extra time again against the same opponents, while the men secured bronze, after losing 3-0 in the semi-final to an Argentina side starring Sergio Agüero, Messi, Javier Mascherano, Ángel Di María and Juan Riquelme which, unsurprisingly, went on to win the competition.

London 2012 seemed the perfect opportunity to rewrite Brazil's Olympic football history. The squad was stronger than in Beijing, being graced by OSCAR, Neymar, Hulk and captain Thiago Silva. En route to the final, they scored three goals in every match. At Wembley, Mexico won 2-1, partly because they played as if their country's reputation depended on the result and Brazil didn't. The curse looked as if it was haunting Brazil when they conceded the fastest goal in Olympic history – Oribe Peralta scoring the first of his two goals after just 29 seconds. Brought on after 32 minutes, Hulk was probably Brazil's best player, and he gave his country undeserved hope when he slammed the ball into the net with his right foot with two minutes to go. Yet when the final whistle blew, the Wembley centre circle was littered with distraught Brazilian players. Dunga is the next coach to attempt to lift the curse. The pressure of expectation may be even greater in Rio, especially with the final at the Maracanã. If Brazil lose their fourth Olympic final in their national stadium, it will be a lot harder for Dunga to exit disguised as a nanny than it was for Flavio Costa in 1950.

GOLF

11–20 AUGUST 2016

RESERVA DE MARAPENDI, BARRA
DA TIJUCA, RIO DE JANEIRO

Athletes: 120 | **Golds up for grabs:** 2

OLYMPIC FORMAT

THE OLYMPIC GOLF EVENT WILL RUN ON THE SAME LINES AS the sport's majors. Sixty men and sixty women, including the fifteen players at the top of the IGF rankings, will play four rounds of eighteen holes. After four rounds, the golfer who has completed the holes in the fewest shots will win each competition. In the event of a tie for any of the medal positions, there will be a PLAY-OFF over three holes. If the scores are still equal, the play-off goes to sudden death.

CONTENDERS

WITH THE TOP FIFTEEN MALE AND FEMALE PROFESSIONAL golfers automatically qualifying, the USA will expect to be on the podium. In the men's event, JORDAN SPIETH and BUBBA WATSON will be among the favourites, though they will face stiff competition from Australia (JASON DAY), Ireland (RORY MCILROY), Sweden (HENRIK STENSON) and Great Britain (JUSTIN ROSE).

The USA will also challenge in the women's event, through Stacy Lewis and Lexi Thompson, but they will not have things all their own way, with New Zealand's LYDIA KO and South Korea's INBEE PARK CURRENTLY at the top of their game.

PAST CHAMPIONS

USA: 3 | CANADA: 1

WHY WATCH GOLF?

THERE IS SOMETHING INTRINSICALLY THRILLING ABOUT watching people thwack a very small ball over long distances, making sure that it avoids a series of obstacles, and guiding it, with skill and efficiency, into a very small hole. Many great golfers – Jack Nicklaus and Tiger Woods in his prime – do this so calmly they appeal to the Apollonian ideal of sport as a pursuit for the mind, not the muscles. Yet others – Seve Ballesteros, Colin Montgomerie, Bubba Watson, Ian Poulter – invite you to revel in the human drama of every shot.

In many Olympic sports, only a handful of favourites are truly in contention for medals. The competitive field in golf is wide, however, and it's entirely possible that ten players may be in contention until the final holes. Victory is never certain until every contestant has completed the course: in 1999, Scotland's Paul Lawrie won the British Open in a play-off despite starting the final eighteen holes ten shots behind leader Jean van der Velde.

The sport has often been damned as slow, almost masonic in its middle-class elitism, and a 'good walk spoiled'. There may be some truth in these criticisms but speed is not a virtue in itself and golf does acquire its own kind of momentum in the final round. Meanwhile, the game has made strenuous efforts of late to become more inclusive. Few sports test a player, mentally and physically, as thoroughly as golf. Like archery or darts, one simple mechanical act can make the difference between triumph and despair. With so much often riding on a two-foot putt, the pundit Bobby Jones claimed the most important distance in golf is the five-and-a-half inches between a player's ears.

THE STORY OF GOLF

THE TRADITIONAL TALE OF GOLF'S ORIGINS STARTS WITH apocryphal accounts of the sport being played on West Sands, a stretch of dunes just along the Scottish coast from ST ANDREWS in the early twelfth century. Certainly, we know that the game was established enough in Scotland by 1547 for King James II, fretting that too many of his subjects were neglecting archery, to pass a law declaring, 'It is ordained and decreed that football and golf be utterly condemned and not practised.'

Yet this view has been challenged in China, where there is intriguing evidence that a game called CHUIWAN ('hit ball') was played in the thirteenth century. In 1282, a book called *Wan Jing – Manual of the Ball Game* became the first known published guide to a game that sounds a lot like golf. A Ming dynasty scroll called *The Autumn Banquet* shows a member of the imperial court swinging something that looks very much like a golf club at a ball. The urge to hit a ball with a stick is so universal that other sports have been suggested as precursors. The most credible contender is *colf*, a game played in what is now Belgium and the Netherlands; illustrations suggest that the aim of the sport was to hit a ball around the village and put it into a small hole. The word 'colf' refers to the club and is the root of the word 'golf'.

What is in no doubt is that SCOTLAND drove the development of the game between the sixteenth and nineteenth centuries. In 1513, James II's grandson, James IV, had a set of clubs made in Paris for a match against the Earl of Boswell. His royal blessing popularised the game in Scotland – the oldest course, St Andrews, dates back to 1574 – and it spread south of the border under the patronage of the STUARTS: James I (James VI of Scotland), Charles I and Charles II. At this point, golf had no real rules – players usually agreed them on the day – and most games were MATCH PLAY, in which each hole was effectively a match in itself, the winner being whoever had hit the fewest strokes, and the ultimate victor whoever has won the most holes at the end of the round.

The world's first golf club, the Royal Burgess Golf Society in Edinburgh, was probably founded in 1735, followed in 1754 by the Royal & Ancient Golf Club in St Andrews (the club, now known as the R&A, jointly governs the game today with the United States Golf Association). The creation of an eighteen-hole course at St Andrews ten years later was an important step in codifying the game; Montrose's course then had 25 holes, while Leith's had just five.

WALTER HAGEN TAKES ON A BUNKER – NO HURRY, NO WORRY

Until the 1850s the sport remained the preserve of a privileged few but the advent of a cheaper ball (see below) and the growth of railways helped popularise golf in the coming decades. It was at this point, too, that the STROKE-PLAY format – in which players were judged against a 'par' score for a course – gained a foothold, being used at the inaugural BRITISH OPEN in 1860. Two years later, the first great professional golfer, a Scot known as OLD TOM MORRIS, won the Open by fourteen shots, a record margin for a major that stood until Tiger Woods won the 2000 US Open by fifteen strokes. This is the preferred format for PGA tournaments and Olympic golf.

By the end of the nineteenth century, the game had been established across Britain and exported across the British Empire and to the United States. Americans with plenty of money and no gadgets to distract them at home quickly adopted the sport. The fact that it wasn't too strenuous, dangerous and took hours to play appealed to industrialists like JOHN D. ROCKEFELLER and ANDREW CARNEGIE who used the sport to meet their peers and make deals between shots. The first US OPEN was held in 1895 but it wasn't until 1913 that the competition ignited public interest, when American golfer FRANCIS OUIMET won a three-way play-off against Britons Harry Vardon and Ted Ray, deemed the best in the world at that time.

The sport made its OLYMPIC DEBUT in 1900 but the issue of professionalism – along with a certain institutional arrogance from the R&A – would lead to its Olympic exile. In golf, professionalism was a complicated issue. In the nineteenth century, gentlemen played the sport for pleasure while professionals were usually working-class men, earning a living by caddying, coaching, making clubs, keeping greens and playing occasional challenge matches. Such class distinctions were imported to America, too, as many of the first professionals hired by clubs were British. The American WALTER HAGEN was probably the first golfer to earn a living purely by playing the game. A charismatic personality, whose relaxed credo was 'Don't hurry, don't worry, and be sure to smell the flowers along the way', he won eleven majors; only Woods (14) and Nicklaus (18) have won more. In 1923, after discovering that professionals were banned from the Royal Troon clubhouse where the British Open was held, he ordered his limousine to park in front of the club where, to the chagrin of members, he was served a lavish lunch. Four years later, the RYDER CUP was launched at the instigation of garden seed magnate Samuel Ryder. The match-play tournament's inclusion of other European golfers in 1979 signalled the game's growing global appeal.

Given that golf was once said to be an acronym for 'Gentlemen Only, Ladies Forbidden' – and the fact that many clubs are still men only – the game has been surprisingly open to WOMEN. Mary Queen of Scots is said to have been an early enthusiast – although some historians argue that she more likely played a similar French game called pall-mall. In 1811, women golfers were competing for a fishing basket and silk handkerchiefs in a competition sponsored by what would become the Royal Musselburgh Golf Club. The oldest independent women's golf club was founded in 1873 at Carnoustie. Twenty years later, the Ladies Golf Union was founded at London's Grand Hotel and was influential enough to have its invention, handicapping – a system which enabled golfers of differing abilities to play against each other – adopted by men. By 1925, the women's game had become established enough for F. Scott Fitzgerald to draw on socialite and amateur golfer Edith Cummings for the character Jordan Baker in *The Great Gatsby*.

Perhaps the greatest golf landmark in popular culture, however, came in February 1971 when the US astronaut ALAN SHEPARD played two shots on the surface of the moon.

ALAN SHEPARD DEBUTS GOLF ON THE MOON. WITH A MAKESHIFT SIX-IRON.

GAME ON: GOLF BASICS

IN ESSENCE, THE OBJECT OF GOLF IS TO HIT A BALL THAT must be at least 1.68 inches in diameter and weigh no more than 1.68 ounces from A (a tee) to B (a hole measuring 4.25 inches in diameter) using as few strokes of a club as possible. The distance from A to B typically varies from around 160 yards to more than 500 yards. Each hole has a PAR SCORE signifying the number of shots it should take to complete – three for the shortest, five for the longest and most challenging. Golfers' scores are determined by whether they play more or fewer strokes than par on a hole. Each course consists of EIGHTEEN HOLES and in many tournaments, including the Olympics, the winner is the player who, after four rounds, is the most BELOW PAR (or the least above).

To get around a course, golfers use an impressive array of equipment: up to FOURTEEN CLUBS (of which more later), tees (essentially little stands to put the ball on so they can hit the ball cleanly), specialist gloves and shoes, bags and trolleys, a scorecard, and some very odd clobber. American golfer John Daly's multi-coloured trousers are so loud they should be issued with a noise abatement order.

BALLS

HOW FAST AND FAR BALLS CAN TRAVEL AND EXACTLY HOW symmetrical they are is defined by the R&A and the USGA, but golfers don't all play with the same ball. The long officially approved list of balls allows golfers to choose from a handful of colours (white, yellow, orange, pink, red, green, purple and grey) and the number of dimples on the ball can vary from 252 to 446.

Golf balls didn't always have dimples. The very first spherical(ish) objects golfers thwacked were called 'featheries' because they were made out of gorse and duck feathers. Expensive to make – and hard to hit very far – these balls were replaced by ones made out of a sap-like material called gutta-percha. The 'gutty' balls were cheaper, could be hit further, flew straighter and were easy to remould if they got damaged during play. When it became apparent that worn, beaten-up balls seemed to fly further than new smooth ones, the ball was covered with dimples. They act as turbulators – creating turbulence in the layer of air surrounding the ball which tends to reduce the drag so that it can travel further. Variations in the number, shape and pattern of dimples can subtly affect the way the ball travels through the air. Less spin usually means more distance on the shot whereas more spin means more control but less distance.

CADDIES

MANAGING ALL THIS PARAPHERNALIA CAN BE LABORIOUS which is why golfers, uniquely in Olympic sports, are allowed to compete with a sidekick called a caddie. These assistants can walk around with the golfer, carrying their bag, going ahead to find the ball, assessing the yardage to the hole and highlighting hazards. They can also assist in the mysterious art of reading the greens – considering such important details as the direction in which the grass is growing (shots in the same direction as the grass go faster), the general slope, any nearby water (if there is some, a ball will usually break toward it) – to make sure the putt is as accurate as possible. It might sound like a thankless task but Seve Ballesteros, Sam Snead and Ben Hogan all started out as caddies and on the PGA tour top caddies can earn $600,000 a year.

··· **THE COURSE** ···

THE OLYMPIC COURSE IN BARRA DA TIJUCA WILL HAVE 18 holes, be a par 71 and cover 7,350 yards for men and 6,500 yards for women. The course is pretty narrow and includes, among the usual obstacles, a couple of lakes.

Most golf courses have a variety of holes with three DIFFERENT PARS: typically a par 3 hole is up to 250 yards long for men (210 for women); a par 4 is 251-470 yards for men (211-400 for women); and a par 5 is 471-690 yards long for men (401-675 for women). The RIO COURSE, created by architect Gil Hanse with advice from former US Women's Open winner Amy Alcott, is designed to encourage golfers to aim for a 'BIRDIE' – one shot under par – with some shorter par 3s and 4s and reachable par 5s.

The action on each hole follows a set pattern. Once the first shot has been played, the golfers who are furthest from the green play first. On par 3 holes, the golfer will hope to reach the green from the tee. On longer holes, the golfer will tee off, looking to place the ball in the FAIRWAY, an area between the tee and the green where the grass is even and short. What they don't want to do is end up in the ROUGH, where the grass is higher and it's harder to play the next shot or, worse still, the WATER – if this happens, most golfers either take a one-shot penalty and play from the point where the ball went into the hazard or take a one-shot penalty and go back to the point where they played the shot and start again.

From the fairway, most golfers will look to land the ball near or on the GREEN, preferably in a position that sets them up for an easy

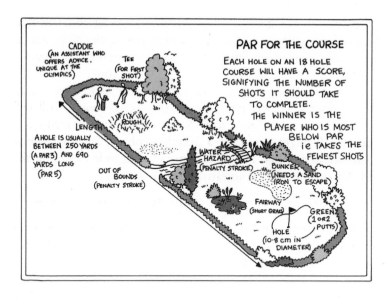

CADDIE
(AN ASSISTANT WHO
OFFERS ADVICE.
UNIQUE AT THE
OLYMPICS)

TEE
(FOR FIRST
SHOT)

PAR FOR THE COURSE

EACH HOLE ON AN 18 HOLE
COURSE WILL HAVE A SCORE,
SIGNIFYING THE NUMBER OF
SHOTS IT SHOULD TAKE
TO COMPLETE.
THE WINNER IS THE
PLAYER WHO IS MOST
BELOW PAR
ie TAKES THE
FEWEST SHOTS

LENGTH
ROUGH

A HOLE IS USUALLY
BETWEEN 250 YARDS
(A PAR 3) AND 690
YARDS LONG
(PAR 5)

OUT OF
BOUNDS
(PENALTY STROKE)

WATER
HAZARD
(PENALTY STROKE)

BUNKER
(NEEDS A SAND
IRON TO ESCAPE)

FAIRWAY
(SHORT GRASS)

GREEN
(1 OR 2
PUTTS)

HOLE
(10·8 cm IN
DIAMETER)

finish. The course designer makes this task harder by strategically placing a few BUNKERS, usually filled with sand, near the green. Although Jack Nicklaus was a master at getting out of these traps, even the best can be troubled: at the 2015 PGA Championship, America's Rickie Fowler took four shots to escape a bunker on a par 3 hole.

On the green, the world's best golfers expect to have the ball in the HOLE, also called a CUP, within one or two putts. Most of them will play a PENDULUM STROKE – in which their arms, hands and putter are mainly controlled by the rocking of their shoulders – and, for two seconds, follow the stroke with their club, rather than with their eyes. Yet different folks have flourished with different strokes. The great Sam Snead in the 1960s putted like he was playing croquet.

A variety of OFFENCES can lead a golfer to have strokes added to their score: having more than fourteen clubs in the bag can cost up to four strokes. Unintentionally hitting the flagstick in the hole with the ball earns a two-stroke penalty. The following misdemeanours all earn a one-stroke penalty: if the ball is lost, goes out of bounds, is deemed unplayable or is accidentally moved by a practice swing.

Jotting down the wrong score on the scorecard will lead to instant disqualification but this is an unlikely Olympic offence.

·· **CLUBS** ··

A GOLF CLUB HAS THREE COMPONENTS: THE HEAD, THE SHAFT and the grip. They are designed to optimise the physics behind a golfer's swing while allowing them to make a decent shot if their swing goes awry. The better the player, the less forgiving the club needs to be. There are twelve golf clubs in a typical set: three WOODS, seven IRONS, one PUTTER and a HYBRID – to which a player might add another hybrid and a WEDGE (a kind of iron used for specific situations, such as lobbing to the green or getting out of a bunker). Clubs are also categorized by their LOFT – the angle of the club face that affects trajectory and controls distance – with a driver, for example, having a loft of 7-12 degrees. The higher the loft, the higher the angle at which the ball can be launched. Clubs are numbered sequentially, so that, until you get to a wood 5, the greater a number, the higher the loft and the shorter the shaft. At wood 5 and above, the shaft stays the same because if it got any shorter, the club wouldn't generate enough speed when it hit the ball.

Despite their name, WOODS no longer have wooden club heads (they are now made of metal because this provides a bigger 'sweet spot' – the area which results in a good hit) but the purpose of these clubs hasn't changed. With their longer shafts, and larger rounder heads, a golfer will typically use these clubs to strike the ball when they are 175 yards or more from the green. The most popular woods are the DRIVER (aka 1 wood) and 2, 3, 4 and 5 (also known as FAIRWAY WOODS because they are often used for the second shot).

With shorter shafts and smaller club heads than woods, IRONS come into their own within 200 yards of the green. Again, the numbers indicate the degree of loft. The 1 IRON has the smallest sweet spot and is considered so hard to hit with that Lee Trevino famously remarked, after almost being struck by lightning on a course, that if he ever played in another storm he would take his 1 iron out and point it at the sky because 'even God can't hit a 1 iron'. The LONG IRONS (2 to 4) are used on the fairway and rough with the 3 iron useful for long approaches to the green. The MID-IRONS are easier to hit with the 6 iron a beginners' favourite and the 7 iron good for shorter approach shots and windy conditions because it helps keep the ball low. The 9 iron is ideal if you want to impart some backspin and land the ball close to the pin without it rolling very far.

Most golfers will also have a specialist iron or two in their bag. With a loft of 50-52 degrees, WEDGES are especially useful for accurate, high, short shots (especially chips and lobs) and getting the ball out of hazardous spots. Yet if the ball lands in a bunker, a golfer will try to get it out using a SAND IRON. With the large club head of a high-lofted wood, and the shorter shaft of an iron, HYBRID CLUBS are catching on because they make it easier for a golfer to swing and harder for them to slice the ball.

A PUTTER only has one purpose: to get the ball into the hole. Because they are designed for short, slow shots, they usually have a loft of 5-6 degrees. Many golfers will have dozens of putters, selecting one to put in the bag depending on recent results. Because touch and feel are so crucial to putting, these clubs come in all shapes and sizes: PERIPHERALLY WEIGHTED, with the club head offset from the shaft for better balance; blade, which has a smaller sweet spot for greater precision; MALLET-HEADED, with a larger club head; and CENTRE-SHAFTED, designed to help a player align their body correctly. Jack Nicklaus won the 1967 US Open with a centre shaft, dubbed White Fang, but less than one in ten professionals use them today.

THE FINER POINTS

RELAX AND SWING

THE PERFECT SWING IS THE HOLY GRAIL OF GOLF AND, LIKE that legendary chalice, is destined never to be discovered. With golfers coming in an array of shapes and sizes, simple biomechanics suggests that there is no one-size-fits-all perfect swing. One that enables you to hit the ball with accuracy and power – a powerful drive can send the ball 300 yards – and do so with such consistency that it feels as if your muscles are remembering the shot, not your brain.

Why is the swing so important? Because its basic principles apply to every shot a golfer plays. When you hear Rory McElroy, who has one of the best swings in the game, describe how he does it you can see why it carries such mystique. A successful swing, for him, starts with the fundamentals – grip, posture, alignment and ball position – but also involves correct manipulation, movement and use of his head, hands, wrists, shoulders, hips, lower body, feet, right thumb, right toe, right elbow and left knee. If one of these factors is wrong, the swing can fail. The young Nicklaus only learned the importance of keeping his head still after his coach grabbed his hair.

The swing can be broken down into several key stages: set-up (preparing the body to hit the ball), takeaway (sweeping the club head back the first few feet, keeping it low), top of the back-swing (when the club should be above the head and parallel to the ground); impact (the fastest drive ever recorded is 167mph); and follow through (here the club head should point towards the target). The most critical stage is the BACKSWING. And, for McIlroy, the key to his backswing is the way he turns his shoulders by 90 degrees while keeping his right knee flexed to generate the energy to drive the ball around 300 yards.

One of the joys of Rio will be watching different swings. American golfer JIM FURYK won the 2002 US Open despite having a swing that was described as 'like an octopus falling out of a tree'. Not every golfer plays this shot with the clean lines of Tiger Woods in his pomp. JB HOLMES, one of the biggest hitters on the PGA circuit, can't move his upper back much and has to bend his left arm slightly to complete his backswing. Whatever coaches might say, the best swing is often the one that comes most naturally.

THE SCORING ZONE

DON'T BE MISLED BY THE AWESOME POWER WITH WHICH THE likes of Bubba Watson (who uncorked a 424-yard drive in a PGA tournament in August 2014) can strike the ball. Most golfers – and coaches – will tell you that the most crucial part of the hole is the last 100 yards, the scoring zone. This where 65–70 per cent of all

TIGER WOODS CELEBRATES WITH HIS CADDIE STEVE WILLIAMS AFTER MAKING THE CHIP OF HIS LIFE AT THE 2005 US OPEN

shots are played and the quality of a player's short game – how well they approach the green, chip, get out of bunkers and putt – will probably decide who is on the podium in Rio. As the great South African golfer Bobby Locke put it: 'You drive for show and you putt for dough.'

Succeeding in the scoring zone isn't just about technical prowess; it's about selection and imagination – seeing shots others can't. TIGER WOODS did precisely that on the sisteenth hole of the final round of the 2005 US Masters at Augusta. Playing from the left of the green, with the tournament effectively riding on his shot, he persuaded the ball to land 25ft left of the flag, turn hard right, roll down and pause on the lip of the cup before trickling into the hole. It was arguably the greatest chip in the (televised) history of golf.

Putting is often about psychology as much as technique. Jack Nicklaus won so many tournaments on the green because he rarely needed three shots and seldom missed from six feet or less. Ben Crenshaw putted like he was attempting a miniature chip but his unusual technique didn't hold him back. When he won at Augusta in 1995, he one-putted or two-putted all 72 greens. So look out for players showing that kind of consistency because that – rather than the occasional 18-foot putt – is the key to victory.

······················ EAGLES, BIRDIES AND ALBATROSSES ······················

GOLF'S LINGUISTIC INVENTIVENESS IS EXEMPLIFIED BY THE terms used to describe a good or bad score at each hole. One over par is a BOGEY – after a Scottish sixteenth-century goblin. One shot under par is a BIRDIE, believed to have derived from the use of 'bird' to denote excellence in American slang. The EAGLE (two under par) followed on naturally, especially as the bird is America's national symbol. In the 1929s, the British chipped in with an ALBATROSS ,because three under par was as rare as a sighting of the bird, but the Americans prefer to call this a DOUBLE EAGLE. This is how they described Gene Sarazen's exploit in 1935, when at the US Masters, he holed with his second stroke, from 235 yards, on a par five, in what was dubbed 'the shot that was heard around the world'.

GOLF GOES TO THE OLYMPICS

THE IDEA OF A GOLF TOURNAMENT HAD BEEN MOOTED FOR the first modern Olympics in Athens in 1896 but, at the time, there were no golf courses in Greece. Four years later, in the shambolic PARIS GAMES, golf made a strange, half-hearted Olympic debut. Some of the twelve men who competed in this event, playing two rounds of eighteen holes at the Compiègne Club, 30 miles north of Paris, didn't realise they were taking part in the Olympics. The victor, America's CHARLES SANDS also competed in the tennis. Coming eighth in the men's event was another American, Albert Lambert, a wealthy businessman better known to posterity for founding the company that invented LISTERINE mouthwash.

The women's event in Paris made an equally strange contribution to Olympic history. A keen golfer, 23-year-old

American MARGARET ABBOTT was in Paris with her mother to study art under Edgar Degas, but persuaded her mother to extend their stay in France so that she could enter the event. She took just 47 shots to compete the nine-hole course and secure gold. Her cause was helped, she admitted later, by the fact that many players 'misunderstood the nature of the game ... and turned up to play in high heels and short skirts'. With Margaret's mother, Mary, finishing a respectable seventh in a field of ten, the Abbotts became the only MOTHER AND DAUGHTER to compete in the same event at the same Olympics.

At ST LOUIS in 1904, golf had the enthusiastic backing of the American organisers – but was shunned by almost everyone else. Out of 77 competitors, the only non-Americans were a trio of Canadians, one of whom, GEORGE LYON, won gold in the men's individual event. The organisers had rung some changes: the women's event had been replaced by a team event and the scoring was decided by who won each hole rather than the total number of

GEORGE LYON SHOWS OFF HIS 'COAL HEAVERS' SWING' TO WIN GOLD AT THE 1904 OLYMPIC GAMES.

strokes played. The team event was an all-American affair, with the Western Golf Association triumphing. One of the stars of that side, US Amateur champion CHANDLER EGAN, was expected to win the other gold but was outpsyched on a wet final day by George Lyon. An all-round sportsman – he also played cricket, baseball and held Canada's pole vault record – the 46-year-old Lyon used his powerful drives from the tee to exhaust Chandler and underlined his stamina at the celebratory banquet by walking across the dining room on his hands.

Lyon sailed to LONDON in 1908 to defend his title but it was not to be. As golf was so popular in Britain, its inclusion in the Olympic programme seemed assured but a dispute over contestants' eligibility between the Olympic Committee and the Royal & Ancient Golf Club at St Andrews led to the withdrawal of all British golfers and, subsequently, to the cancellation of the event.

Golf's return to the Olympic arena, agreed in 2009 after a PR campaign led by Tiger Woods, Padraig Harrington and Michelle Wie, is recognised as vital to the sport's future. Although the game is more popular than ever in Asia, it is struggling in its core market, the USA, and in Europe. In the UK, for example, the number of people playing golf once a month fell by 25 per cent between 2007 and 2014. The oxygen of Olympic publicity could halt the decline.

Yet many doubt that an Olympic gold will ever mean as much to the best golfers as the green jacket they get if they win the US Masters at Augusta. Some IOC delegates also wondered about the sport's cost, accessibility and inclusivity. Golf has been pencilled in for TOKYO 2020 but, with Olympic status due to be reviewed in 2017, much will depend on the quality of the golfers in Rio.

GYMNASTICS

6–21 AUGUST 2016

ARENA OLÍMPICA DO RIO, BARRA
DA TIJUCA, RIO DE JANEIRO

Athletes: 324 | **Golds up for grabs:** 18

OLYMPIC PRESENCE

MEN: ARTISTIC SINCE 1896; TRAMPOLINE SINCE 2000.
WOMEN: ARTISTIC SINCE 1928; RHYTHMIC SINCE 1984;
TRAMPOLINE SINCE 2000.

OLYMPIC FORMAT

MEN'S AND WOMEN'S EVENTS IN ARTISTIC GYMNASTICS AND
TRAMPOLINE. RHYTHMIC GYMNASTICS is for women only.

CONTENDERS

THE USUAL SUSPECTS – RUSSIA, BELARUS, CHINA, ROMANIA,
JAPAN and the USA – are expected to do well in the ARTISTIC
division, but are likely to face a challenge from BRAZIL, GREAT
BRITAIN, GREECE and NORTH KOREA. Russia will expect to win
both RHYTHMIC golds. China usually dominate TRAMPOLINE events.

PAST CHAMPIONS

USSR/RUSSIA: 91 | USA: 33| JAPAN, CHINA: 29 |

WHY WATCH GYMNASTICS?

AT ITS ENCHANTING BEST, OLYMPIC GYMNASTICS OFFERS THE
fleeting illusion that the laws of gravity can be escaped. It requires
immense self-discipline and grace, and, in the case of artistic gymnastics, great strength, courage and preternatural spatial awareness.

ARTISTIC GYMNASTICS, the classic form of the sport, involves fixed pieces of equipment and the men's rings. In TRAMPOLINING, the competitors repeatedly launch themselves to heights of up to ten metres, which means they are in the air for much longer than divers, and thus can perform astounding acrobatic manoeuvres: quadruple somersaults are routine. RHYTHMIC GYMNASTICS often seems closer to dance than to a measurable sport, and there are many who query its inclusion in the Olympic programme. It remains a great spectacle nonetheless.

THE STORY OF GYMNASTICS

THE WORD 'GYMNASTICS' IS DERIVED FROM THE GREEK FOR 'exercise', which in turn derives from the word for 'naked', which is exactly how the men of ancient Greece liked to work out. Every self-respecting Greek city had its own gymnasium, and records show that boxing, wrestling and swimming were all practised within their walls. What is less clear is the precise form of the activities that would now be classified as gymnastic.

The streams that fed into the modern gymnastics are numerous. The BULL-LEAPING MINOANS of Ancient Crete (2700–1450 BC), for example, are known to have vaulted over the animals' backs by using HANDSPRINGS, a technique reminiscent of modern VAULTING. The POMMEL HORSE can count among its ancestors the wooden horses used by ROMAN cavalrymen to refine their mounting and dismounting skills. Disciplines such as the floor exercise and rhythmic gymnastics are rooted in ACROBATIC DISPLAYS, which have a similarly long pedigree: they were held in CHINA as part of harvest festival celebrations, and at the Imperial Court by the seventh century BC. In addition to tumbling routines, these displays frequently involved props such as chairs, bowls and wicker rings, which can be seen as counterparts to the BALLS, RIBBONS AND ROPES used in the rhythmic form of the sport today. In medieval times, acrobatics was a regular entertainment in Europe's castles and palaces.

Another source for modern gymnastics was the CIRCUS, which became popular in its modern form during the late eighteenth

NOT JUST A CUTE FACE: OLGA KORBUT ON THE UNEVEN BARS, MUNICH 1972

century. The influence of the trapeze is easy to detect in the HIGH
BAR, UNEVEN BARS AND RINGS. The safety nets used by circus performers prompted GEORGE NISSEN of the University of Iowa to
build the first modern TRAMPOLINE in 1934. His invention had
actually been anticipated by the INUIT, who have a long tradition
of bouncing on stretched walrus or bearded seal skins, as in the
nalukataq (spring whaling festival) of northern Alaska.

In the nineteenth century, various MASS GYMNASTIC MOVE-
MENTS emerged in Central Europe, the most important of which

was developed by FRIEDRICH LUDWIG JAHN, a Prussian nationalist who called his system TURNEN because he couldn't bear to use the Greek word 'gymnastics'. Jahn's initial motivation was to produce a generation of young Germans fit and disciplined enough to drive Napoleon's armies from his country. In 1811, he opened the first *Turnplatz* (open-air gymnasium) in a field outside Berlin, replete with platforms, ropes and rings. Jahn also invented the PARALLEL BARS (by removing the rungs from a ladder), created an early version of the HIGH BAR, and refined and developed the POMMEL HORSE and BALANCE BEAM.

In 1819, the Prussian authorities, tired of Jahn's grandiosity, passed an edict banning *Turnen*. But his ideas had already taken root. In the run-up to the Franco-Prussian War of 1870, a curriculum based on Jahn's system was adopted by the German educational system and the DEUTSCHE TURNERSCHAFT was founded. By 1914 it boasted more than a million members.

The emphasis in the *Deutsche Turnerschaft* was firmly on paramilitary collective manoeuvres – competitive sports were despised as decadent English inventions. But there was less antipathy towards competition in the rival SOKOL movement that swept through the Slavic world in response to the *Turnen* explosion.

The other major nineteenth-century European gymnastic movement was based on the health-oriented teachings of PER HENRIK LING, who opened, in Stockholm, the Royal Gymnastic Central Institute in 1813. The so-called SWEDISH SYSTEM, like *Turnen*, focused on synchronised team displays, but shunned the use of apparatus. An Olympic discipline in its own right in 1912 and 1920, it made a particularly important contribution to the development of the FLOOR EXERCISE.

RHYTHMIC GYMNASTICS grew from the eighteenth-century ideas of the likes of JEAN-GEORGES NOVERRE and FRANÇOIS DELSARTE, who believed that the best form of exercise was based on freely expressive dance-like movements. The rejection of the rigidity of ballet by the great American dancer ISADORA DUNCAN also contributed to the emergence of the sport, as did the Swiss teacher ÉMILE JACQUES-DALCROZE, whose EURHYTHMIC SYSTEM (note that spelling, Annie Lennox) combined movement with music.

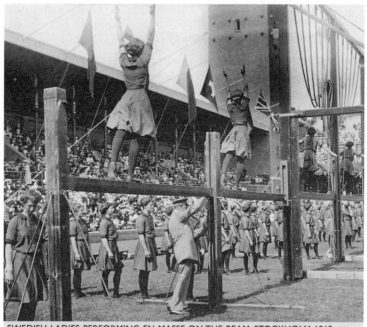

SWEDISH LADIES PERFORMING EN MASSE ON THE BEAM, STOCKHOLM 1912

The final stage in the pre-Olympic evolution of gymnastics was the formalisation of its constituent disciplines into competitive sports. In the case of ARTISTIC GYMNASTICS, the organisation primarily responsible was the European Federation of Gymnastics; founded in 1881 in Liège, it was the world's first international sports organisation. It had just three member nations (France, Belgium and the Netherlands) until 1921, when non-European countries were admitted and the organisation changed its name to the FÉDÉRATION INTERNATIONALE DE GYMNASTIQUE.

The first competitive RHYTHMIC GYMNASTICS events were held in the Soviet Union, where a national championship was established in 1942. The FIG brought the discipline under its wing in 1961 and two years later the first World Championship was held in Hungary. In 1948 the first national TRAMPOLINE CHAMPIONSHIPS were held in the USA. Trampoline's inaugural World Championship took place in 1964 and in 1999 this sport, too, came under the FIG's umbrella.

Game On: Gymnastics Basics

Artistic Gymnastics

THERE ARE FOUR DISCIPLINES IN WOMEN'S ARTISTIC GYM-
nastics and six in men's. Two of the disciplines – the VAULT and
the FLOOR EXERCISE – are contested by both genders. Women also
compete in UNEVEN BARS and BALANCE BEAM. Men add POMMEL
HORSE, RINGS, HORIZONTAL BAR and PARALLEL BAR.

The Olympic programme consists of three competitions for each
gender: TEAM, INDIVIDUAL ALL-ROUND and INDIVIDUAL APPARATUS.
Qualification for the finals is determined by qualifying rounds in
which five of the six competitors from each team perform on each
piece of apparatus, and their scores are used to determine qualification for the individual all-round and apparatus finals as well as
the team final. Scores from the preliminary round are not carried
forward – competitors start each final with a clean slate.

In the TEAM FINAL, three gymnasts from each team compete on
each piece of apparatus, and their scores contribute to their team's
points total. A maximum of two competitors per nation take part
in the INDIVIDUAL ALL-ROUND FINAL, in which each contestant
performs on all pieces of apparatus, with their cumulative scores
determining their finishing positions. A maximum of two gymnasts
per nation also qualify for the INDIVIDUAL APPARATUS FINAL, which
is contested by the eight gymnasts who scored highest on each
piece of apparatus in the qualifying round.

In all the exercises, pay particular attention to the form of the
gymnasts: limbs should be straight, toes should be pointed and there
should be a general air of tightness about the body. HEIGHT is particularly important in airborne manoeuvres, as are perfect LANDINGS.

·· **THE VAULT** ··

THERE ARE SEVERAL STAGES TO A VAULT. A TYPICAL ROUTINE
is the YURCHENKO. In this, the gymnast sprints down a 25m runway and performs a HANDSPRING at the end, propelling themselves
towards the springboard in such a way that they land on it feet first,

facing back in the direction they came from. During the spring, they do another half rotation to ensure that they land on the vaulting table in a hands-down position. During their brief contact with the table, they push downwards, which sends them still higher. This action, plus the forward momentum generated by their run-up, launches them into the flight phase, during which they perform a combination of twists and/or somersaults, before (hopefully) landing neatly on both feet.

Until 2001, vaulting involved a canvas-covered 'horse' set at right angles to the runway for women and parallel for men. This has now been replaced by a more stable VAULTING TABLE 1.2m long and 95cm wide. It is set at a height of 1.25m for women and 1.35m for men. Gymnasts perform two vaults and the one receiving the higher marks counts towards their score.

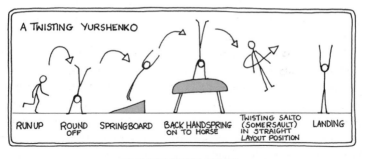

A TWISTING YURSHENKO

RUN UP — ROUND OFF — SPRINGBOARD — BACK HANDSPRING ON TO HORSE — TWISTING SALTO (SOMERSAULT) IN STRAIGHT LAYOUT POSITION — LANDING

································· **FLOOR EXERCISE** ·································

IN SOME WAYS THE FLOOR EXERCISE IS 'FREER' THAN THE OTHER disciplines in artistic gymnastics – it's the competitors doing what they can with their bodies on a 12m × 12m mat set on top of a sprung floor. Women's routines are longer – 70–90 seconds as against 60–70 seconds for the men – and are accompanied by MUSIC, whereas the men's are not. The differences are revealing: women are expected to incorporate DANCE-LIKE MOVEMENTS into their routines, whereas the emphasis for men is on STRENGTH. Competitors must use the whole area of THE MAT. The most spectacular elements of floor routines are the TUMBLING PASSES, which consist of a variety of somersaults, twists, handsprings and cartwheels performed in succession. The top women typically get four or five passes into their routines; the men rarely manage more than four because they have less time.

UNEVEN BARS (WOMEN ONLY)

THIS DRAMATIC APPARATUS CONSISTS OF TWO PARALLEL BARS made of wood-sheathed fibreglass set at different heights (1.66m and 2.46m above the ground) and separated by a gap of between 130cm and 180cm (adjustable in 2cm increments to suit individual competitors). Back in the 1950s, gymnasts basically clambered between the bars, albeit gracefully. Now they fly around at scarcely believable speeds. To comply with Olympic specifications, a routine must include one AERIAL MANOEUVRE from the lower bar to the higher bar, one in the reverse direction and one that starts and finishes on the same bar. Competitors must also perform at least one HANDSTAND TURN.

BALANCE BEAM (WOMEN ONLY)

MANY OF US WOULD STRUGGLE EVEN TO WALK ALONG A 5M strip of wood 10cm wide and 1.25m above the floor. The best Olympic gymnasts leap around on it as if they were performing on a piece of apparatus ten times as wide. This discipline is all about courage, confidence and elegance. Competitors have up to 90 seconds to impress the judges, during which time they must perform a variety of jumps, turns and balancing postures. They must also use the entire length of the beam.

POMMEL HORSE (MEN ONLY)

THE MILITARY ROOTS OF THE POMMEL HORSE ARE CLEAR: essentially you are watching cavalrymen showing off on their stationary mounts. The 'horse' is a leather-covered structure 1.6m long and 35cm wide, with a top surface 1.15m above the ground. The pommels are a pair of 12cm high upward-standing 'D' handles set each side of the centre of the top of the horse.

The first commandment for gymnasts performing on the horse is not to touch the apparatus with their legs. Instead, they move around its surface (they must use all three sections) on their HANDS, while constantly swinging their legs, which sometimes are separated scissor-style – FLAIRS – and at other points are held together and moved in a circular or pendulum fashion. When circling his legs above the horse, the gymnast must lift his hands with immaculate timing to allow the limbs to pass.

Pommel routines end with a DISMOUNT, which must involve the gymnast dropping to the ground after a handstand.

Too Much Too Young?
The Age of Teen Gymnasts

B efore the era of NADIA COMANECI, who was just fourteen when she wowed the world at Montreal 1976, champion Olympic female gymnasts were invariably in their twenties, and sometimes even older: ÁGNES KELETI of Hungary was 35 when she won four gold medals in Melbourne. As the technical demands of the sport increased, the age of successful gymnasts plummeted. Prepubescent girls, being smaller and lighter than fully grown women, found it is easier to overcome the force of gravity. The top two competitors in 1992, for example, were both fifteen years old, 4ft 6in tall, and weighed around 31.5kg/70lbs.

Male gymnasts also tend to be on the small side – the great SAWAO KATO of Japan, who won eight gold medals between 1968 and 1976, was 5ft 3in and weighed 125lbs/56.7kg – but the emphasis on strength in the men's sport means that they aren't at their best until their musculature has fully developed.

Up to and including the Moscow Games, the minimum age for competing in senior FIG tournaments like the Olympics was fourteen. In 1981, amid growing concerns about the effect of intense competition on the muscular and skeletal development of young girls, the age limit was increased to exclude gymnasts who wouldn't have turned fifteen by the end of the calendar year. In 1997, the age requirement was bumped up another year.

Opinion is divided about the rule changes. Supporters point to statistics showing that young female gymnasts are much more prone to stress fractures than their non-gymnastic peers. They also argue that girls in their early teens are poorly equipped emotionally to deal with the pressures of international competition. On the other side are former gymnasts like

NELLIE KIM, who argue that younger girls are better equipped for the sport as they are typically more fearless. Others point out that FIG under-16 competitions are judged according to the same points system that applies to the seniors in the Olympics, so the rules are scarcely protecting younger gymnasts from the physical hardships that affect older competitors.

Not surprisingly, given the advantages possessed by gymnasts in their early teens, one effect of the rule changes has been a growing temptation to cheat. DANIELA SILIVAS, who won three golds at Seoul in 1988, later revealed that the Romanian Gymnastics Federation had added two years to her age in 1985 (when she was actually thirteen) to make her eligible for that year's World Championships. Nicolae Vieru, head of the Romanian Federation at the time, later claimed that 'changing the ages was a worldwide practice'. The issue resurfaced in Beijing, when four Chinese gymnasts were strongly suspected of being under age, though an FIG inquiry exonerated them.

RINGS (MEN ONLY)

THE MOST DEMANDING PIECE OF APPARATUS, THIS INVOLVES A pair of rings with an internal diameter of 18cm suspended at a height of 2.75m by way of cables hanging from a bar 5.8m above the ground. The gymnast grips one ring in each hand and performs a variety of swings (e.g. from handstand to handstand), holds (such as L-SITS, in which the legs are extended forward with the body bent at the hips), and strength moves.

The last of these include various forms of CRUCIFIX (or IRON CROSS), in which the body is held motionless by the fully out-stretched arms. Competitors must endeavour to keep the rings stationary, except when moving them apart in a controlled manner when going into an iron cross or similar position. They are also expected to perform spectacular dismounts.

HIGH BAR (MEN ONLY)

ALSO KNOWN AS THE HORIZONTAL BAR, THIS PIECE OF APPARATUS consists of a steel bar 2.8cm thick and 2.4m long, fixed 2.75m above the ground. Competitors swing from it continuously, except when performing RELEASES (aerial manoeuvres which involve

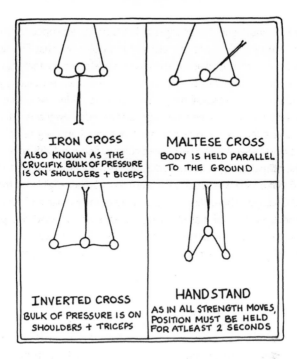

IRON CROSS
ALSO KNOWN AS THE
CRUCIFIX. BULK OF PRESSURE
IS ON SHOULDERS + BICEPS

MALTESE CROSS
BODY IS HELD PARALLEL
TO THE GROUND

INVERTED CROSS
BULK OF PRESSURE IS ON
SHOULDERS + TRICEPS

HANDSTAND
AS IN ALL STRENGTH MOVES,
POSITION MUST BE HELD
FOR ATLEAST 2 SECONDS

temporarily letting go of the bar). Extra variation is provided by one-handed ROTATIONS, changes of grip, changing the direction of rotation and switching the lead part of the body from front to back. DISMOUNTS tend to be even more dramatic than from the rings as the gymnasts are able to generate more momentum by means of GIANTS (powerful extended body rotations). TRIPLE TWISTING SOMERSAULTS are considered almost routine at Olympic level.

······························ **PARALLEL BARS (MEN ONLY)** ······························

THE PARALLEL BARS ARE WOODEN, 3.5M LONG, 2M HIGH AND between 42cm and 52cm apart (the distance can be adjusted within this range to suit the gymnast). Competitors grip the bars with their hands, sometimes with their arms fully extended, at other times with them bent and the upper arms resting on the apparatus. No other part of the body is allowed to touch the bars. A gymnast is expected to make full use of the possibilities provided by the equipment, which include SWINGS, HANDSTANDS and AERIAL

THE GREATEST MALE GYMNAST EVER? VITALY SCHERBO AT ATLANTA 1996

MANOEUVRES. For much of the time he will have a hand on each bar, leaving his body free to swing in the gap, but on occasion he will place them both on the same bar, which provides scope for UNDER-SWINGS. A typical DISMOUNT would be a double somersault either from the end of the bars or off to one side.

SCORING

THE ERA OF THE PERFECT 10, LED BY NADIA COMANECI, WAS certainly thrilling but it left the sport with nowhere to go. FIG has consequently revised the scoring system several times to dispense with the delightful but troubling notion of perfection. Performances on each piece of apparatus are now marked by two panels of judges. The first, which has two members, calculates the DIF-FICULTY OF THE ROUTINE on the basis of a standard list of values for its elements. The difficulty score is open-ended, which has led some critics to claim that the results of a competition can effectively be decided before it has started (though, of course, the harder the routine, the greater the risk of losing points in its execution).

The second judging panel, which has six members, marks the EXECUTION on a scale of one to ten. The highest and lowest scores are discarded and the remaining four scores are averaged. This figure is then added to the difficulty score to give a final mark for the performance. Any total of sixteen or more is exceptional – even the phenomenal South Korean vaulter YANG HAK-SEON, famed for his trademark triple-twisting handspring front somersault, only just managed it, scoring 16.533 when winning gold in London.

RHYTHMIC GYMNASTICS

RHYTHMIC GYMNASTICS TAKES PLACE ON A MAT WITH THE same dimensions and qualities as the floor exercise. Although practised by men in some countries, notably Japan, it is a WOMEN-ONLY DISCIPLINE at the Olympics. All routines are accompanied by MUSIC, which must be free of vocals and alarming sound effects. INDIVIDUAL ROUTINES must be between 75 and 90 seconds in duration. The parameters for TEAM ROUTINES are 60 seconds longer. The key to success is keeping the equipment CONTINUALLY IN MOTION, handling it with as much variety as possible, and producing routines that feel like unified performances. Demonstrations of BODILY FLEXIBILITY are also rewarded by the judges.

For rhythmic gymnastics there are separate qualifying rounds for the team and individual competitions. No more than two gymnasts from the same nation can qualify for the individual final, in which each gymnast performs with all four accessories: the ribbon, hoop, ball, and clubs. The team final consists of two rounds: in the first, five of the six members of the team perform with the same piece of equipment; in the second, two pieces of equipment are used simultaneously, three team members using one, two the other.

·· **HOOP** ··

THE HOOPS USED IN RHYTHMIC GYMNASTICS MUST BE SEMI-rigid and 80–90cm in diameter. Competitors throw them, catch them, rotate them around their hands and bodies, swing them, jump through them and roll them along the ground. Any flutter while the hoop is travelling through the air is penalised.

BALL

SURPRISINGLY 'STREET', THE BALL EXERCISE COMBINES elements of basketball, freestyle soccer and seal-like joie de vivre. Gymnasts perform with a single ball 18–20cm in diameter. They are not allowed to grip the sphere but must let it rest on their hands, unless they are bouncing, throwing or rolling it, or balancing it on some other part of their anatomy. The ball is probably the most elegant of the rhythmic gymnastic disciplines.

CLUBS

THIS IS DRUM MAJORETTING TAKEN TO ANOTHER DIMENSION. Each gymnast performs with two 40cm-long wooden or synthetic clubs which are shaped like skinny bowling pins, with graspable 'knobs' on their heads. Successful performance requires many of the same skills as juggling, including high levels of hand and eye co-ordination and ambidexterity. Competitors throw and catch the clubs, balance them on their hands and swing them in a variety of visually appealing ways, while performing leaps and other acrobatic moves. Some rhythmic gymnasts grip them between their toes.

RIBBON

THE RIBBON IS A 7CM STRIP OF SATIN OR SIMILAR MATERIAL attached at one end to a 50–60cm stick. Visually this is perhaps the most appealing of the rhythmic disciplines, with competitors creating ever-shifting calligraphic shapes in the air. Large, free-flowing movements are rewarded and the gymnasts employ a wide range of throws and catches.

SCORING

RHYTHMIC DISPLAYS ARE GIVEN MARKS OUT OF TEN IN THREE categories: EXECUTION (where marks are deducted for mistakes such as losing control); ARTISTIC EXPRESSION; and DIFFICULTY. There are four judges for each category, whose marks are averaged.

TRAMPOLINE

OLYMPIC TRAMPOLINES ARE 5.05M LONG, 2.91M WIDE AND 1.155m high. The bouncy bed is around 6mm thick and is made from nylon or string-based material. The centre of the bed – the springiest part – is marked with a cross to help competitors position themselves. The closer they land to it the better, from both a safety and a technical perspective.

An Olympic routine consists of TEN ELEMENTS or bounces, although competitors can make preliminary bounces to achieve suitable heights, plus one manoeuvre-free bounce at the end to control their height and prepare to 'STICK' their landings. Each element must be different – if one is repeated, the second occurrence receives a difficulty score of zero. While performing their elements, trampolinists must keep their legs together with the toes pointed. They should keep their bodies in one of three positions: STRAIGHT, in which the body and limbs are held as the adjective suggests, PIKE, in which the straightened legs are grasped near the ankles, and TUCK, in which the bent knees are clasped to the chest.

Competitors must start and end their routines on their feet. In theory they are allowed to land on their seats, fronts or backs at other stages, but this rarely happens in top-class competition. The final landing should be 'STUCK', i.e. ended abruptly and in a controlled manner with both feet on the bed. The gymnast must remain standing still for approximately three seconds.

Both male and female competitions start with two-routine qualification rounds. The best eight progress to the finals, where they perform another routine to determine their final placing. As with other gymnastic disciplines, no more than two finalists may come from any nation.

SCORING

THERE ARE TWO ELEMENTS TO A CONTESTANT'S SCORE. THE DIFFICULTY SCORE is calculated by adding up the set tariffs of all the moves within a routine: manoeuvres like the QUADRIFFUS, a quadruple somersault with half a twist or more, are very valuable. Top male performers typically perform routines with difficulty values of around 16.5; the equivalent figure for women is 14.5. Five judges score each routine for EXECUTION, with a maximum of ten points. The verdicts of the most and least generous judges are discarded; the remaining three are added together and this figure is added to the difficulty mark to give an overall score.

The more controlled a performance the higher it will be marked. Both feet should touch the bed simultaneously every time a gymnast lands, and they should land close to the cross.

GYMNASTICS GOES TO THE OLYMPICS

GYMNASTICS, IN ONE FORM OR ANOTHER, HAS FEATURED AT every modern Olympics, but it took some time for the authorities to establish its parameters. There were eight gymnastic events at the first modern Games in ATHENS, all of them for men: ROPE CLIMB-ING, TEAM HIGH BAR and PARALLEL BARS competitions, plus all the disciplines of today's male ARTISTIC GYMNASTICS except the floor exercise. GERMAN gymnasts carried off five of the eight gold medals but there were home victories in the rings and rope climbing.

There was just one event at PARIS 1900, a sixteen-exercise all-round competition. FRENCH gymnasts occupied the first eighteen places, though the odds were stacked in their favour, as 108 of the 135 entrants were from the home nation. The ratio of Americans to other competitors was even higher in ST LOUIS but one title did go to Switzerland's ADOLF SPINNLER, who won the triathlon, which consisted of routines on the high and parallel bars plus the horse.

LONDON 1908 hosted two events: an all-round individual com-petition, won by ALBERTO BRAGLIA of Italy, and a group team event, won by SWEDEN. Braglia won the individual all-round title again in Stockholm, adding another gold to his collection in the apparatus-based team contest, while Sweden (predictably) won the Swedish System team event. They did it again at ANTWERP in 1920.

The list of events was expanded to nine for PARIS 1924, with individual apparatus titles back on the agenda. SWITZERLAND, ITALY and YUGOSLAVIA each notched up two wins. Swiss gymnasts won five gold medals at AMSTERDAM 1928, where women's synchronised calisthenics joined the party. This last event – the first Olympic gymnastics competition for women – was won by the DUTCH, four of whose team were Jewish; three were to perish in the Nazi gas chambers.

There were no women's events at LA 1932 but at BERLIN 1936 they competed individually for the first time in the Olympics, albeit in the context of a team competition. GERMAN gymnasts won six of the nine gold medals on offer. The FINNS won six out of eleven golds at LONDON 1948, in a tournament that was marked by weird scoring – one judge awarded 13.1 points out of 10 for a performance in the women's team competition. This event, which included the rings for the one and only time, was won by CZECHO-SLOVAKIA, whose victory was made particularly poignant by the death from polio of intended team member ELISKA MISÁKOVÁ on the first day of the competition.

INDIVIDUAL WOMEN'S EVENTS (all-round and apparatus) made their debut at HELSINKI 1952, where the SOVIETS competed in the Olympics for the first time. They made an immediate impression, winning nine gold medals, including four for 30-year-old VIKTOR CHUKARIN. The USSR's policy of hot-housing talented young children would ensure that this was no flash in the pan. The practice later spread to other Eastern bloc nations (notably ROMANIA and EAST GERMANY), where generous state sponsorship went hand in hand – it is widely believed – with chemical assistance. Puberty-arresting drugs, among other substances, are thought to have been commonly administered to young female gymnasts in both countries during the 1970s and 1980s.

At MELBOURNE 1956, the star of the show was ÁGNES KELETI of Hungary, who won four gold medals at the age of 35 – she remains the oldest female Olympic gymnastics champion by quite a margin. She was pipped to the all-round title by LARYSA LATYNINA of the USSR. Chukarin showed that age was no barrier in the men's division, either. At the age of 34, the great Soviet added two golds to his collection, including a second successive men's all-round title.

In 1960, JAPAN won the first of five successive men's team titles, while Latynina took the women's all-round gold again. She claimed two more medals at Tokyo 1964, taking her total Olympic haul to

THE BOHEMIAN BET LYNCH: VERA ČÁSLAVSKÁ ON THE BEAM AT MEXICO 1968

eighteen, the most won by any competitor in any Olympic sport. But she lost her all-round crown to the rising star of the women's sport, VERA ČÁSLAVSKÁ of Czechoslovakia.

Čáslavská did it again four years later in MEXICO CITY, where she was a huge hit with spectators, partly because of her prominent role in the Prague Spring earlier that year and partly because she used the Mexican Hat Dance as the accompaniment for her floor routine. Čáslavská won four golds and two silvers at the 1968 Games, joining Latynina as the only female gymnast to have won the all-round title at two Olympics. She also managed to squeeze in a wedding to Czech 1500m champion Josef Odlozil. But things turned sour for her thereafter. Časlavaská's conduct at the Games – she had snubbed the Soviet anthem at a medal ceremony – led the Czech authorities to banish her from gymnastics. Then in 1992, a son she and Odlozil had produced during their marriage killed his father with a punch in a bar room brawl.

If Čáslavská had raised the profile of women's gymnastics, then OLGA KORBUT sent it into orbit at MUNICH 1972. The coquettish seventeen-year-old Belarusian won golds in the team competition, floor and beam, and performed the first-ever back flip on the uneven bars, but what secured her popularity was her bursting into tears after falling twice on the uneven bars during the all-round competition. Many purists preferred the elegance of her compatriot LUDMILLA TOURISCHEVA, who won the all-round title.

In 1976, at Montreal, Romania's NADIA COMANECI became the first gymnast to score a PERFECT 10 in the Olympics – she went on to score six more in the course of securing three golds, a silver and a bronze. Her great Soviet rival, NELLIE KIM, also achieved two perfect scores, and took three golds and a silver.

The exploits of Japan's SHUN FUJIMOTO in the men's team competition were even more remarkable. During the last tumbling pass of his floor exercise routine, he fractured his knee-cap. As the Japanese were going for their fifth successive victory in the face of stern competition from the heavily fancied Soviet team, he decided not to tell the team medics. He proceeded to score 9.5 on the pommel horse and a lifetime best of 9.7 on the rings, albeit at terrible cost – when he landed, after a twisting somersault dismount from a height of eight feet, he dislocated the broken knee-cap. His efforts proved enough to secure victory for his team; when asked if he would do it all again, Fujimoto tersely replied 'No'.

Fujimoto wasn't the only Japanese hero in Montreal. SAWAO KATO's victories in the team competition and parallel bars brought him his 7th and 8th Olympic golds, establishing a record in the sport that still stands.

NADIA AND THE PERFECT TENS

Nadia Comaneci had been awarded perfect scores in competitions preceding the Montreal Games, but it was nonetheless one of sport's transcendent moments when, on 18 July, 1976, the scoreboard finally registered 10 at the Olympics – or 1.00 as it actually read, the designers not having considered the possibility of perfection.

Comaneci's literally faultless performance occurred during the uneven bars segment of the women's all-round competition. Unusually self-possessed for a fourteen-year-old, she couldn't see what all the fuss was about. 'I've had nineteen tens in my career,' she revealed at a press conference. 'It's nothing new.' Comaneci ended the Games with seven perfect scores, Nellie Kim of the USSR with two. The pony-tailed Romanian had already wowed the gymnastic world at the 1975 European Championships, winning every event except the floor exercise.

Being the first Olympic gymnast to achieve perfection ramped up the pressure on her. At fifteen, after the Romanian sports establishment had forced her to stop training under Béla Károlyi, her coach and mentor, Comaneci apparently drank bleach, a protest that persuaded the government to reverse its decision. In 1981, however, Károlyi defected, and in November 1989, just weeks before the overthrow of the Ceausescu regime, Comaneci followed suit. Her escape was facilitated by Constantin Panait, a Romanian roofer living in Florida, whose price appeared to be that he should thereafter manage her affairs and never let her out of his presence. Comaneci soon extricated herself from Panait's clutches: an old friend who had been a rugby coach in Romania intervened and invited her to live with his family in Montreal.

In 1996, Comaneci married the American Bart Conner, who had won two gymnastics golds at the 1984 Olympics. Today, the most famous gymnast in history runs a training facility in Oklahoma with her American husband. Its name? The Bart Conner Gymnastics Academy.

THE SCOREBOARD BLOWS A FUSE AS NADIA COMANECI SCORES TEN,
MONTREAL 1976

The pre-tournament favourite for the all-round women's gold at MOSCOW 1980 was YELENA MUKHINA (USSR), who had beaten Comaneci and Kim to the World Championship title two years before. Two weeks before the opening ceremony, she broke her spine during floor practice and was paralysed from the waist down. Mukhina had seen the tragedy coming. Unhappy at having been rushed back into training after breaking a leg in 1979, she had expressed grave misgivings at her coaches' insistence that she incorporate a 'Thomas salto' into her floor routine. It was a mistimed attempt at this one and three-quarter somersault with one and a half twists that left her quadriplegic.

In Mukhina's absence, the competition came down to a head-to-head between YELENA DAVYDOVA of the Soviet Union and COMANECI. The Romanian seemed to have done enough to win with a near-perfect performance on the beam, but after a furious debate lasting 28 minutes, the judges gave her a score of 9.85, leaving her 0.05 points behind Davydova. Comaneci nevertheless took two golds and two silvers, while Nellie Kim again won a couple of golds.

AMERICAN GYMNASTS exploited the Eastern European boycott of LOS ANGELES 1984 by winning five gold medals, including the men's team and women's all-round titles. The latter was secured by MARY LOU RETTON in the only way possible – by scoring a 10 on the vault. In Los Angeles, CHINESE gymnasts made their Olympic debut, winning five titles. The first RHYTHMIC GYMNASTICS event was, surprisingly, won by LORI FUNG of Canada, who had only managed 23rd place at the 1983 World Championship. Four years later in Seoul, the rhythmic gold went to MARINA LOBATCH of the USSR, who received a perfect score for each routine. During the club exercise, she was saved by her pianist, who increased the pace to ensure she finished in the allotted time.

The gymnastic star of the Barcelona Games was VITALY SCHERBO of BELARUS, who won six of the eight titles available to men, including four in a single day. Away from the swimming pool, no Olympian has won as many gold medals at one Games. By 1994, Scherbo had claimed world titles in every discipline, a unique achievement that probably makes him the greatest male gymnast of all time. As Scherbo's triumph emphasised, the collapse of the Soviet Union had done little to harm the fortunes of the former nation's gymnasts – the one-off UNIFIED TEAM carried away four other golds.

At Atlanta in 1996, KERRI STRUG of the USA did an imitation of Shun Fujimoto, performing her second vault in the artistic team event after badly damaging her ankle in her first. Her score of 9.712 helped the so-called Magnificent Seven to the women's team title. But overall the Americans had to play third fiddle to the Ukrainians and Russians, who won four and three titles respectively.

At the Sydney Games, the MEN'S AND WOMEN'S TRAMPOLINE made their Olympic debut: both were won by RUSSIANS, as were the two rhythmic titles. CHINA won the men's artistic team event and ROMANIA the women's. The latter came top of the artistic medal table at Athens 2004 by winning four of the six women's events, but the performance of the Games came from PAUL HAMM of the USA, who recovered from a fall on the vault to win gold in the men's all-round competition by 0.012 points, the closest margin in the history of Olympic gymnastics.

CHINESE gymnasts were the dominant force at BEIJING 2008, winning all but one title in the men's artistic division, two golds in the women's events and both the trampoline titles. As was by now customary, Russia claimed both rhythmic golds. China were again the most successful nation at LONDON 2012, but had to share the golds with nine other nations, notably Russia and the US (who each won three). Two countries secured their first Olympic gymnastic titles: BRAZIL, with Arthur Zanetti triumphing in the rings, and the NETHERLANDS, with Epke Zonderland giving a dazzling performance to win the high bar. The bitterest disappointment for GREAT BRITAIN came in the men's team final when the silver medal won by Louis Smith, Daniel Purvis, Max Whitlock, Kristian Thomas and Sam Oldham was awarded to Japan, after the latter had appealed against the scoring, leading them to be bumped up from fourth to second. The Britons had to settle for bronze, the first podium medal won by a British gymnastics team since 1912.

HANDBALL

6–21 AUG 2016

OLYMPIC TRAINING CENTRE, BARRA
DA TIJUCA, RIO DE JANEIRO

Athletes: 336 | **Golds up for grabs:** 2

OLYMPIC PRESENCE

MEN: 1936 (FIELD HANDBALL); INDOOR HANDBALL SINCE 1972.
WOMEN: INDOOR HANDBALL SINCE 1976.

OLYMPIC FORMAT

THERE ARE TWELVE TEAMS IN EACH COMPETITION. THEY ARE
divided into groups of six, each nation playing all the others in
their section. The four best teams in each group qualify for the
knock-out stages.

CONTENDERS

NORWAY'S WOMEN'S TEAM AND FRANCE'S MEN'S TEAM CAN
make history in Rio, becoming the first sides to win three Olympic
golds in a row in handball. In the women's tournament, Denmark,
South Korea and Russia are strong, while 2013 world champions
– and hosts – Brazil will hope to win their first Olympic medal.
In the men's competition Sweden, Croatia and Spain are serious
contenders.

PAST CHAMPIONS

USSR/RUSSIA: 6 | YUGOSLAVIA: 3 | DENMARK: 3

Why Watch Handball?

Fast-paced, skilful and free-scoring, handball is the second most-played sport in Europe, though it remains a minority interest in Britain. However, football fans will find the object of the exercise – propelling a ball into a netted goal – reassuringly familiar. Matches often feature 40-50 goals and shots

As with basketball, the game is well suited to giants with ball-handling talent. But one of the more surprising aspects of handball is the degree of body contact permitted. Body checking is perfectly legal provided the defender is directly between the attacking player and the goal. Another unusual aspect of the game is the absence of midfield players. Matches are end-to-end affairs, with teams either attacking or defending.

Recently, the sport has gone professional, raising the stakes and adding to the intensity. With its burgeoning commercialism, handball has seen big transfer fees (in a world record deal, Croatian defender Domagoj Dubnjak cost Hamburg just under £1m in 2013), dubious officials, raucous (and occasionally violent) fans and significant investment by Qatar as the oil-rich kingdom strives to become the 'world capital of sport'.

Handball at the Movies

Oddly, handball has spawned a double bill of hit movies: *Machan*, directed by *Full Monty* producer Uberto Pasolini, and *Forever the Moment*, which topped the box office charts in South Korea following the country's silver medal in the women's tournament at Athens 2004.

Based on a true story, *Machan* concerns a posse of happy-go-lucky Sinhalese would-be-emigrants to Germany, who fail to get visas but then find a magazine on

FOREVER THE MOMENT, PROBABLY THE BEST KOREAN HANDBALL MOVIE EVER MADE

the beach inviting entries to a Bavarian handball tournament. Undeterred by the sport's non-existence in Sri Lanka, they form a squad and after a few knock-backs make it to Germany. Having initially planned to leg it from the airport, they get swept up in the tournament and can't resist playing a couple of matches first …

Forever the Moment, similarly based on real life, celebrates the brief period when the entire South Korean nation found itself gripped by an Olympic sport about which it normally doesn't give a stuff. A cobbled-together team of inexperienced youngsters, veterans pulled out of retirement and a sacked coach who decides to stay on as a player fights its way to the final in Athens, where it nearly, *nearly* pulls off a dramatic upset. The fact that the heroes fail to win makes a refreshing change but viewers are still left with a feel-good glow.

THE STORY OF HANDBALL

IT WASN'T QUITE HANDBALL AS WE KNOW IT, BUT THE ancient Greeks certainly liked to chuck a ball around. If this account in Homer's *Odyssey* is anything to go by, they did it in a celestial and rather elegant manner:

> *They took at once in their hands the lovely ball*
> *Which Polybos, with cunning art, had woven from purple wool.*
> *One cast this up to heaven to reach the sparkling clouds,*
> *Bent hard back; the other then sprang high up in the air*
> *And caught it nimbly, ere his foot touched ground again.*

Alexander the Great was known to enjoy SPHAIRISTERION, a Greek ball court game named after the boxing room in a classical gymnasium, and the ROMANS played ball in their baths and spas. Team games involving the throwing of balls continued through the Dark Ages. There are medieval accounts of ladies of the court tossing around ribbon-wrapped balls, and British knights were so partial to a form of handball that Kings Edward II and Henry VIII banned it because of the detrimental effect it was having on archery practice.

Intriguingly, given Denmark's pre-eminence in the modern sport, the INUIT of Greenland were known to be fans, with records of their matches dating back to 1793.

MODERN HANDBALL emerged in the 1890s in two parallel forms. CZECH teachers created and set down the rules of HAZENA, a seven-a-side game played on an indoor court. Meanwhile in Denmark, where football had been banned in schools due to too many broken legs and windows, a PE teacher called HOLGER NIELSEN, who had won fencing and shooting medals at the Athens Games, created HAANDBOL. An instant hit, it spread throughout Scandinavia, and its rules form the basis of the modern game.

The game developed further in *fin de siècle* Germany, where the gymnastic movement was a serious business, training minds and bodies for a powerful and regimented nation. The intransigent, ultra-nationalist proponents of gymnastics never reconciled themselves to ball games, but for those who did, KONRAD KOCH, not content with introducing football to Germany in 1874, came up with RAFFBALLSPIEL. This evolved into TORBALL, a game for the women's branch of the gym, not unlike the Scandinavian version of handball. In the 1920s, CARL SCHELENZ, a German PE professor, decided that the game needed to be more masculine, revising the rules to create an eleven-a-side sport to be played outside on a football field, with body checking allowed for the first time.

While Scandinavians and Central Europeans preferred the indoor version, the Germans began to organise international matches in the new format and showcased outdoor handball at the 1936 BERLIN OLYMPICS. Predictably, the Germans walked the competition, beating Austria 10-6 in the final in front of 100,000 rain-drenched spectators to win the first and only FIELD HANDBALL gold medal.

GAME ON: HANDBALL BASICS

THE OBJECT OF HANDBALL IS TO PUT THE BALL IN YOUR OPPONENTS' net more often than they put it into yours. A match consists of TWO

DENMARK'S RIKKE SKOV 'MAKES HERSELF BIG' IN THE 2004 WOMEN'S FINAL

30-MINUTE HALVES separated by a interval which can last ten or fifteen minutes. If the scores are level at the end of regulation time and a definitive outcome is required, up to two five-minute periods of EXTRA TIME are played. If the scores are still level at this point, a PENALTY SHOOT-OUT takes place.

Olympic handball is played on courts 40m long by 20m wide, with 3m-wide goals pleasingly striped in the manner of barbers' poles. The GOAL AREAS are bounded to the front by lines 6m from the centre of the goals, and to the sides by quarter circles. FREE THROW LINES curve across the court 9m from the goals, while PEN-ALTY THROW LINES are 7m from the goals.

Each team has seven players: six outfielders and one goalkeeper. Seven SUBSTITUTES are allowed per side. Players can be changed at any time during a match and as often as the coach wishes. Each side is allowed a one-minute TIME OUT period in each half but must be in possession of the ball when it is called.

Matches are officiated by TWO REFEREES, who direct the action using various hand signals. The one denoting a two-minute suspension, for example, looks very like an earthy Anglo-Saxon gesture meaning 'go away'. The refs have equal authority, which you might think would be a recipe for chaos. Luckily, there are set protocols. If they have different opinions about how an infraction should be punished, the more severe option must be taken. If the refs cannot agree about a straight either-or, for instance which

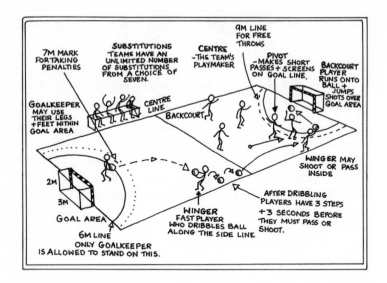

team should be awarded possession after the ball goes out of play, the matter is referred to the COURT JUDGE.

.... **FOUR KEY RULES** ....

NO KICKING: Handball is hands only, though goalkeepers can use their lower legs or feet to move the ball. The keeper is also the only player allowed to stand within the goal area.

THREE STEPS TO HEAVEN: Players can take up to three steps with the ball, after which you must pass or dribble (by bouncing it). Once you stop moving you have three seconds to pass or shoot. If you jump before shooting you must let go of the ball before you land.

IN AND OUT OF PLAY: If the ball goes out of play along the sides of the court, the team that didn't touch it last is awarded a throw-in. If it goes out behind the goal line, the attacking team is awarded a corner throw if the ball was last touched by a defender; the defending team is awarded a goal throw if it was last touched by an attacker. In other words, it's just like soccer.

GETTING THE BALL BACK: Players can steal the ball by slapping it out of an opponents' hands and can disrupt their opponents by body checking, provided they approach them directly from the front. They may not, however, snatch the ball, use their hands to hold or check an opponent, or indulge in tripping or any other rough stuff.

IF ANY OF THE ABOVE RULES ARE BROKEN, THE OPPOSING team is awarded a FREE THROW from the spot where the foul was committed. If the infringement occurred between the free throw and penalty throw lines, the free throw is taken from the former. For more serious misdemeanours, especially crossing into or playing the ball into your goal area, the official can award a PENALTY THROW taken from the 7m line.

A player's first reasonably serious foul or display of unsportsmanlike conduct gives rise to a warning, indicated by a YELLOW CARD. The next offence of a similar magnitude is punished by a TWO-MINUTE SUSPENSION. A player who has not been warned can also be suspended if they commit a suitable offence and their team has accumulated three warnings in total. Fighting and repeated or very serious fouls are punished by RED CARDS and permanent expulsion.

THE FINER POINTS

······························ A BIG SLICE OF GOAL PIE ·······························

NEARLY ALL OF THE ACTION OCCURS AROUND THE GOAL areas, which is why the final scoreline in so many games is in the region of 28-24. Following a game is partly about sensing the momentum of scoring and the balance of opportunities taken and missed over time, rather than the impact of any single goal.

Handball is loaded against goalkeepers, with big nets, small balls and players as little as 6m away when throwing. Nevertheless, keepers do make saves – and often spectacular ones.

···················· THE ARTS OF DEFENCE AND ATTACK ····················

LOOK AT THE DEFENDERS – HOW ARE THEY ORGANISING themselves? Most start with a 6-0 formation with all the outfield players close to their goal area line, moving forwards and backwards to engage the opposition as the ball moves among them. More attacking teams will use a 5-1 or even a 4-2 formation in which one or two players consistently stand further out trying to disrupt the attack and force a mistake.

As players can't use brute force to get round a defender, keep an eye out for feints, swerves, high leaps and sudden body checks as ways of gaining an inch of space from which to pass or shoot. Players close to their opponents' goal will also try spin shots that bounce around defenders and goalkeepers.

HANDBALL GOES TO THE OLYMPICS

AFTER THE SECOND WORLD WAR, GERMANY WAS TEMPORARILY excluded from the international community and consequently lost control of international handball. The new centre of power was DENMARK. The IHF (International Handball Federation) was created in Copenhagen in 1946 and though the outdoor Germanic sport hung on for a decade, the indoor game, now known as TEAM or OLYMPIC HANDBALL, became the international standard. Not that anyone outside of continental Europe took much notice. The Anglo-Saxon world and Latin America were indifferent to handball and it was virtually unknown in Africa and Asia. Even in its heartlands, the culture of handball was unassuming and non-commercial.

Nevertheless, by the 1970s the sport had become sufficiently international to warrant inclusion in the Olympics. A men's competition was introduced at the 1972 Games and a women's followed at Montreal in 1976. For the next twenty years, both events were dominated by Warsaw Pact nations, whose state-sponsored athletes consistently outperformed the amateurs of the West.

Since then, things have been stirring in the world of handball. The sport has turned professional, with TV contracts worth tens and sometimes hundreds of millions of pounds. The men's game is closely followed in GERMANY, FRANCE, SPAIN and GREECE, while the women's version has become the sporting phenomenon of the last decade in DENMARK and NORWAY. The Posh and Becks of Norway were the celebrity couple GRO HAMMERSENG and KATJA NYBERG, stalwarts of the women's handball team, but they split and Hammerseng married another Norwegian handball international, Anja Edin. The Women's World Handball Championship gets higher TV ratings in Denmark than any sporting event bar the football World Cup. This westward shift in power, led by the all-conquering Danish women's team (Olympic champions in 2000 and 2004), is reflected in successive gold medals for FRANCE in the men's competition and NORWAY for the women's.

Handball's journey from northern European amateurism to global commercialism has not been smooth. In Greece and Egypt, where the sport has become immensely popular, the ULTRAS culture of the football stadium has reached the handball court. Games between Olympiakos and Panathinaikos in Athens regularly descend into punch-ups. In Egypt in 2010, the Cairo derby between Al Ahly and Zamalek was preceded by street riots and attacks by Zamalek fans on the Al Ahly club complex.

The arrival of so much money in handball is changing the game in ways that aren't always welcome. Rumours of MATCH-FIXING and BRIBERY abound. France's most famous handball player, Nikola Karabatic and fellow Olympic champion Samuel Honrubia, were BANNED in 2013 after a betting scandal. A blatantly mis-refereed qualifier for the 2008 Olympics between Kuwait and South Korea had to be replayed after the IOC threatened to drop handball from the Games.

QATAR's investment in handball has not been without controversy. In 2015, it staged the men's World Championship and reached the final amid accusations of biased refereeing: after losing the semi-final to the hosts, Poland's players sarcastically applauded the officials. Qatar fielded a squad containing at least ten naturalised players – IHF rules allow anyone who has not played internationally for three years to switch countries – hired Spain's World Cup-winning coach Valero Rivera Lopez and paid for 60 Spanish fans to fly in and cheer on the hosts. It is hard to know how competitive this team will be if it qualifies for Rio.

HOCKEY

7–20 AUGUST 2016

OLYMPIC HOCKEY CENTRE,

DEODORO, RIO DE JANEIRO

Athletes: 384 | **Golds up for grabs:** 2

OLYMPIC PRESENCE

MEN: 1908, 1920, 1928–PRESENT; WOMEN SINCE 1980.

OLYMPIC FORMAT

THERE ARE TWELVE TEAMS IN BOTH THE MEN'S AND THE women's events, divided into two qualifying groups of six, with the top two from each group going through to the semi-finals. Lower-ranked teams play a series of classification matches.

CONTENDERS

THE DUTCH, GERMANS AND AUSTRALIANS ARE TRADITIONALLY strong but in the women's event, Argentina and Great Britain pose a real threat. Although Brazil are hosts, they will only field a men's team – their women's team failed to meet the minimum qualification level.

PAST CHAMPIONS

INDIA: 8 | NETHERLANDS: 5 | AUSTRALIA: 4 | GERMANY: 4

WHY WATCH HOCKEY?

ONE COULD DO WORSE THAN HEED THE WORDS OF LORD Lyttelton, the old Etonian Under-Secretary of State for War and the Colonies in the 1840s. A lifelong hockey fanatic, he explained his love of the sport in the *Eton College Magazine*: 'It is a game in which, as in poetry, mediocrity is not tolerable: indeed, a bad game at hockey is one of the most stupid sights ... but, on the other hand, when it is played, as at Eton, with a considerable degree of dexterity, we think it one of the most elegant and gentlemanlike exercises, being susceptible of very graceful attitudes and requiring great speed of foot.'

The best part of two hundred years later, hockey is recognisably the same game that Lyttelton gushed over, and at the Olympics it will be played with more dexterity, speed and elegance than was ever managed in early Victorian England. Olympic hockey offers the flow and teamwork of football, combined with skilled stick play and drilled, small-ball precision. It's also very physical. Struck correctly, a hockey ball can travel at 100mph, and in the modern era the fitness of players produces a game of relentless ebb and flow. Don't expect mediocrity; do expect poetry.

THE STORY OF HOCKEY

THE URGE TO SWIPE THE NEAREST OBJECT WITH A STICK AND send it soaring into the air or scuttling along the ground is surely universal. There are records of hockey being played in Persia as long ago as 2000 BC. From North America to Africa and East Asia, the game has been invented and reinvented a dozen times, but the version that is now the global standard has its roots in Western Europe.

Europeans have been devising their own versions of the sport for over a millennium, most enthusiastically on the continent's Celtic fringe, where the Irish variant became HURLING. During the Peasants' Revolt of 1381, hurley sticks were the weapons of choice for many of the rural poor who marched on London; in the aftermath of the uprising, Richard II ordered the burning of every last hurley stick in the realm. However, the game was too much a part of rural life across the British Isles and Ireland to be eradicated.

Like many other rural games, hockey was fashioned into a proto-sport in nineteenth-century public schools, and in the 1860s the first hockey club was formed at BLACKHEATH in south-east

London. Here, the local rugby club developed a variant of 'Union Hockey' which pitted two rampaging fifteen-man teams against each other, belting a small leather cube – more hacky-sack than hockey ball – with one-handed sticks.

On the other side of London, the more genteel members of TEDDINGTON CRICKET CLUB were looking for a winter game. Adapting their flat-rolled cricket pitch and cricket balls, they devised an eleven-a-side version of hockey which forms the basis of the modern sport, with dribbling, passing, running and positional play. In 1875, Teddington joined forces with four other south London clubs to create the HOCKEY ASSOCIATION. This body set down the first written rules of hockey, introducing the scoring circle and banning high swinging, tripping and charging.

By the early 1890s, hundreds of clubs had formed across Britain and there were calls for leagues, cups and proper contests. The conservative Hockey Association promptly outlawed them all, to the delight of the editor of *Hockey*: 'Such a vital decision has undoubtedly saved hockey from disaster and being sacrificed upon the altar of popular, but ruinous competition.' The edict saved hockey for the upper classes in Britain, but not for long.

GAME ON: HOCKEY BASICS

HOCKEY IS AN ELEVEN-A-SIDE GAME IN WHICH EVERYONE, goalkeepers included, must carry a wooden stick at all times. The J-shaped sticks are all RIGHT-HANDED, which is tough on the lefties. One face is flat, the other rounded. Using the flat side only, the players must pass, push and flick a small hard plastic ball up the field and try to put it in their opponents' net.

The FIVE KEY RULES are: no using your LEGS OR FEET to move the ball (though unintentional deflections are overlooked); no CARRYING OR HANDLING the ball; GOALKEEPERS (of whom more below) may use their limbs and hands inside the defence zone around their goal; there is NO OFFSIDE, so the play is stretched right across the field; you can SCORE only from a shot taken inside the SCORING CIRCLE.

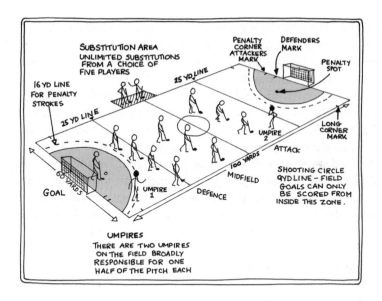

Tackling is allowed and encouraged. Players may use their sticks to intercept and take the ball from opponents.

·················· **FOULS, PENALTIES AND SET PIECES** ··················

A FOUL IS CALLED IF A PLAYER DOES THE FOLLOWING: PLAYS the ball with the ROUNDED SIDE of the stick; plays the ball in a DANGEROUS way (too high or at an opponent); uses any part of the BODY rather than the stick to move the ball; RAISES THE STICK in an intimidating way; CHARGES, SHOVES OR TRAPS an opponent; deliberately OBSTRUCTS the movement of the ball or another player; hits, hooks or holds an OPPONENT'S STICK, or plays any part in the game WITHOUT HOLDING THE STICK.

The punishment for committing a foul depends on where the offence occurs. Outside the shooting zone, the other team gets a FREE HIT from where the misdemeanour was committed. The opponents must retreat 5m. Foul inside the shooting zone or commit an intentional foul in your own 25-yard area and the other team is awarded a PENALTY CORNER. Defenders who deliberately put the ball out of play behind their goals also concede penalty corners.

The most egregious sin is to commit a FOUL INSIDE THE SHOOTING CIRCLE against a player in possession who is deemed to have a chance on goal. This is punished by the award of a PENALTY STROKE or FLICK, taken from a spot 7 yards in front of goal.

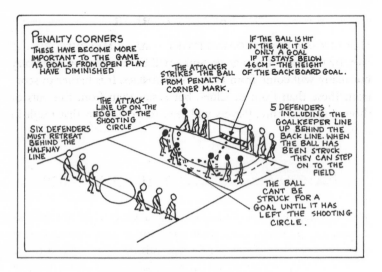

PENALTY CORNERS
THESE HAVE BECOME MORE IMPORTANT TO THE GAME AS GOALS FROM OPEN PLAY HAVE DIMINISHED

IF THE BALL IS HIT IN THE AIR IT IS ONLY A GOAL IF IT STAYS BELOW 46 CM – THE HEIGHT OF THE BACKBOARD GOAL.

THE ATTACKER STRIKES THE BALL FROM PENALTY CORNER MARK.

THE ATTACK LINE UP ON THE EDGE OF THE SHOOTING CIRCLE

SIX DEFENDERS MUST RETREAT BEHIND THE HALFWAY LINE

5 DEFENDERS INCLUDING THE GOALKEEPER LINE UP BEHIND THE BACK LINE. WHEN THE BALL HAS BEEN STRUCK THEY CAN STEP ON TO THE FIELD

THE BALL CANT BE STRUCK FOR A GOAL UNTIL IT HAS LEFT THE SHOOTING CIRCLE.

THE FINER POINTS

FORMATIONS

ALTHOUGH HIGH-LEVEL HOCKEY IS A FLUID GAME, WITH NO formal positions apart from the goalkeeper, most teams have a basic shape with three lines of players – defence, midfield and forward line. An attacking 5-3-2 formation is favoured in Australia. The Dutch prefer 3-3-3-1, with a SWEEPER behind the back three as an insurance policy. Great Britain traditionally play 2-3-2-3.

SPECIAL DUTIES

LIKE MANY SPORTS, HOCKEY HAS ACQUIRED A SPECIALISED division of labour. Players are not just midfielders, but will be defensive or attacking midfielders with specific roles and duties. Some defenders have licence to move up the field, others will sit back.

THE SPEED, DEXTERITY AND CREATIVITY OF TOP-CLASS STICK work are joys to behold. Players at Olympic level have a variety of tricks and moves to evade opponents when dribbling, or to extract themselves from tight marking.

HOCKEY IS A LOW-SCORING SPORT – MANY MATCHES WILL BE won by just one or two goals. Some will be scored from open play but many will come from PENALTY CORNERS. It is harder to score from these than from penalties, but easier than from free hits or shots under pressure. Players will seek to draw fouls that result in penalty corners.

HOCKEY GOES TO THE OLYMPICS

THE ORGANISERS OF THE 1900 PARIS OLYMPICS ASKED THE British HOCKEY ASSOCIATION if they would care to field a team, but were politely declined on the grounds that there would be no international opponents to play. In 1904, St Louis didn't even bother to ask. However, despite the insularity of the Hockey Association, the sport had made its way to elite athletic clubs in the USA and continental Europe and, at the instigation of the French, a hockey tournament was played at LONDON 1908. The British presence, contrary to usual Olympic practice, was split into the four home nations, in order to make up the numbers with the French and Germans. England won. Absent again in 1912, hockey returned at ANTWERP 1920 – another small affair, won by the English, despite a fiendish ploy by the French team, who invited them to an immense dinner party the night before in the hope of slowing them down.

In the early 1920s the IOC insisted that to qualify for the Games, a sport had to have an international federation with whom they could do business. The Hockey Association in London, which retained copyright over the game's rules, remained aloof and uninterested, so hockey was omitted from the 1924 Games. Finally, a small group of European nations formed an international federation, the FIH,

THE LOST WORLD OF INDIAN HOCKEY

When Indian hockey ruled the world from the 1930s to the end of the 1950s, the game was at least the equal of cricket in the nation's affections. While cricket brought great pride and honour to India, it could hardly compete with hockey's six Olympic golds. In another universe, hockey would have become India's national sport, with all the razzmatazz of today's IPL Twenty20 cricket league. The introduction of synthetic turf as the international norm certainly hurt the south Asian nations, but political conflict and corruption in India's hockey federation also contributed to the country's declining competitiveness, allowing the sport to be marginalised by the juggernaut of cricket.

The hit Bollywood movie of 2007, *Chak de India* (Go! India!), provides a taste of what Indian hockey might have been and indicates the abiding popular affection for the sport. Shah Rukh Kahn stars as a former captain of the national hockey team, disgraced by defeat to Pakistan, ostracised from the sport and forced from his ancestral home. Redemption comes seven years later, when Khan welds the fractious members of the national women's team into a side that wins Olympic gold.

THE GOLDEN AGE: INDIA TROUNCE GERMANY AT BERLIN 1936

with the tacit permission but not the involvement of the Hockey Association. This was enough to get hockey back into the Games at AMSTERDAM in 1928, where it was the INDIANS not the Europeans who proved to be the masters of the sport.

Hockey had arrived in India via officers of the British army, who were playing at the Calcutta Club as early as 1885. The game quickly spread to the British, Indian and Anglo-Indian ranks, and was enthusiastically taken up by members of the Indian urban elite working for the imperial administration. By the beginning of the First World War, there were several teams sponsored by army regiments or by the Indian railways, telegraphs and customs departments. A network of provincial teams and competitions had also been established.

The Indians swept all before them in Amsterdam, winning every game without conceding a goal. They also provided hockey with its first global star, in the person of leading scorer DHYAN CHAND, known as 'the Wizard' because of his superb ball control. India won again at Los Angeles in 1932, thrashing the hosts 24-1 with a team described in the local press as '... like a typhoon out of the east. They trampled under their feet and all but shoved out of the Olympic stadium the eleven players representing the USA.' In 1936, the Indian team arrived in Berlin with a huge burden of expectation on their shoulders. Seen as representatives of the simmering nationalist unrest at home, they saluted the Indian Congress flag in the dressing room before meeting the hosts in the final. The Germans held them to 1-1 in the first half, but were swept aside in the second as India won its third gold in a row, 8-1.

The subcontinent's domination of the sport survived partition and independence, with India winning its fourth gold in London in 1948, beating Pakistan 1-0 in the final. This amazing streak was sustained at the next two Games. PAKISTAN finally broke the Indian stranglehold in Rome in 1960, a victory celebrated by delirious crowds in Lahore and other Pakistani cities. India won again in 1964 and Pakistan in 1968, but the great turning point in global hockey came in Munich in 1972, when WEST GERMANY beat Pakistan 1-0 to win Europe's first gold in more than half a century. The losers did not take it well. The Pakistani players were so incensed by the refereeing of the game that on the final whistle they doused the Belgian president of the FIH with a bucket of water. Then they refused to wear their medals or face the flags during the medal ceremony. Every member of the team was subsequently barred from the Olympics, but miraculously received pardons and reappeared at the 1976 Games.

The Pakistanis returned to a changed hockey universe. The competition at Montreal was played on SYNTHETIC TURF, as have been all subsequent Olympic tournaments. Unable and unwilling to spend money on new pitches, the south Asian nations have lagged behind ever since. The 1976 final was played between rising stars from the Antipodes, AUSTRALIA claiming gold at New Zealand's expense. The hockey at Moscow 1980 was distorted by the absence of many leading nations who boycotted the Games in protest at the Soviet invasion of Afghanistan. A scratch team of Soviet-sponsored ZIMBABWEANS won the women's tournament, while India enjoyed a last hurrah in the men's.

Since then, the golds in men's and women's hockey have been divided among the DUTCH, GERMANS and AUSTRALIANS, with two notable exceptions. The SPANISH women won miraculously

'WHERE WERE THE GERMANS?' THE OLYMPIC MEN'S FINAL, SEOUL, 1988

in Barcelona in 1992 and in 1988 GREAT BRITAIN's men slew the giants of West Germany by three goals to one in Seoul. The occasion was bejewelled by the unashamedly partisan TV commentary of the BBC's Barry Davies. 'Where were the Germans?' he asked after one British goal, ' … but frankly, who cares?'

The Germans were conspicuously present in 2012, beating Netherlands 2-1 in the men's final. The Dutch, in turn, defeated Argentina 2-0 to win gold in the women's event. Germany's victory was a third successive gold for Markus Weise, the only coach to triumph in the women's event (in 2004) and the men's (2008 and 2012).

In London, hockey pitches were blue, to provide better contrast for players, officials and spectators. The pitches will also be blue in Rio where, for the first time in Olympic history, hockey will be a game of four 15-minute quarters rather than two halves. New 40-second time outs for the award of a penalty corner and goals are designed to minimise dead time during the 60-minute matches.

JUDO

6–12 AUGUST 2016

OLYMPIC TRAINING CENTRE, BARRA
DA JIJUCA, RIO DE JANEIRO

Athletes: 386 | Golds up for grabs: 14

OLYMPIC PRESENCE

MEN 1964 & 1972–PRESENT; WOMEN 1992–PRESENT.

OLYMPIC FORMAT

SEVEN WEIGHT CATEGORIES FOR BOTH MEN AND WOMEN.

CONTENDERS

AT LONDON 2012, JAPAN WON ONLY ONE GOLD, A SHOWING
that seemed to confirm its long dominance of the sport was at an
end. Golds went to Europeans (X, Y and Z), the Americas (A, B and
C) and the two Koreas. In Rio, look out for the men's heavyweight
champion, the French Guadeloupian TEDDY RINER, who has been
all but unbeatable since London 2012, and for Brazil's SARAH ME-
NEZES, who will be looking to win her second successive gold in
the extra-lightweight division (under 48 kg), plus Rafael 'Bobby'
Silva, who won bronze in the heavyweight event in London.

PAST CHAMPIONS

JAPAN: 36 | FRANCE: 12 | SOUTH KOREA: 11

WHY WATCH JUDO?

IN THE *KOJIKI*, AN EIGHTH-CENTURY CHRONICLE THAT GATHERED
the foundation myths of the Japanese people, the god Takemikazuchi
fights a divine wrestler called Takeminakata for control of the earth,

winning the islands for the sun goddess and her descendants – the people of Japan. Literally translated as 'the gentle way', JUDO is a ritualised duel that may be seen as a manifestation of the Japanese soul. Embodying a profound tradition of self-discipline and self-improvement, it remains one of the purest expressions of sport as ruthless competition, hence its global popularity.

JUDO BOUTS are sometimes tactical and wary, with each contestant – or *JUDOKA* – searching for a micro-advantage. Some tussles are bruising and apparently unstructured. Some are protracted battles in which fitness is as crucial as technique. And some are over in a moment's flurry of jackets and limbs – so you need to concentrate on the action right from the start.

THE STORY OF JUDO

IN MEDIEVAL JAPAN UNARMED COMBAT WAS POPULAR AMONG the warrior elites, though less prestigious than the real business of killing with weapons. That said, a whole school of armoured wrestling was devised for samurai who, dismounted and unarmed, still wished to fight on.

In 1603 the TOKUGAWA SHOGUNATE began its long rule over Japan. Sidelining the emperor, the dynasty created a centralised state that was powerful enough to defeat and disarm the samurai clans who had terrorised the country for much of the previous five hundred years. In this new context, martial values were maintained largely by the practice of unarmed combat systems or JUJITSU – best translated as 'the gentle technique' or 'the technique of pliancy'. These systems flourished in a hundred different schools: in some the practice was infused with an aesthetic that prized the beauty of a fighter's movements; in others it served to train new generations of thugs and enforcers.

The shogunate lasted until 1868, when the old order was overturned. The Meiji restoration returned symbolic power to the emperor, while keeping real executive power with a core of modernisers, who embarked on half a century of systematic industrialisation, reverse-engineering western institutions for a Japanese context. Sport was part of that transformation, and the Japanese embraced the newly imported games of baseball, athletics and basketball as emblems of modernity.

This was the milieu in which JIGORO KANO, born in 1860, grew up. Learning English and German as a child, Kano became a key figure in the educational establishment, and was simultaneously a moderniser and a traditionalist. In the evenings he liked to spar and fight, old style. From the age of seventeen, he attended Tokyo's leading ju-jitsu schools and systematically collated the fragmented fighting systems that had survived from the Tokugawa era. The crude and often violent teaching methods fell short of the spiritual, aesthetic and moral dimensions that Kano believed a modernised Japanese martial art should possess. In 1882 he founded his own school in a corner of the Eishoji temple in Tokyo. It did not teach ju-jitsu, it taught JUDO; not the gentle technique, but the gentle way, which represented a journey of moral, personal and social progress.

Excising brute force and lethal techniques, judo focused on three forms of combat: THROWING (*nage waza*), and the concomitant skills of FALLING AND LANDING; GROUNDWORK (*newaza*), which consisted of PINNING HOLDS, STRANGLE HOLDS and JOINT LOCKS; and STRIKING (*atemi waza*). Judo would forge 'noble and vigorous characters' who, imbued with the values of self-perfection, mutual welfare and maximum efficiency, were perfectly equipped for the social complexities of the new Japan. Its style of fighting – always seeking to turn an opponent's strengths and weaknesses against him, applying minimum force for maximum results, favouring technique and style over size and power – reflected the ethos of Meiji Japan, a rising power in a world of giants.

Within a few years judo was on the curriculum at Japan's teacher-training institutes, police and naval academies, and its most prestigious universities. By the eve of the First World War it had become central to secondary-school education, and was widely taught in the armed forces. For Kano, judo was a DISCIPLINE rather than a competitive sport or an instrument of nationalism. But after the invasion of China in 1937 and Kano's death the following year, judo became inevitably aligned with the imperialist ideology of

Japanese fascism. Consequently it was banned by the American occupation authorities in 1946, along with all other martial arts. When judo was allowed to re-emerge publicly in 1951 it was as a sport rather than a martial philosophy.

The following year the INTERNATIONAL JUDO FEDERATION (IJF) was created, with seventeen founding national associations, signalling an end to Japan's automatic role as the heartland of the sport. The new judo nations were primarily European. JU-JITSU had been popular in Britain and France since the start of the twentieth century ('Ju-jitsu is everything! The streets, the newspapers and magazines, the theatres, the music halls – they all sound the triumphant clarion of this almost magic world,' proclaimed *Le Sport Universel Illustré* in 1906), and after the First World War judo clubs – many led by Kano's students – sprang up in ENGLAND, FRANCE, GERMANY and the LOW COUNTRIES.

Meanwhile, in the SOVIET UNION, VASILI OSHCHEPKOV, another of Kano's students, was commissioned with ju-jitsu expert Viktor Spirindov to devise a self-defence system for the Red Army. His creation blended elements of the many combat sports in the new Soviet republics with the core dynamics of judo. In 1937, Oshchepkov fell victim to the great purges and his name was

JIGORO KANO, THE MASTER OF THE GENTLE WAY, THROWS AN OPPONENT

obliterated from the official records, along with all references to the foreign and imperialistic influence of judo on the Red Army's SAMBO school of self-defence. Closely aligned to judo, SAMBO followed its own independent path for the next two decades, but after Stalin's death a generation of Soviet *judoka* emerged, famed for their disciplined but high-energy aggression. The sport remains popular in Russia: in 2008, president VLADIMIR PUTIN celebrated his 56th birthday by releasing a training video starring himself for use at martial arts centres throughout the country.

GAME ON: JUDO BASICS

THE PLAYING SPACE

JUDO BOUTS ARE CONDUCTED ON A TATAMI, BASED ON THE traditional Japanese domestic floor mat but now made of foam and covered in vinyl. The tatami must be scrupulously clean – if blood is inadvertently spilt during a fight, the contest will be stopped and a maniacal cleaning process will follow. The contest area is a bounded inner square at least 8m by 8m and no larger than 10m by 10m. BOUTS last for five minutes for men and four for women. If no one is ahead at the end of 'regular time', the contest continues on a 'first scorer wins' basis.

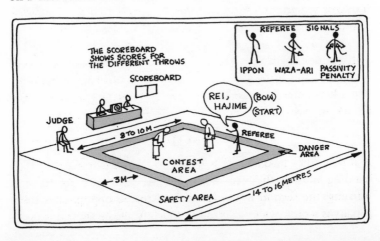

.... **NEW KIT** ....

THE DIFFICULTY OF DISTINGUISHING WHITE-CLAD JUDOKA IN action has led, at the insistence of the IJF, to the introduction of contrasting coloured suits, a move bitterly opposed by the All Japan Judo Federation. Japanese competitions are still conducted in all-white JUDOGI, with one contestant wearing a red belt.

.... **HOW TO WIN A BOUT** ....

KANO ENVISAGED JUST ONE WAY OF WINNING A BOUT – AN IPPON, scored from a throw that puts the opponent directly on to his back, or from a long hold or submission. For Kano this system aligned judo with the all-or-nothing peril of real combat. Such are the demands of sporting competition and TV schedules that endless bouts without *ippons* could not be tolerated, so lesser scores were introduced for imperfect throws – the WAZA-ARI and the YUKO – which function as tie-breakers.

IPPON is scored for a 30-second pin, a throw direct onto the back or a submission in a lock or choke hold. An *ippon* scores one full point and ends the match.

WAZA-ARI is scored for a throw not directly onto the back or of insufficient power to qualify as an *ippon* and for holds of twenty seconds. If a *judoka* is awarded two *waza-ari* in the same match they make an *ippon* and the game is over.

YUKO is scored for a throw of inferior quality to a *waza-ari*. One *waza-ari* beats any number of *yukos*.

If a bout ends in a draw, the contestants effectively fight a second bout, with the first *judoka* to register any kind of score winning. If neither scores, the result is decided by HANTEI – a vote by the referee and two corner judges.

.... **PENALTIES** ....

A *JUDOKA* IS PENALISED FOR INACTIVITY, ILLEGAL MOVES, AND standing outside the mat area. The first penalty is issued as a warning, the second is a *yuko* awarded to the opponent. A third penalty is scored as a *waza-ari* and a fourth (called HANSOKU-MAKE) constitutes an *ippon*. *Hansoku-make* are also awarded for extremely serious acts of dissent or rule-breaking.

The Finer Points

THE PROCESSION

THE COMPETITORS' PROGRESS TO THE MAT IS WORTH WATCHING: each *judoka* is flanked by an official and their coach, rather like a condemned prisoner en route to the firing squad. The warm-up routines can be idiosyncratic and instructive. Expect much ear-rubbing to stimulate adrenaline and sumo-esque squats to maximise suppleness. Competitors are called to the edge of the mat, then to their marks, where they must bow, before the call to engage (*Hajime!*).

THE BATTLE OF GRIPS

MOST BOUTS BEGIN WITH A STRUGGLE FOR THE BEST GRIP AS A prelude to a throw. British champion Neil Adams says that in the initial EXCHANGE OF GRIPS 'volumes of subtle tactical information are picked up … in a few seconds'. Note how *judoka* on the defensive move, bend and use counter-attacks to free themselves

LOOKING GOOD ON THE DANCE FLOOR

JUDOKA CONSTANTLY MOVE THEIR FEET AND SHIFT THEIR WEIGHT IN response to the smallest change in their opponent's position and stance. If you look closely, the contestants' interlocking footwork is suggestive of a dance.

Judo Goes to the Olympics

WHILE JUDO'S OWN WORLD CHAMPIONSHIPS ARE CENTRAL to the sport, its broader cultural history has been written at the Olympics. The inclusion of judo at the 1964 TOKYO GAMES made it the first Olympic sport that had been formalised and codified outside the West. The Games themselves were emblematic of Japan's return to the international community as an economic superpower shorn of its aggressive militarism. Rather than epitomising Japan's uniqueness and superiority, judo appeared in the guise of a gift to the world – although the Japanese expected to win.

They certainly put on a show. A large corner of the Imperial Palace's gardens were occupied by the NIPPON BUDOKAN, a 15,000-seat octagonal temple to judo which was easily the largest purpose-built arena ever constructed for the sport. In the presence of the emperor, Japan took the first three gold medals, but for the fourth event, the OPEN WEIGHT final, Hirohito stayed home, perhaps fearing the humiliation of defeat.

To the Japanese, the open weight was the most important judo medal – in Kano's conception of judo, mere body mass should never prevail over technique. As Japan's champion, AKIO KAMINA-GA, faced the gigantic Dutchman ANTON GEESINK, parliament was closed and companies put TVs on factory floors so that workers could watch the contest. They were to be disappointed: in an imperious display, Geesink ground Kaminaga down before trapping him in an unbreakable hold. Jubilant Dutch spectators were about to invade the mat when Geesink stopped them – a gesture that made him a hero in Japan.

DUTCH COURAGE: ANTON GEESINK WINNING THE MEN'S OPEN
GOLD AT TOKYO 1964

Though absent from the Games in Mexico City, judo has been a constant presence since Munich 1972. The pinnacle for Japan came in 1984 with the gold medal won by Yasuhiro Yamashita, the greatest judo star of post-war Japan. Yamashita was revered for his fighting prowess, demeanour, style and meticulous planning (from 1977 to 1984 he did not lose a single bout). He won the two final bouts in 1984 heroically, fighting and triumphing despite a torn muscle in his ankle.

Japan remained the most successful nation in the following decades, but the drug-fuelled winning machine of EAST GERMANY was quite successful in the 1980s, while the FRENCH, AUSTRIANS, AMERICANS and DUTCH all produced their share of champions. From outside Europe, *judoka* from BRAZIL, SOUTH KOREA and most recently CHINA have all won gold. The sport's widening global appeal is reflected in the success of CUBA'S WOMEN, whose medal haul includes gold in the heavyweight (over 48kg) event for IDALYS ORTIZ at London 2012. At the same Games, teenager WOJDAN SHAHERKANI made sporting history: although her heavyweight bout only lasted 82 seconds, she was the first woman to represent Saudi Arabia at the Olympics.

MODERN PENTATHLON

19–20 AUGUST 2016

DEODORO MODERN PENTATHLON PARK

Athletes: 72 | Golds up for grabs: 2

OLYMPIC PRESENCE

MEN 1912–PRESENT; WOMEN 2000–PRESENT.

OLYMPIC FORMAT

THE PENTATHLON KICKS OFF WITH EITHER A 200M FREESTYLE SWIM, or A ROUND-ROBIN ÉPÉE FENCING tournament, followed by SHOW JUMPING. The scores from these events are then combined to decide the starting positions for the last event, a combined RUN/SHOOT. Competitors have to run four 800m laps but, before each lap, they have to shoot and hit five targets (or wait 50 seconds if they can't do so). The first athlete to cross the line wins the event.

CONTENDERS

EAST AND CENTRAL EUROPEANS HAVE DOMINATED THE OLYMPIC modern pentathlon, along with Sweden. In the women's competition, Lithuania's LAURA ASADAUSKAITE has a good chance of winning a second successive gold, with BRAZIL'S hopes resting on Yane Marques, a bronze medallist in 2012. Germany's LENA SCHÖNEBORN, who won in Beijing, remains a contender. In the men's contest, Russia's ALEKSANDR LESUN and Ukraine's PAVLO TYMOSCHENKO will be among the favourites.

PAST CHAMPIONS

HUNGARY: 9 | SWEDEN: 9 | USSR/RUSSIA: 8

Why Watch Modern Pentathlon?

Imagine a nineteenth-century soldier trapped behind enemy lines, cornered in an island castle. He has to fight his way out with his sword before swimming across the lake and grabbing the nearest available horse. After galloping the animal to exhaustion, he has to abandon his mount and run across the countryside. Every now and again he might need to fire off a few rounds at the enemy, but eventually he escapes and returns home to a hero's welcome.

This is the kind of scenario Baron Pierre de Coubertin, father of the modern Games, had in mind when he devised the only sport specifically created for the Olympics. It's hard not to love an event based on a proto-Bond fantasy: pentathlon is anachronistic, but the old-fashioned strangeness is part of its charm. In some ways the modern pentathlon's presence in the Olympics is like The Boomtown Rats' slot at Live Aid in 1985. Nobody can really begrudge the organiser a place at his own party but does his creation deserve to be there on merit? Despite recent changes to enhance the drama – and make it safer – the jury is still out as far as the modern pentathlon is concerned.

The Story of Modern Pentathlon

At the fourteenth session of the IOC in Budapest in 1911, Baron de Coubertin reported that 'the Holy Ghost of sport illuminated my colleagues and they accepted a competition to which I attach great importance'. Just as the organisers of the ancient Games had used the original pentathlon as a training for war and an alternative to it, De Coubertin wanted the modern pentathlon to improve the world by involving the world's soldiers in friendly competition. He believed that the sport would test 'a man's moral qualities as much as his physical resources and skills, producing thereby the ideal, complete athlete'. It's just as well he never met Boris Onishchenko – of whom more below.

Not surprisingly, given its origins, the history of the modern pentathlon is closely intertwined with that of the Olympics. Before the UIPM (Union Internationale de Pentathlon Moderne) was founded in 1948, the sport was administered directly by the IOC.

GAME ON: PENTATHLON BASICS

THE STRUCTURE OF THE PENTATHLON AND THE DETAILS OF the events that comprise it have changed several times over the years. In Rio, as in London, the men's and women's events will both take place on a single day. The scoring system is based on a set of standard times and performances; a total score of 5000 points is considered 'par'.

FENCING

IN THIS DISCIPLINE, EVERY COMPETITOR HAS ONE SIXTY-second fencing bout with each of the others. The swords used are épées (see 'Fencing') and the bouts are sudden death, i.e. the first dueller to score a hit wins. If neither fencer wins the bout in the allotted time, both register a defeat.

An Olympic pentathlete who wins 70 per cent of their fencing matches (in other words 25 out of 35 bouts), earns 250 points. Deviations from that total are punished/rewarded to the tune of six points for every bout. In Rio, for the first time at the Olympics, pentathletes will also compete in a new bonus round. The athlete in 36th place after the first round will fence the athlete in 35th. Whoever wins, faces the 34th best athlete and so on. Contestants gain bonus points for every fight they win – and aren't penalised for defeats.

SWIMMING

SWIMMING IS CONSIDERED THE HARDEST DISCIPLINE FOR athletes to improve in substantially if they come late to the sport. As a result, many of the best pentathletes have a swimming back-ground. Men and women both compete in 200M FREESTYLE RACES, with the heats seeded according to personal best times. For both sexes, completing the course in 2min 30sec earns 1000 points. Deviations are punished/rewarded at the rate of one point for every third of a second.

RIDING

FOR THE SHOW JUMPING, CONTESTANTS ARE ALLOTTED horses in a draw made shortly before the event begins, the idea being to test their ability to ride an unfamiliar beast. The athletes then have twenty minutes to practice with their new equestrian partners. The COURSE itself will include twelve obstacles, one of which must be a double and one a triple jump. The fences may be up to 1.2m high and at least five of them must be at this maximum.

POINTS are awarded on the basis of the optimum time for completion of the course, which varies according to its distance. A rider who achieves a clear round within the time limit earns 300 points. Each additional second incurs a PENALTY of one point. If a competitor fails to complete the course within twice the standard time they must stop riding, as must any rider who has fallen twice. They are then eliminated and receive no points.

Other penalties include ten points for each fence knocked down, every refusal to jump and every time they fall off. If a horse baulks twice at the same jump, the rider must move on to the next one.

COMBINED EVENT

IN 2008, THE UIPM COMBINED THE SHOOTING AND RUNNING disciplines into a new event, which closes each competition. It has a staggered start, the athletes being handicapped on the basis of the scores they have accumulated in the preceding events.

The race begins with a RUN OF ABOUT 20M to a SHOOTING RANGE, where each pentathlete has 50 seconds to hit five 59.5mm targets from a distance of 10m with a LASER PISTOL. Lasers replaced air pistols in 2010 in a bid to make the sport cheaper – they reduce the cost of shooting by two-thirds – and safer, to encourage more youngsters to take part. There is no limit to the number of shots competitors can fire within the time permitted but they must keep their pistols in contact with the shooting table throughout reloading. They must also leave them in a safe position, i.e. open, unloaded and pointing at the target area. Each infringement of these rules results in a TIME PENALTY of ten seconds. These are paid on the spot: guilty parties are held back from continuing the event until they have done their time.

If athletes manage to hit all five targets within the allotted time, they can immediately set off on the first of four 800m RUNS. If athletes have failed to hit all of their targets within 50 seconds, they will be allowed to leave the range. There are no other penalties for missed targets – if you don't hit all five, you might as well miss the lot.

The shooting procedure is repeated after each 800m run. The fourth run ends at the finishing line. As a result of the handicapping system, the FIRST TO CROSS the line wins the entire competition.

In the combined event, a time of 13:20 is worth 500 points. Deviations from that are rewarded/punished at the rate of 1 point for every second.

THE FINER POINTS

MANY SPORTS ARE BETTER WATCHED LIVE THAN ON TV AND the modern pentathlon is a prime example. The tension builds throughout the day, creating a buzz around the last event that it is impossible to feel if you haven't watched the drama unfold in real time.

For some spectators, the modern pentathlon can suffer from a problem afflicting all multi-disciplinary sports: there are better performers of each of the individual elements elsewhere. But with this sport, you have to think cumulatively. If you watch only a couple of the disciplines, make them the RIDING and the COMBINED EVENT. The former can be especially dramatic, with some competitors scuppering their chances by ploughing into obstacles and others setting themselves up with immaculate rounds. The combined running/shooting provides an element of novelty and an exciting denouement.

MODERN PENTATHLON
GOES TO THE OLYMPICS

THE MODERN PENTATHLON MADE ITS DEBUT AT STOCKHOLM in 1912. The SWEDES took to the new sport in a big way, filling six of the first seven places in the inaugural competition and winning eight of the first nine Olympic titles. Future US General George Patton came fifth in 1912, let down, ironically, by his shooting. He came 21st in that leg, though he claimed that he had been wrongly penalised for missing a target when, in fact, his bullet had passed through an existing hole. This kind of chutzpah would serve him well in wartime, but in Stockholm nobody believed him.

Before the shooting event at the 1932 Games, Swedish aristocrat Johan Oxenstierna decided to fire off a few practice rounds in the woods. He was accosted by an LAPD officer, who threatened to arrest him. Oxenstierna insisted that he was about to take part in an Olympic competition; the policeman, though suspicious, eventually relented, and Oxenstierna won the gold.

At Helsinki 1952, Lars Hall, a carpenter from Gothenburg, rode his luck to become the first non-military winner of the modern pentathlon. In the equestrian competition, the horse he initially drew proved to be lame and he was then given the best show jumper in Finland. Hall also turned up late for the shooting and would have been dis-

qualified if a protest by the Soviet team hadn't delayed the start of the event. The Helsinki Games also saw the introduction of a TEAM COMPETITION, which endured until Barcelona. The most gifted pentathlete of the 1960s (indeed the most decorated Olympic pentathlete ever) was Hungary's András Balczó. He struck gold in the team event in 1960 and 1968, won silver in the individual event in 1968, and gold in 1972. Such was his talent, many historians of the sport say he should have won even more medals.

WILLIAM GRUT SHOOTS HIS WAY TO GOLD, LONDON 1948

The pentathlon competition at the 1968 Games in Mexico was marred by an incident involving West Germany's HANS-JÜRGEN TODT, who became so frustrated after his horse Ranchero balked at three obstacles that he attacked the animal and had to be dragged away by team-mates. At the same Games, Sweden's HANS-GUNNAR LILJENWALL became the first athlete to fail an Olympic drugs test; he claimed he'd had a couple of beers to steady his nerves ahead of the shooting. Four years later, in Munich, fourteen pentathletes were discovered to have taken TRANQUILISERS ahead of the shooting contest. The drugs in question, Librium and Valium, were banned by the UIPM but not the IOC, whose verdict trumped that of the sport's governing body.

The pentathlon at Montreal in 1976 got off to a poor start when CAPTAIN ORBEN GREENWALD of the USA was court-martialled for insubordination by his own team manager, Lieutenant-Colonel Donald Johnson. Things went from bad to worse when Red Army Major BORIS ONISHCHENKO was discovered to have cheated in the team competition. The Soviet Union was disqualified, paving the way for Great Britain's JIM FOX, DANNY NIGHTINGALE and ADRIAN PARKER to win the gold.

NOT SO ONISHCHENKO

B ORIS ONISHCHENKO went into the 1976 Montreal Games as a much-respected modern pentathlete, having won team gold and an individual silver in 1972, and a team silver in 1968. By the time he left, the Soviet volleyball team had threatened to throw him out of a window if they ever came across him in the Olympic village.

The episode that shattered Onishchenko's reputation occurred during the USSR team's fencing contest against Great Britain. British captain Jim Fox had sensed something fishy when the Ukrainian registered a hit against Fox's team mate Adrian Parker without seeming to have touched him. When the same thing happened to Fox, he protested. While the officials inspected his épée, Onishchenko continued to fence – remarkably well – with a substitute weapon. He won his duel with Fox but shortly afterwards it was announced that he had been disqualified.

It transpired that Onishchenko had equipped his sword with a hidden circuit breaker that allowed him to register a hit at the push of a button. The incident was particularly embarrassing given the modern pentathlon's connection with notions of military honour. Whisked away from the Games, Onishchenko was kicked out of the Red Army, stripped of his medals and, months later, spotted working as a taxi driver in his hometown, Kiev. He has never been seen outside the USSR since.

THE SOCK OF SHAME: ONISCHENKO AFTER HIS DISQUALIFICATION AT MONTREAL 1976

The organisers of the modern pentathlon at Los Angeles in 1984 took two important steps to restore the sport's reputation. To combat the problem of doping, they decided to move the shooting – the most common occasion for pill-popping – to a slot a few hours before the running competition. No one wanted to be tranquillised before a run, so the measure proved very effective. The second big decision was to stagger competitors' starting times in the final event, the cross-country, on the basis of their cumulative scores going into the race. The athlete who first crossed the line would win the gold medal. The move undoubtedly improved the pentathlon as a spectacle.

In 1992 the UIPM tinkered with the formula again by moving the riding to the end of the team and the individual competitions. The logic was that this portion of the pentathlon was subject to wilder score swings than the other disciplines, so bad showings in the riding could knock participants out of contention for the rest of the competition. Holding riding at the end would maintain the suspense for longer. The individual final did indeed produce a dramatic reversal – Russia's EDUARD ZENOVKA started the final round 106 points ahead of Poland's ARKADIUSZ SKRZYPASZEK and finished it 198 behind, having to settle for bronze – but the sport's authorities voted to return to the previous structure at the following Games.

The modern pentathlon at Atlanta was enlivened by the presence of Swedish-American actor DOLPH LUNDGREN as non-competing US team leader. Even though the team competition had been dropped from the Games after Barcelona, Lundgren did much to raise the profile of the event. Two years earlier, he had starred in a movie called *Pentathlon*, as an East German gold medallist escaping the clutches of a sadistic trainer, played by David Soul.

A WOMEN'S MODERN PENTATHLON competition was added to the Olympic menu at Sydney 2000, with Great Britain's STEPHANIE COOK taking the gold medal ahead of American Emily de Riel. Subsequent golds have been won by Hungary's ZSUZSANNA VÖRÖS, Germany's LENA SCHÖNEBORN and Lithuania's LAURA ASADAUSKAITE. Asadauskaite's triumph completed a family set of medals: her husband Andrejus Zadneprovskis won silver and bronze in the pentathlons in Athens and Beijing.

A significant recent development in modern pentathlon was the UIPM's creation of a COMBINED RUNNING AND SHOOTING EVENT, which made its Olympic debut in 2012. Traditionalists grumbled – the *New York Times* greeted the move with the headline 'modern pentathlon gets a little less penta' – but it certainly added to the excitement: the combined event, which decided the final medals of the London games, was watched by 23,000 spectators in Greenwich Park. DAVID SVOBODA from the Czech Republic won the men's event.

In the long run, will the UIPM's tinkering be enough to counter the many critics of the sport's Olympic status, who argue that it's too esoteric, elitist and ill-suited to television? The sport's finances aren't in great shape either: being a modern pentathlete is costly, and national funding has diminished substantially since the demise of the team event. But the modern pentathlon survived a vote on its Olympic future in 2005 and looks safe until 2024.

ROWING

6–13 AUGUST 2016

LAKE RODRIGO DE FREITAS,

COPACABANA, RIO DE JANEIRO

Athletes: 550 | **Golds up for grabs:** 14

OLYMPIC PRESENCE

MEN'S 1900–PRESENT; WOMEN'S FROM 1976.

OLYMPIC FORMAT

FOURTEEN EVENTS ARE HELD OVER SIX DAYS (EIGHT MEN'S, SIX WOMEN'S), in classes organised by number of rowers (SINGLES, PAIRS, FOURS and EIGHTS) and types of rowing (SCULLS and SWEEPS).

CONTENDERS

IN MEN'S ROWING, GREAT BRITAIN, GERMANY AND NEW ZEALAND were especially strong in 2012 and will expect to do well again. Because of the number of events, AUSTRALIA, CANADA, CROATIA, the CZECH REPUBLIC, DENMARK, FRANCE, ITALY, SOUTH AFRICA and the US all have realistic hopes of gold. In the women's events the strongest crews tend to come from the USA, NETHERLANDS, CHINA and BRITAIN. Hosts BRAZIL are making strenuous efforts to break their Olympic duck in rowing in Rio.

PAST CHAMPIONS

EAST GERMANY: 33 | USA: 32 | GREAT BRITAIN: 28

WHY WATCH ROWING?

IN 1996, AFTER WINNING HIS FOURTH CONSECUTIVE GOLD, an exhausted STEVE REDGRAVE declared that if anyone saw him near a rowing boat again they should shoot him. As a sport, rowing demands a colossal amount of training, and an ability to endure immense physical pain. Because rowers FACE BACKWARDS during a race, they gain a tactical and psychological advantage by being in front; consequently, they must start with an EXPLOSIVE SPRINT that floods the body with lactic acid, which in turn means that their muscles are burning through the whole race.

Despite all this, Redgrave came back and won his fifth gold medal in the coxless fours at Sydney in 2000. What brought him back? A shot at making Olympic history? Or the adrenaline rush of making these lightweight boats fly through the water, of working in telepathic harmony with a team of superlative athletes?

THE STORY OF ROWING

ROWING BEGAN WHEN SOMEBODY WORKED OUT THAT YOU got more bang for your buck if you moved a paddle on a fixed fulcrum rather than just dabbing at the water. It worked even better if you could corral a lot of people to row in time, and for longer and harder than they would otherwise choose to do. The battleships of antiquity, from Egypt to Phoenicia, and Greece to Rome, were invariably rowed by banks of chained slaves. For over two millennia, maritime empires stuck with slave rowers where they could, though the Vikings, in a spirit of commando imperialism, rowed their own long boats. The BATTLE OF LÉPANTO in 1571, at which the combined forces of Spain, Venice and the papacy defeated the fleet of the Ottoman Empire, was the last great naval engagement fought by rowing boats. Thereafter, oar power was the preserve of the domestic waters of rivers, harbours and canals.

Rowing's emergence as an ORGANISED SPORT began in seventeenth-century England. The Thames thronged with oarsmen and rowing boats, and the quays were thick with gentlemen itching for a wager. The first regular ROWING RACE was established by the Georgian actor and comedian THOMAS DOGGETT. On a late-night journey from the West End to his home in the City, he had trouble persuading any ferryman to row him through the stormy weather.

OXFORD POWERS TO VICTORY IN THE FIRST UNIVERSITY BOAT RACE, 1829

One finally agreed and got Doggett home, and in his honour Doggett established in 1715 an annual race on the Thames for ferrymen, offering a badge and coat as prizes. The craze for rowing races reached such heights that Joseph Strutt, the great chronicler of Georgian sport, wrote in 1801, that, 'when a rowing match takes place near London, if the weather be fine, it is astonishing to see what crowds of people assemble themselves on the banks of the Thames as spectators, and the river itself is nearly covered with wherries, pleasure boats and barges, decorated with flags and streamers and sometimes accompanied by bands of music.'

Through the nineteenth century the British public's appetite for rowing races grew, but in two almost entirely separate social spheres. On the one hand was PROFESSIONAL RACING, which thrived in London and on the Tyne. On the other was a world of elite amateur rowing clubs such as the LEANDER, which flourished as the sport became a central element of the culture of Thames-side public schools like Eton and Westminster. Schoolboys took their enthusiasm to university and by the 1820s rowing races had begun in Oxford and Cambridge. The first OXBRIDGE BOAT RACE was held in 1829, with considerable wagers at stake; by 1845 it had, like the Derby, become an unofficial national holiday, with crowds packing the banks of the Thames.

Rowing's brief life as a commercial spectacle was over by the end of the nineteenth century. In part the sport was driven from England's rivers by the ships of the industrial revolution and the arrival of steam power. Its demise was also encouraged by the rowing establishment which, from the 1850s onwards, prosecuted an increasingly fearsome war against professionals, excluding them from all major rowing events. The definition of PROFESSIONALISM, originally confined to just watermen, was extended to anyone who was a tradesman, artisan or labourer. The result, inevitably, was a decline in the competitiveness of British rowing. By the late nineteenth century the sport had spread widely across NORTH AMERICA, AUSTRALIA and NORTHERN EUROPE and by the time rowing became an Olympic sport in 1900, Britain's early lead was waning.

GAME ON: ROWING BASICS

ROWING RACES COME IN MANY FORMATS, BUT AT THE OLYMpics the competition is simple. In all events, up to six boats race side by side in LANES, over a dead straight 2000M COURSE. The current race length was first tried in Stockholm in 1912 but became the norm only in 1952. WOMEN'S RACES, first held over 1000m, were lengthened to 2000m in 1988. Early Games saw head-to-head match racing but the side-by-side format became standard in 1956.

All Olympic competitions combine HEATS, a REPECHAGE (second-chance round) and FINALS. If enough crews are entered there may be quarter-finals and semi-finals too.

Boats are allowed one FALSE START; any more and you are out. A RESTART is called if a boat suffers a mechanical failure, such as an oar splitting, before it has travelled 100m. In the final of the men's lightweight double sculls event at London 2012, Britain's defending champions Zac Purchase and Mark Hunter stopped because Purchase's seat had broken. (After the restart, they led with 500m to go before being overtaken by Denmark's Mad Rasmussen and Ramus Quist.) The LANES, though marked by buoys, are optional. Crews can take any course they like as long as they don't interfere with others.

························· **OLYMPIC ROWING CLASSES** ·························

ROWING TAKES TWO FORMS: SCULLING, IN WHICH THE rower has two oars, and SWEEPING, in which the rower has just one oar, held with both hands. SCULLS are raced with one, two or four rowers, called SINGLES, DOUBLES and QUADS. SWEEPS are raced with two, four or eight rowers, called PAIRS, FOURS and EIGHTS. In eights, a coxswain or COX sits at the back of the boat, steers the craft and directs the crew's stroke rate. In STRAIGHT or COXLESS craft, the boat is directed by the STEERSMAN, a rower who has the rudder cable attached to a shoe.

Men compete in all of these boats, with an additional category of LIGHTWEIGHT men (no one heavier than 72.5kg) in the coxless fours and double sculls. Women compete in all boats except the coxless fours and have a lightweight event (no one heavier than 59kg) in the double sculls.

Sculls go faster than sweep boats with the same number of rowers, and the more rowers a boat has the faster it will be. Men's eights can reach speeds of 28kmh.

These are the CLASSES:

SINGLE SCULL *Average length: 8.2m; Minimum weight: 14kg. Events: men and women.* The SINGLE – or the SKIFF, as it is known in Europe – is the only individual event in rowing. There's nowhere to hide.

DOUBLE SCULL *Average length: 10.4m; Minimum weight: 27kg. Events: men, women and lightweight for men and women.* Like all pair events in rowing, double sculls favour partnerships made up of different kinds of rowers: POWER ROWERS are often combined with more TECHNICAL athletes. Personal chemistry between the pair is crucial.

QUAD SCULL *Average length: 13.4m; Minimum weight: 52kg. Events: men and women.* Eight blades and four rowers makes for the fastest boats after the eights. Great precision and team work are required to keep time and avoid blade clashes.

PAIR OR COXLESS PAIR *Average length: 10.4m; Minimum weight: 27kg. Events: men and women.* The coxless pair is one of the most technically demanding boats, responding poorly to indiscriminate use of power. Balance, stability and elegance are essential.

FOUR OR COXLESS FOUR *Average length: 13.4m; Minimum weight: 50kg. Events: men, lightweight men.* The same blend of power and technique is required to get the best from this boat, but with four rowers the degree of complexity is even greater. The crew spend more time rowing at maximum stroke rate than in any other class.

EIGHT *Average length: 19m; Minimum weight: 96kg. Events: men and women.* Considered by many the premier regatta format – and the only coxed event at the Olympics – the EIGHTS is an unbelievably demanding competition with rowers achieving close to four-minute-mile pace and constantly on the verge of a lactic acid burn-out.

THE FINER POINTS

THE ROWING STROKE

EACH STROKE CONSISTS OF FOUR ELEMENTS: THE CATCH, IN which the oar is lowered into the water; the DRIVE, in which the oar is pulled through the water as the rower slides back in their seat, driving the boat forward; the EXTRACTION, where the oar is lifted out of the water, and the SLIDE or RECOVERY, which returns the rower to their original position. After the extraction, the rower FEATHERS the oar (rotates it through 90 degrees) to minimise air resistance during the recovery. At the end of the slide, they SQUARE the blade, twisting it back into a sideways-on position before dropping the end into the water for the next catch.

Rowers sit on SLIDING SEATS, which allow them to contract and expand their bodies during the stroke sequence to maximise leverage.

RACE TACTICS

IN MANY RUNNING EVENTS, ATHLETES HANG BACK, GAINING advantage by monitoring their opponents. In rowing, where you face backwards, you want to be OUT FRONT from the start, so you can see and cover any attack.

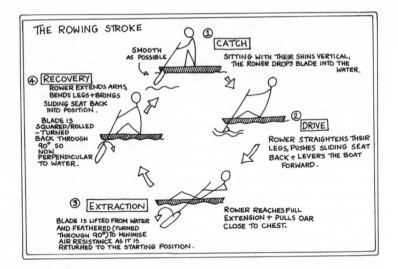

Nearly all crews will row fastest in the FIRST 500M of the race, at a stroke rate of around 45–48 a minute. For the MIDDLE 1000M they drop down to around 35 strokes a minute and then pick the pace up again in the FINAL 500M.

The explosive effort required to get the boat up to 48 strokes a minute means that rowing is a game of STRATEGIC PHYSIOLOGY. The opening 500m burns more oxygen than any athlete can take in, and as a consequence they experience the LACTIC ACID BUILD-UP and MUSCLE PAIN that comes with anaerobic respiration.

Rowers have to decide how much lactic acid they can tolerate and carry throughout the race, balancing the advantage of being ahead early on against the risk later of complete fatigue, induced by lactate accumulation. Towards the finish the rate of energy consumption increases again as does the amount of lactic acid the body produces. If the rowers time it correctly, the FINAL STROKE of the race is the last they are able to pull.

ROWING GOES TO THE OLYMPICS

CANCELLED DUE TO BAD WEATHER AT THE INAUGURAL modern Olympics in 1896, rowing made its debut at the PARIS

GAMES of 1900, in predictably chaotic fashion. Disagreements over the rules saw two final runs for the men's coxless fours, with two different boats awarded gold medals. In the men's coxed pairs, the Dutch team ditched their portly cox after the semi-final and plucked a slender – and sadly still anonymous – Parisian youth from the crowd to replace him. They duly won the title.

ST LOUIS 1904 was a near walkover for the home nation, as only a Canadian eight showed up from outside the USA, winning a silver medal. The oddball 1906 INTERCALATED GAMES featured a suitably eccentric rowing programme, including the seventeen-man naval rowing boat, which provided GREECE's first and only rowing gold.

GREAT BRITAIN won all four golds at LONDON in 1908, when the regatta was held in HENLEY. In the inter-war era, the British were less successful, despite the best efforts of JACK BERESFORD, who won rowing medals at five consecutive Games (1920–36), including three golds. SWISS and ITALIAN teams won Olympic titles during this period, but the USA was the leading rowing nation, with JOHN B. KELLY their leading rower. The son of an Irish immigrant, Kelly learned his rowing while working as a bricklayer, and was excluded from competing at the prestigious Henley Royal Regatta because of his status as an artisan. Undaunted, he went on to win two golds at the 1920 Antwerp Games and a third in 1924. His son JACK won a bronze rowing medal at the 1956 Games and his daughter GRACE became Princess Grace of Monaco. A more conventional Harvard eight of the era, gold medallists in 1924, included BENJAMIN SPOCK, the future childcare guru.

MASTERS OF THE RIVERVERSE:
THE USA'S ROWING AND RULING ELITES

CAMERON AND TYLER WINKLEVOSS are best known as the Harvard graduates who received $65 million from Mark Zuckerberg, the founder of Facebook, in a lawsuit that tried to resolve who owned and invented which bit of the ubiquitous social media site. But they are also top-class sportsmen: at college they were the engine room of a Harvard men's eight that won the US national championship and finished sixth at the World Cup in 2006. The twins went on to compete in the coxless pair at Beijing in 2008, finishing sixth.

The Winklevosses are the latest in a long line of blue bloods in American rowing. Both Yale and Harvard have supplied gold-winning eights to the

STATUS UPDATE: THE WINKLEVOSS TWINS AFLOAT

US team. Other competitive rowers from America's ruling and celebrity elites include Secretary of State DEAN ACHESON (Yale), AVERELL HARRIMAN (Yale), ADMIRAL CHESTER NIMITZ (Navy), the actors GREGORY PECK (Cal-Berkeley) and VINCENT PRICE (Yale), PRESIDENT TEDDY ROOSEVELT (Harvard) and astronaut ALAN B. SHEPARD (Navy).

The balance of power changed in 1936, when the GERMANS won five of the seven events, but in the post-war era the dominance of northern Europe (SWITZERLAND, GERMANY and SCANDINAVIA) and the ANGOLOPHONE nations (USA, CANADA, GREAT BRITAIN and AUSTRALIA) began to weaken. Up against a rigidly amateur or college-based framework in the West, the new state professionals of EAST GERMANY and the SOVIET UNION were increasingly successful. VYACHESLAV IVANOV won three consecutive gold medals in the single scull (1956, 1960, 1964) with his blistering turn of speed. At the Moscow Olympics in 1980, East Germany nearly swept the board, winning eleven of the fourteen rowing titles on offer.

Since the break-up of the Soviet Bloc, Eastern Europe's fortunes have varied. In 2012, Czech rower Miroslava Knapková won the single sculls while Ukraine triumphed in the quad sculls. Women's teams from ROMANIA have consistently done well: no rower has won more medals than ELISABETA LIPA, who has claimed five golds (1984, 1992–2004) in three different classes. KATHRIN BORON of Germany

SHOOT ME NOW: HAVING FORESWORN ROWING FOUR YEARS EARLIER, STEVE REDGRAVE WINS A FIFTH GOLD IN THE MEN'S COXLESS FOUR, SYDNEY 2000

runs her close, though: she won four straight golds between 1992 and 2004 and narrowly missed out on a fifth at Beijing.

In MEN'S ROWING the dominant figure has been Britain's STEVE REDGRAVE, the only rower to win five gold medals at consecutive Olympics (1984–2000). MATTHEW PINSENT, his team-mate for three of those golds, went on to win a fourth himself in 2004, in a coxless four. Together they have inspired a considerable revival in British rowing. At London 2012, Great Britain topped the medal's table with four golds, three in the women's event, with Anna Watkins and Katherine Grainger (double sculls), Helen Glover and Heather Stanning (coxless pair) and Katherine Copeland and Sophie Hosking (lightweight double sculls) all victorious.

AUSTRALIA'S 'OARSOME FOURSOME' (originally NICK GREEN, JAMES TOMKINS, MIKE MCKAY and SAM PATTEN; Patten was replaced by ANDREW COOPER in 1991–92 and he by DREW GINN in 1995), won the men's coxless fours in 1992 and 1996, and brought a welcome dash of populism to a sport which has remained narrowly based. It was only in 2004 that the first black African rower, Kenya's IBRAHIM GITHAIGA, took part in an Olympic rowing regatta.

RUGBY 7s

OLYMPIC PRESENCE

MEN'S EVENTS: 1900, 1908, 1920, 1924 (15-A-SIDE), SEVENS (2016–); WOMEN'S EVENTS: SEVENS (2016–).

OLYMPIC FORMAT

IN BOTH MEN'S AND WOMEN'S EVENTS, THE TWELVE TEAMS are divided into three groups of four. The top two from each section and the two best-placed third teams will reach the quarter-finals, where the top side will face the eighth-best qualifier, second-best face seventh and so forth. The winners then proceed to semi-finals, finals and a bronze runner-up event.

CONTENDERS

AS IN THE 15-A-SIDE GAME, NEW ZEALAND ARE AUTOMATIC favourites, although they will be tested by AUSTRALIA, FIJI (twice winners of the Sevens World Cup,)and possibly GREAT BRITAIN (a combined England, Scotland, Wales and Northern Ireland team). In the women's event, the main challenge to Australasia is likely to come from CANADA and the US. BRAZIL have never entered the men's Sevens World Cup but their women's team beat Fiji in the group stage in 2013 and, no matter how they perform, they will be deemed to have brought 'samba style' to the competition.

PAST CHAMPIONS (15-A-SIDE)

USA: 2 | AUSTRALIA, FRANCE 1

WHY WATCH RUGBY SEVENS?

WHY IS RUGBY SEVENS ONE OF THE FASTEST GROWING SPORTS in the world? Partly because it is one of the fastest sports in the world. Any player with the ball has the chance to score at any given time. Possession can change at any moment. The rules are a lot easier to grasp than in the 15-a-side game (or NFL for that matter), there are hardly any stoppages and the matches are over in 15 minutes. If you want non-stop action, where the outcome can be changed in an instant by a piece of breathtaking athleticism or a bone-crunching tackle, rugby Sevens is the sport for you.

The sport seems to work a mysterious alchemy in the stadiums, too. The usual competitive tension is replaced by feel-good bonhomie, with fans from different nations revelling in the camaraderie and dressing to impress, masquerading as anything from Shrek to Star Wars stormtroopers. Will this goodwill survive the partisan pressures of Olympic contest in Rio?

THE STORY OF RUGBY

IT MUST BE ONE OF THE MOST INFLUENTIAL RUNS IN THE history of sport: in 1823, so legend has it, sixteen-year-old Rugby schoolboy William Webb Ellis picked up the ball in the middle of a football match and ran with it. And lo, the sport we now know as rugby – after the school where this run occurred – was born. It's also why the game's most prestigious prize, the World Cup, is officially known as the William Webb Ellis trophy.

If you're thinking that this all sounds a bit too neat, then you're right. Games involving feet, hands and spherical objects have been played across the world for a millennium or three. Roman generals such as Julius Caesar encouraged their troops to keep fit by playing *harpastum*, a game in which players threw or kicked a 20cm-diameter ball from one end of a pitch to another (while trying to evade rough tackling) in order to score. The Romans probably exported this game across their empire and therefore to Britain. *Harpastum* may in turn have been a Roman makeover of the Greek game *phaninda*, derived from the word 'pretend' because players would deceive opponents by faking a pass. In the third century BC, the Athenian playwright Antiphanes recalls one spectator instructing a player to 'pass it back in the scrum'.

In the centuries since, many games were played in Brittany and Britain in which the object of the exercise was to seize a ball – sometimes more of a leather bag – and take it back to your village. In the Breton version, *la soule*, competitors were supposed to run with the ball, while in Cornwall, where such games were known as *hurling*, the ball could be thrown, and in the contests played on Shrove Tuesday in such villages as Ashbourne, you could do pretty much whatever you wanted with the ball – even, if the fancy took you, playing the entire match on the river.

The game of football played by the privileged nineteenth-century pupils at Rugby School allowed players to handle the ball but not pick it up and run with it. Yet by the late 1830s, possibly thanks to Webb Ellis's inspirational example, such runs had become

THE YOUNG GENTLEMEN OF RUGBY HONING THEIR SKILLS

accepted and were legalised in 1845 when three senior boys drew up the first laws of rugby. The games were played with balls supplied by a local cobbler and, being made from inflated pig bladders, were plum-shaped. Later, they evolved into the familiar oval shape, believed to be easier for players to hold on to while running. The split between rugby and football became official when in 1863 Blackheath FC refused to agree to its eleven fellow Football Association members outlawing handling of the ball, paving the way for the creation of the Rugby Football Union in 1871.

RUGBY SEVENS arrived in the early 1880s, when Scottish butcher Ned Haig, racking his brains for ways to save Melrose Football Club from closure, came up with the idea of hosting an afternoon tournament with shorter games, played between two sides of seven men. The world's first sevens tournament was hosted at Melrose's Greenyards ground on 28 April 1883. The philosophy of the time was to play what Mike Williams, in his 1975 book *Rugby Sevens*, called 'a bodily contact style', a direct, aggressive brand of rugby that relied on using possession to test an opponent for weaknesses. Resembling, ironically, the very physical play of rugby league, this was the original rugby Sevens style. It would be reinvented, in devastating fashion, by New Zealand in the 1980s.

Haig's innovation soon spread across Scotland but took a while to cross the border: the first Middlesex Sevens event was held at Twickenham in 1926, organised by a London-based Scot. Like football and 15-a-side rugby, Sevens was exported across the British Empire, but the first international tournament wasn't held until 1973. In a competition between seven countries (the eighth side was a President's VII marking the centenary of Scottish Rugby Union), England beat Ireland 22–18 in the final at Murrayfield. Three years later, the first Sevens tournament was staged in HONG KONG, instigated by cigarette brand Rothmans. This proved successful enough to become an annual affair and, since 1999, the most famous event in the RUGBY SEVENS WORLD SERIES.

In 1993, when 24 nations contested the first RUGBY SEVENS WORLD CUP, England triumphed at Murrayfield, winning a trophy officially known as the MELROSE CUP. By this point, globalisation had begun to change the game, encouraging new playing styles (of which more later) and helping nations such as FIJI and KENYA to challenge rugby's traditional superpowers.

The game's seismic shift to the southern hemisphere was confirmed in 1997, in Hong Kong, when Fiji, led by the great WAISALE SEREVI, became world champions, beating South Africa 24–21, after trailing 0–14 in a final still considered one of the finest Sevens matches of all time. In 2001, in Argentina, winger JONAH LOMU, rugby's first global superstar, scored three tries in the Sevens World Cup final as the All Blacks overcame Australia. The growing global popularity of the format was underlined in 1998 when it made its debut at the Commonwealth Games and, six years later, with the successful launch of USA SEVENS in Las Vegas.

In 1997, the WOMEN'S GAME began to make its mark with its own competition at the Hong Kong Sevens. The participation of women eased the sport's way onto the Olympic programme. In 2009, after Australia won the inaugural WOMEN'S SEVENS WORLD CUP in Dubai, the sport was chosen, by a landslide vote of 81–8, for inclusion at Rio. Fittingly, Lomu and CHERYL SOON, captain of the reigning women's world champions, were in Lausanne to savour the moment. Four years later, in an event that confirmed Sevens had begun to acquire all of the accoutrements expected of a modern global sport (sponsorship, TV deals, dodgy kits), England launched what is widely regarded as the worst strip the sport has ever seen. The RFU allowed Umbro to create an acid house-influenced kit, with a Magic Eye-style motif. Sevens had become accustomed to the presence of outrageously dressed people in the stadium – but they were usually fans, not players.

THE GLORY OF LOMU

' Sevens is exactly how the game should be played – fair play, speed, skill, everything that needs to be done.' That's how Jonah Lomu – one of rugby's true legends – described this variant of his sport in 2014, only a year before his untimely death.

Lomu's commitment to Sevens went beyond mere rhetoric. He had first caught the eye at the 1994 Hong Kong Rugby Sevens tournament and

JONAH LOMU (RIGHT) LEADS HIS NEW ZEALAND SEVENS TEAM IN A VICTORY HAKA AT THE 1998 COMMONWEALTH GAMES.

in 1998 won a gold medal with New Zealand when the sport made its Commonwealth Games debut in Kuala Lumpur. In 1999, his eight tries at the 15-a-side Rugby World Cup were not enough to win the competition. But he made up for that, two years later in Argentina, in the Sevens World Cup, introducing the rap music of Tupac Shakur alongside the traditional All Blacks haka in pre-match build-ups, to lead New Zealand to victory. By his exalted standards, his contribution looks ordinary: he only scored four tries – but three of them did come in the final, against Australia.

Lomu was born to play Sevens. His unprecedented combination of pace (he once ran 100m in 10.7 seconds) and physical power (6ft 5in tall, he weighed a shade under 19 stone in his prime) enabled him to make the most of the space created by having 14 players compete on the same size pitch as 30.

The idea of players running through defences at will has become a cliché but Lomu gave a definitive example of such attacking play in the 2001 final. His first try, a 50-metre run during which opponents bounced off him without disturbing his stride, was the most spectacular. For his third, he just collected the ball in the centre of the pitch and powered towards the posts with the kind of effectiveness that prompted commentator Bill McLaren to remark: 'And there goes Jonah Lomu, proving once and for all that the shortest distance between two points is a straight line.' His performance is all the more poignant because, only a year later, a kidney disease forced him to retire from international rugby at the age of 27, and led little more than a decade later to his death.

GAME ON: RUGBY SEVENS BASICS

THE BASIC RULES OF RUGBY 7S FOLLOW THE 15-A-SIDE GAME: the object is to score tries and drop-kicks, and to do so the ball must be passed backwards by hand (it can also be kicked forward and then caught by a player who starts behind the kicker). The single most important aspect of rugby sevens is that, even though there are only seven players in each team, the pitch is the same size as for the 15-a-side game: 100m long and a maximum 70m wide. So players and teams have a lot of space to play in – and defend. To prevent exhaustion, each half lasts only seven minutes (unless it's a final, in which case they are ten minutes long) and three of the seven players can be substituted. Stamina is nonetheless tested as sides may play three or more matches in a day.

·················· SCORING: TRIES AND DROP-KICKS ··················

Points are scored when a player either runs over the opposing team's goal line and touches the ball on the ground, or kicks the ball into the goal (the space above the bar, between two tall posts). A player who 'touches down' scores a TRY, which is worth FIVE POINTS. Their side can earn another TWO POINTS if one of their players drops the ball into the air and half volleys it into the goal to score a CONVERSION. (This kick has to be taken from a spot verti-cally in line with the point where the try scorer touched the ball down.) If a player DROP-KICKS A GOAL during normal play, they score THREE POINTS. If a team is awarded a penalty for a serious foul or dangerous play, they can score three points by drop-kicking the ball into the goal.

LINE-OUTS, SCRUMS AND POSITIONS

Like the 15-a-side game, Sevens has LINEOUTS and SCRUMS (as scrummages are usually called) though they are subtly different. For certain offences – for example, a KNOCK-ON (when a player inadvertently knocks the ball forward) or a FORWARD PASS (when a player throws the ball ahead of himself to a team-mate) – the opposing team is allowed to throw the ball into a scrum, in which three players from each side lock together and try to back-heel the ball towards their team-mates. If the ball goes out of play on either side of the pitch, a LINEOUT is awarded – a throw-in in which both sides line up to jump and attempt to catch the ball before the opposition. In Sevens, unlike 15-a-side, lineouts are infrequent and usually only feature two or three players from each side.

The POSITIONS in a Sevens team will be familiar to fans of the 15-a-side game. Three of the team are, for obvious reasons, called FORWARDS – two PROPS and a HOOKER. The props are principally there to anchor their side in the scrum, provide lifting strength for team-mates who jump in the lineouts and bring their strength to bear in the rucks, as they try to drive opposing players away from a loose ball, and MAULS, in which one or more players from either side grapples with the ball carrier. The hooker is so called because it's their job to use their feet to 'hook' the ball backwards a team-mate during a scrum. They also usually take lineout throws.

The other four players are called BACKS: a SCRUM-HALF, a FLY-HALF, a CENTRE and a WING. Traditionally, in a soccer team, one player – often described as a No.10 – will be the PLAYMAKER who sets the style and tempo of play, makes goals and, when needed, scores them. In rugby, playmaking duties are shared between the scrum-half and fly-half, with the onus falling more on the latter. As the term suggests, the scrum-half's most obvious contribution is to throw the ball into the scrum. But their duties are much broader: they link the forwards and backs and decide where and how best to distribute the ball. They need to read the game so they can decide, almost instantly, whether it is best to throw a quick pass to a back or keep the ball nearer the forwards as they drive upfield. They will often pass to the fly-half, the team's creative fulcrum,

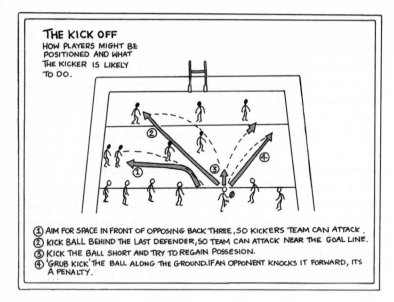

THE KICK OFF
HOW PLAYERS MIGHT BE
POSITIONED AND WHAT
THE KICKER IS LIKELY
TO DO.

① AIM FOR SPACE IN FRONT OF OPPOSING BACK THREE, SO KICKERS TEAM CAN ATTACK.
② KICK BALL BEHIND THE LAST DEFENDER, SO TEAM CAN ATTACK NEAR THE GOAL LINE.
③ KICK THE BALL SHORT AND TRY TO REGAIN POSSESION.
④ 'GRUB KICK' THE BALL ALONG THE GROUND. IF AN OPPONENT KNOCKS IT FORWARD, ITS A PENALTY.

who, in a split second, with opponents looking to press them, must calculate whether it is best to pass, run with the ball or go for a drop goal.

When their side is not in possession, the centre's job is to tackle an attacker and get the ball back. When they have won the ball, they will look to unlock defences with their speed, power and flair. The winger's job is to outrun an opponent and score a try – and make sure that no opponent outruns them to score. They need to be strong and handle the ball well but, above all, they must be fast. In Rio, America may look to CARLIN ISLES, who has run 100m in 10.24 seconds (Usain Bolt's world record time is 9.58) and is known as the fastest man in rugby. For many purists, the best example of audacious attacking wing play came in the 1990 Hong Kong Sevens final between FIJI AND NEW ZEALAND. The All-Blacks were caught out in the closing minutes by a superb one-handed overhead pass by SEREVI and, when the ball made its way to TOMASI CAMA, he sprinted two-thirds of the pitch, turning inside to leave a chasing defender in his wake, and placed the ball between the posts to win the final.

Though many players – Lomu, England's Lawrence Dallaglio and Australian scrum-half George Gregan – have proven their worth in both rugby codes, Sevens does suit a particular physique. In Sevens, scrums are not grinding heavyweight struggles so even the forwards are likely to be smaller and thinner. The backs don't tend to be as big as in the 15-a-side game either because they spend so much time running and have so much grass to cover. The division between roles is less rigid in sevens. With so few players in so much space, everyone has to tackle, ruck, run and pass.

The tempo and fluidity of Sevens has enabled countries such as FIJI, KENYA and SAMOA to compete with the established giants. As a youngster, despite his magical sidestep and immaculate ball-handling, Fijian legend Serevi was rejected by some 15-a-side clubs because he was too small, yet his unorthodox brand of rugby suited Sevens – in four World Cups, two of which he won, he accumulated 297 points. Could the openness of sevens suit the hosts in Rio?

THE FINER POINTS

STYLE COUNSEL

IN THE BEGINNING, THERE WAS ONE WAY OF PLAYING SEVENS: the robust BODILY CONTACT style, honed on the Scottish borders. The first serious challenges to this philosophy emerged in the 1960s when London Scottish developed – and Australia later adopted – what is now known as the POSSESSION STYLE, a tactic that prioritises keeping the ball so that it can be passed backwards to disturb a defence's shape. In the same decade, a dynamic, ALL-ACTION GAME emerged at Loughborough College with teams looking to run through the opposition as soon as they won the ball. This gung-ho style found particular favour in the Pacific with TONGA, SAMOA and, to a degree, FIJI.

In the 1980s, under coach BRYCE ROPE, NEW ZEALAND revolutionised the Scottish bodily contact style. He told his team: 'We will change our pattern, we will never go backwards on attack or defence.' One sign of this attacking intent was the way in which they defended, getting rid of the sweeper who covered from deep and using all seven players in the frontline, with the one furthest away from the ball charged with covering kicks. Rope thought his side's new approach had 'destroyed the game of seven-a-side rugby as it had been played for 100 years', yet many said that what was truly different about his side wasn't the tactics, but how brilliantly the players put them into practice.

Whichever style a team chooses – and many mix them up during a match depending on the circumstances – the imperative is to KEEP THE BALL. As a rule of thumb, a player with the ball is urged to be 95 per cent sure of scoring if they take a chance. In the 15-a-side game, possession is often sacrificed to gain territory so a side, for example, will kick the ball upfield and out of play in the hope of winning a lineout near their opponents' byline. In Sevens, KICKING is a last resort – unless you're converting a try or scoring a drop goal. With Sevens players having virtually twice as much space to manoeuvre in, one mistake can lead to the other side scoring within seconds. Coaches often train their teams to pass the ball away from pressure, as they try to move defences from side to side looking for an opening.

RUGBY GOES TO THE OLYMPICS

MODERN OLYMPICS FOUNDER BARON PIERRE DE COUBERTIN watched a game of 15-a-side rugby on a visit to Rugby School and declared the game 'truly the reflection of life, a lesson in experimenting in the real world, a first-rate educational tool.' He became such a fan that he refereed the first French rugby cup final in 1892, and made sure that the sport was featured in the programme for the 1900 PARIS OLYMPICS.

The inaugural event was, however, a modest affair, contested by just three countries: FRANCE, GREAT BRITAIN (represented by Moseley Wanderers) and GERMANY (then a bit of a powerhouse, represented by a team from Frankfurt). Germany and Great Britain never actually played each other, but shared silver after losing

17-27 and 8-27 respectively to France, who secured gold. One of France's players, Haitian-born winger and centre CONSTANTIN HENRIQUEZ, became the first black player to have competed at the Olympics – and the first to win a gold medal.

Rugby was a predictable absentee at ST LOUIS 1904 but returned, rather ingloriously, for LONDON 1908. With the Games held in the homeland of rugby, this should have been a vintage tournament. Unfortunately, the best English and Welsh players were in New Zealand at the time, so CORNWALL's county side, only three of whom had appeared for England, represented the host nation in another tripartite competition with France and an Australian side made up from the WALLABIES, who were touring Britain. Predictably, the Wallabies thrashed England 32-3 to win gold. Two of the Aussies would secure golds in other events: SYDNEY MIDDLETON (with Australia's rowers in 1912) and DANNY CARROLL (with the US rugby team in 1920).

Such unconvincing action persuaded the Olympic organisers to ignore rugby in 1912 but the sport returned for ANTWERP 1920, with Carroll leading a US squad drawing on players from the universities of Berkeley, Santa Clara and Stanford. However,

THE AMERICANS DEFEATING ROMANIA AT PARIS 1924 ON THEIR WAY TO FOMENTING A RIOT IN THE FINAL AGAINST FRANCE.

by the time the Americans arrived in Belgium, Czechoslovakia, Great Britain (concerned about the impact on the start of the new domestic season) and Romania had all withdrawn. This meant that the gold medal came down to one match, in which America beat France 8-0. The only notable feature of the entire tournament was that America's MORRIS KIRKSEY became one of four athletes to win golds in different sports at the same Olympics, triumphing in the rugby and the 4 × 100m relay sprint team.

The US successfully defended their title at PARIS 1924, defeating Romania before winning an ill-tempered final against favourites France 17-3. Infuriated by a tackle two minutes after kick off that left Adolphe Jauréguy unconscious, having to be stretchered off with blood pouring down his face, the home fans threw bottles and rocks at the American team and invaded the pitch at full time. Boos and hisses drowned out the Star Spangled Banner at the medal ceremony and the Americans needed police protection to get back to their dressing room. This hardly epitomised the Olympic spirit and, with so few countries competing and the British not really bothered about the sport's place at the Games, rugby was dropped from the programme for 1928.

Rugby's return was proposed by the Soviet Union (in 1980) and South Korea (1988) but World Rugby, the international ruling body, began a serious campaign to have RUGBY SEVENS included in 2000. Sevens was deemed more internationally competitive than the 15-a-side version, suited the Olympic ethos and was fast and fluid enough to be compelling on TV for the uninitiated. In 2009, after noting the sport's efforts to create more opportunities for women players, the IOC endorsed Sevens' place on the programme at RIO.

SAILING

5–21 AUGUST, 2016

MARINA DA GLÓRIA, GUANABARA

BAY, COPACABANA

Athletes: 380 | Golds up for grabs: 10

······························ **OLYMPIC PRESENCE** ······························

MEN AND WOMEN: 1900, 1908–PRESENT

······························ **OLYMPIC FORMAT** ······························

THERE ARE TEN EVENTS IN 2016, FIVE FOR MEN, FOUR FOR WOMEN and one event OPEN TO ALL. Different yacht classes are used for each. Men and women have their own events in the WIND-SURFING, LASER, 49ER CLASS and 470 CLASS. Men alone compete in the FINN CLASS. In the NACRA 17, mixed crews are compulsory.

······························ **CONTENDERS** ······························

AT LONDON 2012, AUSTRALIA WAS THE TOP SAILING NATION, winning three out of ten golds. With so many Aussies at, or near, the top of the ISAF world rankings, they will expect to do well again in Rio. For GREAT BRITAIN, BRYONY SHAW, who won bronze in windsurfing in 2008, could do even better, while in the men's 49er, two crews – DYLAN FLETCHER AND ALAIN SIGN and JOHN PINK AND STUART BITHELL (the latter a silver medallist in 2012) – have been in medal-winning form. Other countries in serious contention include NEW ZEALAND, CROATIA, DENMARK, ITALY and BRAZIL. The host nation's hopes rest on RICARDO SANTOS, the world's best windsurfer in 2015, and MARTINE SOFFIATTI GRAEL, daughter of two-time Olympic champion Torben Grael, in the women's 49er.

······························ **PAST CHAMPIONS** ······························

GREAT BRITAIN: 25 | USA: 19 | NORWAY: 17

Why Watch Sailing?

Once the preserve of aristocrats and millionaires, Olympic sailing has become a somewhat more open and democratic sport in recent decades: standardised equipment has reduced the costs of participation, and since its Olympic debut in 1900 the sport has been open to women as well as men. The sport's global reach has extended too: in 2012 fifteen nations shared the medals, with Argentina, China, Cyprus and Poland on the podium alongside such traditional powers as Australia and Great Britain. Nonetheless, sailing retains much of the élan and glamour of its high-society origins, while offering a complex and compelling spectacle, combining TACTICAL SOPHISTICATION and ATHLETICISM with the unpredictability of WIND AND WAVE. What it does not offer is a spectacular experience for those watching the event in person: although the races will be close to the shore in Rio (as they were in 2012), the best seat in the house will still be at home, watching television.

The Story of Sailing

The word yacht derives from the Dutch word *JAGHTE*, itself derived from the verb *jagen,* to hunt or pursue. In the seventeenth century, the NETHERLANDS was arguably the world's leading maritime nation, with fleets of advanced sailing ships criss-crossing the oceans for the purposes of trade and war. The Dutch spent some of their newly accumulated wealth by messing about in boats at home: the wealthy built sumptuously fitted *jaghte* for gentle cruises, parties, parades and mock battles. They did not, however, race them.

An injection of competitive spirit was introduced, predictably enough, by the BRITISH. CHARLES II was in exile in the Netherlands when the monarchy was restored in 1660, and he returned to London in a yacht gifted to him by the Prince of Orange. Charles was entranced by his new toy, as was his younger brother, the DUKE OF YORK (the future James II). Back home, each brother commissioned a version of the ship, and named it after his wife. The two vessels raced against each other in October 1661, and the British ARISTOC-RACY soon followed the royal lead, racing their yachts on rivers and down the coast, for honour, pleasure and – above all – wagers.

The first properly organised YACHT-RACING CLUB was established in London in 1815 as the Yacht Club, which, with the patronage of George IV, became the ROYAL YACHT CLUB in 1820. Six years later the Club held its first regatta at COWES on the Isle of Wight, which established itself as the premier festival in the sailing calendar.

For much of the late nineteenth and early twentieth century, the sport's most public face was racing between very large ocean-going yachts. In 1851 the Royal Yacht Squadron announced a race around the Isle of Wight, for which a silver trophy – the RYS £100 Cup – was offered as a prize. The New York schooner *America* won the race, and the cup was donated to the New York Yacht Club as 'a perpetual challenge cup'. The trophy, now known as the AMERICAS CUP, has remained the most prestigious prize in

AMERICA WINS THE RACE THAT WILL BECOME THE AMERICAS CUP, 1851

yacht racing, but SMALL-CRAFT RACING became popular in the late nineteenth century and it was this form of the sport that entered the Olympics.

Game On: Sailing Basics

COMPETITION RACING

There are two forms of sailing race: match racing and fleet racing. In match racing, two boats race head-to-head, with competitors trying to outmanoeuvre each other and force their opponents into rule violations and penalties. Fleet racing involves more than two boats, usually many more, and generally consists of more than one race. Points are awarded according to race position (the higher the position the lower the score) and are accumulated over a series of races. The boat with the lowest total wins. In Rio, all events will follow the fleet-racing format.

At the Olympics, after much tinkering and experimentation, a uniform system is now in place. The competitions begin with an opening series of fleet races (ten for the laser, 470 and Finn classes; twelve for the windsurfing, 49er and Nacra 17). The vagaries of wind and current being what they are, crews discard their worst score after this series of races. The top ten boats then enter a final medal race on a shorter course. Double points are awarded for positions in this race and these are added to the opening series scores to determine the winners. In the event of a tie, whoever finishes higher in the medal race is favoured.

Two different types of course are used: trapezoidal and wind-ward/leeward. Their precise location and orientation will depend on the prevailing patterns of wind and current on race day. The trapezoidal course has a separate start and finish line and three points around which boats must turn to complete the four-leg course. The windward return course is a two-leg affair but orientated so that the first leg is a leeward sail against the wind (called a beat) and the second leg a sail with the wind (called a run). When boats are sailing neither with nor against the wind, the leg is called a reach.

···················· **THE LAW OF THE SEA** ····································

THE RULE BOOK OF INTERNATIONAL SAILING IS LONG AND complex. A century of fearsome competition has produced a vast case history of wrangles over what constitutes a RIGHT OF WAY when two boats want to occupy the same space or path. Broadly speaking, when the boats are on OPPOSITE TACKS (angles to the wind) the onus is on the PORT-TACKING BOAT (lying to the left of the wind) to stay clear. When two boats on the SAME TACK overlap or sit side to side, the boat CLOSER TO THE WIND must stay clear of the other boat.

Sailing remains a highly self-regulated sport in which, like golf, competitors are expected to declare their mistakes and violations. If competitors think they have committed a VIOLATION they can avoid disqualification by taking a penalty (it can be points, one 360-turn or a double 720-turn). In the case of a really serious breach of the rules, boats are expected to retire. Injured parties may protest after a race to a panel of FIVE JUDGES, which can disqualify perpetrators.

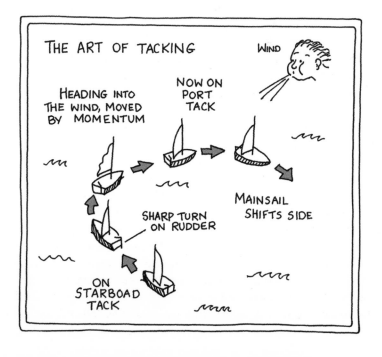

······························· **OLYMPIC SAILING CLASSES** ·······························

YACHTING USED TO BE ALL ABOUT HOW BIG A BOAT YOU could afford and how much you could spend on technology. In its survey of the 1920 Olympic competitions, *Yachting World* asked: 'Are they intended to be a test of seamanship or a test of Yachts? Or both?' While ocean-going racing retains elements of both, Olympic sailing is now focused on seamanship, as events are raced with virtually identical equipment. At Rio 2016, eight classes will be used across the ten events – a WINDSURFING BOARD, six variants on the DINGHY and, in the Nacra 17, a CATAMARAN. Dinghies have movable centreboards that can be taken up into the boats.

470 (DINGHY) *Crew: 2; Events: men and women; Olympic debut 1976. Designer: André Cornu (France).* Exactly what it says on the tin: the light and manoeuvrable 470 is 470cm long. The two crew members are usually little and large: a lightweight skipper who steers, and a heavyweight second crew member who hangs outside the boat in a trapeze to balance it on sharp turns and in high winds.

LASER (DINGHY) *Crew: 1; Events: men and women; Olympic debut 1996. Designer: Bruce Kirby (Canada).* Since making its Olympic debut in 1996, the laser has become the most popular one-person sailing boat in the world. Women will race the LASER RADIAL, which has a reduced sail area and a shorter mast, making it easier for light sailors to manage in heavy winds.

RS:X (WINDSURF BOARD) *Crew: 1; Events: men and women; Olympic debut 2008. Designer: Jean Bouldorres and Robert Stroj.* The RS:X was introduced at the 2008 Olympics, replacing the Mistral class windsurfing board. While former Olympic-class sailboards were all the classic long-board shape, the RS:X is a compromise between traditional longboards and the wider formula racing boards not used at the Olympics.

49ER (DINGHY) *Crew: 2; Events: men and women; Olympic debut 2000. Designer: Julian Bethwaite (Australia).* The 49er is the fastest craft in the Games, but speed comes at the price of instability, so both crew members need to get outside of the craft in a double trapeze to balance it. In Rio, women will compete in the 49ER FX, a revamped version designed to suit a crew weighing 120kg.

FINN (DINGHY) *Crew: 1; Events: men; Olympic debut 1952. Designer: Richard Sarby (Sweden).* In 1949 Richard Sarby, a Swedish polymath who put his hand to sailing, marine engineering and hairdressing, designed the Finn, a single-handed dinghy considered to be the purest athletic experience in sailing. Getting the best from its large sail area and heavy boom requires a lot of strength. Introduced in 1952, when Sarby won bronze in his own creation, the Finn is basically unchanged from its original design.

NACRA 17 (CATAMARAN) *Crew: 2; Events: open; Olympic debut 2016. Designer Gino Morrelli, Pete Melvin (USA).* Taking to the Olympic waves for the first time in Guanabara Bay, the Nacra-17 is a multi-hull catamaran with a distinctive wave-piercing design to help it cut through water with minimum drag and sail at high speed. This will be the only sailing event in Rio with a mixed crew.

THE FINER POINTS

ON THE START LINE

SAILING BOATS DON'T BEGIN A RACE FROM A STANDING START; they are already in motion. Timing their run to the starting line is crucial. If crews go too fast or too early and cross the line before the beginning of the race they are sent back to start all over again. However, if a crew plays it too cautiously they will start behind bolder boats, at a lower speed.

TACKING AND JIBING

TACKING IS THE MOST BASIC MANOEUVRE IN SAILING. WHEN a boat is sailing into the wind, it must chart a ZIG-ZAG COURSE in order to use the wind's energy to move it forward. Boats accomplish this by shifting the direction of the BOW (the front of the craft) and altering the position of the MAINSAIL. JIBING is a similar manoeuvre used by boats that are sailing with the wind or downwind; it involves turning the STERN (the back of the boat).

########### **KEEP AN EYE ON THE NUMBERS** ###########

In rio, every sailing event will be won on a cumulative points basis, with twice as many points awarded for the ten contestants in the final race. Keep an eye on the boats' points totals before that decisive round. A crew might only need to come in fourth or fifth to win a gold medal.

########### **LOOK OUT FOR DEAD CATS AND SOFAS** ###########

In their bid document the Rio organisers pledged to completely refit the city's awful sewage systems and clean the city's polluted water courses, beaches and bays. This has not happened. The IOC insist that the waters of Guanabara Bay (sailing), the Rodrigo de Freitas lagoon (rowing and canoeing) and Copacabana Beach (triathlon) are perfectly safe. However, sailors have encountered 'mattresses, cars, washing machines, tables, TVs, couches and chairs as well as dead dogs, horses and cats.' The Brazilian sailor Lars Grael reported finding four human corpses in the bay, while colleague Thomas Low lost a championship race after sailing into a sofa. Rio's government has claimed that a last minute sewage pipe program is going to make all the difference.

Sailing Goes to the Olympics

For its first three decades at the Games, the event – known as yachting until 1996 – was characterised by a prevalence of upper-class participants and an element of chaos, as it lacked an international sporting body, agreed rules or defined boat classes.

A sailing event was planned for the inaugural Olympics in Athens in 1896, but the weather in the Bay of Piraeus made racing impossible. Things picked up in Paris in 1900, but only marginally. There were two separate courses: on the Seine at Meulan, for smaller boats; and on the coast at Le Havre, for larger vessels. In contrast to the values of amateur sportsmanship that De Coubertin and the IOC had hoped to showcase at the Games, the sailing events were contested with considerable prize money at stake, and skulduggery duly ensued – two boats were disqualified for using means of propulsion other than sail. High society was well represented in the 1–2 Tonne class, with ÉDOUARD ALPHONSE JAMES DE ROTHSCHILD losing out to his Swiss rival, COUNT HERMANN DE POURTALÈS.

St Louis, 1500 miles inland, passed on the sport in 1904, and in 1908 LONDON outsourced the sailing to Ryde and Hunters Quay on the Clyde in Scotland. Britain monopolised the medals, as not one foreign team competed. A boat owned by CONSTANCE EDWINA CORNWALLIS WEST, Duchess of Westminster, came third in the 8m class, thus making the duchess the first woman to win a medal in sailing; how active a role she played in the event is debatable.

By 1936, when Kiel hosted the sailing events for the BERLIN GAMES, the sport had acquired standardised rules, classes and equipment, yet it hadn't lost much of its aristocratic air: CROWN PRINCE OLAF OF NORWAY (the future Olav V), who won a gold in 1928, was the first member of a royal household to compete in Olympic sailing; his son HARALD (Harald V – the current king) has competed in three Olympic regattas, and members of the SPANISH, GREEK and THAI royal families have represented their countries in the sailing events.

The dominant figure in post-war Olympic sailing was the Dane PAUL ELVSTRØM, who won gold medals at four consecutive Games, three of them in the Finn class (1948–60). Elvstrøm came out of retirement to sail with his daughter TRINE in 1984 in the Tornado class and finished fourth. Four years later, at the age of sixty, he competed in his eighth Olympics and finished fifteenth. Tenacious and skilled, he brought new levels of innovation and experiment to the design of racing boats, inventing new rigs, sails, bailers and training techniques. In 1996 he was voted 'Danish Sportsman of the Century'. Separate women's events were established in 1988, the year of Elvstrøm's last Olympic appearance.

Over the last two decades sailing has become ever more professionalised and technocratic. It has also become more internationally competitive. In 1992, on home waters, SPAIN won four gold medals. HONG KONG claimed its very first Olympic gold medal when LEE LAI SHAN won the women's windsurfing at the Atlanta Games. GAL FRIDMAN triumphed for Israel in the men's windsurfing in 2004. AUSTRIA, an entirely land-locked nation, won

TEAM GB EXPERIMENTS WITH NEW TECHNIQUE FOR
PAUL GOODISON, LASER-CLASS VICTOR IN BEIJING

two sailing gold medals in the now discontinued Tornado class.

YIN JIÀN won CHINA's first sailing gold in the women's WINDSURFING at Beijing 2008, while Brazilians ROBERT SCHEIDT, TORBEN GRAEL and MARCELO FERREIRA have four golds between them. The leading sailor of the era, though, is Britain's BEN AINSLIE. The son of a round-the-world racer, he started sailing at the age of four and began competing at ten. A silver medal at Atlanta 1996 was followed by a gold at each of the last four Games. He was Britain's only Olympic champion in the sailing events in London. The ISAF was encouraged to see the likes of Cook Island and Trinidad & Tobago entering for the first time at these Games and expect more new entrants in Rio.

As an Olympic sport, sailing is known for changing course. In Rio, there will be no keelboat events, with the women's Elliott 6m race and the men's star race absent – the latter's omission was particularly controversial as it had featured at every Games since 1932. Despite a plea from Brazilian president Dilma Rousseff to reinstate an event in which her country has traditionally excelled – Grael and Ferreira are among the past Olympic champions – the IOC axed it in favour of such events as the Nacra 17, which showcase high-performance boats. Expect more demands for the star's reinstatement ahead of Tokyo 2020.

SHOOTING

6–14 AUGUST 2016

SHOOTING CENTRE, DEODORO, RIO DE JANEIRO

Athletes: 390 | **Golds up for grabs:** 15

OLYMPIC PRESENCE

MEN'S EVENTS: 1896–PRESENT, EXCEPT 1904 AND 1928. WOMEN'S SHOOTING arrived in 1984. Up until Barcelona 1992, men and women competed together.

OLYMPIC FORMAT

THERE ARE FIVE COMPETITIONS EACH FOR RIFLE, PISTOL AND SHOTGUN. Pistol and rifle competitors shoot at small FIXED TARGETS. In shotgun events competitors shoot at CLAY PIGEONS. There are five events for both sexes (10M AIR PISTOL, 10M AIR RIFLE, 50M RIFLE THREE POSITIONS, SKEET and TRAP), four events for just men (25M RAPID FIRE PISTOL, 50M PISTOL, 50M RIFLE PRONE and DOUBLE TRAP) and one event for just women (25M PISTOL).

CONTENDERS

IN LONDON, SOUTH KOREA AND THE US WON THREE GOLDS each, with seven other countries – led by CHINA and ITALY – producing Olympic champions. China will expect to do better in Rio, especially in the men's events. The standout male shooter is South Korean JIN JONG-OH, reigning champion in – and world record holder for – the 10m air pistol and 50m pistol events. In the women's competition, look out for Iran's ELAHEH AHMADI, ranked No. 1 in the 10m air rifle event and Croatia's SNJEZANA PEJČIĆ, who has been in record-breaking form in the 50m rifle three positions event.

PAST CHAMPIONS

USA: 53 | SOVIET UNION/RUSSIA: 26 | CHINA: 21

Why Watch Shooting?

The first medal of the 2012 Games was won by a Chinese shooter, Yi Siling, who triumphed in the women's 10m air rifle, capitalising on a disappointing eighth shot by Poland's Sylwia Bogacka, to win by 502.9 points to 502.2. Yi Siling cried with relief when victory was secured. The excruciating tension of the final, with its minuscule margins of error, illustrated why shooting can be a compelling sport. The demands it places on competitors – on their skill, concentration and heart rate – are extraordinary and victory is often clinched with the mind, not the trigger finger.

It might seem unlikely that a sport that is all about intense self-absorption, static posture and micro-movements of the trigger finger could generate fervour in a live crowd or television audience, but the ISSF has made strenuous efforts to make shooting spectator-friendly. Crowds are no longer expected to maintain a rigid silence. Clay pigeons now explode in puffs of purple smoke when hit. Big screens and shoot-offs have been introduced, and tiny cameras are now placed on competitors' guns. In Rio, for the first time in the sport's Olympic history, gold and silver medals will be decided by a duel between the two best finalists.

Be patient. Imagine what is going on behind the shooter's sunglasses and blinkers. Let the competition unfold and the margins of error diminish. Enjoy the tension, for the pressure on spectators and competitors alike can be deliciously unbearable.

The Story of Shooting

Shooting as a target sport has its roots in Central Europe. There are records of arquebus competitions sponsored by the municipal authorities in Geneva as early as the 1450s. From the middle of the sixteenth century the leading edge of European rifle technology was in Switzerland and Germany where they made guns that could shoot straight over a reasonable range – a basic precondition of target shooting. Across the Alps, in Italy and France shooting competitions were held on religious holidays.

In nineteenth-century Europe – especially in SCANDINAVIA, GERMANY, FRANCE and SERBIA – shooting was fostered by gymnastic clubs, where the sport was encouraged in a spirit of nationalistic, militarised self-defence. In Switzerland, shooting became compulsory for schoolboys between the ages of sixteen and nineteen and a lifelong commitment to a citizens' army meant that shooting skills were widespread, while in France and Italy rifle skills were honed by legions of rural small-bird hunters. Meanwhile, in Britain and the USA, National Rifle Associations were established in the middle of the century with the dual intention of promoting shooting sports and raising the level of military marksmanship. In BRITAIN they signally failed in the latter task. After the South African War of 1899–1902 had exposed the disastrous state of shooting in the army's ranks, the government supported the creation of civilian rifle clubs, providing them with free ammunition and subsidising rifles for members of the NRA.

While COMPETITIVE RIFLE AND PISTOL SHOOTING evolved primarily in a military milieu the SHOTGUN as a sporting event has its roots in the hunting of birds in Britain and the United States. Shooting grouse and pheasants is a seasonal activity and in the mid-nineteenth century there emerged a niche for a sport that could simulate the game shoot without the game. Initial efforts included glass-ball shooting (as featured in Buffalo Bill's Wild West shows), in which catapults – or traps – fired glass balls stuffed with bird feathers straight up into the air. Alongside live pigeon shooting, this simulated form of hunting formed a staple of marathon competitions between professional shooters like CAPTAIN ADAM H. BOGARDUS and DOC CARVER.

However much the glass ball was refined (it was coloured, covered in ridges, filled with flour, explosives and shredded newspaper), it could not simulate the flight of a bird. Inventors experimented with pitch and concrete variants, wooden balls, tin pigeons and brass globes filled with charcoal, but all proved disappointing. In 1880 American GEORGE LIGOWSKY patented a compressed clay disc for shooting. Initially known as MUD SAUCERS, Ligowsky's targets swept the competition aside and quickly came to be known as CLAY PIGEONS. While their flight was just what was required, the early clays were almost impossible to break, and though a hit could be heard – the pigeon would ring like a bell when struck – it could only be registered once the pigeon had been found. They were superseded by more fragile targets made of limestone and pitch that fragmented on being hit. When these were combined with the new mechanised traps the sport acquired its modern technological form.

GAME ON: SHOOTING BASICS

THE ISSF IS REINVENTING SHOOTING TO MAKE IT MORE attractive to the global TV audience so the basics aren't as basic as they used to be. As of 2015, two major changes to the format of the finals had been announced for Rio: all scores will be reset to ZERO in the final round (or in some cases the semi-finals, which the ruling body counts as part of the final, and reset again when the matches to decide the medals start) and all finals will proceed on a 'DEVIL TAKE THE HINDMOST' basis in which the lowest scorers are successively eliminated until two contestants are left to SHOOT-OUT for gold. The other key difference in Rio is that the scoring systems have become more varied, sometimes confusingly so.

Traditionally in most RIFLE AND PISTOL competitions, contestants shot at a circular target divided into rings, with the centre circle worth TEN POINTS. The best eight shooters then progressed to the final round where the inner zone of the target was itself subdivided into concentric rings so scores from 10.1 to 10.9 were possible rather than just ten. Yet in Rio, in a bid to reduce the number of competitors tied on maximum scores – and make it harder for one shot to change the outcome – the ISSF has decided that the decimal format of scoring used in the final, with the target subdivided, will apply to the qualifying round for the 10m air rifle (men and women) and the 50m prone rifle (men) events. The qualifying round in the 50m 3P rifle (men and women) will still be scored in the traditional way using integers (8s, 9s, 10s).

Integers are also used in the qualifying rounds of the 10m and 50m pistol events, with the best eight proceeding to a final that is

scored decimally and ends in a shootout. The two 25m pistol events
are scored on a hit and miss basis, with contestants getting a point
if they find the target and nothing if they don't.

SHOTGUN EVENTS use a similar format as the 25m pistol events
but competitors are shooting at flying targets released from traps,
which is an either-or business. Each shot scores either a hit or a
miss. The guns are double-barrelled and fire sprays of pellets. In
these events, only six athletes progress from the first round.

You can see the ISSF's logic – the individual finals should be
easier to follow and more enthralling, with each contestant starting
from zero and a golden duel at the finale – but the variety of scoring
systems and differing routes to the final may leave the casual
spectator a bit bemused.

RIFLE

50M THREE POSITIONS

IN THE MEN'S EVENT THE COMPETITORS FIRE FORTY SHOTS IN A
limited time in each of the three positions: PRONE, STANDING AND
KNEELING in the qualifying round (in the women's event competitors take twenty shots in each position). In both competitions, the
top eight go into the final which, in Rio, will be considerably
tougher than it was in 2012, when each contestant fired ten shots
while standing. At the 2016 Games, they have up to 45 shots at the
target, all scored decimally. All the finalists shoot three series of five
shots in each of the kneeling and the prone positions and two series
of five shots while standing. At this point, the two athletes with the
lowest cumulative score are eliminated. There are five more single
shots with the worst performer eliminated after each one until two
athletes are left to duel for gold and silver on the 45th shot. The
target they are aiming at is just over 15cm in diameter and the ten-
point ring at the centre a minuscule 1.4cm across.

50M PRONE

A MEN'S EVENT IN WHICH SIXTY SHOTS ARE FIRED IN THE
qualifying round and up to twenty in the final. Again, the top eight
proceed to the final. This time, the elimination process kicks in

after the eighth shot until the last two left shooting contest gold and silver.

10M AIR RIFLE

MEN SHOOT SIXTY TIMES IN THE OPENING ROUND; WOMEN FORTY TIMES and, in both cases, the top eight contest the final which follows the format of the 50m prone competition. The target for this event is even smaller, just 4.5 cm in diameter with a bullseye of 0.5cm diameter. That is really very small – smaller than a 5p piece!

PISTOL

50M PISTOL

A MEN'S EVENT IN WHICH SHOOTERS HAVE 120 MINUTES TO fire sixty shots at a target that's 5cm across and 50m away. The top eight then qualify for a twenty-shot final, with the usual elimination process culminating in a duel for gold.

25M RAPID FIRE

A MEN'S EVENT IN WHICH SHOOTERS FIRE SIX ROUNDS OF five shots, within time limits (4, 6 or 8 seconds). There are five different targets, slightly larger than those used in free pistol shooting. In this event, as in the women's 25m, contestants score one for a hit and nothing for a miss. The best six then progress to the semifinals where, after the fourth series of five shots, the lowest scorer is knocked out. The elimination process continues after every series of shots until two contestants are left to dispute gold.

25M PISTOL

A WOMEN'S EVENT THAT COMBINES FREE AND RAPID FIRE shooting. The qualification round consists of thirty free shots and thirty rapid fire shots. The final round is just rapid fire. Just to ensure spectators are alert, the competition format is slightly different here: the eight best go through to the semi-finals but this time, the top two from the first round contest gold, third and fourth compete for bronze, and the others vie for fifth to eighth. The medals are decided on a similar basis to match-play golf: after every series of five shots, two points are awarded to the athlete with the most hits; if they have the same number, they get one point each. The first athlete to notch up seven points wins. If they reach the magic number in the same series, they keep firing until one of them wins a series.

10M AIR PISTOL

MEN HAVE 105 MINUTES TO FIRE SIXTY SHOTS, WOMEN 75 MINUTES for forty. Here too, the top eight in each competition progress to a final round of up to twenty shots with the lowest scoring athletes dropping out until only two are left.

SHOTGUN

TRAP

COMPETITORS MOVE ROUND FIVE SHOOTING STATIONS, taking two shots at a single target at each. MEN shoot five circuits (25 targets), WOMEN three (15 targets). The top six progress to a semi-final round with the bottom two eliminated, third and fourth playing off for bronze and the two best competing for gold and silver. In both the semi-finals and the medal matches, contestants only get one pop at each of their fifteen targets.

SKEET

COMPETITORS MOVE ROUND EIGHT SHOOTING STATIONS AND take it in turn to fire at two targets, one thrown from a high position and one from a low position, with a random gap of zero to three seconds between their release. The first target mimics an oncoming bird approaching swiftly overhead, while the path of the second approximates to the flight of a grouse launching itself from the heather. The top six progress from the qualifying round with the medals decided in similar fashion as in the trap event. At London 2012, KIM RHODE made history: by winning the women's event, she became the first American to win a medal in five successive Olympics.

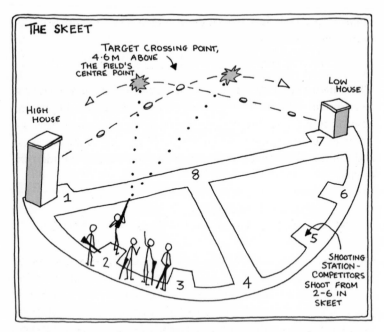

THE SKEET

TARGET CROSSING POINT,
4·6M ABOVE
THE FIELD'S
CENTRE POINT

LOW HOUSE

HIGH HOUSE

7

8

1

6

5

2

3

4

SHOOTING STATION –
COMPETITORS
SHOOT FROM
2–6 IN
SKEET

DOUBLE TRAP

Only men contest this event; the women's version was dropped from the Olympic programme after 2004. Shooters fire one shot at each of two targets released simultaneously on set paths. They rotate through five shooting stations, firing thirty shots from each. The six best shooters enter the semi-finals where they have thirty shots to qualify for the medal matches and secure gold, silver or bronze.

The Finer Points

WHAT TO WATCH

One of the best events for spectators is the shotgun, in which you get a nice swing of the arm as the shooters track the clays out of the traps and pleasing puffs of purple smoke when the targets shatter. The rapid fire pistol competitions have a manic intensity, particularly the rounds in which shooters are firing at more than one target.

·························· **SHOOTING'S NEW DRESS CODE** ··························

CLOTHING HAS BECOME A CONTENTIOUS ISSUE IN SHOOTING. Because thick apparel might offer some additional support or absorb more recoil than thinner material, the authorities have introduced stringent and unbelievably detailed rules on the thickness and stiffness of competitors' clothing – and that includes undergarments.

SHOOTING GOES TO THE OLYMPICS

SHOOTING APPEARED AT THE INAUGURAL MODERN GAMES IN 1896 with five events, and it proved to be enormously popular: the 200m army rifle attracted one hundred and sixty contestants, under the personal supervision of the Greek CROWN PRINCE NICHOLAS. Two brothers from Harvard, JOHN and SUMNER PAINE, whose weapons were far superior to those of their opponents, dominated the pistol shooting. John won the Military Pistol and Sumner took the silver, while John fraternally withdrew from the free pistol competition leaving the field clear for Sumner to bag the gold. It saved his bacon. In 1901 Sumner was charged with assault after firing four shots at his daughter's music teacher who he had found at home with his wife in a compromising position. The case was dropped when it was argued that his marksmanship would have allowed him to hit the music teacher with ease had be really wanted to.

LIVE PIGEON SHOOTING came and went with the PARIS OLYMPICS of 1900: nearly three hundred pigeons were killed in the course of the event, leaving blood and feathers all over the participants, officials and spectators. Thankfully, such slaughter is no longer a feature of the Olympics. Rather more regretfully, the DUELLING PISTOL competition – in which the targets were mannequins dressed in frock coats, with bullseyes on the throat – made its last appearance in 1912.

A YOUTHFUL OSCAR SWAHN (BEARDED) AT STOCKHOLM 1912, EIGHT YEARS BEFORE BECOMING THE OLDEST EVER OLYMPIC MEDALLIST

Shooting was absent from the 1904 Games, having been displaced by archery, but it returned at LONDON 1908 with a vengeance: more than two hundred competitors took part in fifteen events, with TRAP SHOOTING included for the first time. The sport has been a feature of every Games bar 1928, when the IOC decided to get strict about its AMATEURISM rules – most leading shooters of the time were winning prize money in tournaments.

Because shooting requires mental and physical composure rather than athleticism, its list of Olympic champions is rather more diverse than that of other sports. At ANTWERP 1920 the Swede OSCAR SWAHN, a gold medallist at the two previous Olympics, won a team silver in the RUNNING DEER contest and at the age of 72 became the Olympics' OLDEST MEDALLIST. (The deer, by the way, were moving targets made of cardboard; the event has, alas, been lost from the Olympic programme.) At the other end of the scale, at ATLANTA in 1996 KIM RHODE became the youngest shooting medallist when she won the double trap at the age of seventeen.

In 1924 LT SIDNEY HINDS helped the USA to the gold in the team rifle with a perfect score that was achieved after he had been wounded by an accidental discharge. Even more remarkable was the Hungarian KÁROLY TAKÁCS. By the mid–1930s he had become a top-class pistol shooter, but he was unable to compete in the 1936 Berlin Games because the event was open only to commissioned officers and he was a mere sergeant. Worse, in 1938 his right hand was maimed in a grenade accident. Undaunted, he learnt to shoot with his left hand, and went on to take gold in the rapid fire pistol competition in 1948 and 1952. French world champion FRANCK DUMOULIN showed similar pluck: he broke his arm in a motorcycle accident in 1999 but came back to win gold in the 10m air pistol in 2000.

Athens 2004 provided Olympic shooting's first love match. Czech shooter KATERINA KURKOVÁ, who won a bronze in the 10m air rifle, became romantically linked to American shooter MATTHEW EMMONS. Emmons provided the Games' big hard-luck story. Leading in the men's 50m rifle, triple position, he hit the bullseye with his last shot but had fired across the shooting lanes into an opponent's target; he scored zero for that shot, and so lost out on a medal. The pair married in 2007 and both returned to the Beijing Games in 2008. Kurková (now Emmons) won the first gold

'I DID WHAT?' – MATTHEW EMMONS LEARNS HE'S SHOT THE WRONG TARGET AT ATHENS 2004

medal of the Games. Matthew once again lost a winning position on the last shot and ended up with silver.

The silver and bronze medallists in the WOMEN'S AIR PISTOL in Beijing were Russia's NATALIA PODERINA and Georgia's NINO SALUKVADZE, who embraced on the podium and called for their warring nations to desist. At the same Games, 61-year-old Latvian shooter AFANASIJS KUZMINS became the first athlete to appear in eight Olympics, while ABHINAV BINDRA won India's first-ever individual gold medal in the 10m air rifle; the nation rewarded him with heaps of cash and a lifetime pass on Indian railways. In a final narrative twist, North Korean shooter KIM JONG-SU, who had won silver in the men's 50m pistol and a bronze in the 10m air pistol, was stripped of his medals after testing positive for the beta-blocker propranolol.

At LONDON 2012, Malaysian shooter Nur Suryani Mohamed Tabi became the first Olympian to compete while eight months pregnant. (She finished 34th.) Nine nations shared the gold medals including GREAT BRITAIN: farmer Peter Wilson, who had taken up shooting on his father's advice because he couldn't play squash or cricket after a snowboarding accident, won the double trap. Two years later, at the relatively young age (for a shooter) of twenty-eight, he announced his retirement.

SWIMMING

6–16 AUGUST 2016

OLYMPIC AQUATICS STADIUM, BARRA DA TIJUCA, RIO DE JANEIRO (Pool events)

FORT COPACABANA, RIO (Open water Marathon)

Athletes: 950 | Golds up for grabs: 34

OLYMPIC PRESENCE

MEN, 1896–PRESENT; WOMEN, 1912–PRESENT

OLYMPIC FORMAT

MEN AND WOMEN BOTH CONTEST FOURTEEN INDIVIDUAL races and three team relay races.

CONTENDERS

AMERICA WON SIXTEEN GOLD MEDALS AT LONDON 2012; CHINA, their nearest challenger, picked up just five. AUSTRALIA'S meagre haul of one gold was regarded as a national scandal – an official review blamed a 'toxic culture' within the squad – and they will be keen to make amends in Rio. Great Britain, who also disappointed in 2012, will look to ADAM PEATY (50m and 100m breaststroke) and JAMES GUY (200m freestyle), who won their events at the 2015 FINA World Championships. China has grown stronger since 2012, with SUN YANG favoured to retain his titles in the 400m and 1500m freestyle, but expect strong challenges from FRANCE and RUSSIA. Brazil's brightest prospects are ETIENNE MEDEIROS (women's 50m backstroke) and THIAGO PEREIRA (silver medallist in the 400m individual medley in 2012).

PAST CHAMPIONS

USA: 230 | AUSTRALIA: 57 | EAST GERMANY: 38

Why Watch Swimming?

Swimming is an elemental and sensual experience familiar to almost every culture. Swimming and ceremonial bathing were celebrated in the art of ancient Egypt and Assyria, and inscribed in the military training manuals of the Romans, the Japanese samurai and the knights of medieval Europe. In classical Greece, where races were held in honour of the god Dionysius, swimming was held to be on a par with literacy – indeed, the fundamentals of education were 'the alphabet and swimming'.

In its modern super-conditioned and competitive forms, swimming is a rather different beast, demanding of its athletes immense cardiovascular reserves and muscular power combined with supple grace and perfect technique. A top-class swimmer has to master the art of extreme but relaxed effort – if you start fighting the water, speed and power are lost. As the great American coach Bill Bachrach once remarked, 'you can't do anything violently or suddenly in water; it even takes time for a stone to sink.'

The Story of Swimming

With the self-assurance characteristic of the age, a Victorian treatise on swimming opened: 'There is no instance of any foreigner, civilised or uncivilised, whose achievements in the water surpass those of the British.' The modern craze for swimming began in Georgian England, when the aristocracy discovered the benefits and pleasures of sea bathing. Once public swimming had become acceptable, it wasn't long before races were being held on the Thames, off the Kent coast and across Portsmouth harbour. A small circuit of professional swimmers, known as 'the professors', found an audience for feats of endurance, exhibitions of diving stunts, fancy swimming, and races in lakes, rivers and ponds.

In 1828 the world's first MUNICIPAL SWIMMING POOL opened in Liverpool. Although private pools had already existed in Britain for fifty years, the municipal version was to provide the sport's infrastructural backbone; a spine greatly stiffened by the passage of the

1846 Baths and Washhouses Act. This law was designed to improve urban hygiene by encouraging local authorities to build laundries and bathhouses for the poor. Large plunge pools – the most economical way of cleansing the masses – provided space for swimming as well as washing. Those of a more refined sensibility could use the first-class pools, in which the water was changed more regularly.

Britain's NATIONAL SWIMMING SOCIETY, formed in 1837, organised races in the Serpentine and embarked on a programme of instruction. Its successors tried to bring more organisation and order to the sport, and the rule book established by the BRITISH AMATEUR SWIMMING ASSOCIATION (founded 1869) defined the principles on which international and Olympic swimming are still based today.

While competitive swimming took off in Europe's elite ATHLETIC CLUBS AND SCHOOLS from the mid-nineteenth century, the popular expansion of the sport occurred in the 1880s. Pools became widespread and water quality improved. In 1875 CAPTAIN MATTHEW WEBB became the first man to swim the English Channel, becoming a global celebrity and lending swimming an aura of heroic manliness. Thirty years later, the Australian film star ANNETTE KELLERMAN's (unsuccessful) attempts to do the same helped bring women into the swimming mainstream and ensure that it became the FIRST REGULAR WOMEN'S SPORT at the Olympics.

GAME ON: SWIMMING BASICS

FOR FREESTYLE THERE ARE FIVE RACES – 50M, 100M, 200M, 400M and 1500M (800M for women). The other strokes are raced over 100M and 200M, apart from the individual medley (200M and 400M). In 2008, the 10KM MARATHON was introduced. Swum in open water, the 2016 competition will be held against the world famous backdrop of Copacabana beach.

···················· **BREASTSTROKE** ····················

BREASTSTROKE IS A TWO-PART STROKE: A FROG-LIKE KICK OF the legs is followed by an arm movement sweeping the water behind the swimmer. The oldest of the four racing strokes, it was

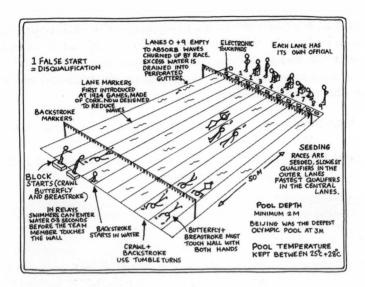

often depicted and described in ancient art and literature, and was practised with the swimmer's head out of the water. Over the years swimmers have increased their speed by keeping the HEAD SUBMERGED as much as possible.

At the 1956 Olympics, Japanese gold medallist MASARU FURU-KAWA swam entire lengths without surfacing. While this raised speeds it also led to oxygen deprivation and health concerns. Under modern rules, the head must break the surface on every full stroke, although the swimmer is allowed just one stroke underwater after turning.

100M BREASTSTROKE | MEN: 58.46, CAMERON VAN DER BURGH (SOUTH AFRICA) LONDON 2012. WOMEN: 1:05.17, LEISEL JONES (AUSTRALIA) BEIJING 2008.

200M BREASTSTROKE | MEN: 2:07.28, DÁNIEL GYURTA (HUNGARY) LONDON 2012. WOMEN: 2: 19.59, REBECCA SONI (USA) LONDON 2012.

··· **BUTTERFLY** ···

IN THE 1930s AMERICAN BREASTSTROKE SWIMMERS AT THE University of Iowa began to experiment with a new action in which the arms were brought through the air together, over the head and into the water, rather than being pushed through the water. This was combined with a newly invented dolphin or fin-tail kick. First seen at the 1936 Olympics, the butterfly stroke proved faster than traditional breaststroke within two years, and in 1952 it was codified as a separate event, making its full Olympic debut in Melbourne four years later.

100M BUTTERFLY | MEN: 50.58 MICHAEL PHELPS (USA) BEIJING 2008. WOMEN: 55.98 DANA VOLLMER (USA) LONDON 2012.
200M BUTTERFLY | MEN: 1:52.03, MICHAEL PHELPS (USA) BEIJING 2008. WOMEN: 2:04.06, JIAO LIUYANG (CHINA) LONDON 2012.

MARK SPITZ OVERCOMING 'TACHE DRAG' IN THE 200M BUTTERFLY, MUNICH 1972

BACKSTROKE

BACKSTROKE BEGAN LIFE AS A GENTEEL AFFAIR, WITH BOTH hands brought up and over the head simultaneously and then pulled through the water to propel the swimmer. But at the 1912 Olympics American backstroker HARRY HEBNER powered the competition aside with the straight-armed, alternate arm stroke that is still used today.

In the 1930s Australian swimmers figured out that a BENT ARM under water was better than a straight arm. At the 1988 Seoul

Games the Japanese swimmer DIACHI SUZUKI and the American DAVID 'BLAST-OFF' BERKOFF blew their competition away in the 100m event away by swimming up to 30m under water using a butterfly kick. The technique was promptly banned. Today, underwater backstroke swimming is restricted to 15m after turning.

100M BACKSTROKE | MEN: 52.16, MATT GREVERS (USA) LONDON 2012.
WOMEN: 58.77, KIRSTY COVENTRY (ZIMBABWE) BEIJING 2008.
200M BACKSTROKE | MEN: 1:53.41, TYLER CLARY (USA) LONDON 2012.
WOMEN: 2:04.06, MISSY FRANKLIN (USA) LONDON 2012.

FREESTYLE (CRAWL)

ANY KIND OF STROKE IS ALLOWED IN FREESTYLE RACES – you could use sidestroke or doggy paddle if you wanted – but everyone uses FRONT CRAWL because it is the fastest. As with backstroke, 15m of underwater swimming is allowed per length in Olympic freestyle racing.

Widely practised in the PACIFIC and SOUTH AMERICA, it was first seen in Britain in 1848 when an ex-army officer and impresario called Arthur Rankin brought a troupe of OJIBWA INDIANS to London. In Holborn Baths two of their number – THE FLYING GULL and TOBACCO – took on one of the London swimming 'Professors', a Mr Harold Kenworthy. After giving a long display in the water, in which *The Times* saw them 'lash the water violently with their arms like the sails of a windmill', the Americans were soundly beaten by the fresher Kenworthy, doing the breaststroke. Disconcerted by the inelegance of the crawl, the British persisted with breaststroke, and it fell to the Americans to modernise the technique. CHARLES DANIELS, American gold medallist at the 1904 Games, was an early exemplar, and at the 1912 Olympics the Hawaiian swimmer DUKE KAHANAMOKU, gold medallist in the 100m freestyle, introduced the world to the six-kicks-a-cycle technique, in which the kick starts from the hips, producing more power.

50M FREESTYLE | MEN: 21.30, CESAR CIELO FILHO (BRAZIL) BEIJING 2008.
WOMEN: 24.05, RANOMI KROMOWIDJOJO (NETHERLANDS)
LONDON 2012.

100M FREESTYLE | MEN: 47.05, EAMON SULLIVAN (AUSTRALIA) BEIJING 2008. WOMEN: 53.00, RANOMI KROMOWIDJOJO (NETHERLANDS) LONDON 2012.

200M FREESTYLE | MEN: 1:42.96, MICHAEL PHELPS (USA) BEIJING 2008. WOMEN: 1:53.61, ALISON SCHMITT (USA) LONDON 2012.

400M FREESTYLE | MEN: 3:40.14, SUN YANG (CHINA) LONDON 2012. WOMEN: 4:01.45, CAMILLE MUFFAT (FRANCE) LONDON 2012.

800M FREESTYLE | WOMEN: 8:14.10, REBECCA ADDLINGTON (GREAT BRITAIN) BEIJING 2008.

1500M FREESTYLE | MEN: 14:31.02, SUN YANG (CHINA) LONDON 2012.

-------------------------------------- **MEDLEYS & RELAYS** --------------------------------------

THERE ARE TWO INDIVIDUAL MEDLEY EVENTS, THE 200M AND 400m, in which each swimmer must swim four sequences of 50m or 100m in the following order: BUTTERFLY, BACKSTROKE, BREAST-STROKE and FREESTYLE.

Finally, there are the TEAM RELAY RACES in which swimmers take it in turns to compete. These races are the 4 × 100M FREESTYLE, the 4 × 200M FREESTYLE and the 4 × 100M MEDLEY, in which each of the four members of the team swims a different stroke in the same order as the individual medley.

200M INDIVIDUAL MEDLEY | MEN: 1:54.23, MICHAEL PHELPS (USA) BEIJING 2008. WOMEN: 2:07.57, YE SHIWEN (CHINA) LONDON 2012.

400M INDIVIDUAL MEDLEY | MEN: 4:03.84, MICHAEL PHELPS (USA) BEIJING 2008. WOMEN: 4:28.43, YE SHIWEN (CHINA) LONDON 2012.

4 × 100M FREESTYLE RELAY | MEN: 3:08.24, USA, BEIJING 2008. WOMEN: 3:33.15, AUSTRALIA, LONDON 2012.

4 × 200M FREESTYLE RELAY | MEN: 6:58.56, USA, BEIJING 2008. WOMEN: 7:42.92, USA, LONDON 2012.

4 × 100M MEDLEY RELAY MEN: 3:29.34, USA, BEIJING 2008. WOMEN: 3:52.05, USA, LONDON 2012.

-------------------------------------- **MARATHON SWIMMING** --------------------------------------

INTRODUCED AT BEIJING 2008 FOR MEN AND WOMEN, THE 10km marathon race for men and women harks back to the sport's roots and the exploits of Captain Webb, conqueror of the

English Channel. Twenty-five swimmers race over a 10km open water course, normally using the FRONT CRAWL, in a race that tests strength, strategy and endurance. The inaugural winner of the men's event, Dutch swimmer Maarten van der Weiden recovered from leukemia to triumph in Beijing. This is the one Olympic swimming competition where coaches can play a key part during the race – they have four opportunities to dispense drinks and advice to their swimmers during the race. Four years later in the Serpentine in Hyde Park, Tunisia's OUSSAMA MELLOULI, the 1500m freestyle Olympic champion in Beijing, won the men's marathon, even though it was only his third race in the event. Underlining how gruelling the course can be, two swimmers in the women's race couldn't complete the course and received medical attention.

10KM MARATHON RUN | MEN: 1:49:55.1, OUSSAMA MELLOULI (TUNISIA) LONDON 2012. WOMEN: 1:57:38.2, ÉVA RISZTOV (HUNGARY) LONDON 2012.

THE FINER POINTS

SUITED AND BOOTED

IN RECENT YEARS, OLYMPIC AND WORLD SWIMMING RECORDS have fallen like nine pins. Twenty-five world record times were set at BEIJING 2008 and twenty more at London 2012.

While technique, nutrition and training have undoubtedly played a part in this, the consensus was that NEW BODY SUITS and POOL TECHNOLOGIES had introduced a step change into the sport. The all-body polyurethane suits – which can change a swimmer's body shape and seriously REDUCE DRAG – proved so controversial that FINA (the sport's governing body) banned them in 2010. At London 2012, only six records were broken in the men's events – but it is hard to know if this reflected the change in swimsuit technology.

A Brief History of Swimming Kit

PRE-NINETEENTH CENTURY Medieval knights and samurai warriors had to learn to paddle in their armour, but the BIRTHDAY SUIT was the kit of choice for most swimmers.

EARLY TWENTIETH CENTURY Knitted WOOLLEN ONE-PIECE SUITS were the norm. They preserved modesty but were incredibly heavy and hard to swim in.

1924 SILK SUITS make their debut at the Paris Olympics.

1956 Men's NYLON SWIM BRIEFS arrive at Melbourne. The Australian men are the first known Olympic competitors to shave their bodies. This has a minor impact on drag, but the innovation gave them a psychological edge – they won eight out of 13 golds.

1976 At Montreal swimmers use GOGGLES for the first time. Persian divers had been using tortoiseshell examples three thousand years earlier. The first modern version of goggles was created in the 1930s by Guy Gilpatrick, who tried to waterproof a pair of aviator goggles with window putty.

PANTS OF POWER: GERMANY'S EMIL RAUSCH, DOUBLE GOLD MEDALLIST AT ST LOUIS 1904

1980s NYLON/LYCRA becomes the material of choice. Men's long trunks (or JAMMERS) are introduced.

2004 All-in-one BODY SUITS make their Olympic debut at the Athens Games.

2010 FINA bans polyurethane body suits.

SWIMMING SPRINTS REQUIRE EXPLOSIVE STARTS, ABSOLUTE concentration and almost flat-out effort for much of the race. The longer events are tactically more complex: some competitors like to lead from the front, others prefer to conserve energy and reel in the front runners.

The MEDLEYS, where each swimmer will be stronger at certain strokes than others, are often more eventful than single-stroke disciplines, as competitors can build and lose large leads.

In all these disciplines the smoothness and speed of TURNS are crucial – and watch how much power and speed a swimmer can get into the UNDERWATER GLIDES AND STROKES permitted at the beginning of each length.

SWIMMING GOES TO THE OLYMPICS

THEY WANTED A POOL BUT MONEY WAS TIGHT, SO THE ORGANISERS of the first modern Olympics held four races in the frigid waters of the BAY OF ZEA, south of Athens. 20,000 spectators saw Hungarian ALFRED HAJÓS, whose father had drowned in the Danube when he was a child, win two gold medals. It sounded tough out there. Hajós remembered, 'The icy water almost cut into our stomachs ... My will to live completely overcame my desire to win. I cut through the water with a powerful determination and only became calm when the boats came back in my direction and began to fish out the numbed competitors who were giving up the struggle.'

The murky waters of the RIVER SEINE provided the setting for two brilliant but one-off races at PARIS 1900. In the UNDERWATER RACE contestants swam submerged for up to 60m, and were awarded two points for each metre swum, and one point for each second that they stayed under water. Frenchman CHARLES DEVENDEVILLE took the gold. Curiously the Danish bronze medallist PEDER LYKKEBERG actually swam for nearly thirty seconds longer than Devendeville, but did not travel as far, as he went in a circle. Meantime, in the AQUATIC OBSTACLE RACE, competitors had to climb a pole, scramble over a row of boats and then swim (against the river's currents) under a second row of boats. The winner, FREDERICK LANE of Australia, received a 50-pound bronze horse instead of a gold medal. In the more conventional events, the star of the Games was Great Britain's JOHN JARVIS. Described as 'fat all over … his breasts fall like a woman's, but he has powerful shoulders and tremendous thighs', he won the 1000m and 4000m freestyle events.

In the bacteria-infested boating lake of the ST LOUIS GAMES of 1904, the 50-yard freestyle race came down to a contest between the American J. SCOTT LEARY and the Hungarian ZOLTÁN HAMAY. Hamay appeared to lead from start to finish, but American judges stationed some distance from the finishing line claimed that he'd stopped swimming short of the line. Leary then got out of the water and complained that the Hungarian had obstructed him. The debate degenerated into a brawl involving athletes and officials, and was only resolved by all parties agreeing to a swim-off. After two nervy false starts, Hamay won his gold.

The 1908 London Games saw the first tailor-made OLYMPIC POOL, which was 100 yards long and placed inside the athletics track in the White City Stadium. It was the first and last Games at which Britain topped the swimming medals table. At Stockholm in 1912, women made their debut in the Olympic pool. SARAH 'FANNY' DURACK won a gold for Australia, while the British women won the relay. The Austrian team, which won the relay bronze, was entirely JEWISH. In Vienna, and all over Central Europe, swimming had become a defining feature of a modern, muscular *mitteleuropa* Judaism, countering the stereotypes of the unathletic Jew who was too timid to get in the water.

In the inter-war years, AMERICAN SWIMMING began its rise to global domination, driven by a combination of well-funded university programmes and a craze for all forms of aquatic sports and entertainments in the beach metropolis of Southern California. The swimming star of the 1920 Antwerp Games was the Hawaiian DUKE KAHANAMOKU, best known for his pioneering role in the development of surfing. At Antwerp he added to the gold and silver he had won in Stockholm in 1912 with two golds, powered by his innovative freestyle flutter kick. He took silver at the 1924 Paris Games before launching into parallel careers as surfer, Hollywood actor and sheriff of Honolulu. He lost out in Paris to JOHNNY WEISSMULLER who won three titles that year and a further two in Amsterdam 1928, before himself heading off to Hollywood.

The next swimming powerhouse was JAPAN. The Japanese had first competed in Olympic swimming in 1920, disastrously; schooled in the nineteenth-century tradition of SAMURAI SWIMMING, they were utterly uncompetitive. After a furious reaction at home, the modernisers prevailed, with pioneering photographic stroke-analysis combined with the iron discipline of the warrior life at the Lake Hamman training complex.

By 1932 the Japanese were ready: they won five out of the six men's events and all three medals in the 100m backstroke. Their coach argued that there was something more than technique at work: 'our swimmers are imbued with the national spirit … and what superiority we have can be attributed to this'. At Berlin the men won another three medals and HIDEKO MAEHATA, in the 200m breaststroke, became the first Japanese woman to win a swimming gold. Japan was excluded from the first post-war Games in 1948, which meant that the great HIRONOSHIN FURUHASHI – the fastest swimmer on the planet – was unable to compete.

HOLLYWOOD'S OLYMPIC TARZANS

Many actors have played Edgar Rice Burroughs' 'King of the Jungle' on TV and in the cinema, but in the classic black-and-white era Tarzan was defined by four American Olympians, two of them swimmers.

JOHNNY WEISSMULLER, who won five swimming gold medals in 1924 and 1928, got his break as Tarzan in 1932 and kept the part until 1948. As well as his Tarzan water dives, he invented the ululations that defined the movie version of the character. He had no illusions about the quality of his performances on screen, saying: 'The public forgive my acting because they know I was an athlete.Æ

BUSTER CRABBE, who won a swimming bronze medal in 1928 and a gold in 1932, was cast as Tarzan in 1933 by a competing studio. A twelve-movie run was planned but Crabbe jumped ship and is now best known for playing Flash Gordon and Buck Rogers.

HERMANN BRIX, silver medallist in the shot put in 1928, was selected to play Tarzan but broke his shoulder and lost the gig to Weissmuller. He got a second chance in 1935, cast in *The New Adventures of Tarzan*, from which a second film – *Tarzan and the Green Goddess* – was spun off in 1938. He then changed his name to Bruce Bennett and played character parts for a couple of decades.

GLENN MORRIS, who took gold in the decathlon in 1932, made *Tarzan's Revenge* in 1938 with another Olympian swimmer Eleanor Holm effectively cast in the Jane role. Morris's acting was rightly lambasted

THE RACING DIVE WAS NEVER HIS STRONG SUIT: OLYMPIC CHAMPION JOHNNY WEISSMULLER IN *TARZAN FINDS A SON* (1939)

and, after an injury-shortened career with the NFL's Detroit Lions, he moved into selling insurance; he later fought in the Pacific and, as a result, suffered from post-traumatic stress disorder.

After their annihilation in the men's events in 1932, the Americans improved at Berlin 1936. Their medal haul would have been even greater if ELEANOR HOLM, the reigning Olympic champion in the 100m backstroke, had not been kicked out of the squad for drunken misbehaviour during the Atlantic crossing. After the war, the USA swept everyone aside, winning eight out of eleven gold medals in 1948, and ten out of twelve in 1952. A rare non-US champion was the Frenchman JEAN BOITEAUX, whose victory in the 400m freestyle in Helsinki prompted his overwrought father to leap into the pool fully clothed.

Throughout the 1950s, 1960s and early 1970s America ruled the swimming world, challenged occasionally by Australia. MARK SPITZ's seven golds at the Munich Olympics was both a personal triumph and a measure of American supremacy. In the 1970s, EAST

GERMANY became a force to be reckoned with, accumulating 38 golds in just two drug-fuelled decades of top-level competition. The women's team was particularly strong: in Montreal in 1976 KORNELIA ENDER won four gold medals, while in Seoul twelve years later KIRSTIN OTTO won six gold medals.

Since the demise of European communism, the USA has resumed its place as the most powerful presence in swimming, albeit with consistent challenges from AUSTRALIA, CHINA and the NETHERLANDS – and, despite a disappointing medal haul in 2012, a significantly improved BRITISH team. The US just keeps discovering swimmers as great as – or greater than – Spitz. In 2008, MICHAEL PHELPS went one better than his illustrious compatriot, winning eight golds. He won four more at London 2012 although this feat was slightly overshadowed by his 17-year-old compatriot MISSY FRANKLIN who dominated the women's events, winning four gold medals, and a bronze and breaking the Olympic record in the 200m backstroke.

GOLDRUSH: 10 GREAT OLYMPIC SWIMMERS

TEN OF THE GREATS – IN ORDER OF APPEARANCE.

I. CHARLES DANIELS, USA (Gold 5, Silver 1, Bronze 2)
The leading swimmer of his era, Daniels was a well-heeled banker who loved to swim and was pretty damn good at golf, too. He went to three consecutive Games – 1904, 1906, 1908 – and won gold medals at all of them, having been the first Olympic swimmer to perfect the powerful six-beat kick.

2. DAWN FRASER, Australia (Gold 4, Silver 4)
Fraser, too, won golds at three consecutive Games (1956, 1960 and 1964) and was the first woman to go under one minute in the 100m freestyle. Her career was cut short after she stole an Olympic flag from outside the emperor's palace at the 1964 Tokyo Games. The emperor forgave her – and gave her the flag – but the Australian swimming authorities froze her out.

3. MARK SPITZ, USA (Gold 9, Silver 1, Bronze 1)

A rising star at Mexico 1968 where he won two gold medals in the relays, Spitz arrived in Munich in 1972 with a luxuriant drag-inducing coiffure and epoch-defining moustache. He blew the field away, retired at 22, and rode the emerging sports-sponsorship-celebrity nexus all the way to a very comfortable retirement. He was a dentist, too.

---

4. KORNELIA ENDER, East Germany (Gold 4, Silver 4)

At just thirteen years of age Ender won three team silvers at the Munich Games in 1972. Four steroid-boosted years later she swept the competition and won four golds and a silver.

---

5. DARA TORRES, USA (Gold 4, Silver 4, Bronze 4)

Torres had won four golds, a silver and four bronzes between 1984 and 2000. She saved her most amazing performance for Beijing 2008 where, at the age of 41, she was the first women over forty to swim at the Olympics. She won two silvers in the relays and an individual silver in the 50m freestyle, which she lost by just 0.01 of a second.

---

6. KRISZTINA EGERSZEGI, HUNGARY (Gold 5, Silver 1, Bronze 1)

Egerszegi is Hungary's greatest swimmer and a national hero. She was immortalised in popular culture by commentator Tamás Vitray who roared her home to gold in Seoul in 1988, shouting 'Come on Mouse, come on little girl.'

---

7. GARY HALL JR, USA (Gold 5, Silver 3, Bronze 2)

Modern swimming's brashest personality, Hall won five golds at three Olympic Games with a trademark boxing robe and a shadow-boxing routine before races. Mid-career, in 1998, he was banned from competition for a year for smoking marijuana. He's had en eventful time since retiring, too, notably saving his sister from a shark attack – Hall punched the fish in the head until it gave in.

---

8. AMY VAN DYKEN, USA (Gold 6)

Van Dyken won four golds at Atlanta in 1996 and two in Sydney in 2000 – not bad for an asthmatic who took up swimming to strengthen her lungs.

9. IAN THORPE, AUSTRALIA (Gold 5, Silver 3, Bronze 1).

The 'Thorpedo' won three golds at Sydney 2000 and two more in Athens in 2004 – and there would almost certainly have been a sixth medal if he hadn't fallen off his starting blocks and been disqualified in a heat of the 400m freestyle. Massively popular in Australia and across Asia, he retired from swimming in 2006 to devote more time to his sponsors Armani.

10. MICHAEL PHELPS, USA (Gold 18, Silver 2, Bronze 2)

The 'Baltimore Bullet' is without question the greatest swimmer ever. He has won 22 medals at three Olympic Games. At Beijing in 2008 he won eight golds, seven of them with world record times. His capacious breakfasts, required to fuel his gruelling training schedule, have received almost as much coverage as his drag on a bong at a college frat house party. Stoner blogs around the world marvelled at his drawing strength. Although he has personally won more Olympic gold medals than the nation of Mexico has in the entire history of the Olympics, he is contemplating a comeback at Rio 2016.

THE 'BALTIMORE BULLET':
MICHAEL PHELPS AT ATHENS 2004

SYNCHRONISED SWIMMING

15–20 AUGUST 2016

MARIA LENK AQUATICS CENTRE,

BARRA DA TIJUCA, RIO

Athletes: 104 | **Golds up for grabs:** 2

OLYMPIC PRESENCE

EXHIBITION SPORT 1952 AND AT FOUR OTHER GAMES. FULL medal event since 1984.

OLYMPIC FORMAT

SYNCHRONISED SWIMMING LAUNCHED AS A SOLO AND A duet event in 1984, became just a team event in 1996, but since 2000 has been a duet and a team event. Like rhythmic gymnastics, synchronised swimming is a WOMEN-ONLY Olympic sport.

CONTENDERS

IN BOTH EVENTS, THE RUSSIANS ARE THE SWIMMERS TO BEAT, having won every gold medal since Sydney 2000. In 2012, CHINA and SPAIN shared the other medals. Other serious challengers include CANADA, USA, JAPAN, FRANCE and AUSTRALIA.

PAST CHAMPIONS

RUSSIA: 8 | USA: 5 | CANADA: 3

Why Watch Synchronised Swimming?

Benjamin Franklin was extraordinary: inventor, scientist, man of letters, signatory to the American Declaration of Independence, US Postmaster General, and ambassador to France. In his spare time he was a keen swimmer and at one point contemplated becoming a swimming coach. Fortunately for American public life he devoted his considerable energies to more elevated occupations, but his contribution to aquatic pursuits was significant, which is why he's now a member of the International Swimming Hall of Fame. He re-engineered the swimming flipper, carried out an early form of kite water-skiing, and in 1726, in London, he gave the first recorded exhibition of 'ornamental swimming'.

'At the request of the company, I stripped and leaped in the river, and swam from near Chelsea to Blackfriars, performing on the way many feats of activity, both upon and under water, that surprised and pleased those to whom they were novelties. I had from a child been ever delighted with this exercise, had studied and practised all Thevenot's motions and positions, added some of my own, aiming at graceful and easy as well as useful. All these I took occasion of exhibiting to the company, and was much flattered by their admiration,' Franklin wrote.

For the next two hundred years or so we find occasional references to swimmers performing water ballet and other such forms of aquatic art, but swimming as a sport has long been about speed rather than grace. Synchronised swimming, the direct descendant of Franklin's ornamental swimming, appeared on the Olympics stage at Los Angeles 1984 – and then only for women. Men do not yet have an Olympic event although, in 2014, governing body FINA agreed that men can participate in mixed duets in its competitions.

Derision is often heaped upon the sport for its cheesy aesthetics and its reliance on subjective scoring, but don't let this deter you: synchronised swimming is a mercilessly demanding sport, requiring immense core strength, great agility, perfect timing and huge lungs. Yes, it's sequin-heavy and the grins are unnervingly fixed, but that's to be expected in an event that's a cousin to the Hollywood musical. And who, in their heart, doesn't love a song and dance act?

The Synchronised Swimming story

The story of synchronised swimming really begins with Annette Kellerman – 'The Venus of the South Seas', as she was sometimes known. Born to a middle-class family in New South Wales, in 1887, Kellerman was a teenage swimming sensation. She broke records for sprints and distance swims as well as taking her first steps in vaudeville, performing as a MERMAID in a glass fish tank at the Melbourne Aquarium in 1903. Three heroic, but unsuccessful, attempts to become the first woman to swim the English Channel brought immense coverage for Kellerman and her revolutionary one-piece bathing suit.

She headed for America and in 1907 performed in a large glass tank at the New York Hippodrome. Her subsequent appearance on a Massachusetts beach in her one-piece swimming attire led

MAKING MATTERS WORSE: ANNETTE KELLERMAN IS ARRESTED FOR INDECENT EXPOSURE, MASSACHUSETTS 1910

to her arrest for indecency – just one of several such incidents in Kellerman's lifelong campaign to democratise aquatic sports (and costumes) for women. Inevitably, Hollywood came calling and in 1911 Kellerman debuted in her first movie, rather predictably entitled *The Mermaid*. Further aquatic adventures followed, most notably in *A Daughter of the Gods* (1916), the first movie with a million-dollar budget, which caused a sensation by giving cinema-goers glimpses of her naked body.

Hollywood's enthusiasm for water ballet dried up in the mid-1920s, but the style of AQUATIC GYMNASTICS pioneered and popularised by Kellerman found a new home in women's swimming clubs across North America. Swimming coach KAY CURTIS, who experimented with combining aquatic routines with music while a student at the University of Wisconsin, founded a WATER BALLET CLUB at the University of Chicago in 1923. In 1939 the first recorded water ballet competition, between the Chicago Teachers' College (coached by Curtis) and Iowa's Wright Junior College, was held in Iowa.

MILLION DOLLAR MERMAID: ESTHER WILLIAMS STARRING IN THE EPONYMOUS MOVIE, 1952

American colleges and amateur sports clubs helped this form of swimming develop as a sport, but Hollywood and vaudeville defined its aesthetic and increased its popularity. In 1934, sixty of Curtis's students performed as the 'MODERN MERMAIDS' at the Chicago World's Fair. The event announcer, Olympic swimming gold medallist Norman Ross, used the phrase 'SYNCHRONISED SWIMMING' to describe it, thereby coining the name under which that sport would be accepted as a competitive event by the American Athletic Union in 1941.

The rave reviews for the Chicago show encouraged vaudeville entrepreneur BILLY ROSE to stage *Aquacade* at the Great Lakes Exhibition in 1937. Success there prompted Rose to stage a much more extravagant version of the show at the 1939 New York World's Fair. Held in a specially built 11,000-seat outdoor amphitheatre, with the accompaniment of a full orchestra, *Aquacade* starred Olympic swimming gold medallists JOHNNY WEISSMULLER and ELEANOR HOLM, plus a cast of hundreds. The performance combined formation swimming, comic clowning on the high board and synchronised diving – and it went down a storm. When the show transferred to San Francisco the following year, Holm was replaced by a new star: ESTHER WILLIAMS.

Williams had been a top level competitive swimmer, but with no Olympics to go to in 1940, *Aquacade* seemed like the best gig going. MGM scouts signed her up, casting her in romantic comedies, frothy musicals and lightweight dramas, inevitably with a swimming subplot. In 1952 Williams starred in the defining movie of the aqua-musical genre, *Million Dollar Mermaid*, a super-hydrated Technicolor pageant perfectly attuned to its subject – it was a biopic of Annette Kellerman. Choreographed by Busby Berkeley, Williams cavorted against a backdrop of water slides, surfers and river nymphs, defining for ever the image of the artistic swimmer: effortless, despite the enormous difficulty of what she was doing, and flawlessly made-up, with a preference for gold lamé, tiaras and cherry-red lipstick. The public loved the movie, and flocked to Esther's follow-ups, such as the following year's *Dangerous When Wet*.

Williams retired in the early 1960s and a decade passed before the baton of theatrical synchronised swimming was taken up again, by choreographer Charlie Phillips. In the mid-1970s Phillips formed a troupe called THE KROFTETTES who peaked in popularity when they danced with Miss Piggy in *The Great Muppet Caper*, ensuring that another generation of young American women would come into the sport.

Away from Hollywood, the sport slowly gained acceptance. America held its first national championships in 1940. FINA was founded in 1954 and recognised synchronised swimming as a competitive sport – it had already been exhibited at the HELSINKI GAMES in 1952. And in 1967, the sport gained some welcome credibility when Pamela Morris, who had won the solo, duet and team event at America's national championship two years before, became the first synchronised swimmer to enter the International Swimming Hall of Fame.

GAME ON: SYNCHRONISED BASICS

SYNCHRONISED SWIMMING IS A FORM OF COMPETITIVE DANCE, in which swimmers must move in time with each other and the music, performing a variety of strokes, twists, turns and lifts. Participants may not touch the bottom of the three-metre-deep pool and must keep themselves aloft with a combination of SCULLS (small hand movements) and EGGBEATER STROKES (made with the legs).

·········· **SHALL WE DANCE? COMPETITIVE FORMATS** ··········

THE OLYMPIC COMPETITIONS ARE BETWEEN PAIRS OF DANCERS (duets) and eight-women teams. In both events, participants perform a TECHNICAL ROUTINE (lasting two minutes and twenty seconds for duets; two minutes and fifty seconds for teams) and a FREE ROUTINE (three minutes for duets; four minutes for teams). The technical competition involves a set series of moves and lifts. In the free competition, swimmers choreograph their own routines.

·········· **ART AND INDUSTRY: JUDGING AND SCORING** ··········

EACH ROUTINE IS SCORED BY TEN JUDGES. FIVE JUDGES GRADE the technical qualities and five the artistic qualities. Technical

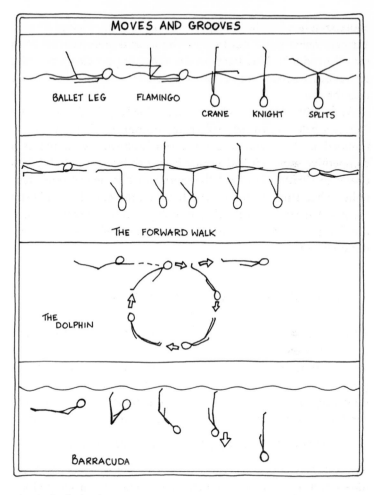

MOVES AND GROOVES

BALLET LEG   FLAMINGO   CRANE   KNIGHT   SPLITS

THE FORWARD WALK

THE DOLPHIN

BARRACUDA

criteria include the DEGREE OF SYNCHRONISATION, the PRECISION OF MOVEMENT and the DIFFICULTY OF THE ROUTINE. ARTISTIC CRITERIA, although voluminously detailed in the regulations, remain a grey area: points are scored for – among other things – flair, creativity and feel for the music.

After the five judges have given their scores, the highest and lowest are discounted and the three remaining scores are averaged. The FINAL SCORE for each routine is calculated by multiplying the technical score by six and the artistic score by four, with the results added to give a maximum of 100. A team or duo's total score is determined by adding the results for the two routines together, with the free routine counting for more than the technical one (they are multiplied by 0.65 and 0.35 respectively). Anyone still with us?

The Finer Points

···················· JUST FOR SHOW: DECKWORK ····················

ROUTINES BEGIN ON THE POOL SIDE WITH ELABORATE WAVING and diving – this is called DECKWORK and it does not have to be synchronised. Great as it is, the judges are instructed not to include deckwork in their scoring.

···················· LOOK MA, NO GOGGLES ····················

THE ONLY EQUIPMENT ALLOWED, APART FROM SWIMSUITS and gelatine (to keep the hair in place), are nose clips: amazingly, synchronised swimmers manage their complex manoeuvres underwater without wearing goggles.

···················· MOVES AND GROOVES ····················

THERE ARE THREE MAIN COMPONENTS TO ANY SYNCHRONISED swimming routine: positions, movements and lifts. POSITIONS or postures generally involve competitors sticking their legs in the air in some way. Judges are looking for precision of movement and the synchronicity of the team. MOVEMENTS are structured series of positions that move the athletes forward, like the WALK, or allow them to descend gracefully, like the BARRACUDA. Underwater speakers help athletes keep time with the music and with each other.

The most dramatic elements of the sport are the LIFTS. All of them have one designated BASE – the member of the team on which the lift is built – plus a FLYER, a lighter member who is lifted up on the back of the base. The rest of the team are the PUSHERS, who swim around the base and lift the flyer up out of the water. Flyers are increasingly likely to perform acrobatic dismounts at the end of lifts.

Synchronised Swimming
Goes to the Olympics

It's been a long haul for synchronised swimming: five Olympic exhibition performances, starting with Helsinki 1952, and a global tour by the US synchronised swimming team in 1960 to promote the sport finally paid off with its full medal debut at the 1984 Los Angeles Games. At the next three Olympics the USA and Canada won all the solo and duet events. Atlanta 1996 was the high point for the US team: performing on home soil, they struck gold with a perfect score of 100 in their free routine, 'Fantasia on an Orchestra'.

This long period of North American dominance was broken in Sydney 2000, where the Russians took both golds. They have held on to them ever since, exploiting the nation's strong background in artistic disciplines such as ballet and acrobatics. They also introduced new hybrid figures and higher lifts, performing at speeds that no one thought possible. It is a mark of their dominance that Svetlana Romashina, who is only 26, has already won three Olympic golds.

Trailing in the Russians' wake in a scramble for silver and bronze, other nations have resorted to the most extraordinary themes and

THE WORLD TURNED UPSIDE DOWN: RUSSIA'S WOMEN AT SYDNEY 2000

costumes. The trend was initiated by the JAPANESE at the 1995 World Championship with a routine entitled 're-enactment of the Kobe earthquake'. The FRENCH team at the 1996 Games hardly enhanced the sport's reputation when they planned a performance on the theme of the HOLOCAUST. Dressed in black bathing suits, team members were to goose-step to the side of the pool before re-enacting, in the water, the arrival of Jewish women in the death camps, the selection by Nazi doctors and the final march to the gas chambers. In the end, after much protest, they thought again.

The USA duo at Athens 2004 mined GREEK MYTHOLOGY for inspiration, appearing in swimsuits adorned with sequinned snakes and performing movements that were meant to suggest the Medusa. In 2008, the SPANISH duet team took months to perfect a swimsuit with built-in fairy lights, batteries and circuit breakers which, inevitably, FINA deemed unacceptable. Four years later in London, MEXICO rose – or should that be sank? – to the challenge. In the duet event, during a routine paying homage to the endangered Mexican wolf, Isabel Delgado Plancarte and Nuria Diosdado Garcia spat out pool water like a spout.

TABLE TENNIS

6–17 AUGUST 2016

RIO CENTRO PAVILION 3, RIO DE JANEIRO

Athletes: 172 | **Golds up for grabs:** 4

···················· **OLYMPIC PRESENCE** ····················

BECAME AN OLYMPIC SPORT IN 1988.

···················· **OLYMPIC FORMAT** ····················

STRAIGHT KNOCK-OUT TOURNAMENTS FOR MEN'S AND WOMEN'S SINGLES and TEAMS, seeded according to ITTF World Rankings. In the team competitions (which replaced the doubles event after Athens 2004) teams of three players play between them four singles matches and one doubles match per round.

···················· **CONTENDERS** ····················

CHINA WON ALL FOUR GOLD MEDALS IN 2012 AND WILL consider anything less than another clean sweep a national disgrace. The ranking tables show why: the top five women and four of the five top men are Chinese. The one exception is Germany's Dimitrij Ovtcharov, currently ranked second ranked in the men's game.

···················· **PAST CHAMPIONS** ····················

CHINA: 24 | SOUTH KOREA: 3 | SWEDEN: 1

WHY WATCH OLYMPIC TABLE TENNIS?

AT ITS VERY BEST, TABLE TENNIS HAS THE SPEED AND INTENSITY of a martial art. It has become so fast – balls fly around at more than 70mph – that the uninitiated find it hard to follow. But the pace is what makes it so thrilling.

As fast as it is, top-class table tennis is a game of great subtlety. It is all about sending your opponent the wrong way, mentally as well as physically, and to do this you need plenty of TRICKS. Among these are DISGUISE, a knack for SECOND-GUESSING and the ability to suddenly CHANGE TACTICS mid-point. QUICK FOOTWORK is essential. The most important element is SPIN – both delivering it and reading and exploiting your opponent's. The greatest players can make it seem as if the ball is defying the laws of physics.

The sport has acquired a small but intriguing niche in global POPULAR CULTURE. The cheapness of its basic equipment and the relatively small space required for the table has made it a staple of youth clubs everywhere and a favourite of groups as diverse as Premiership footballers, American hipsters who frequent table tennis-themed diners (one owned by actress Susan Sarandon) and Zen warrior monks in contemporary Tokyo. Table tennis has even made its impact on cinema, featuring notably in *Forrest Gump*, the drama *As One* about the unified Korean team at the 1991 World Championships, and the cult Japanese movie *Ping Pong*.

THE STORY OF TABLE TENNIS

'PING PONG'S COMING HOME!' QUIPPED LONDON MAYOR BORIS JOHNSON after taking possession of the Olympic flag at the end of the Beijing Games. The genius of his remark was that it managed to be cheekily flattering to his hosts, yet true. Table tennis was born on the dining tables of Victorian Britain but found its spiritual home in East Asia, with China becoming so dominant it has won nineteen out of the last twenty gold medals.

According to table tennis lore, the sport was invented by a group of BRITISH OFFICERS in India (or possibly South Africa) in 1881. Looking for after-dinner entertainment, they carved a champagne cork into a ball and started hitting it over a net made of cigar-box lids. They brought the game back to England, where it proved a big hit among the upper classes. At this stage, the embryonic sport went by such splendid onomatopoeic names as 'WHIFF WAFF' and 'FLIM FLAM', and was frequently played with a golf ball.

In 1891 JOHN JACQUES of London introduced a game called GOSSIMA, played with long-handled racquets that had drum-like heads of stretched parchment, but such early forms of table tennis were held back by the poor quality of the projectiles. This was resolved in 1900 by the introduction of HOLLOW CELLULOID BALLS, which bounced predictably, offered the possibility of spin, and sped the game up dramatically. Sensing the beginning of a full-blown craze, John Jacques reintroduced Gossima as 'PING PONG'. The firm also quickly trademarked the name – by now the standard term for the sport – and sold the American rights to PARKER BROTHERS. Henceforth, competitors in any event that described itself as 'ping pong' were legally obliged to use Jacques/Parker equipment.

This restriction might have strangled the sport in its infancy. Luckily, a group of free-spirited enthusiasts decided to form an association based on the generic name 'TABLE TENNIS'. The Table Tennis Association, formed in England in 1901, four days before the establishment of the rival Ping Pong Association, is the direct ancestor of the ITTF (International Table Tennis Federation), the body that governs the sport today.

Although the game remained popular in parts of Eastern Europe, the initial craze for table tennis quickly burned out elsewhere. By the early 1920s a revival was underway, particularly in Britain, where the laws of the game were codified. A colourful aristocrat named IVOR MONTAGU, the prime mover behind the establishment of the ITTF in 1926, spearheaded this organisational effort. The first World Championships were held that same year. All the medals went to HUNGARIANS, who would dominate the championships for most of the pre-war period, with VIKTOR BARNA and MARIA MEDNYANSZKY each collecting five singles titles. A young FRED PERRY, of future lawn tennis and shirt fame, was the only non-Hungarian to win one of the first nine men's World Championships.

The period between 1926 and 1952 is often described as the 'HARD BAT' ERA, because bats then consisted simply of thin sheets of pimpled rubber stuck on to plywood blades. They offered little scope for spin and lacked spring, making the sport much slower than it is today. The route to victory was guile, with players striving

SPIN DOCTOR: FIDEL CASTRO PLAYING BARE CHEST PING PONG, 1963

relentlessly to manoeuvre their opponents out of position. RALLIES could be interminable – one at the 1936 World Championships lasted for more than two hours. That said, some still hanker after this simpler, purer form of the sport, with 'old school' hard bat clubs increasingly popular in the USA and Western Europe.

Everything changed in 1952. At that year's World Championships, JAPAN'S HIROJI SATOH blew away all-comers with a bat that, in the words of one commentator, resembled a handheld mattress. Featuring a thick layer of SPONGE between the blade and the pimpled rubber surface, it enabled Satoh to hit shots with the kind of speed and spin his opponents could only dream of. His success triggered an intense competition to develop ever more sophisticated combination bats, transforming the sport forever.

Satoh's triumph was also significant for ushering in an era of ASIAN SUPREMACY that, aside from a brief period in the late 1980s and early 1990s, has continued ever since. The dominant force, however, would not be Japan but CHINA. Ominously for the rest of the table tennis world, MAO ZEDONG declared *pinpang qiu* the national sport. It was an idiosyncratic choice – although he and his colleague Zhou Enlai had played it often during their years of exile, table tennis had made little impact on China before the Communist Revolution – but an inspired one. The game required little space or expensive equipment and its emphasis on quick reflexes and nimble movement fitted the Chinese psyche perfectly. Almost uniquely among global bodies of the era, the ITTF was willing to admit the People's Republic into its ranks. The sport therefore offered a rare opportunity for Chinese athletes to succeed on the world stage.

Once Mao had his heart set on table tennis glory, concrete tables were constructed everywhere, from collective farms to suburban railway stations. The effort paid off. In 1959, a mere six years after China's admission to the ITTF, RONG GUOTUAN won the World Championship, becoming the first Chinese national to hold such a title in any sport. The country went table tennis crazy.

Chinese dominance might have continued unabated had not Mao unleashed the chaos of the Cultural Revolution. Missing the 1967 and 1969 World Championships was the least of their worries for the nation's top players, as three of them were hounded into suicide by the Red Guards. When it suited Mao politically to rehabilitate the sport after a six-year hiatus, the top Chinese players picked up more or less where they had left off.

PING PONG DIPLOMACY

As the 1960s drew to a close, China and the USA had many reasons for wanting to cosy up. The Cultural Revolution had devastated China's economy and the Mao regime was desperate that it, rather than the exiled government in Taiwan, should enjoy international recognition. US president

High Lob

PIGGY IN THE MIDDLE: ZHOU ENLAI AND RICHARD NIXON OUTMANOEUVRING
TAIWANESE LEADER CHIANG KAI SHEK THROUGH 'PING PONG DIPLOMACY'

Richard Nixon needed China onside for his planned withdrawal from Vietnam and recognised that closer relations with Beijing would strengthen his negotiating hand with the Soviets. Yet neither party could admit to wanting a rapprochement without losing face. What was needed was a 'chance encounter' that could be exploited to kick start discussions. Opportunities were limited – the two superpowers had broken off diplomatic relations in 1949 and contact of any kind between Chinese and American citizens was extremely rare – but there was one international body to which both nations belonged: the International Table Tennis Federation.

And so it was that the chance encounter took place at the World Championships in Nagoya, Japan. On 4 April 1971, nineteen-year-old GLENN COWAN, a member of the US team with hippyish tendencies, found himself stranded after a training session and jumped on to the People's Republic team bus to grab a lift. Initially, the Chinese players were as dumbfounded as if a Martian had appeared in their midst. After an awkward silence, Cowan said: 'I know my hat and hairstyle and clothes must look funny to you but in the US lots of people look like this.' China's team captain Zhuang Zedong walked up to Cowan with an interpreter and presented him with a silk painting of the Huangshan Mountains.

Cowan rummaged in his bag for a suitable gift but all he could find was a comb, so he promised to reciprocate with something more appropriate the next day (a 'Let It Be' T-shirt, as it transpired).

By the time the coach reached its destination, the world's media had assembled to cover this seminal moment in Sino-American relations. One journalist asked Cowan whether he would like to visit China. 'Of course', the athlete replied. The idea of the US team visiting China was mooted, rejected by Premier Zhou Enlai but passed on to Mao. Although the Chinese leader had previously told his players, 'Regard a ping-pong ball as the head of your capitalist enemy. Hit it with your socialist bat, and you have won the point for the fatherland,' it took him just two days to order the Chinese team to invite their American counterparts to Beijing. Less than a week after Cowan's bus trip, the US table tennis team crossed from Hong Kong to the Chinese mainland to begin a week-long tour. Four days later, the US government lifted a twenty-year trade embargo on China. Within ten months, Richard Nixon paid his historic visit to Beijing. The Great Thaw had begun.

At least, that's the most widely accepted version of the story. It later transpired that Zhou Enlai had raised the possibility of inviting the US to compete in China at a high level meeting held seventeen days before the World Championships began.

But in 1989, the unthinkable happened. In the team event final at the World Championships in Dortmund, China lost 5–0 to SWE-DEN. The coaches knew that the country's table tennis was being inhibited by the same force that was paralysing so much of national life – the omnipresent influence of Chairman Mao – but to say so in public was unthinkable.

In the 1950s, Mao had approved a COACHING MANUAL that had acquired the status of a holy document. Unquestioned adherence to its doctrines, particularly its insistence on the use of the 'distinctively Chinese' PENHOLD GRIP which only allowed one side of the bat to be used, had stultified the nation's table tennis. At the start of the 1990s DENG XIAOPING began to put into practice his famous remark that 'it doesn't matter whether the cat is black or white as long as it catches mice.' The doors were opened to reform in all areas of Chinese life, ping pong included.

Leading players like WANG LIQIN abandoned the sacred grip and the diminutive DENG YAPING, the top ranked women's player for the first eight years of the 1990s, used a Western 'SHAKEHAND' GRIP. Yaping was later voted the greatest female Chinese athlete of the twentieth century. Meanwhile, LIU GUOLIANG developed a swivel-wristed variant of the penhold that allowed him to use both sides of the bat, thus overcoming the traditional grip's one great weakness. By the time table tennis became an established Olympic event, the top Chinese players were catching mice with astonishing regularity.

GAME ON: TABLE TENNIS BASICS

FORMAT

OLYMPIC TABLE TENNIS IS A KNOCK-OUT TOURNAMENT. Each nation can enter up to three men and three women, with a maximum of two in each of the singles events.

SINGLES MATCHES are the BEST OF SEVEN GAMES, TEAM MATCHES the BEST OF FIVE. A TEAM CONTEST consists of two singles matches and then a DOUBLES MATCH, followed, if necessary, by up to two more singles matches until one team has chalked up three victories.

RULES

EACH POINT BEGINS WITH A SERVICE AND ENDS WHEN A player fails to make a legitimate return. When a player SERVES, the ball must bounce once on each side of the net; all other shots during a rally must land on the opponent's side only. As in lawn tennis, if a service clips the net but lands in play it is counted as a 'LET' and the point is replayed, whereas if a shot clips the net during a rally play continues regardless. There is also a DEUCE SYSTEM, which kicks in when both players are one point away from what would normally be a winning score. Thereafter, the first player to draw two points ahead wins the game. Unlike in lawn tennis, volleys are not allowed and servers get only one attempt per point (barring 'lets').

For most of the sport's history 21 POINTS were required to win a game but in 2001 the ITTF took the seismic decision to reduce the figure to eleven, with SERVICE TO ALTERNATE EVERY TWO RATHER THAN FIVE POINTS. The consensus is that the changes have heightened the tension and drama in a sport that already had plenty of both.

A less familiar aspect of the scoring system is the 'EXPEDITE' RULE. If a game is unfinished after ten minutes and both players have fewer than 9 points, service alternates for the remainder of the match and a receiver who makes thirteen good returns in a rally automatically wins the point.

··· **EQUIPMENT** ···

AMERICANS KNOW THEM AS 'PADDLES', IN EUROPE THE WORD is 'bat' and the official ITTF terminology is 'RACQUET'. Whatever they are called, in the quest for more spin and speed the devices used to hit table tennis balls have evolved dramatically since Satoh first used his sponge-filled instrument in 1952.

The modern table tennis bat is rather like a sandwich. The core structure, known as the blade, must be 85 per cent wood, but the remaining 15 per cent gives plenty of scope for the use of other materials: carbon fibre, for example, stiffens a blade and gives it a bigger 'SWEET SPOT'. The 'filling' consists of a layer of sponge on either side of the blade, which can be thick, thin, hard or soft according to player preference. The outer layers of the sandwich are formed by

THE WEIGH-IN: TABLE TENNIS BALLS MUST TIP THE SCALES AT 2.7G

two thin pimpled sheets of rubber. Depending on the precise petrochemical formula used in their manufacture, rubbers can impart varying degrees of spin and speed. They are usually adhered to the sponge layers with their smooth sides outward but 'PIMPLES–OUT' RUBBERS are used by players who specialise in neutralising their opponent's spin or turning it against them.

It is perfectly legitimate, indeed normal, for players to use bats with completely different characteristics on each side. To help players 'read' their opponents' shots, one surface of the bat must be BLACK and the other RED.

The BALLS at Rio will be made of plastic, not out of celluloid as they were at London 2012. They must bounce at least 24cm when dropped on to the table from a height of precisely 30.5cm. After the Sydney Games in 2000, the ITTF increased the diameter of regulation balls from 38 to 40mm, partly to make them more visible to television audiences and partly to slow the action slightly.

Other key pieces of equipment include the TABLE, which must be 2.74m (9ft) long, 1.525 m (5ft) wide and topped by a smooth, low-friction coating; the net is 15.25cm (6in) high. PLAYERS' CLOTHING must not be white, as this would make it harder to see the ball.

THE FINER POINTS

HOLDS

THERE ARE TWO BASIC WAYS OF HOLDING A TABLE TENNIS bat. The PENHOLD GRIP, favoured in China and north Asia, involves wrapping the thumb and index finger around the handle with their tips touching the front of the bat while the remaining fingers support its back. Penhold grip players were restricted to using just one side of the racquet until the 1990s, when the Chinese developed the REVERSE PENHOLD BACKHAND. The SHAKEHAND GRIP, as its name implies, involves a player holding the bat as if he or she were shaking a hand. Traditionally the hold of choice of EUROPEAN and SOUTH ASIAN players, it is increasingly favoured because it makes it much easier to play backhand shots than the penhold.

SERVICE

AS IN TENNIS, THE SERVER HAS A SIGNIFICANT ADVANTAGE AS they can dictate the initial 'shape' of a rally. The HIGH SERVE, initiated by the server tossing the ball up to four metres in the air, has become standard among top-class players. The ball gathers speed on its descent, enabling it to take more spin from the bat when the two connect. Serves are usually played with heavy SIDE SPIN but a NO-SPIN SERVE can be thrown into the mix to catch an opponent off-guard.

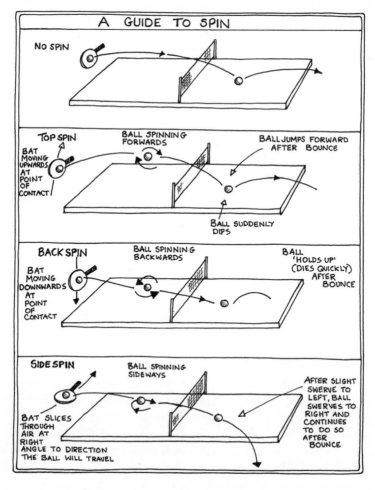

A GUIDE TO SPIN

·· **SPIN** ··

Spin is crucial. Topspin, executed through an upward movement of the bat, causes the ball to dip then leap forward when it hits the opponent's side of the table. In contrast, backspin shots, generated by a downward chopping motion, 'hold up' when they strike the table. Sidespin, imparted with a slicing action, causes the ball to move in the opposite direction to the original slice. Just to add to the devilment, sidespin is frequently applied in combination with top- or backspin.

·· **FOOTWORK** ··

The quality of players' footwork is easy to miss with so much action going on above the table, but take a look below. The nimbleness required at this level is astonishing.

·· **PLAYING STYLES** ··

top players vary their style according to circumstance, but they invariably have a 'default setting'. They are usually categorised in terms of aggression and can generally be divided into those who play to win and those who play not to lose. Fortunately, defensive play can be every bit as thrilling to watch as all-out attack. As with many one-on-one sports, the most thrilling matches often involve players with contrasting styles.

Table Tennis Goes to the Olympics

Despite the global popularity of table tennis, the sport did not feature in the Games until 1988. This was largely down to ITTF founder Ivor Montagu, who ruled the sport for more than forty years. (He also produced several Hitchcock movies, worked as *The Observer*'s first film critic and, as a Communist Party member, was suspected of spying for the Soviet Union.) Montagu was resolutely opposed to table tennis becoming an Olympic sport on the grounds that he already ran a perfectly good World Championship.

A further obstacle was the issue of professionalism. As early as 1935, the ITTF had erased the distinction between professional and amateur players in its constitution, setting it at odds with the IOC's insistence on amateurism. Montagu's successor, H. Roy Evans, suitably amended the ITTF's constitution in 1979. Two years later, the IOC voted to admit table tennis into the Olympic fold. Ironically, by the time the sport made its debut in Seoul, the IOC had dropped the 'amateurs only' clause from its charter.

Four events were scheduled at SEOUL: MEN'S and WOMEN'S SINGLES and DOUBLES. To no one's astonishment, CHINA captured gold in the women's singles and men's doubles. Rather more surprising were victories for SOUTH KOREA in the other events. (The doubles were replaced by team events in 2008.)

Further evidence that Chinese table tennis had allowed itself to be caught napping was provided by the country's thrashing by SWEDEN at the 1989 World Championships. The presence of this new kid on the ping-pong block was confirmed at Barcelona in

1992 when the great Swede JAN-OVE WALDNER collected Olympic gold playing a dazzling close-to-the-table game. Often described as the Mozart of table tennis, Waldner is as big a celebrity in China as in his own country. He has acquired the affectionate Chinese nickname 'the evergreen tree' and been celebrated on one of the country's stamps.

The humiliating losses to Sweden, combined with a new openness to foreign influences, spurred the Chinese coaches to amend their game. They dropped their insistence

EYES ON THE PRIZE: DENG YAPING, CHINA'S FEMALE ATHLETE OF THE 20TH CENTURY

on the unreconstructed penhold grip and dispatched the top players' training partners to study the best European players. The new approach has certainly paid off: the only player from outside China to win gold since 1996 is South Korea's RYU SEUNG-MIN, the men's singles champions at Athens 2004. At LONDON 2012, both singles' finals were all-Chinese affairs. One intriguing subplot at these Games was that the draw created two politically charged ties between North and South Korea, two countries that are still technically at war with each other. Both nations saved face – the North's Kim Hyok-Bong won the men's singles clash, while the South's men's team triumphed.

TAEKWONDO

17–20 AUGUST 2016

OLYMPIC TRAINING CENTRE, BARRA DA TIJUCA, RIO

Athletes: 128 | Golds up for grabs: 8

-------------------------------- **OLYMPIC PRESENCE** --------------------------------

DEMONSTRATION SPORT 1988, 1992; FULL STATUS SINCE 2000.

-------------------------------- **OLYMPIC FORMAT** --------------------------------

FOUR WEIGHT DIVISIONS FOR MEN (58KG, 58–68KG, 68–80kg, 80kg+) and women (49kg, 49–57kg, 57–67kg, 67kg+). All events are KNOCK-OUT CONTESTS, with eight contestants in each competition seeded on the basis of World Taekwondo Federation (WTF) rankings and the other eight subject to a random draw. The two BRONZE MEDALS awarded in each weight division go to the winners of a pair of REPECHAGE TOURNAMENTS, one contested by everyone who lost to the first finalist during the main phase of the competition, the other by those who lost to the second.

-------------------------------- **CONTENDERS** --------------------------------

THE SOUTH KOREANS USED TO BE DOMINANT – AFTER ALL, taekwondo is their national sport – but in 2012, for the first time, the eight gold medals were divided between eight countries – ARGENTINA, CHINA, GREAT BRITAIN, ITALY, SERBIA, SOUTH KOREA, SPAIN AND TURKEY – and, in another first, South Korea did not top the medals table. The introduction of a new electronic scoring system, smaller mats and instant video replays rendered the form book irrelevant. The WTF world rankings suggest that the contest for medals could be just as open in Rio.

-------------------------------- **PAST CHAMPIONS** --------------------------------

S. KOREA: 10 | CHINA: 5 | USA, TAIWAN, MEXICO, IRAN: 2

WHY WATCH TAEKWONDO?

TAEKWONDO IS ONE OF THE MOST POPULAR MARTIAL ARTS, and one of the fastest growing: it has been around for less than sixty years but there are already more than 60 million practitioners, including *Buffy the Vampire Slayer* star SARAH MICHELLE GELLAR, a black belt, and BARACK OBAMA, who studied the sport for four years, but is only a green belt. If you like your sports full of aggression, taekwondo should appeal. It is spectacular, lightning-quick and brutal – which is why contestants wear head and body protectors. Yet, with its graceful movements and super-high kicks, it also has a balletic quality. These elements combine to form what can seem like a video game transmuted into reality.

Aside from its inherent attractions, taekwondo offers a fascinating insight into KOREAN CULTURE – the history of the sport and the nations are intimately entwined. Until now, the Olympics has not witnessed any momentous clashes between NORTH and SOUTH because the North Koreans practise taekwondo in a slightly different form to the version sanctioned by the IOC. That may change in Rio – or at Tokyo 2020 – as the countries' competing federations have agreed to allow athletes to contest each other's events, as long as they abide by that competition's rules.

THE STORY OF TAEKWONDO

ALTHOUGH THE ANCIENT FIGHTING ARTS OF THE KOREAN peninsula fuelled the development of taekwondo, the sport is essentially a modern invention, amalgamating elements of Japanese karate and Chinese kung fu. It came into existence formally on 11 April 1955, when the masters of several South Korean *kwan* (martial art schools) agreed to merge their styles into a new, unified discipline, to be known as TAE SOO DO. Two years later, at the instigation of GENERAL CHOE HONG HI, the name was changed to TAEKWONDO to foster a sense of continuity with TAEKKYEON, a martial art with roots stretching back to the fifth century.

Although little is known about its precise techniques during this era, *taekkyeon* was a subset of SUBAK, a leg-oriented fighting system that emerged in Goguryeo, one of three kingdoms that shared the Korean peninsula from 57 BC to AD 668. The smallest kingdom, Silla, was raided regularly by Japanese pirates. When the Sillans asked the Goguryeons for help, part of the aid package was training a few Sillan warriors in *taekkyeon*. This elite group, which also studied Confucian philosophy and Buddhist ethics, became known as the *Hwarang* ('flowering of manhood'). As they travelled around the Korean peninsula, they helped popularise *taekkyeon*.

In 936, the three kingdoms were united under Goryeo, the successor state to Goguryeo, from which the name Korea is derived. During a long, relatively peaceful era, *taekkyeon* and related disciplines declined, all but disappearing by the close of the nineteenth century. Interest was rekindled by the Japanese invasion of Korea in 1909. The occupiers tried to suppress all aspects of the nation's culture, including its martial arts, which naturally increased their appeal to the natives. In remote Buddhist temples, small groups of nationalistic Koreans kept the flame of *taekkyeon* alive.

ALEXANDROS NIKOLAIDIS LANDS A NICE 3-POINTER IN THE 2008 MEN'S HEAVYWEIGHT FINAL

In 1943 the Japanese officially introduced karate, judo and kung fu to Korea as aspects of military training for conscripted locals: thus, by the time Korea was liberated in 1945, all the ingredients were in place for the new hybrid of TAEKWONDO to blossom.

The crucial role of Choi Hong Hi in formulating the rules of taekwondo and popularising the sport is covered below, as is the acrimonious split between its ruling bodies. Another key moment in the rise of this martial art was a demonstration in front of President Syngman Rhee in 1952, during which a master named TAE HI NAM broke thirteen roof tiles with a single blow. Rhee was sufficiently impressed to order that all Korean troops be trained in the evolving martial art.

The growth of taekwondo has been phenomenal: by 1974 there were around six hundred ITF trained instructors distributed across the globe. But it was the newly formed WTF, which held its first WORLD CHAMPIONSHIP in Seoul in 1973, which took its version of the sport into the Olympic Games, thanks to some intense South Korean lobbying. Today the organisation encompasses 205 countries.

THE DISOWNED FATHER OF TAEKWONDO

GENERAL CHOI HONG HI developed taekwondo, gave the sport its name and inspired its global spread. Yet today the sport's governing body can scarcely bring itself to mention his name.

Born in what is now North Korea in 1918, Choi Hong Hi studied calligraphy under a tutor called Han Il Dong, a master of *taekkyeon*, an ancient Korean form of foot fighting. When his pupil showed interest, Han Il Dong taught it to him, even though it had been banned by the country's Japanese occupiers.

During the war, Choi was imprisoned by the Japanese for attempting to avoid conscription. During captivity, he created a hybrid of *taekkyeon* and karate. After his release, he joined the new Korean army and began teaching his method. On the outbreak of the Korean War in 1950, he formed a crack regiment on the island of Cheju, which marched under a flag displaying his clenched hand over a map of Korea.

GENERAL CHOI HONG HI SEEMS UNHAPPY WITH HIS EASEL

The 'Fist Division' provided taekwondo instructors for the entire South Korean army and Choi was promoted to the rank of major general. His star continued to rise and he demonstrated the new martial art in the Far East and America. But the coming to power of General Park Chung Hee in 1961 was a major problem for Choi; back in the 1940s he had been a member of a military panel that had sentenced the general to death.

Choi had no choice but to leave the army, though for a time he continued to live and teach in South Korea, founding the INTERNATIONAL TAEKWONDO FEDERATION (ITF) in 1966. Life under the Park regime became increasingly intolerable and in 1972 he went into exile in Canada, taking the ITF with him. The South Korean government promptly founded a rival body, the WORLD TAEKWONDO FEDERATION (WTF), and set its intelligence unit on Choi. Told that his son and daughter, who had stayed in South Korea, would be executed if he didn't return, he replied: 'I chose taekwondo over my son' (his daughter doesn't appear to have got a mention).

Choi's reputation in Seoul took one last nosedive when he introduced taekwondo to North Korea in 1980. He eventually moved to Pyongyang, where he died in 2002.

Game On: Taekwondo Basics

As with most oriental martial arts, taekwondo is a philosophy of life as much as a method of fighting: the extreme concentration required to smash through a stack of wooden boards is an aspect of the mental discipline that will lead one to the truth. But competitive taekwondo requires measurable criteria of success, as well as certain measures to prevent serious injury. Olympic taekwondo is therefore confined to SPARRING (GYEO-RUGI), a form of constrained combat in which points are awarded for striking various points of the opponent's body. Other elements of taekwondo include self-defence, breaking boards and tiles, and POOMSAE – set movements based on imaginary contests against multiple attackers.

Taekwondo can be loosely translated as 'the way of the foot and the fist', and that in a nutshell is what the sport is about. Contestants can only strike each other with their feet and the leading part of their closed hands. The LEG is the primary weapon, which is logical as it is the longer and more powerful limb. The FISTS are of secondary importance – although they are invaluable for blocking, strikes with them score fewer points. In boxing parlance, hand-strikes are the jabs, while the kicks are the hooks and uppercuts.

THE FORM OF THE BOUT

Olympic taekwondo bouts are held on a square measuring 8m × 8m, with a 2m margin which is not a part of the fighting area. The fighters begin facing each other, standing on starting positions 1m from the centre of the mat. They return to these positions at the beginning of each round. After they have bowed to each other, the referee calls out 'SHI-JAK' and the fighting begins.

Bouts consist of three TWO-MINUTE ROUNDS separated by ONE-MINUTE REST PERIODS. If the scores are level at the end of the final round, the bout goes into sudden death – the first combatant to score a point wins the match. If no victor has emerged after two minutes, the officials choose a winner on the basis of aggression shown during the sudden death round.

The WTF guidance states that, for a blow to score a point the judges must deem it to have been 'accurate and powerful'. Glancing or half-hearted contact does not count.

OFFICIALS

A SINGLE REFEREE CONTROLS EACH BOUT AND KEEPS IT FLOWING. In the normal course of events, referees do not award points. This is the job of the four CORNER JUDGES, whose main task is to score shots to the head (body strikes are recorded electronically). If the judges fail to reach a majority decision about the award or deduction of a point(s), the referee has the casting vote.

EQUIPMENT

TAEKWONDO IS PRACTICED IN A TRADITIONAL UNIFORM known as a DOBOK, with a protective jacket called a HOGU worn over the top. At the Olympics and other major competitions, *hogu* are fitted with SENSORS that automatically register hits to the parts of the torso that must be struck to earn points (the front and the sides). This technology has made the judges' job easier, but hasn't ended all controversy: it has been argued that the sensors are too sensitive, and cannot distinguish between a legitimate strike and a part of the wearer's body hitting the *hogu* in a counter-reaction to a successful block. KICKS TO THE HEAD are scored solely by the judges.

Contestants wear plenty of SAFETY EQUIPMENT. If they didn't, few bouts would last long. In addition to their blue or red *hogu*, they sport head and hand protectors, groin, forearm and shin guards and gum-shields.

SCORING

PUNCHES TO THE HEAD ARE FORBIDDEN BUT KICKS TO IT ARE positively encouraged by the award of up to four points.

Points are scored as follows:

KICK OR PUNCH to the *hogu* – 1 point

KICK to the *hogu* involving a partial turn of the assailant's body – 2 points

KICK to the face or side of the head – 3 points

KICK to the head or face involving a full spinning turn – 4 points.

To WIN A BOUT before the end of the third round, a fighter must achieve a LEAD OF TWELVE POINTS at the end of the second round or at anytime in the third. In the event of a KNOCKDOWN, the referee counts to ten – in Korean. As in boxing, there is a mandatory eight count. If a fighter fails to get up in time, or if the referee concludes that they are in no state to continue, their opponent wins.

PENALTIES AND WARNINGS

FOR EVERY TWO WARNINGS (KYONG-GO) A FIGHTER RECEIVES, HE is punished with a ONE-POINT DEDUCTION (GAM-JUM). If a fighter accumulates FOUR POINT DEDUCTIONS he forfeits the bout. Warnings are issued for the following offences: attacking below the waist; inadvertently striking an opponent's face with the hand; both feet going over the boundary of the fighting area; feigning injury; avoiding combat; turning the back to an opponent except in the course of executing a spinning kick; holding, pushing, butting or kneeing.

MORE SERIOUS OFFENCES such as attacking a fallen opponent or deliberately striking them in the face are punished with an instant *gam-jum*.

THE FINER POINTS

COMPETITIVE TAEKWONDO REQUIRES MASTERY OF A WIDE range of kicks, punches, blocks and dodges. A selection is shown in the diagram on the previous page. The contestants in Olympic taekwondo go at each other hammer and tongs from the word go, because aggression is rewarded (and the new rules, introduced at London 2012, make it harder for athletes to run down the clock). The kicks and punches are so attention grabbing that it's easy to miss the blocks and dodges, but avoiding being hit is as important as hitting: developing an eye for this aspect of taekwondo will greatly enhance your enjoyment of the sport.

TAEKWONDO GOES TO THE OLYMPICS

THE OPENING CEREMONY AT THE 1988 SEOUL GAMES WAS AN emphatic pitch for taekwondo's elevation to the ranks of full Olympic sports: several hundred white-clad South Koreans performed a perfectly co-ordinated taekwondo routine, accompanied by spine-tingling sound effects on the stadium PA. The crowd went wild. South Korea then proceeded to win nine of the sixteen demonstration events.

It wasn't until 2000, however, that taekwondo made its FULL OLYMPIC DEBUT. South Koreans won three of the eight golds on offer in Sydney, but the diversity of the nationalities of the other medallists (GREEK, CUBAN, AUSTRALIAN, IRANIAN and CHINESE) was equally striking. In Athens four years later, CHINA and TAIWAN tied with KOREA, taking two titles each. The South Koreans were back on form in Beijing, winning half of the events, but the main talking point was Cuban fighter ÁNGEL MATOS, the men's middleweight champion at Sydney, who kicked the referee in the face after being disqualified for exceeding a time limit. Matos was banned for life; Fidel Castro expressed his 'total solidarity' with the fighter.

More consequential for the future of the sport was the quarterfinal between SARAH STEVENSON (Great Britain) and CHEN ZHONG (China). Four seconds before the end, with the Chinese fighter

YOU CANNOT BE SERIOUS! SARAH STEVENSON REACTS IN DISBELIEF TO HER APPARENT DEFEAT IN BEIJING

leading 1–0, Stevenson landed a clear match–winning kick on her opponent's face. Unaccountably, two of the four corner judges failed to register the strike, as did the referee, who had the authority to cast the deciding vote and Zhong was awarded the fight. The British team protested vigorously and the judges, after watching a video replay, reversed their decision, infuriating the Chinese crowd. Such incidents made the introduction of replay technology inevitable.

Yet the competition in Beijing had its inspirational moments. ROHULLAH NIKPAL, who had worked as a barber in Kabul to finance his training, won AFGHANISTAN'S first Olympic medal, securing bronze in the 58kg division. Four years later, he repeated the feat in London – in the 68kg event. The sport's growing international appeal was underlined in 2012 when Anthony Obame won silver in the heavyweight contest, securing GABON'S first Olympic medal. In the women's 57kg class, JADE JONES, who trained on a diet of pasta and jelly, won Great Britain's first Olympic gold in taekwondo.

TENNIS

6–14 AUGUST 2016

OLYMPIC TENNIS CENTRE, BARRA DA TIJUCA, RIO

Athletes: 172 | **Golds up for grabs:** 5

OLYMPIC PRESENCE

1896–1924; 1988–PRESENT.

OLYMPIC FORMAT

THE FIVE EVENTS ARE MEN'S AND WOMEN'S SINGLES, MEN'S and WOMEN'S DOUBLES and MIXED DOUBLES. All competitions have a knock-out structure, with players and pairs SEEDED according to ITF rankings. All matches are the BEST OF THREE SETS, except the men's singles final, which is the best of five.

CONTENDERS

THE FAVOURITES AT RIO 2016 WILL BE THE USUAL SUSPECTS, adjusted according to how they perform in the Grand Slams and whether their game suits the hard courts in Rio's new Olympic tennis centre. Four years ago, at Wimbledon, ANDY MURRAY became the first British man to win the Olympic singles since Josiah Ritchie in 1908. Could he become the first man to retain the title? Or will ROGER FEDERER or NOVAK DJOKOVIC, neither of whom have won this event, put that right in Rio? In the women's events, it is hard to see past the Williams sisters – Serena won the singles and the women's doubles (with sister Venus) in 2012. In the mixed doubles, aficionados can't wait to see MARTINA HINGIS partner with FEDERER in a Swiss dream team, but INDIAN duo LEANDER PAES and SANI MIRZA should also be in contention.

PAST CHAMPIONS

USA: 20 | GREAT BRITAIN: 17 | FRANCE: 5

WHY WATCH OLYMPIC TENNIS?

TENNIS IS A SPLENDID SPECTATOR SPORT: FAST, INTENSE AND intimate. You can get to know the competitors surprisingly well during a match, or at least you feel as if you do, as the TV cameras zoom in to catch every emotion that flickers across their faces. But you know this already. The question is therefore not so much why you should watch the sport as why you should watch the Olympic version.

Twenty years ago, this would have been a tricky question to answer. When tennis was reintroduced as an Olympic sport in 1988, few of the world's top performers were interested: the tournament had no prestige, fell right in the midst of an already packed season, and there was no prize money. But the decision of the sport's governing bodies to award RANKING POINTS for Olympic tennis – to men from 2000 and women from 2004 – transformed its relevance to hard-bitten pros, who now appreciate that a gold medal looks nice in the trophy cabinet. Barring injury, most of the top seeds will be there in 2016.

Admittedly, some still doubt whether tennis really belongs in the Olympics. A gold medal should be a pinnacle of an athlete's career, but no tennis player would rather win an Olympic title than a GRAND SLAM. That said, Murray's two Grand Slam titles – the 2012 US Open and Wimbledon in 2013 – followed his Olympic triumph, so a gold medal can prove a game changer for players. Expect the competition in Rio to be fierce.

THE STORY OF TENNIS

LAWN TENNIS IS OFTEN ASSUMED TO HAVE DESCENDED FROM REAL or ROYAL TENNIS, an indoor game involving a droopy net and asymmetrical racquets, played by Henry VIII. Yet the two sports have little in common, although both ultimately derive from *jeu de paume*, a game played in medieval France using bare hands (*paume* = 'palm') rather than racquets. The principal creator of LAWN TENNIS was Major Walter Wingfield of Llanelidan, who experimented with various permutations for the amusement of his summer guests in the 1860s and 1870s. A hybrid of several pre-existing games, his invention went by the name of SPHAIRISTIKÈ (from the ancient Greek for 'playing ball'), was played on a court shaped like an hourglass, and in 1874 was deemed original enough to earn a patent.

The game swiftly morphed into LAWN TENNIS. Indeed, the world's first 'tennis club' had already been founded in Leamington Spa in 1872, and within months of the patent being granted a court had been laid in NEW YORK. In BRITAIN, Oscar Wilde became a devotee, and in 1878 women's colleges at Oxford and Cambridge began organising doubles competitions.

In 1877, three years after Wingfield's patent, the ALL ENGLAND CROQUET CLUB in WIMBLEDON held its first MEN'S TOURNAMENT. A WOMEN'S TOURNAMENT followed in 1884. Women initially played in voluminous bustle dresses, but in 1887 a teenager named LOTTIE DOD took the title wearing shortish skirts, in defiance of Victorian convention. (Twenty-one years later she won an Olympic silver medal for archery.)

Other centres of the new sport began to organise their own national championships: England was followed by the USA (1881), FRANCE (1891) and AUSTRALIA (1905). These tournaments, collectively known as the GRAND SLAMS, became the heart of the international tennis circuit and remain so today. The other innovation driving the game's development was the establishment in 1900 of the DAVIS CUP, an annual competition for men's national teams; the women's equivalent, the FEDERATION (NOW FED) CUP, arrived 63 years later.

The British dominated the sport until the 1920s, when the pendulum bifurcated towards AMERICA and FRANCE. The latter's so called 'Four Musketeers', featuring RENÉ LACOSTE of crocodile fame, won twenty singles and twenty-three doubles Grand Slam titles between them in the men's division, while the great SUZANNE LENGLEN lost only two sets in seven years.

The winners' lists from the Davis and Federation Cups show how power has shifted over the years. Until 1975, the men's championship was invariably held by one of the Grand Slam nations, usually either the USA or AUSTRALIA (the British dropped off

'LA DIVINE' SUZANNE LENGLEN, WHO LOST JUST TWO SETS IN SEVEN YEARS

the radar after 1936 and France went almost sixty years without a win after 1932). Since then, new countries have entered the fray, with SWEDEN, GERMANY, CROATIA, RUSSIA, SERBIA, SPAIN, the CZECH REPUBLIC and SWITZERLAND successively challenging the supremacy of the old guard. The women's game has followed a similar pattern: AMERICA and AUSTRALIA dominated the picture in the 1960s and 1970s, but since 2000, the Fed Cup has been monopolised by Europe, with the continent's eastern half especially powerful. Only the redoubtable Williams sisters have kept the American flag flying.

GAME ON: TENNIS BASICS

THE COURT

TENNIS IS PLAYED ON A RECTANGULAR COURT 78FT (23.77M) long, divided by a net 3ft high at its centre. The WIDTH of the playing area is 27ft (8.23m) in singles matches and 36ft (11m) in doubles, hence the TRAMLINES on either side of the court. Balls other than services hit into these tramlines are deemed 'in' in doubles matches but 'out' in singles matches.

SCORING

WHOEVER INVENTED THE SCORING SYSTEM IN TENNIS WAS equal parts genius and lunatic. The logic is hardly obvious, yet the system is such that a match can remain tense and in the balance right to the death. Indeed a single point can prove a player's undoing or salvation, turning a whole match.

There are three fundamental units: points, games and sets.

A GAME is made up of several exchanges ('POINTS'), all beginning with services delivered by the same player. Each point ends either with a 'double fault' (failure to deliver a valid serve in two attempts) or with a player failing to make a legitimate return. The game is won by the first player or doubles pair to ACCUMULATE 4 POINTS, with the proviso that they must be at least 2 points ahead of their opponents. If the score reaches 3 points all, it is described as 'deuce', and the game continues until one player wins by drawing 2 points ahead. Except it's not that simple. Tennis scoring does not operate on a single-point system: instead, a player earns 15 points for the first exchange they win during a game, another 15 for the second and 10 for the third. A score of nil is described as 'love', a term derived from the French *oeuf* (egg), a suitably zero-shaped object. The server's score is always announced first, so a typical progression might be 0-15, 15 all, 30-15, 40-15, game to the server. If 40–40 (DEUCE) is reached and a player draws one point ahead, they are described as having 'advantage'. Andre Agassi, men's singles champion at Atlanta 1996, had a succinct explanation for the origins of the points' names: 'It was invented to cause frustration to those who chose to play.'

A SET is made up of several games, with the service changing sides after each one. The first player to win 6 games wins the set, provided they are at least two games ahead of their opponent. If the score reaches five games all, a player can win the set by winning the next two games, but if it reaches 6-6, the players enter a TIE-BREAK. Thankfully, at this point the accounting system reverts to normal. The first player or pair to reach 7 points wins the set, provided there is a 2-point lead; if the score reaches 6-6, play continues until one player has a 2-point lead. (In the final set of an Olympic mixed doubles match, the target is 10 points rather than 7; the 2-point rule applies.) The player whose turn it was to serve in the set serves the first point of the tie-break; his or her opponent serves the next two points and after that the serve rotates after every two points.

Olympic tennis matches are the best of THREE SETS, with the exception of the MEN'S SINGLES FINAL, which is, as per tradition, the BEST OF FIVE.

PLAY

PLAY BEGINS WITH ONE PLAYER SERVING THE BALL FROM BEHIND the baseline on the right-hand side of their end of the court. For a service to count, it must land in the box diagonally opposite the server, who changes sides after each point. Servers get two chances to deliver a legitimate serve per point. If they fail, they register a DOUBLE FAULT and concede the point to their opponent. If the ball clips the net en route to landing in the correct box, a LET is played and the service is retaken with no penalty. If the receiver fails to get their racquet to a winning serve, it is known as an ACE.

If a legitimate service is returned, a RALLY ensues, with the players alternately hitting the ball over the net until one of them loses the point by committing a fault, either by missing a ball that lands in the court, or by hitting it into the net or out of bounds. If a shot ends with the ball clipping any part of a boundary line, it is deemed valid.

EQUIPMENT

PLAYERS IN THE FIRST OLYMPIC INCARNATION OF TENNIS used RACQUETS made of laminated wood, with animal gut strings forming a head with a surface area of around 65 square inches. Today, racquets are typically made of carbon fibre mixed with fibreglass and all manner of high tech substances. They have much larger heads than their predecessors (up to 137 square inches) and far bigger 'SWEET SPOTS' – the part of the striking surface that delivers maximum power and control. Strings are now synthetic.

The BALLS used in tennis are made of felt-covered vulcanised rubber. They rapidly lose their bounce and 'nap' (fluffy coating), once released from the pressurised cans in which they are stored and then knocked around the court, and start behaving oddly. This is why they are changed so often during the course of a match.

································· **EVOLUTION OF THE RULES** ·································

THE RULES OF TENNIS HAVE CHANGED LITTLE SINCE THE 1890s. Between 1908 and 1961, players were required to keep one foot on the ground when serving. TIE-BREAKS were instituted during the 1970s and latterly the sport has introduced a points challenge system, based on 'Hawk-Eye' technology: players can call for a video-based review of an official's decision any time they like, although they lose this right for the remainder of any set in which they have made three invalid challenges. They get another 'life' if there is a tie-break.

THE FINER POINTS

HARD COURT TENNIS HAS ITS OWN PECULIARITIES. IN RIO, the surface has been chosen to minimise disruption for players who compete in the US OPEN only two weeks after the Games. The decision has been questioned by some, notably RAFAEL NADAL, winner of the men's singles in Beijing, who wondered why Brazil wasn't sticking to its traditional clay surface. Hard courts place more strain on a player's legs and the tennis balls – which can be virtually bald after half an hour of play. In recent years, the difference between the surfaces – clay, grass and hard – has had less influence on the outcome and the Rio organisers will presumably create a surface that encourages rallies, the most exciting aspect of the game.

If you are lucky enough to attend a match, make the most of the opportunity to see the action from a different angle to the one invariably used in television coverage. You don't appreciate how

FAST tennis is until you see it live. Watch how the players try to manoeuvre their opponents into positions where wide expanses of court open up, allowing them to deliver killer shots.

You'll appreciate, too, the diverse playing styles of the competitors. SERVE-VOLLEYERS typically rush to the net after serving, trying to narrow the angle of possibility for their opponents' returns. BASELINE PLAYERS only approach the net when they have to, for instance when retrieving a drop shot.

For those only accustomed to watching Grand Slam tournaments, the THREE-SET FORMAT of the men's singles and doubles will be a novelty. The effect is to reduce the margin for error. Losing a set is far more serious than in five-set matches, where a player who falls far behind in one may choose to kiss it goodbye and conserve their energy for the next one.

TENNIS GOES TO THE OLYMPICS

TENNIS WAS ONE OF THE NINE SPORTS THAT FEATURED IN the 1896 Games in ATHENS, and the men's singles title was won by an Irishman named JOHN BOLAND, representing 'The United Kingdom of Great Britain and Ireland'. Not having expected to participate in the competition (he was drafted in by a Greek friend who was a member of the organising committee), Boland played in heeled shoes with leather soles.

In 1900, CHARLOTTE COOPER of the UK defeated Hélène Prévost of France in the women's singles final, becoming the first female to win an Olympic title – her gender having been forbidden to compete in the ancient Games.

Americans won all the tennis medals in ST LOUIS in 1904, which is hardly surprising as there was only one foreign entrant. British players won gold in all six tennis events at the subsequent Games in LONDON – but this time there weren't any Americans. There was just one American in 1912, when medals were divided fairly equally between FRANCE, BRITAIN and SOUTH AFRICA, and none again when France and Great Britain split the golds at Antwerp in 1920. But the USA was back with a vengeance four years later, winning all five titles. HELEN WILLS MOODY, the greatest female tennis player of the era, triumphed in the women's singles in Paris without dropping a set and won the women's doubles with her coach, Hazel Wightman.

Wills could have won many more medals but, at this point, the issue of PROFESSIONALISM ruined Olympic tennis. The International Lawn Tennis Federation, formed in 1913, banned any player who turned pro from the competitions under its control, which included the Olympic Games. It was fighting a lost cause. In 1926 the promoter C.C. Pyle lured SUZANNE LENGLEN and American star VINNIE RICHARDS, double Olympic gold medallist in Amsterdam two years earlier, to join his lucrative travelling tour. Within a few years the 'PRO SLAMS' established in the USA (1927), France (1930) and England (1934) had effectively replaced the old Grand ones. Deprived of its stars, tennis was always likely to fade out of the Olympic programme, and after the 1924 Games it did.

In 1968, the ILTF finally bowed to pressure and admitted professionals to its tournaments. The IOC eventually followed suit in the 1980s, and tennis reappeared at the SEOUL GAMES, after an absence of 64 years. The men's singles title was won by Czechoslovakia's MILOSLAV MEČÍŘ, the women's by STEFFI GRAF, whose victory secured her a unique

GOLDEN SLAM FOR THE GOLDEN GIRL: STEFFI GRAF ADDS THE OLYMPIC TITLE TO HER 1988 GRAND SLAM

'Golden Slam' – all four Grand Slam titles and an Olympic gold in the same year.

The tennis tournaments at the next few Games were marked by the inconsistent attendance of the world's best players – the top five men in the world all participated in the men's singles in BARCELONA but only three of the top ten pitched up in ATLANTA – and some surprising results, notably when Switzerland's MARC ROSSET pipped the likes of Pete Sampras and Boris Becker to gold in 1992.

The growing status of Olympic tennis and the introduction of ranking points for participation have gone some way to solving the attendance problem. In 2012, ANDY MURRAY had to overcome Roger Federer (who he had lost to four weeks earlier in the Wimbledon final) to win the men's singles event and such was his enthusiasm for the Olympic cause that, later that same day, he and Laura Robson contested the mixed doubles final, losing to Belarus's VICTORIA AZARENKA and MAX MIRNYI. Yet the tournaments still produce the occasional unexpected champion. NICOLÁS MASSÚ anyone? The Chilean won both the men's singles and doubles titles in 2004.

TRIATHLON

18–20 AUGUST 2016

FORT COPACABANA, RIO DE JANEIRO

Athletes: 110 | **Golds up for grabs:** 2

··· **OLYMPIC PRESENCE** ···

SINCE 2000.

··· **OLYMPIC FORMAT** ···

THERE ARE NO HEATS: EVERY ATHLETE JUST TRIES TO COMPLETE a 1500M SWIM, 40KM BICYCLE RACE, and a 10KM RUN as quickly as possible.

··· **CONTENDERS** ···

SWITZERLAND, AUSTRALIA, NEW ZEALAND, CANADA AND GERMANY occupy the first five places in the all-time Olympic medals table, followed by Great Britain and Austria. If the UK's Alistair Brownlee is make history as the first athlete to win a second successive gold, he must see off the challenge of his brother Jonathan (a bronze medallist in London), SPAIN'S Mario Mola and Javier Gómez, FRANCE'S Vincent Luis and GERMANY'S Jan Frodeno, a gold medallist in 2008. In the women's competition, AMERICA'S Gwen Jorgensen has been in scintillating form and will be keen to erase the disappointment of 2012, when she suffered a flat tyre.

··· **PAST CHAMPIONS** ···

SWITZERLAND: 2; AUSTRALIA, NEW ZEALAND, CANADA, GERMANY, GREAT BRITAIN and AUSTRIA: 1 each.

WHY WATCH TRIATHLON?

ONE OF THE FASTEST-GROWING SPORTS IN THE WORLD, triathlon is an excruciating endurance event: the cumulative effects of its three disciplines – swimming, cycling, running – are extremely gruelling. Success hinges on an athlete's ability to overcome levels of pain that would incapacitate ordinary mortals. To put the event into perspective, the world's best times for the INDIVIDUAL COMPONENTS of the triathlon give a cumulative time of a little over 1hr 20min. Given that a triathlete has to do the three events back-to-back, swimming in an outdoor pool, and running and cycling on tarmac, it's amazing that ALASTAIR BROWNLEE took only 1:46:25 to complete the triathlon when winning gold in London.

As a spectacle, triathlon offers all the pleasures of its constituent disciplines plus some that are uniquely its own. The changeovers are particularly gripping. Watching a competitor zero in on a bicycle racked among 54 similar machines is always impressive and there is the tantalising possibility of an athlete coming to grief while changing out of a wetsuit or being penalised if they start running while wearing their cycling helmet. Amazingly, given the demands the sport makes on contestants, the margin of victory in the Olympics is usually less than fourteen seconds. In Rio, the contestants will swim off Copacabana beach, a spectacular setting marred only by worries over the cleanliness of the water and the risk of viral infection.

THE STORY OF TRIATHLON

MULTI-SPORT RACES OF VARYING DEGREES OF FORMALITY HAVE been around for a long time. For example an event called LES TROIS SPORTS has been held at Joinville-le-Pont in France since 1902. It originally featured running, cycling and canoeing, but by 1920 the canoeing had been replaced by a swim across the river Marne. The Olympic form of triathlon took shape in the USA in the 1970s, as the country became obsessed by jogging. The triathlon is one of the few Olympic sports with an identifiable date of birth. It came into existence in California on 25 September 1974, heralded by an announcement in the San Diego Track Club newsletter.

The event was the brainchild of JACK JOHNSTONE, a 38-year-old who had taken to jogging to rein in his expanding waistline. An enthusiastic but mediocre runner, Johnstone had grown accustomed to finishing down the field in road races. He had, however, been an excellent swimmer in his youth, so when he heard about an event dubbed the DAVID PAIN BIRTHDAY BIATHLON, which consisted of a 4.5-mile run followed by a quarter-mile swim, he thought 'this could be the event for me'.

Encouraged by finishing in the top ten in the 1974 event, Johnstone decided to stage a race with a longer swimming section. He then joined forces with DON SHANAHAN, a fellow member of the San Diego Track Club, who was also planning a multi-sport race. When Johnstone reluctantly acceded to Shanahan's demand for a cycling event, the format for the newly christened triathlon was established. Forty-six men and women took part in the inaugural race, the Mission Bay Triathlon. Johnstone came sixth and everyone went out for a pizza.

IRON MEN AND WOMEN

The Mission Bay Triathlon started the fire but the event that really drew the world's attention to the infant sport was conceived by the man who finished 22nd in that race. In 1977, US Navy Commander JOHN COLLINS was attending the awards ceremony for the Oahu Perimeter Relay in Hawaii when he overheard members of the Waikiki Swim Club and the Mid-Pacific Road Runners debating whether swimmers or runners were fitter athletes. He cited a *Sports Illustrated* article which said that Belgian cyclist Eddie Merckx had the highest maximum oxygen uptake ever recorded and wondered if cyclists were fitter than either group.

To settle the argument, he devised the mother of all triathlons, consisting of a 2.4-mile swim followed by a 112-mile bike race and a full marathon. 'Whoever wins, we'll call him the Ironman,' Collins declared. On 18 February 1978, GORDON HALLER, now a programmer analyst for Walmart,

TRIATHLETES EMERGING FROM THE WAVES AT ATHENS 2004

became the first man to earn that accolade, completing the course in a shade under 11hr 47min. He might have gone quicker had he not popped into a hotel for a shower after his swim. But his performance would still have looked lame compared to today's Ironpersons. The official male record now stands at 7:5:8, the female at 8:18:13.

As the sport evolved, the early happy-go-lucky spirit gave way to a more professional and scientific approach. One of the symptoms – mega-events like the Ironman notwithstanding – was the standardisation of the 1500M/40KM/10KM FORMAT, which was developed in the mid-1980s for the US TRIATHLON SERIES. Another was the emergence of techniques and training regimes specifically tailored to the triathlon, as opposed to borrowed from its constituent disciplines. TRANSITIONING (changing equipment and clothes between stages as rapidly as possible) became a particular focus, as did the quest for maximally efficient balance between expenditure and conservation of energy at every point in the race.

One major debate that has coloured the first four decades of the triathlon has been the legitimacy of DRAFTING, the practice of SLIPSTREAMING during the cycling and swimming races to save energy. This would have been anathema to the earliest triathletes but is legal at the Olympics.

In 1989, the INTERNATIONAL TRIATHLON UNION was established in Avignon, France. Aside from organising an annual World Championship, which was first held that year, its specific goal was to get the sport on the Olympic agenda. The ITU took just five years to accomplish its aim. The sport was awarded full medal status at the 1994 IOC Congress in Paris and made its debut at Sydney 2000. Famous triathlon enthusiasts include F1 driver JENSEN BUTTON and actress and singer JENNIFER LOPEZ.

GAME ON: TRIATHLON BASICS

SWIMMING

OLYMPIC TRIATHLON RACES BEGIN WITH THE COMPETITORS diving en masse off a pontoon or on-shore launching platform. During the swimming section, athletes may use any stroke they like but it will be a Richter-worthy shock if anyone deviates from front crawl. They can take a breather by treading water, floating or holding on to a marker buoy but it's a bad sign if they do. Swimming caps must be worn at all times. If the water temperature exceeds 20°C, as it probably will in Rio, contestants will not be allowed to wear WETSUITS; if it is below 14°C they are mandatory.

CYCLING

AFTER EMERGING FROM THE WATER, ATHLETES ENTER THE first transition zone, where they take off their wetsuits and put on their cycling shoes, which may be placed on their bicycles in advance. Before taking their bikes from the racks, they must put on CYCLING HELMETS and fasten them properly. Failure to do so leads to disqualification, as does removing a helmet at any point before racking the bike in the second transition zone, unless stationary and doing something desperate like repairing a puncture.

RUNNING

ATHLETES MUST DISMOUNT WHEN THEY REACH A LINE JUST ahead of the second transition zone. Here they will find their running shoes placed as close to their personal racks as possible. Having racked their bikes, removed their helmets and changed their footwear (in that order), they can set off.

THE FINER POINTS

PACING

BE AWARE THAT ATHLETES WILL BE PACING THEMSELVES UNTIL the final stages of the race: if they cycle like a time-trialler they're not going to make it to the finish line.

SIGHTING

IN THE SWIMMING SECTION, WATCH OUT FOR COMPETITORS 'SIGHTING'. This is where they raise their heads above water to look for course markers, using modified strokes that allow them to do so with minimal expenditure of energy and loss of speed.

TRANSITIONING

PAY CLOSE ATTENTION TO TRANSITIONS. TOP TRIATHLETES can perform them very smoothly but they can also come a cropper. Many a triathlon has been lost by a tangle with a wetsuit or the clumsy placement of a bicycle in its rack. The best athletes anticipate their transitions. In the closing stages of the swimming, for example, they will kick out a bit more to get some blood to their legs so that, when their hand hits terra firma, they can run hard to their bikes. When cycling, athletes will try not to dip below 90 revolutions per minute believing that this will help them hit 90 strides a minute during their run.

Triathlon Goes to the Olympics

The inaugural Olympic triathlons were held in the photogenic environs of the Sydney Opera House. The women went first, with Switzerland's Brigitte McMahon pipping local favourite Michellie Jones in a sprint finish. The men's champion was Canada's Simon Whitfield.

At Athens in 2004, the women's race again went to an athlete with a British-sounding name from an alpine nation. Austria's Kate Allen was in 28th place after the cycling and her victory was a dramatic illustration of the importance of keeping something in reserve for the 10km run. The men's title was won by New Zealand's Hamish Carter, who finished just under eight seconds ahead of his compatriot Bevan Docherty.

At Beijing 2008, Australia's Emma Snowsill won the women's event by an astounding margin of 66 seconds, with a recorded

ALL CHANGE PLEASE: THE SWIMMING TO CYCLING TRANSITION ZONE AT SYDNEY 2000

time of 1:58:27. (This is the fastest women's time but, because of the variability in conditions between locations, the Olympics does not keep records for the triathlon.) In the men's race, German champion JAN FRODENO took gold, leaving hot favourite Javier Gómez in fourth. Four years later in London, Gómez won silver as the Brownlee brothers secured gold and bronze in front of a fervent crowd of around 300,000 in Hyde Park. In the women's event, Switzerland's NICOLA SPIRIG clinched gold after a photo finish decided she had crossed the line in the 10km run just six inches ahead of Sweden's Lisa Nordén.

VOLLEYBALL

INDOOR: 6–21 AUGUST 2016

GINÁSIO DO MARACANÃZINHO, MARACANÃ, RIO

BEACH: 6–21 AUGUST 2016

COPACABANA BEACH, RIO

Athletes: 288 (INDOOR), 96 (BEACH) | **Golds up for grabs:** 4

OLYMPIC PRESENCE

INDOOR: DEMONSTRATION SPORT 1924; FULL MEDAL SPORT since 1964. BEACH VOLLEYBALL since 1996.

OLYMPIC FORMAT

IN INDOOR VOLLEYBALL TWELVE NATIONS COMPETE IN GROUPS to produce eight qualifiers for the knock-out rounds. On THE BEACH twenty-four nations compete in groups to produce sixteen qualifiers for the knock-out rounds

CONTENDERS

IN THE MEN'S VOLLEYBALL, THE FIELD HAS OPENED UP WITH POLAND and ITALY competing with the traditional powers: USA, BRAZIL AND RUSSIA. In the women's volleyball, BRAZIL are the reigning champions and will face serious competition from JAPAN, CHINA, the USA and possibly RUSSIA and SERBIA. In the beach version, RUSSIA, GERMANY, BRAZIL and the USA shared the gold medals in 2012, but expect AUSTRALIA and possibly the NETHERLANDS to challenge in Rio.

PAST CHAMPIONS

INDOOR: USSR/RUSSIA: 8 | BRAZIL: 4 | JAPAN: 3 |
USA: 3 | CUBA: 3
BEACH: USA: 6 | BRAZIL: 2 | AUSTRALIA: 1 | GERMANY: 1

Why Watch Volleyball?

Volleyball has a split personality. Its indoor version, with six-a-side teams, began as a wholesome sporting recreation for paunchy Massachusetts Christian businessmen that positively revelled in its honourable amateurism. Beach volleyball is a hedonistic, flamboyant and acrobatic variant, born on the beaches of Hawaii and California, that inhabited the same milieu as beauty pageants, and entered the world of globalised TV sport as a fiesta of hot bodies, tiny swimsuits and garish commercialism.

In reaction, indoor volleyball is now trying to sex itself up, introducing new rules and skimpier outfits to make the game faster and more television-friendly, while beach volleyball finds itself battling the constant accusation that it is not a serious sport. Neither version should worry: both are intensely athletic, tactically sophisticated and absorbingly competitive.

The Story of Volleyball

Like basketball, its muscular Christian cousin, volleyball began life as a project for YMCA physical educators in Massachusetts. Codified in 1891 by James Naismith at the Springfield YMCA, basketball was designed to fill the organisation's underused gyms. But not everyone could cope with the game's physicality, least of all the kind of slow-moving businessmen that came to William G. Morgan's classes in Holyoke.

Morgan experimented with various options for a new sport played with bare hands and a ball. He liked the idea of a court divided by a high net, as in badminton, and after experimenting with a basketball (too heavy) and a basketball bladder (too light) he convinced sports goods manufacturer Spalding to create a ball that was just right. Basic rules for batting the ball back and forth were drawn up, and a demonstration game of what was initially known as Mintonette was played at the YMCA conference of 1895. A member of that first audience, Professor Alfred T. Halstead, suggested that the sport be known as VOLLEY BALL (the two words officially became one in 1952).

In 1897 the rules were refined, and subsequently, through the YMCA's gym network, the sport spread to countries such as Canada, Cuba, Japan, Mexico, South America, China and India. The game really took off in the PHILIPPINES, where players were the first to perfect the attacking SET-AND-SPIKE routine, which they showcased at the 1913 Far Eastern Games.

In AMERICA volleyball became a craze, as colleges and the army introduced it into the curriculum. The US Overseas Expeditionary Force, stationed in Europe after the First World War, distributed 160,000 volleyballs to the public and played the game in front of huge crowds at the 1919 INTER-ALLIED GAMES in Paris – a mini-Olympics for the Allies' armies. Spreading into Central and Eastern Europe, volleyball became a popular minority sport in the inter-war era. Its rise continued after the Second World War and in 1947 an international governing body, the FIVB, was founded. The first volleyball World Championships were held in Prague in 1949.

The precise origins of BEACH VOLLEYBALL are disputed. Some say it originated with surfers on WAIKIKI BEACH near Honolulu, in the 1910s; others trace it to SANTA MONICA, California, in the following decade. Either way, it was only a matter of time before volleyball hit the beach: playing on sand, the most arduous aspects of the game – falling and rolling on the court – became part of the fun. The sport took hold in Southern California, evolving into its established TWO-A-SIDE format. Initially played on family outings, beach volleyball grew more popular through the 1930s as Californians flocked to the shore for exercise and fun. The scene was big enough to support organised tournaments after the Second World War and Pepsi, alert to the game's close association with beach culture, started sponsoring it in 1948.

For the next two decades, beach volleyball hovered between sport and showbiz. Proper competitions were organised in California but they were invariably paired with beauty pageants, bathing-suit contests and musical entertainments. MARILYN MONROE and JFK both thought the sport cool enough to be

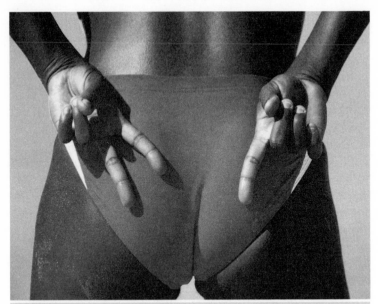

WATCH THOSE HAND SIGNALS – CRUCIAL IN BEACH VOLLEYBALL

photographed in the audience. By the 1970s beach volleyball had turned professional in the USA, was spreading to other major beach cultures – notably BRAZIL and AUSTRALIA – and was attracting so much attention and money that the FIVB, much to the old guard's displeasure, took the sport under its wing in 1986. The move was one of many controversial acts by the Mexican FIVB president, Rubén Acosta, a relentless commercialiser who was investigated by the IOC ethics committee and quit his post in 2008 amid allegations that he and his family had raked off millions in commissions on contracts.

As one of the world's most iconic beaches, the Copacabana should provide a spectacular setting for beach volleyball. In 1987, Rio de Janeiro hosted the sport's very first international event. The atmosphere inside the Maracanãzinho for the indoor version could be intense too: in 1983, Brazil and the USSR faced each other at the Maracanã in front of 95,000 spectators – the largest crowd in the history of the sport.

GAME ON: VOLLEYBALL BASICS

INDOOR VOLLEYBALL

INDOOR VOLLEYBALL IS PLAYED SIX-A-SIDE WITH A HIGH NET dividing the court. Teams hit the ball back and forth over the net until one side grounds the ball in the opponents' half or puts it out of play or into the net. Players may use any part of their bodies above the waist to hit the ball, but may not hold it. Individuals may touch the ball only ONCE before it goes back over the net, but the team as a whole is allowed THREE HITS before the ball is returned.

DIG, SET, SPIKE!

PLAY BEGINS WITH A SERVE FROM THE BACK LINE. THE RECEIVING side will look to DIG THE BALL (cushion and control it with their forearms), then play a SET UP, putting the ball into a position where it can be struck hard and downwards over the net – a shot known as the SPIKE. The opposing team will try to BLOCK the ball as soon as it comes over the net so that it drops straight back on the other side and is hard to return. Players must not TOUCH THE NET at any time.

SERVING UP

SERVICE ROTATES AMONG THE PLAYERS OF THE TEAM, EACH player continuing to serve until their team loses the point. Each time the side wins back the serve the players ROTATE clockwise around the court, consequently the best defensive players – with the exception of the libero (see below) – must sometimes play attack and vice versa. Serves may be UNDERARM or OVERARM, but at the Olympics most players throw the ball high, leap and attempt an overarm jump serve.

THE SPECIAL ONE

THE LIBERO IS A SPECIALISED POSITION. THE PLAYER MUST wear different kit from the rest of the team, can play only in the back row, and is not allowed to serve or spike the ball. The libero

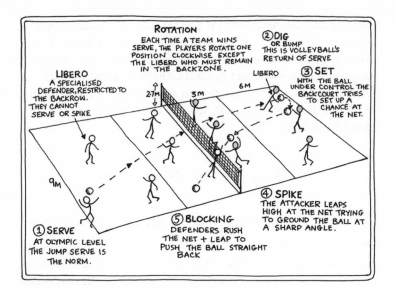

is usually a defensive specialist, who receives serve and cushions attacks from the back of the court

POINTS, SET, MATCH

POINTS ARE SCORED ON EVERY RALLY, WITH THE WINNER OF the point taking the next serve. SETS are won by the first team to 25, provided they are two points clear. If they aren't, play continues until one side goes two points ahead. MATCHES are the best of five sets. The fifth set is played to fifteen points.

SUBSTITUTIONS

SUBSTITUTIONS CAN BE MADE AT THE START OF A SET OR during a time out. A maximum of six changes can be made per set. Each team has twelve members.

BEACH VOLLEYBALL

THE BEACH RULES ARE THE SAME AS FOR INDOOR VOLLEYBALL except that the game is played TWO-A-SIDE, with no fixed player positions and no substitutions. The court is fractionally smaller and is played on SAND which must be at least 40cm deep; the ball is slightly bigger and pumped to a lower pressure; a BLOCK counts as one of the three hits; and games are the best of THREE SETS – in the first two the victor is the first to reach 21 by two clear points (or to pull two points ahead), while in the third set the first to reach fifteen wins.

THE FINER POINTS

SERVICE WITH A SMILE

LOOK OUT FOR TOP-SPIN SERVES, WHICH ARE HIT WITH THE wrist and drop sharply once they cross the net, and FLOATS, in which the ball is given no spin and has a very unpredictable flight. In 1982, Brazilian player Bernard invented what became known as the 'Star Trek' serve, launching the ball so high it nearly touched the ceiling before plummeting into the opposition court.

DEFENSIVE TACTICS

ALTHOUGH TEAMS USUALLY PLACE THREE PLAYERS AT THE BACK of the court to receive serve, they sometimes use just two, leaving the third player free to occupy a better position for setting the ball.

Many teams will gamble on where a return is going to cross the net. Team members will jump high at the net before the ball is released by the opposition. When it works the effect is devastating. Watch for blockers who reach over the net to play the ball sharply down, thus immediately turning defence into attack.

ATTACKING TACTICS

LOOK FOR THE TANDEM ATTACK, WHERE TWO PLAYERS approach the ball at the net simultaneously, forcing defenders to choose which of them to block and giving the attackers the chance to pass to an unmarked hitter. A similar play is the CROSSOVER, in which the two attackers make crossing diagonal runs. In the PIS-TON move, two attackers are at the net, one behind the other, again

forcing the defender to decide which one to follow and potentially giving the other an open shot.

ON THE BEACH

In beach volleyball keep an eye on the signals players make behind their backs, indicating what kind of serve or defensive play they want their team-mates to make. For example, if a player has two hands behind a back, they wiggle a finger on their top hand to show which side of the court they want the ball served to and wiggle a finger on their lower hand if they want the serve hit deep.

Volleyball Goes to the Olympics

Volleyball's first moment in the Olympic limelight may have been its finest. Seventy per cent of the Japanese population watched the opening ceremony of the 1964 Tokyo Olympics and nearly all of them turned on again for the hosts' most celebrated sporting triumph, the women's volleyball. The match that decided who won gold and who had to settle for silver was an epic battle between the tall, powerful squad from the Soviet Union and the shorter, lighter but indefatigable Japanese team. The latter had begun life in 1953 when DAIMATSU HIROFUMI, a manager at the Nichibo Spinning Mills near Osaka, started up a women's volleyball programme. A former soldier, his methods were notoriously harsh and his team trained six hours a day after work. Hirofumi's regimen worked, and Japan – effectively the Nichibo team – arrived at the Olympics as defending World Champions, hailed by Pravda as 'the witches of the Orient' after winning the title in Moscow in 1962. In the decisive fixture in Tokyo, Japan raced into a two set lead, but the Soviets stormed back in the third, nearly stealing the set before the hosts took back the serve and won 15-13. The winning shot was watched by 94.5% of the Japanese population.

Though Olympic volleyball has never quite reached such an emotional pitch since, the women's game has provided many of the sport's biggest stories. The victory by the CHINESE women's team at the 1984 LOS ANGELES Games, the first time the country had competed in this event, was acclaimed at home as a huge national triumph. LANG PING, the team's star, earned the heroic soubriquet 'iron hammer'. A trio of golds for the CUBAN women (in 1992, 1996 and 2000) was followed by the brilliant recovery of the CHINESE women in the 2004 Olympic final, from two sets down against the Russians, a victory greeted with euphoria by a Chinese population that was now glued to its television sets. The women's volleyball was duly one of the hottest tickets at BEIJING 2008, where the competition was made all the spicier by the presence of Lang Ping as coach of the US women's team. The Americans took the silver ahead of China, with BRAZIL winning gold. The 2008 finalists met again in the 2012 final, with Brazil once more defeating America.

In the MEN'S GAME the Olympics were dominated by the SOVIET UNION and EASTERN EUROPEAN nations until the 1980s. Since then the USA (1984, 1988 and 2008) and BRAZIL (1992, 2004), both benefiting from the decline of communist volleyball and the rise of the professional game, have won the competition, as have the DUTCH (1996) and the YUGOSLAVS (2000). In London, RUSSIA fought back from two sets down in the final against Brazil to win gold.

Since volleyball first arrived at the Olympics in 1964, it has become faster and more acrobatic. Yet outside of Japan and China it

BRAZIL'S WOMEN ATTEMPT A TRIPLE BLOCK, BEIJING 2008

has not attracted the kinds of audience and TV ratings you might expect from a game played so widely. On and off the court, volleyball remains bound to its amateur roots, with strict forms of etiquette applied to player behaviour. Bad language, for example, is regularly punished and over-emotional displays are frowned upon.

BEACH VOLLEYBALL offers much of what the traditional game has lacked. When it debuted at the 1996 ATLANTA OLYMPICS, it was the third event to sell out – though cynics suggested that was as much down to the bikinis and well-toned flesh on display as the sporting experience. Indeed, in 1999 the FIVB rewrote the sport's sartorial rules, insisting on the two-piece bikini kit for women (with a maximum size for the bottom half) and making more revealing kit compulsory for men, too. The beach discipline has proved enormously popular at every Olympics since. At LONDON 2012, the American women's team of Kerri Lee Walsh Jennings and Misty-May Treanor cemented their claim to be 'the greatest beach volleyball team of all time' by winning their third successive gold medal. Beach volleyball will certainly be one of the main attractions in Rio, with Brazil going for gold in the men's and women's events, against the famous backdrop of the Copacabana.

WATER POLO

6–20 AUGUST 2016

MARIA LENK AQUATIC CENTRE,

BARRA DA TIJUCA, RIO

Athletes: 260 | **Golds up for grabs:** 2

OLYMPIC PRESENCE

MEN SINCE 1900; WOMEN SINCE 2000.

OLYMPIC FORMAT

BOTH MEN AND WOMEN'S TEAMS PLAY IN PRELIMINARY GROUPS
with eight teams progressing to the quarter-finals.

CURRENT CONTENDERS

IN THE MEN'S TOURNAMENT THE ESTABLISHED NATIONS ARE
ITALY, HUNGARY, RUSSIA, SERBIA and CROATIA – though Spain,
Australia, Montenegro and the USA are all contenders and BRAZIL
have recently been in good form. In the women's tournament, the
AMERICANS have never failed to make the podium and AUSTRALIA
have been almost as consistent. They will face strong competition
from SPAIN, CHINA, CANADA and RUSSIA.

PAST CHAMPIONS

HUNGARY: 9 | ITALY: 4 | GREAT BRITAIN: 4

WHY WATCH WATER POLO?

'FISTS FLEW AND BLOOD FLOWED,' RAN THE HEADLINE IN THE
New York Times on 6 December 1956. You might have been
expecting a boxing report and in a way you would have been
right, but the *Times* was actually reviewing Hungary's 4-0 victory

against the Soviet Union in the men's water polo competition at the Melbourne Olympics. By far the most famous moment in the sport's history, it was also the biggest ever Olympic brawl.

The swimming caps with huge ear protectors worn by water polo players wouldn't look out of place on a rugby field and they wear two pairs of trunks for a reason. Ears get mauled, trunks get ripped and these are merely the least of the shenanigans that go on in this furious form of aquatic handball. The game is insanely demanding. Players must constantly tread water, beating out egg-beater patterns of strokes with their legs, lift themselves up out of the water when necessary and switch to lung-burning sprints as the play surges from end to end.

Dominated in modern times by Australia, Hungary, Russia, Italy, the US and Yugoslavia (and its descendant states), water polo is invariably played at an intense emotional and physical pitch, with players, coaches and fans given to outbreaks of volcanic temper. What the sport lacks in elegance it more than makes up for in tempestuousness and titanic competitiveness.

The Story of Water Polo

The precise origins of water polo are unclear. Some sources trace it back to members of the British Army of the Raj attempting an aquatic version of the horse-bound form of polo, but it seems more likely to have been developed for a lark by young men in Britain swimming in lakes and the first generation of Victorian municipal baths.

Players took their cues from rugby and football, attempting to score goals with much fighting, rucking, ducking and punching along the way. Early variants included scoring by placing the ball on a buoy or at the end of the pool, and goalies standing outside the water and only jumping in when their goals were threatened.

A measure of rationality, if not civility, was introduced by Scottish pioneer William Wilson, whose 1877 rules for the game of 'water football' forbade the tackling of players not in possession of the ball. The first organised competition, the London Water Polo

VICTORIAN GENTLEMEN EXPERIMENT WITH AQUATIC FORMS OF POLO

League, was established in 1888 and two years later Scotland beat England 4-0 in the sport's international debut. Interestingly, the Scottish players' preference for collective passing over the English taste for individual dribbling mirrored the nations' contemporary approaches to football. By 1900, water polo was popular enough to be the first team sport to be selected for the Olympics.

In the years before the First World War, young, often college-educated men were introduced to the game in cities across continental Europe and North America. The Italians were especially keen, despite a Milanese paper describing the sport in 1890 as being 'like football but more tiring and difficult, requiring energy and strength beyond the ordinary'. The game also proved popular in France, Belgium, the United States and, above all, in Hungary and Yugoslavia.

Controlled by FINA since 1930, the game has been steadily refined to speed up play and to persuade players to focus on the ball rather than the man or woman. The Hungarians were the first to use the dry pass, in which the ball moves from hand to hand rather than the receiver picking it up out of the water. This was the basis of their long era of superiority either side of the Second World War. In 1956, they even pioneered a form of zonal marking, decades before this style of defending became popular in European football.

Leather balls, which absorbed water and got slower and heavier as the game progressed, were replaced by rubber-coated versions during the 1930s. As with basketball, which was suffering from low-scoring and over-physical play, shot clocks were introduced in the 1950s. Henceforward, a team had 45 seconds (now down to 30) to shoot on goal before possession passed to the opposition. Similarly, accumulated fouls and violent play were increasingly punished, ultimately leading to players being temporarily excluded from play. It is in these situations, with one side a player down, that most goals are scored.

Game On: Water Polo Basics

WATER POLO IS A GAME OF ATTACK, DEFENCE AND TRANSITION. Each team consists of six players and a goalkeeper. When one side has the ball, it moves it by dribbling, passing and hopefully shooting on goal. When a team loses possession, it blocks, tackles and tries to snatch the ball back. Whenever the ball changes hands there is an almighty sprint by both sides from one end of the pool to the other.

THE POOL must be at least two metres deep and players are not allowed to touch the bottom, which means that they must constantly tread water, including during STOPPAGES. There are a lot of these in most games, which, despite being scheduled for just 28 minutes of play, can last over an hour. The MAIN NO-NOS are taking the ball underwater, tackling a player without the ball and using two hands to hold the ball (unless you are a goalkeeper). When a FOUL is called against a team it concedes possession to the opposition. If it commits a foul inside its own 5-metre line, the opponents get a PENALTY THROW on goal.

DANGEROUS, VIOLENT AND UNSPORTSMANLIKE PLAY, which abounds, results in an exclusion foul being called and a 20-SECOND PENALTY imposed on the guilty party. Examples include splashing water in an opponent's face, and holding or sinking them. Brutal

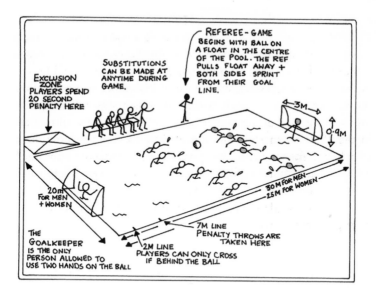

play, such as kicking or punching with malicious intent, leads to permanent exclusion, with substitution only allowed after four minutes.

THE FINER POINTS

·· **WATCHING THE ATTACK** ··

FOR MUCH OF THE TIME, BOTH TEAMS CLUSTER AROUND ONE of the goals. The key player to look for is the 2-METRE or 'HOLE' MAN positioned in the centre, and the defender who has been tasked with guarding him. As well as absorbing a lot of fouls, the 2-metre man is the pivot of most attacking moves, passing the ball along to team-mates along the semi-circular perimeter of the 2-metre line.

Some of the best SKILLS in the game can be seen when attacking players find an angle around the defence, using a body feint, a sudden leap or a flick of the wrist to change direction. At LONDON 2012, Hungary's Marton Szivos found the net after flicking the ball up in the air with his foot and scoring with a backhand shot over his shoulder into the goal.

····························· **WATCHING THE DEFENCE** ·····························

DEFENDERS look to block their opponent's paths to goal and to contest and block passes and shots. They can also tackle players with the ball and attempt to steal it from their grasp.

The best defenders play the ball not the man and concentrate on turning possession over. However, there is a lot of aggressive body contact, especially underwater. Look out for illegal grapples, punches, scratching with fingers and toes (even though officials check players have filed their nails down before a game starts), elbowing and GROIN GRABBING.

WATER POLO GOES TO THE OLYMPICS

THE FIRST OLYMPIC WATER POLO TOURNAMENT TOOK PLACE in the River Seine in 1900 and was contested by clubs from Brussels, Lille and Manchester. The Osborne Swimming Club from Manchester took gold for Great Britain, which went on to win another three titles (1908, 1912 and 1920) before disappearing from the world of competitive water polo altogether. Britain last qualified for an Olympic tournament in 1956, where it finished seventh of eight.

At the 1904 Games, the USA monopolised the medals, but as all three teams were American this was scarcely surprising. A team from Germany had travelled to St Louis but found itself at odds with the American officials, who decided that a goal could only be scored by holding the ball in the net and deemed a partially deflated volleyball perfectly adequate for the competition. Accustomed to different rules and better equipment, the Germans derided this 'softball water polo' and refused to compete. Maybe they knew something the Americans didn't. Suffering from their long immersion in the bacteria-ridden lake, four of the American players died within a year from typhoid.

In 1932 the HUNGARIANS, who had taken the silver medal in 1928, crossed the Atlantic by liner, practising in a tiny on-board pool, and made for Los Angeles. One of the stars of this victorious team was Oliver Halassy, who had lost his left foot in an accident when he was eight. Their triumph was the first of the country's nine gold medals. Since then, all but one Olympic tournament has been won by Hungary, Italy, Yugoslavia, the Soviet Union or descendent states of the last two.

Hungary's gold in 1932 established the new global water polo aristocracy but Brazil's experience at the same tournament was a harbinger of controversies to come. The Brazilians almost failed to make the Games at all, the government having initially responded to a collapse of the world coffee market by refusing to fund the trip to LA. Then, in a stroke of administrative genius, it decided to send an Olympic squad to America, accompanied by a 50-strong marine band and 25 tonnes of coffee. Squad members would serve as crew and sell coffee en route, to cover their expenses.

Things didn't quite work out. An attempt to pass the ship off as a military vessel to get free passage through the Panama Canal was rumbled by the Panamanian authorities despite the presence of two rusty cannons on board. Coffee sales were so poor that on arriving in the USA, the athletes could only muster $24 between them, enough to send 24 representatives ashore, each paying the $1 immigration tax. Fortunately for the water polo team, its members were among them. While the rest of the squad headed for Portland and Seattle to sell coffee, they travelled to Los Angeles and wrote

Hungary v. USSR 1956

The Melbourne Olympics were played in the shadow of the Hungarian revolution and the recent invasion of the country by the Soviet Army. As luck would have it, the Hungarian and Soviet water polo teams shared a boat for the journey to Australia – and the fighting began on board. Once in Australia, the large expatriate Hungarian community in Melbourne made sure that the Hungarian team were well aware of their feelings – and when the two teams met in their final group game, nearly 5,000 Hungarian Australians came along to watch.

The Hungarians went into the match intending to wind up their opponents. It didn't take long for their shouts of 'You dirty bastards, you come over and bomb our country' to take effect. In the second minute, one Soviet player gripped his Hungarian opponent in a hammer lock, whereupon he was excluded, to a hail of catcalls. This set things up nicely. Early in the second half, with the Hungarians leading 2-0, Boris Markarov delivered a haymaker punch to the eye of Hungary's Belvari. All hell broke loose; the pool was engulfed in fighting and the ball all but forgotten. In the final minutes of the game, a Russian hit Hungarian Ervin Zador so hard that he split his brow, opening a wound that bled profusely into the water. The crowd spilled out of the stands and on to the tiles around the pool, screaming at the Soviets and forcing the police to intervene.

Hungary held on to win 4-0. Afterwards Zador made clear what had been at stake: 'We felt we were playing not just for ourselves but for our whole country.' Several members of the Hungarian team defected and stayed in Australia. Zador settled in America where, as a swimming coach, he trained a talented teenager called Mark Spitz.

ERVIN ZADOR AFTER THAT PUNCH

themselves into Olympic history at the conclusion of their first round 7-3 defeat by the Germans. Incensed by what they perceived as the Hungarian referee's bias, they finished the game with a polite cheer for their opponents and a mass attack on the judges' stand, an assault eventually halted by the LAPD.

And so it has gone on. The greatest Olympic PUNCH-UP of all took place at the 1956 Hungary-USSR semi-final (see opposite page) but there has been many another ruckus. In 1992, with King Juan Carlos in the audience, Italy beat hosts Spain 9-8 in the final, with Ferdinando Gandolfi scoring the winner with 32 seconds to go – but only after the players had climbed out of the pool to scuffle with each other, the coaches had had a pushing match and an Italian official had shouted: 'The referee is a thief.' The swimsuit

HELLO BOYS! THE SINGAPOREAN GOVERNMENT WASN'T BEST PLEASED WITH THIS SARTORIAL COCK-UP

ripping and punching that marked women's water polo's Olympic debut at SYDNEY 2000 proved that the boys have no monopoly on this roughhouse of a sport.

In 2012, Croatia won the men's competition but their victory will probably be best remembered for a Geoff Hurst-style controversy in a group match against Spain. The Croatians won 8-7 but only because a last-gasp goal by Spain's Ivan Perez was not given. As the BBC commentator put it: 'Everybody in this stadium saw that ball pass behind the line of the goal.' To be accurate, everybody in the stadium saw that except for Slovenian referee Boris Margeta who declared it was not a goal – even though the line judge was convinced it was. In the women's event, Spain were involved in a very different kind of controversy when NBC was slammed for inadvertently showing a contestant's nipple after America's Kami Craig pulled on a Spanish player's swimsuit, briefly exposing her opponents' breast. The incident was not repeated when the sides met in the final, which the US won 8-5.

Water polo offers occasional fun for fashion spotters. At the 2010 Asian Games, Singapore's male players were sharply criticised by their government for their undignified swimsuits. Designed by the team themselves, the trunks, like the national flag, were red with five white stars and a white crescent. Unintentionally or not, the crescent was positioned directly over the players' groins.

WEIGHTLIFTING

6–16 AUGUST 2016

RIOCENTRO PAVILION 6, RIO DE JANEIRO

Athletes: 260 | **Golds up for grabs:** 15

OLYMPIC PRESENCE

MEN: 1896, 1904, 1920–PRESENT; WOMEN SINCE 2000

OLYMPIC FORMAT

ATHLETES IN ALL WEIGHT CATEGORIES PERFORM TWO LIFTS: the snatch, in which they raise the bar over their heads in one movement, and the clean-and-jerk, in which they do it in two. The maximum weights a competitor lifts in each are added together to give their final score.

CONTENDERS

GREECE, TURKEY, RUSSIA, BULGARIA AND CHINA ARE THE leading nations in men's weightlifting, though Iran, North Korea and Ukraine all won gold in London. Lifters from China, Kazakhstan and North Korea dominated the women's competition in 2012.

PAST CHAMPIONS

RUSSIA/USSR: 47 | CHINA: 24 | USA: 16 | BULGARIA: 12

WHY WATCH WEIGHTLIFTING?

IF THE 100 METRES IS THE PUREST TEST OF THE CITIUS ('FASTER') portion of the Olympic motto, and the high jump and pole vault of the *altius* ('higher'), the *fortius* ('stronger') bit unquestionably belongs to weightlifting. The sport provides some of the most compelling theatre at the Games. It may have a drug record to rival the Tour de France but there are few Olympic sights as exhilarating as an athlete psyching himself up to an almost unbearable pitch before hoisting three times his body weight over his head, a feat rendered all the more spectacular because it is often accompanied by a vivid soundtrack of grunts, groans and wails.

The mechanics of the sport favour short, squat athletes who don't have to hoist the weight as far as their longer-limbed peers. The ultimate example was JOE DI PIETRO of the USA, who won bantamweight gold in 1948. Standing just 4ft 10in, he had arms so short he could barely raise the bar above his head.

Aside from the need for SHORT ARMS and BRUTE STRENGTH, the sport is intensely PSYCHOLOGICAL: if a lifter doesn't believe they can lift a weight, they haven't a chance. Conversely, if they convince themselves that they can, they may prove themselves right. The fact that competitors can only attempt THREE LIFTS in each discipline allows them to play fearsome mind games with opponents. The most common is to select an intimidating STARTING WEIGHT. This policy can backfire – it isn't unheard of for a weightlifter to make the initial bar so heavy that they fail to register a single lift. One favourite tactic of Turkey's Naim Suleymanoglu, of whom we shall hear more later, was to pass up his turn to lift, let his rivals exhaust themselves, and then stride out, ask for more weight on the bar, and lift it easily, beating everyone.

The Story of Weightlifting

HUMANS HAVE BEEN COMPARING STRENGTH BY LIFTING HEAVY objects since we developed opposable thumbs. The earliest historical record of the practice is a mural of men exercising with weights (possibly sacks of sand) in the ANCIENT EGYPTIAN tomb of Beni Hassan, c. 3500 BC. Weightlifting was an important aspect of military training in the ancient world. In CHINA, two distinct forms of contest evolved during the first millennium BC. The first was QIAO GUAN, which involved grabbing one end of a heavy door bar and lifting it with one hand. Popular among court warriors, by the Tang Dynasty

(618–907AD) it had become part of the army's entrance examination, with the door bar replaced by tailor-made weights. The other format, KANG DING, entailed the lifting of massive two-handled cooking pots or *dings*. During the Han Dynasty (206BC–220AD), Kang Ding became a professional sport.

Weightlifting was popular in ANCIENT GREECE, as a conditioning activity for soldiers and a demonstration of machismo. A red sandstone block weighing 143kg displayed at the archaeological museum at OLYMPIA bears the inscription 'Bybon son of Phola lifted me over his head with one hand'. Meanwhile, Bybon's contemporary Milo of Croton, the sixth-century BC superman who we will meet again in the Wrestling chapter, is the first lifter recorded as using a progressive system of resistance training. He acquired a male calf, lifted it every day and continued to do so until it had grown into a bull. When he could no longer shift it, he ate it.

The ROMANS inherited the Greeks' penchant for weightlifting but during the Dark and Middle Ages the focus of activity shifted to the CELTIC and SCANDINAVIAN fringes of Europe. Here the sport took the form of elemental battles between man and nature in the shape of enormous rocks. To get work on a fishing vessel in Iceland, a candidate had to be able to hoist a 104kg boulder called a *hálfsterkur* ('half strength') onto a hip-height ledge. The full strength version *(fullsterkur)* weighed 155kg. The SCOTS also used LIFTING STONES as male initiation devices. Known as *clach cuid fir* ('manhood stones'), they included such legendary lumps of mineral as the McGlashen Stones and the Blue Stones of Old Dailly.

Modern weightlifting sprang from the mania for all things classical that swept through Europe and the USA during the eighteenth and nineteenth centuries. One aspect of this was a renewed interest in physical training, which led aristocratic young men to join GYMNASIUMS, and universities to add PE to their curricula. The phenomenon that really glamorised weightlifting, however, was the CIRCUS STRONGMAN. People on both sides of the Atlantic flocked to watch big moustachioed men break chains, lift horses and pick up cannons.

One of the most influential members of this colourful profession was the German LOUIS ATTILA, born Ludwig Durlacher in 1844.

FREDERICK WINTERS, SILVER
MEDALLIST IN THE ALL-ROUND
DUMBBELL EVENT, ST LOUIS 1904

Learning his craft from Italian strongman Felice Napoli, he partnered up with Valerie the Female Gladiator and introduced all kinds of innovations to weightlifting, including the SHOT-LOADED GLOBE BARBELL. This device, which allowed the weight of a single piece of equipment to be varied precisely, spelled the end for the old fashioned dumbbell (originally a shaft with a pair of clapperless bells at either end). People – including crowned heads of state – solicited Attila's advice on strength and fitness, and around 1887 he opened his first gym in Brussels. After running a similar institution in London, in 1893 he founded the wildly successful Attila's Athletic Studio and School of Physical Culture in New York. Among his students were Eugene Sandow, known as the 'father of modern bodybuilding', the boxing champion James J. Corbett and, astonishingly for the era, several women.

Other developments that helped transform weightlifting from sideshow attraction to sport included the DISC LOADING SYSTEM of weights, introduced by M. M. PELLETIER MONNIER in the 1880s, and, in the 1920s, CHARLES RIGOULOT's pioneering use of a LONG, SPRINGY BAR, with which he broke the clean-and-jerk world record. Training became increasingly scientific. In 1906, the nine-stone W. A. PULLUM founded the first weightlifting school that emphasised technique over strength. Six years later, he vindicated his methods by becoming the first Briton to lift twice his bodyweight.

The final pieces in the jigsaw were the establishment in 1920 of a global governing body for the sport, the INTERNATIONAL WEIGHTLIFTING FEDERATION, and the emergence of competitions for women. The first women's event was held in the USA in 1947.

GAME ON: WEIGHTLIFTING BASICS

---------- **FORMAT** ----------

MEN COMPETE IN EIGHT BODY-WEIGHT CATEGORIES (56KG, 62KG, 69kg, 77kg, 85kg, 94kg, 105kg, 105kg+) and women in seven (48kg, 53kg, 58kg, 63kg, 69kg, 75kg, 75kg+). In Rio, 156 men and 104 women will take part in the weightlifting competitions. No nation may enter more than ten individuals in total or more than two in any one event.

---------- **RULES** ----------

COMPETITORS ARE REQUIRED TO REGISTER SUCCESSFUL LIFTS in both the SNATCH and the CLEAN-AND-JERK, which take place in that order. A maximum of THREE ATTEMPTS is allowed in each discipline, whether the lifts are successful or not. After being called to the platform, a competitor has one minute to begin their lift or two if they made the previous lift in the competition themselves. If they succeed in lifting a weight, it must be increased by at least 1kg for their next attempt (though they are usually increased in multiples of 2.5kg).

For a lift to be declared valid it must be performed in the COR-RECT NUMBER OF MOVEMENTS – one in the snatch, two in the clean-and-jerk. Once the weight is above the head, the elbows must be locked, the legs brought together and the competitor must be in complete control for long enough for at least two of the three judges to register a GOOD LIFT.

They do this by pressing buttons which illuminate WHITE LIGHTS. NO-LIFTS are signalled by RED LIGHTS. A jury is on hand to vet the judges' decisions. If a lifter DROPS THE BAR before lowering it to waist height, the lift is technically invalid. If two competitors lift the SAME TOTAL WEIGHT during the competition, the one with the lower body-weight is placed higher in the rankings.

---------- **TECHNIQUE** ----------

THE STANDARD WAY OF GRIPPING THE BAR IS KNOWN AS THE HOOK. The thumb is wrapped around the bar and the first and

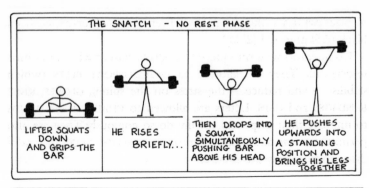

second fingers are placed tightly over it. The SNATCH is the more difficult discipline as the lifter must judge precisely when to position their body under the rising bar for the decisive upwards push. Too early and the bar will come down onto their chest. Too late and it will fall behind, quite possibly dislocating the lifter's shoulders in the process.

Lifters generally place their hands less far apart on the bar for the CLEAN-AND-JERK than for the snatch. Having completed the first movement (bringing the bar to shoulder height), the lifter drops into a squat position before simultaneously straightening the legs and powering upwards with their arms.

··· **EQUIPMENT** ···

LIFTING TAKES PLACE ON A 4×4M WOODEN PLATFORM COAT-ED with a non-slip surface. The DISC WEIGHTS, which are fastened in place with a 2.5kg collar at each end, are colour-coded from black (2.5kg) to red (25kg).

Competitors wear one-piece LEOTARDS, with or without T-shirts underneath. They are allowed to wear SUPPORT BELTS (which stabilise – and reduce – the stress on the spine), GLOVES, KNEE BANDAGES and CAPS. Lifters are allowed to CHALK THEIR HANDS to improve their grips and usually do so copiously. They are also permitted to use ammonium carbonate SMELLING SALTS to render themselves suitably pugnacious.

THE FINER POINTS

PSYCHING UP

ONE OF THE PLEASURES OF WATCHING THE SPORT IS TRYING to guess whether or not a lifter will succeed at a particular weight on the basis of their conduct immediately prior to the attempt. Keep an eye on the way a lifter chalks their hands and to their facial expressions and body language. Do they betray nervousness or convey self-belief? And does the vibe change during the maximum of sixty seconds they have between mounting the platform and attempting the lift?

Some lifters have distinctive ways of getting into the zone. The Iranian Kurd MOHAMMAD NASIRI, who won the bantamweight gold in Mexico, used to pray for thirty seconds, then turn to the bar and shout 'Ya Ali!' in homage to the first leader of the Shiites. Japan's TAKASHI ICHIBA, who came fourth in the same class in 1984, performed a back-flip before each attempt. Other lifters more or less beat themselves up to get their adrenaline pumping.

ELBOWS, EXPLOSIONS AND EXECUTION

WHEN THE MOMENT OF TRUTH COMES, TRY TO GAUGE THE explosivity of the lift or the lack of it. This is a fairly reliable guide to how much the lifter may have left in the tank. SPEED OF EXECUTION is essential to successful weightlifting as the contestant expends less energy. Watch out for whether the elbows lock and the legs come together in the last phase of the lift. If they don't, it should be declared invalid. Allow yourself to get swept up by the crowd's emotions. Weightlifting fans are a vocal lot so feel free to yell at the telly.

THE INSIDE DOPE ON WEIGHTLIFTING

S ince 1968, thirteen male lifters – and one female – have been stripped of their medals after being busted for doping offences. Another eight male gold medallists – and two female Olympic champions – have been banned for doping offences at other times in their careers. Norway's Leif Jenssen, who won gold in 1972, wasn't banned for taking anabolic steroids but has freely admitting using them, on the grounds that, as everyone else probably was, he couldn't have won without them.

The use of performance-enhancing substances in sport is as old as sport itself. Athletes at the ancient Games pepped themselves up by eating lizard meat, nineteenth-century bike-racers were known to ingest nitroglycerine to dilate their blood vessels, and Thomas Hicks, the American winner of the 1904 marathon, staved off exhaustion with two shots of strychnine and a glass of brandy. As a sport that is all about explosiveness and muscle development – attributes which the illicit administration of drugs can profoundly improve – weightlifting has been particularly vulnerable to interference from the laboratories.

The key figure in the evolution of doping in the modern era was the American DR JOHN ZIEGLER. In 1954, he travelled to Vienna with the US weightlifting team, where he fell into conversation with a Soviet trainer. Lubricated by a few drinks, the Russian revealed that 'his boys' had been routinely receiving TESTOSTERONE injections since the mid-1940s. When Ziegler got back to the States, he dosed himself, the great Bob Hoffman and two lifters with the hormone but was unhappy with the side effects.

His dissatisfaction led him to work with the Ciba Pharmaceutical Group to develop an oral ANABOLIC STEROID (a class of drugs that mimic the effects of testosterone) called Dianabol, which became commercially available in 1960. Ziegler administered the drug to the entire US weightlifting squad at that year's Olympics – completely legally, it should be pointed out, as the IOC didn't formally ban performance-enhancing drugs until 1967 – but they were still resoundingly beaten by the Soviets. When Ziegler discovered that some of his lifters had damaged their livers by taking twenty times the recommended dose of Dianabol, he abandoned his experiments. 'I lost interest in fooling with IQs of that calibre,' he said later. But the damage had been done.

Lowlights in the subsequent history of drug abuse and Olympic weightlifting have included the disqualification of the Bulgarian IZABELA DRAGNEVA after winning the first-ever women's weightlifting gold in Sydney, eleven out of thirteen members of the GREEK SQUAD testing positive before Beijing, and the withdrawal of the entire BULGARIAN TEAM from the same Games after dismal test results in the run-in. In London, the organisers narrowly avoided serious embarrassment when an offer to make Bulgarian gold medallist Sevdalin Marinov technical operations manager was withdrawn after it was revealed that, in 1995, he had been given a two-year ban for testing positive for steroids. The first official doping ban at London 2012 was, all but inevitably, issued to a lifter, Albania's HYSEN PULAKU.

The doping record has naturally been acutely embarrassing for the IWF and the IOC. Unfortunately, there is only so much they can do about it. They have devised ever more sophisticated testing procedures but this has only inspired the shady men in white coats to develop cleverer ways of avoiding detection.

WEIGHTLIFTING GOES TO THE OLYMPICS

WEIGHTLIFTING FEATURED IN THE INAUGURAL MODERN Games in Athens but it was a very different animal from the contemporary sport. For one thing, it was deemed a track and field event. For another, there were no weight classes (which remained the case until ANTWERP 1920). Instead, there were just two events, open to all. LAUNCESTON ELLIOT of Great Britain took gold in the ONE-HAND LIFT but had to settle for silver in the TWO-HANDED equivalent. He lifted the same weight (111.5kg) as the winner, Denmark's VIGGO JENSEN, but was adjudged to have done so with less style. Clearly a sporting polymath, Jensen also won a couple of shooting medals and came fourth in the rope climb.

Absent from the 1900 Games, weightlifting reappeared at ST LOUIS. Again there were just two events, this time the two-hand lift and an ALL ROUND DUMBBELL CONTEST, which featured a bewildering nine different lifts. The fields were rather thin – a mere five athletes took part – which may explain why there was no weightlifting at the 1908 and 1912 Games. But the sport made a comeback at ANTWERP in 1920 and has remained ever since.

VASILY 'THE BODY' ALEXEYEV IN ACTION IN MOSCOW IN 1980

There was still some tinkering with the formula to be done. One-handed lifts continued to feature until LOS ANGELES 1932, when the competition switched to a THREE-LIFT FORMAT (snatch, clean-and-jerk, and press, which involved hoisting the bar to the shoulders and waiting two seconds before raising it above the head with arm power alone). This endured until 1972 when the press was dropped.

During the Olympic era, different regions of the world have dominated the sport in turn. If the 1920s belonged to ITALY, FRANCE and CENTRAL EUROPE, the 1930s and 1940s were bossed by EGYPT and the USA. Much of America's success during this period can be attributed to BOB HOFFMAN of York, Pennsylvania, who recruited promising European immigrants to work in his oil burner business and trained them up in his gym. The dramatic decline of the USA's weightlifting fortunes after the Second World War coincided with the ascendancy of the SOVIET BLOC, whose lifters claimed the lion's share of Olympic medals between 1950 and the fall of the Berlin Wall. Latterly, things have come nicely full circle, with the nations with the longest weightlifting pedigree – CHINA plus GREECE, TURKEY and BULGARIA – ruling the roost. In 2012, KAZAKHSTAN and NORTH KOREA were among the medals, with lifters from both countries breaking Olympic records.

SULEYMANOGLU: THE POCKET HERCULES

The featherweight Naim Suleymanoglu is not just the greatest Olympic weightlifter of all time – on a pound for pound basis, he is one of the strongest men ever to have lived. Heaven knows what he would have achieved if he hadn't puffed his way through fifty fags a day, 'to find my inner peace', as he memorably put it.

Born in 1967 in Pitchar, Bulgaria, to a diminutive family of ethnic Turks (his father, a zinc miner, was 5ft tall, his mother, a hothouse worker, 4ft 7in), Suleimanov – as he was originally called – was prodigiously strong from an early age. His strange proportions worried his mother but having 'a back wide enough to play poker on', as an Australian journalist observed, and being only 4ft 11in tall, proved advantageous in his chosen sport. In his first international competition at the age of fourteen, he came within 2.5kg of the adult world record for combined lifts. The following year he went one better, breaking the first of 46 WORLD RECORDS he would claim during his career. At sixteen, he became only the second man to lift three times his own weight. He would have been a shoo-in for gold at the LA Olympics had Bulgaria not joined the Eastern bloc's boycott.

The mid-1980s was a turbulent period for Bulgaria's ethnic Turks, with mosques forcibly closed and the speaking of Turkish forbidden. Suleimanov was tempted to defect while at a training camp in Melbourne in 1985 but told his would-be helpers that he would only do so if the government in Sofia tried to force him to take a non-Islamic name. As soon as he got back to Bulgaria, his passport was confiscated and reissued in the name of NAUM SHALAMANOV.

When he returned to Melbourne for the 1986 World Championship, he slipped away from his minders at a formal banquet, went to the Turkish consulate and requested asylum. A few days later he was flown to Turkey in President Turgut Ozal's private jet; he kissed the tarmac on arrival, securing his status as a national hero. When the Bulgarian government later permitted over 300,000 ethnic Turks to leave as a direct result of the publicity generated by Suleimanov's defection, he ascended to near deity.

Olympic rules stipulated that an athlete who changed nationality had to wait three years before competing in international tournaments, unless he obtained a waiver from his former nation. The Turkish government happily paid the Bulgarians $1m to obtain such a document in time for

THE INCOMPARABLE NAIM SULEYMANOGLU ABOUT TO LIFT THE EQUIVALENT OF THREE-PLUS CHERYL COLES OVER HIS HEAD

Suleymanoglu (as he spelled his name in Turkish style) to compete in the Seoul Games. The money was well spent. The little man cruised to gold, breaking world records in two of his three lifts in each discipline. His best lifts in the snatch and the clean-and-jerk exceeded those racked up by Paul Anderson in winning the super-heavyweight gold in Melbourne 32 years earlier. Anderson had tipped the scales at 303 pounds; the 'pocket Hercules' weighed a mere 132.

Having intended to retire after the 1988 Games, Suleymanoglu was persuaded to think again when a crowd of one million assembled at Ankara airport to greet him on his return. He went on to win featherweight golds at Barcelona and Atlanta.

WRESTLING

17–21 AUGUST 2016 (**Freestyle**)

14–16 AUGUST 2016 (**Greco-Roman**)

CARIOCA ARENA 2, BARRA DA TIJUCA, RIO

Athletes: 344 | **Golds up for grabs:** 18

·· **OLYMPIC PRESENCE** ··

MEN 1896 (GRECO-ROMAN) AND 1904–PRESENT (FREE-STYLE); WOMEN (FREESTYLE) SINCE 2004.

·· **OLYMPIC FORMAT** ··

TWO STYLES FOR MEN: GRECO-ROMAN, IN WHICH HOLDS beneath the waist are forbidden, and FREESTYLE, in which they are allowed. WOMEN only compete in freestyle.

·· **CONTENDERS** ··

IN THE GRECO-ROMAN EVENTS IN LONDON, IRAN, SOUTH KOREA, RUSSIA and CUBA shared the golds. Expect other former Soviet/Eastern bloc nations – notably BULGARIA, AZERBAIJAN, ARMENIA, SERBIA, and HUNGARY – to be in contention. In the men's freestyle, many of the same nations will vie for medals, as will the USA, TURKEY and GEORGIA. In the women's freestyle, JAPAN are dominant, with the other countries mentioned above in pursuit.

·· **PAST CHAMPIONS** ··

RUSSIA/USSR: 80 | USA: 50 | SWEDEN, JAPAN, TURKEY: 28

WHY WATCH WRESTLING?

SEOUL, 1988. WITH THIRTY SECONDS TO GO IN THE FINAL OF the Greco-Roman super-heavyweight competition, RANGEL

GEROVSKI, a twenty-stone Bulgarian, has a seemingly unassailable three-point lead over his Russian opponent, ALEKSANDR KARELIN. Suddenly, the giant Siberian pulls Gerovski over his knee; then, without releasing his grip, he hoists himself to his feet while turning his adversary upside down, flings himself backwards, twisting as he falls, and slams the Bulgarian shoulders-first on to the ground. Gold is secured in an instant. Welcome to Olympic wrestling.

Olympic wrestling may seem somewhat colourless to the unenlightened, particularly those enthralled by the slapstick theatre of WWE or Mexican *Lucha Libre*. It's true that a bout can look rather like two blokes rolling around in an undignified manner. But it only appears that way because the competitors are so good at neutralising each other. Put a bodybuilder on the mat and he'd be flying out of the ring in seconds.

Wrestling may not be the most aesthetically pleasing Olympic event but it is certainly among the most primal, as befits what may well be the most ancient sport of all. The high percentage of flesh-to-flesh contact ensures that the strength and guile of the protagonists are tested in the most direct way possible. And the nations which dominate the sport make a refreshing change from the usual suspects: 38 nations have won gold, including Armenia, Egypt and Georgia. With wrestling so huge in CENTRAL AND WESTERN ASIA, countries ending in '-STAN' also feature in the medal tables.

THE STORY OF WRESTLING

VARIATIONS OF WRESTLING ARE FOUND AMONG THE INUIT, the Maori and pretty much everyone in between, a universality that suggests that the sport has a deep place in the human psyche.

The importance of wrestling in prehistoric times is evident from its presence in the mythologies of several cultures. In the book of GENESIS, Jacob wrestles a mysterious stranger in an all-night bout which ends only when the adversary touches 'the hollow' of Jacob's thigh, wrenching his hip out of joint. (This is regarded by the author(s) as foul play, suggesting that the contest was in the Greco-Roman style.)

BAS RELIEF OF ANCIENT GREEK WRESTLING

According to SHINTO LEGEND, divine ownership of the Japanese archipelago was decided by the victory of the thunder god Take-mikazuchi in a wrestling contest on a beach in Izumo (see Judo chapter). And in Greek myth, Zeus confronted the old Titan deities with his fellow Olympian gods and out-grappled his father Kronos for possession of the Universe.

By the time the first city-based empires were established, wrestling had become a formalised sport. SUMERIAN wall carvings from 3000 BC depict refereed contests accompanied by music. The EGYPTIANS, for their part, elevated the sport into a science. Of the six HOLDS depicted in the tomb of Ptahhotep (c. 2300 BC), five are still used by Olympic athletes.

Wrestling is recorded as making its OLYMPIC DEBUT in 708 BC, and it remained an integral part of the ancient Games, both in its own right and as part of the not-at-all-modern pentathlon.

The ancient Greeks had two main styles of wrestling: KALO PALE (ground wrestling), somewhat reminiscent of modern FREESTYLE, in which a bout was ended by one participant's submission; and ORTHIA PALE (upright wrestling), which appears to have been the dominant form and was closer to modern GRECO-ROMAN wrestling. It was conducted in a standing position and consisted of five rounds, each ending when one of the contestants was thrown to the floor. There were no time limits and no separate weight divisions. The naked participants wrestled on bare earth, which could become a sea of mud in wet weather. They arrived in the arena coated with olive oil (rather like modern Turkish oil wrestlers) and heavily dusted with powder.

By the MIDDLE AGES, there were hundreds of folk wrestling styles, ranging from Icelandic GLIMA, in which contestants wear special leather harnesses to provide gripping points, to a North of England variant known as CUMBERLAND WRESTLING, in which the action commences with the combatants locked in a bear hug.

During the late nineteenth century, two forms of wrestling evolved into internationally recognised professional sports. The first, known as FLAT HAND or FRENCH CLASSICAL WRESTLING, in which holds beneath the waist were banned, had been developed during the 1840s by a former Napoleonic soldier named JEAN BROYASSE (or 'Exbroyat', as he styled himself as a professional strongman). By the end of the century, the style had become extremely popular in France, Italy and the Austro-Hungarian and Russian empires.

In the English-speaking world the dominant wrestling style was CATCH-AS-CATCH-CAN, in which, as the name implies, competitors were allowed to perform holds with – and to – almost any part of the body. Catch-as-catch-can was a well-established fairground attraction in the UK and USA, and was adopted by universities throughout America.

By the eve of the sport's Olympic debut, flat-handed wrestling had evolved into the GRECO-ROMAN discipline and catch-as-catch-can into FREESTYLE.

GAME ON: WRESTLING BASICS

IN GRECO-ROMAN WRESTLING IT IS FORBIDDEN TO GRASP the opponent below the beltline or to use the legs 'actively' to perform any action. In FREESTYLE the first rule doesn't apply, and legs can be used aggressively, though it is not permitted to lock them scissor-style around an opponent's head, neck or body. That aside, the rules are broadly the same for each style.

Freestyle is the more dynamic form of wrestling – competitors spend a lot of time circling each other looking for an opportunity to dive in. Greco-Roman wrestling is more obviously a matter of brute strength, but in both styles, maintaining balance is essential. The action may appear to freeze at times, but the wrestlers are really probing for small losses of equilibrium.

Wrestlers are NOT ALLOWED to talk during a bout. Neither may they pull each other's hair, pinch, bite, headbutt, attack genitals, hold an opponent's singlet, grab the sole of his foot or generally do anything 'with the intention of torturing the opponent', as the rule book puts it. Double nelsons are forbidden in women's wrestling.

Greco-Roman wrestling features one of the most unusual rules in the Olympic sports programme. Either wrestler can call a temporary halt to proceedings – and trigger a kind of steward's inquiry – by casting what looks like a padded coloured brick into the ring.

THE MAT

THE ACTION TAKES PLACE ON A CIRCULAR MAT 9M IN DIAMETER. The outer 1m of this area is known as the RED ZONE. Its function is to alert the wrestlers and officials that the action has moved to the margin of the legitimate wrestling area.

The region beyond the red zone is a 1.5m strip called the PROTECTION AREA. If a wrestler places a foot in the protection area, the bout is stopped, a point is awarded to his opponent and wrestling resumes in the centre of the mat.

In the middle of the wrestling area is the CENTRAL CIRCLE, which is 1m in diameter. Aside from forming the area of the mat where wrestling commences or recommences after a break, the central circle determines how the wrestlers are to disport themselves during curious set pieces called ORDERED HOLDS, of which more later.

DRESS CODE

EACH MALE COMPETITOR MUST BE CLOSELY SHAVEN OR HAVE a BEARD of several months' growth. Moustaches, which are very popular in some of wrestling's dominant nations, are not mentioned in the official rules. Competitors wear either BLUE OR RED SINGLETS made of nylon or Lycra. The use of light, metal-free KNEE PADS is permitted. Women cannot wear underwired bras. Wrestlers are not permitted to apply greasy or sticky substances to their bodies. They must have CLOTH HANDKERCHIEFS with them at all times, to wipe away any escaped bodily fluids. Fingernails must be cut very short. Ear guards are allowed to prevent the notorious 'cauliflower ear'.

··· **THE OFFICIALS** ···

EACH BOUT IS OFFICIATED BY A REFEREE, A MAT CHAIRMAN and a JUDGE. The referee controls the action on the mat, using voice and whistle, and indicates the scoring of points with hand signals. The judge keeps tally of the score and, as a second pair of eyes, will alert the ref if they miss something important. The mat chairman keeps time and arbitrates in any dispute between referee and judge.

······················· **STRUCTURE OF THE TOURNAMENT** ·······················

THERE ARE SEVEN WEIGHT CLASSES, RANGING FROM 50KG upwards. Rather marvellously, there is now a MAXIMUM WEIGHT LIMIT for Olympic wrestlers of 130kg.

The competition for each weight division takes place on a SINGLE DAY. The first part of the contest is a series of knock-out rounds, delivering two finalists. The second is contested by everyone who was beaten by either of the finalists earlier in the competition. They are divided into two groups according to which finalist they lost to. Each group then has a mini-tournament, with the winners claiming the two bronze medals awarded.

··· **HOW A BOUT IS WON** ···

THE RULES AND SCORING SYSTEMS OF OLYMPIC WRESTLING change with infuriating frequency, but a grasp of the following principles should allow you to appreciate what is going on.

If one wrestler manages to PIN THE OTHER'S SHOULDERS to the ground long enough for the referee to determine that they are indeed pinned, a FALL is scored and they win the bout immediately. A wrestler also wins a bout if their opponent is DISQUALIFIED, either through incurring three cautions or, in cases of egregious brutality, through instant dismissal.

In all other cases, a bout is the BEST OF THREE ROUNDS. These can be won in three ways. The first is TECHNICAL SUPERIORITY, in which one wrestler goes so far ahead in a round that they are declared its winner before two minutes have elapsed. The second is simply for a wrestler to SCORE MORE POINTS than their opponent.

The final way of winning a round, if the scores are level, is to be AWARDED IT. In GRECO-ROMAN ROUNDS, the judges use complex criteria based on cautions, high-scoring manoeuvres and so forth. In FREESTYLE, if neither wrestler scores a technical point during the thirty-second round extension, the one who pulled the short straw in the draw for the ordered hold (see p.408–9) is automatically awarded the round.

································ **HOW POINTS ARE SCORED** ································

THE USUAL WAY TO WIN A ROUND IS TO ACCUMULATE THE MOST POINTS. These can be scored in a variety of ways, which will make more sense once you have grasped the definition of the DANGER POSITION. A wrestler is said to be in this undesirable state when the line of their back or shoulders forms an angle of less than ninety degrees to the mat while they are using their upper body to avoid the indignity of a fall.

That established, here are the chief moves and points:

TAKEDOWN A two-point takedown involves gaining control over an opponent from a neutral position, i.e. when the taker-down is on his feet.

A FIVE-POINT takedown involves a throw of GRAND AMPLITUDE which places the opponent in a direct and immediate danger position.

THREE POINTS are awarded for a grand amplitude throw that does not bring the opponent into a direct and immediate danger position, or for a SHORT AMPLITUDE throw which does. ONE POINT is awarded for a short amplitude takedown which does not put the opponent in the danger position.

REVERSAL A wrestler who gains control over their opponent immediately after being in the reverse position (i.e. in the opponent's control) is awarded ONE POINT.

EXPOSURE A wrestler is said to be exposed when they are in the danger position but not via a throw. TWO POINTS are awarded whenever a wrestler exposes their opponent's back to the mat, whether it is pinned or not. An EXTRA POINT is earned if a wrestler keeps their opponent in an exposed position for five continuous seconds.

PENALTIES If a wrestler takes a time out due to injury, their opponent is awarded ONE POINT unless the injured combatant is bleeding. Infractions such as fleeing the mat, openly refusing contact, using an illegal hold or striking an opponent earn the opponent ONE OR TWO POINTS, depending on the severity of the offence. The guilty party also receives a CAUTION: three strikes and you're out.

OUT-OF-BOUNDS If a wrestler puts a foot in the protection area, the match is stopped and ONE POINT is awarded to their opponent. Wrestling then resumes in the centre of the mat.

THE FINER POINTS

················ **GRECO-ROMAN BOUTS: THE PAR TERRE** ················

IN GRECO-ROMAN WRESTLING, ROUNDS ARE NOMINALLY TWO minutes long, but if one wrestler achieves technical superiority the round ends immediately. The combatants begin each round in a standing position and spend sixty seconds trying to take each other down. Then something rather odd happens: a PAR TERRE session. The wrestler who is behind at this stage – or, if the scores are level, the one who loses the toss of a two-coloured disc – kneels in the centre circle, with his hands on the floor; the other wrestler approaches him from the side, placing one knee on the ground if he so desires, and wraps his arms around his opponent's waist, linking his hands.

The combatants are now said to be in the ORDERED HOLD or CLINCH POSITION. The wrestler on top then executes what is known as an UPSIDE-DOWN BELT HOLD. As the thirty second period unfolds, both wrestlers may get to their feet. At the end of the thirty seconds the wrestlers swap positions, with the one who had the advantage in the first *par terre* session assuming the

TWO WRESTLERS GRAPPLING AT THE 1936 BERLIN OLYMPICS

disadvantaged kneeling position in the second. If the wrestler who began a *par terre* session with the advantage fails to score a technical point during his thirty seconds, his opponent is awarded a technical point.

The usual structure of a Greco-Roman round does not apply if one of the wrestlers is in the DANGER POSITION either at the end of the first minute (in which case both *par terre* sessions are cancelled) or at the end of the first *par terre* session, in which case the second one is cancelled.

FREESTYLE BOUTS

A STANDARD FREESTYLE ROUND IS ALSO TWO MINUTES LONG and ends prematurely if one wrestler achieves technical superiority. If the score is 0–0 after two minutes, the action is extended for up to thirty seconds with the wrestlers in an ORDERED HOLD position, also known as THE CLINCH. Advantage in this situation is determined by the toss of a disc.

The freestyle ordered hold is not the same as the Greco-Roman: the contestant who loses the toss must place one leg in the middle of the centre circle (the leg is determined by his opponent) and the other outside the circle. The wrestler with the ADVANTAGE then grabs the leg inside the circle with both arms, placing his head on the outside of his opponent's thigh. The wrestler with the DISAD-VANTAGE must place both hands on the shoulders of his adversary. When the referee is happy with this complex arrangement of limbs, he blows his whistle and action commences. The first point scored ends the round and determines the winner. If the wrestler with the advantage fails to score a point, one is awarded to his opponent.

WRESTLING GOES TO THE OLYMPICS

WHEN BARON DE COUBERTIN AND HIS CRONIES WERE draw-ing up the list of events for the first modern Olympics, wrestling was a shoo-in, as it had featured in the ancient Games. The dif-ficulty was deciding which form of the sport to choose.

In the end, the organisers of the Athens Games selected the French version of the sport – now styled GRECO-ROMAN WRESTLING – partly because of its supposed resemblance to the ancient Olympian version and partly because it had an established World Championship. Unfortunately, as the British and Americans did not recognise the French rules, the top performers were absent from the 1896 Olympics. So too, because of De Coubertin's allergy to professionalism, were most of the big names in European flat-hand wrestling. There was one unlimited weight class in the Athens Games, with the gold medal going to the 5ft 4in CARL SCHUHMANN of Germany, who also distinguished himself by winning three golds in gymnastics.

Possibly as a result of the poor turnout at Athens, wrestling did not feature in the 1900 Games and when it returned at ST LOUIS in 1904, it was in the American-friendly FREESTYLE format, with US athletes winning all seven weight divisions.

In 1908, both disciplines featured at the Olympics for the first time, but all the wrestling events at Stockholm in 1912 were Greco-Roman, with the FINNS and SWEDES taking the four gold medals on offer. As bouts could be ended only by a fall, disqual-ification or withdrawal, they could last for hours. In the most

US WRESTLING TEAM *PAR TERRE* AHEAD OF THE 1932 GAMES

notable contest at Stockholm, the Estonian MAX KLEIN eventually prevailed after an ELEVEN-HOUR middleweight marathon with Finland's ALFRED ASIKAINEN. Klein was too exhausted to compete in the final, so gold went to Sweden's CLAES JOHANSON by default. The unsatisfactory nature of such interminable contests led to the introduction of TIME LIMITS and a SCORING SYSTEM at the Paris Games in 1924.

Since Antwerp 1920, every Olympic Games has featured both freestyle and Greco-Roman events. Highlights have included Sweden's IVAR JOHANSSON winning the freestyle middleweight gold in 1932, then shedding 5kg in a sauna to allow him to win the Greco-Roman welterweight title 24 hours later; Estonia's KRISTJAN PALUSALU becoming the only wrestler to win heavyweight gold in Greco-Roman and freestyle at Berlin in 1936; and American JEFF BLATNICK's victory in the Greco-Roman super-heavyweight competition at LA 1984, two years after being diagnosed with Hodgkin's disease and having his appendix and spleen removed – probably the most inspiring story in Olympic wrestling history. At London 2012, Uzbekistan's hulking heavyweight freestyle wrestler ARTUR TAYMAZOV made his mark, winning his third gold – and fourth medal – in four different Games. Purists often regard the heavyweight event as less stylish than the other classes but Taymazov displayed an athleticism and technical variety seldom seen at this weight.

A murkier kind of Olympic history was made in Rome in 1960 when Eastern bloc politics shaped the outcome. The USSR's AVTANDIL KORIDZE whispered something in Bulgarian DIMITRO STOYANOV's ear a minute before the end of a semi-final that persuaded Stoyanov to roll over and submit to a fall, helping to ensure that the Russian deprived Branislav Martinovic – and Tito's Yugoslava – of gold.

In 2004, Olympic wrestling took the long overdue decision to introduce a WOMEN'S FREESTYLE COMPETITION (female Greco-Roman wrestling has yet to appear). Of the twelve events contested, JAPAN have won seven and CHINA two. Two Japanese wrestlers have monopolised the golds in their events: SAO-RI KOSHIDA (in the 55k event) and KAORI ICHO (in the 63kg heavyweight class) will be aiming for their fourth consecutive Olympic titles in Rio.

Wrestling's Olympic future remains uncertain. In 2013, the IOC executive board voted to drop it as a core sport for the 2020 Games. In competition with seven other non-core sports for a place on the programme at Tokyo, the sport won a reprieve. Even though VWW, the sport's governing body, has made the changes the IOC requested – in an attempt to make wrestling more fun for the casual to watch, to promote more aggressive wrestling, and to give women more opportunities to compete – the pressure is still on. More than most sports, wrestling needs a spectacular Olympics in Rio.

ALEKSANDR KARELIN

The greatest Olympic Greco-Roman wrestler of modern times, Siberian-born ALEKSANDR KARELIN won gold at the 1988 Olympics (with the outrageous takedown described in this chapter's introduction) and then didn't lose another bout until Sydney 2000. Some dubbed him 'The Experiment', hinting that – though Karelin passed any number of doping tests – his awesome record might have had its roots in the laboratory. To his detractors, Karelin had a ready answer: 'I train every day of my life as they have never trained a day in theirs.' One of his defeated opponents said of him: 'Wrestling him is like wrestling King Kong.' A softly spoken man with a penchant for opera, the mighty Karelin once took delivery of a 400lb refrigerator and lugged it up the stairs to his eighth-floor apartment. He has been a member of the Russian parliament since 1999.

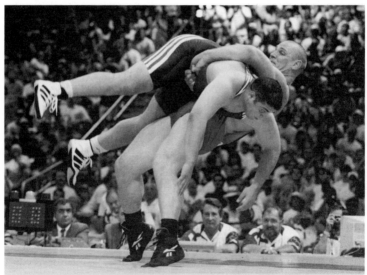

THE EXPERIMENT: ALEKSANDR KARELIN HALFWAY THROUGH A GRAND AMPLITUDE THROW AT ATLANTA 1996

MEDALS
CEREMONIES

THE OFFICIAL OLYMPIC LINE IS THAT IT IS MORE IMPORTANT to participate than to win. This sentiment is not reflected in the MEDALS CEREMONIES. The athletes on the podium have worked unbelievably hard to get there and their governments have paid millions of pounds to share in the glory. As a consequence, the ceremonies are invariably occasions of intense emotion, both for the happy winners and the occasionally sour losers. Viewers may find themselves welling up, too.

MEDAL CEREMONY BASICS

MEDALLISTS MUST BE DRESSED IN OFFICIAL NATIONAL TEAM uniforms and are not allowed to display political affiliations or make statements of any kind during the ceremony. They enter the stage together and then climb on to the podium, with the winner on the highest tier in the centre, the silver medallist on their right and the bronze medallist on their left. The MEDALS are awarded in reverse order (bronze first, gold last) by a member of the IOC, accompanied by volunteers from the host city bearing the now obligatory Olympic BOUQUETS. Then the NATIONAL ANTHEM of the winner is played while the flags of all three medallists' nations are raised, with the winner's elevated above the others. The anthems are now pre-recorded.

The MEDALS themselves must be a minimum of 6cm in diameter and 3mm thick. Despite the different denominations, they are all largely made of silver, but the golds have to be coated with at least 6 grams of the metal. The medals for London 2012 were the biggest to date, 85mm in diameter and weighing in at 400g (nearly a pound).

THE MEDAL CEREMONY STORY

WINNERS AT THE ANCIENT GAMES WERE PRESENTED WITH olive wreaths harvested by boys with golden sickles. When the Games were revived at ATHENS 1896, the victors were presented with crowns of OLIVE BRANCHES, certificates of victory and silver medals, while the runners-up got LAUREL CROWNS and bronzes. Third-placed athletes got nowt. In keeping with the gentlemanly aura, Olympians received their awards in evening dress, at the closing ceremony rather than after each individual competition. Things acquired a more familiar shape at LONDON 1908, with medal ceremonies held on the same days as competitions and GOLD, SILVER and BRONZE MEDALS awarded to first, second and third place. Then at Los Angeles in 1932 came the three-tiered podium, the raising of the medallists' national flags and playing of their national anthems.

The average medal ceremony is graced by trembling lips and a great deal of handshaking, but on occasion the script gets altered. The IOC has never quite recovered from the BLACK POWER SALUTES made on the podium by American sprinters TOMMIE SMITH and JOHN CARLOS in 1968 (white Australian silver medallist Peter Norman wore a badge supporting the protest). Other notable breaches of decorum have included the US BASKETBALL TEAM's no-show in 1972, the bodybuilder poses stuck by the USA 4 × 100m gold medallists at SYDNEY 2000, and Greco-Roman wrestler ARA ABRAHAMIAN tearing off his bronze in disgust at BEIJING 2008.

There have been heart-warming moments, too. At LA 1984, the Yugoslav ANTON JOSIPOVIC, light heavyweight boxing champion, hauled bronze medallist EVANDER HOLYFIELD up on to the winner's rostrum as he had only lost his semi-final due to a ludicrous refereeing decision. At Sydney 2000, American weightlifter TARA NOTT chose not to collect her gold medal, preferring to cheer on her friend Cheryl Haworth at the women's super heavyweight final. More poignantly, the ceremony for the 10m air pistol in Beijing ended with Georgia's NINO SALUKVADZE and Russia's NATALIA PADERINA embracing and calling for an end to the fighting between their nations.

THE CLOSING CEREMONY

21 AUGUST 2016

MARACANÃ STADIUM, RIO DE JANEIRO

Athletes: All 12,000 are invited but many will have gone home.

·· **OLYMPIC PRESENCE** ··

THE 1896 ATHENS GAMES ENDED WITH A SPLENDID MIX OF marching bands, medals, victory laps and laurels, and with the exception of PARIS 1900 some kind of show has been staged ever since. The closing ceremony acquired something close to its settled form with the introduction of the Olympic flag in 1920.

·· **OLYMPIC FORMAT** ··

THE IOC STIPULATES A PROGRAMME OF SPEECHES, FLAGS AND anthems, but there is plenty of scope for the hosts to indulge in all kinds of artistic interpretation.

·· **CONTENDERS** ··

RIO DE JANEIRO IS THE STAR OF THE SHOW BUT, AS IS NOW traditional, the next Olympic host city, TOKYO, will be given a ten-minute slot to do its thing.

WHY WATCH THE CLOSING CEREMONY?

HOW DO YOU BRING THE CURTAIN DOWN ON THE GREATEST show on earth? After seventeen days of intense immersion in sporting competition, tens of thousands of athletes, officials and spectators can't just rush home and put the kettle on. What is need-ed at this stage is a party. A chance to reflect on what has happened, look forward to what is to come and affirm that we are all good friends really, despite our nations having devoted the preceding fortnight to trying to beat the crap out of each other. Throw in a few solemn rituals and pompous speeches and everyone will be primed to do it again in four years' time.

Armchair viewers also need a rite of passage to ease themselves back to normal life. So draw up a chair and watch the show. Share in the feel-good factor as the world's athletes MARCH TOGETHER unsegregated by nationality. Get a foretaste of the flavour of the next Games during the HANDOVER CEREMONY. And watch out for the unexpected. Whether it's a streaker, athletes riding

THE CHINESE SETTING THE CLOSING CEREMONY BAR HIGH AT BEIJING 2008

piggyback or a giant inflatable octopus, the closing ceremony has a habit of coming up with something memorable.

CLOSING CEREMONY BASICS

THE OPENING MOMENTS OF THE CLOSING CEREMONY ARE unpredictable. In the past clocks have chimed, stilt walkers have performed, fireworks have gone off and spaceships have landed. At London 2012, proceedings began with a filmed countdown around the capital, the chimes of Big Ben and an arena that DAMIEN HIRST had turned into a giant representation of the Union flag. It's not clear what the plans are in Rio but expect an injection of street culture in the shape of hip-hop dance, roller skating and skate-boarding.

THE MARCH OF THE ATHLETES

THE MAIN BUSINESS KICKS OFF WITH A PARADE OF EVERY competing nation's flag and name board. Compared to the opening ceremony this is mercifully brisk. The flag-bearers and placard-holders then line up somewhere, probably near the OLYMPIC FLAG, so that the athletes can show up in a great unstructured crowd. Note how well policed they are. The ceremony at Tokyo 1964 was chaotic and Mexico 1968 was memorable for some unscripted sprints by Nigerian athletes who broke out to embrace the crowd.

THE MARATHON MEDALS

EARLIER IN THE DAY THE MEN'S MARATHON WILL HAVE BEEN run, the competitors crossing the finishing line in the Olympic Stadium. Its medal ceremony will feature somewhere in the mix. If you have watched a fraction of the 10,000 hours plus of sport-ing action over the previous fortnight, this can be your medal ceremony too. Relive those late nights when you found yourself mysteriously captivated by the early rounds of the badminton. Feel righteous in your endurance of the very real pain of the initial rounds of the 50m rifle; pat yourself on the back for those hours you put in watching weightlifting and water polo.

FLAGS AND SPEECHES

NOW TAKE A DEEP BREATH: WE'VE GOT TO GET THROUGH the FLAGS, ANTHEMS and SPEECHES bit. There may well be more fanfares and specially commissioned musical concoctions have be-come sadly inevitable. Atlanta took the opportunity to pay tribute to the athletes with a tune called 'Faster Higher Stronger', followed by Gloria Estefan belting out 'Reach'. In London, the concept of a symphony of British music spotlighted an eclectic cast including Freddie Mercury, electronically reincarnated on a big screen.

Next up is the lowering of the GREEK FLAG and the playing of the GREEK NATIONAL ANTHEM. Then there will be lots of introduc-tions in various languages before CARLOS ARTHUR NUZMAN, who represented Brazil in volleyball at the 1964 Olympics and is chief cheese of the Local Organising Committee, gets his slot. There will be an awful lot of thank-yous, possibly hints of relief and a touch of valediction. Finally, the president of the IOC, Thomas Bach, will say:

> I declare the Games of the Thirty-First Olympiad closed and, in accordance with tradition, I call upon the youth of the world to assemble four years from now in Tokyo to celebrate the Games of the Thirty-Second Olympiad.

This is the president's chance to pass judgement. One of Bach's predecessors, Juan Antonio Samaranch got himself stuck on an escalator of superlatives, pronouncing every Games he attended, 'the best ever Olympics' – a comment he pointedly withheld from Atlanta 1996. Bach will perhaps have some fresh adjectives.

THE HANDOVER

SPEECHES DONE, THE NEW HOST NATION'S FLAG WILL BE raised and its NATIONAL ANTHEM played: at Rio 2016, this will be Japan. Then the Olympic flag comes down, to another round of the Olympic anthem (see THE OPENING CEREMONY, p.12), and Rio will pass the baton to the representatives of TOKYO 2020. The floor is now theirs for about ten minutes. At London 2012, the Rio organisers presented a carnival in miniature, with Brazil's most famous model Alessandrio Ambrosio leading a parade including 82 drummers, samba dancer Renato Sorriso, classical singer Marisa Monte and rapper BNegão, before the great PELÉ personally invited the watching millions to come to Rio in August 2016. Inevitably, this segment lacked the emotional charge that infused much of the rest of the ceremony but it was fast and painless.

LIGHTS OUT!

THE FINAL CEREMONIAL ACT IS THE EXTINGUISHING OF THE Olympic flame. Simple as this task might seem, past producers have managed to make a remarkable business of it. In London, Britain's prima ballerina Darcey Bussell flew into the stadium in a flame-coloured catsuit and tried to convey what might happen if the Olympic flame mysteriously acquired the ability to dance. Once the flame is extinguished, the compulsory programme is complete, which is usually the cue for more music. The athletes' morale improves at this point because they know that the end of the ceremony is nigh.

The Closing Ceremony Story

The ancient Olympics closed with oath taking, venerating and feasting. The closing ceremony of the first modern Olympiad didn't stretch to feasting and was delayed by torrential rain for a day but Athens 1896 did sign off with fanfares and odes, silver medals for the champions and a victory parade for all the medallists led by Spyridon Louis, winner of the marathon. The King of Greece (the Danish-born George I) declared the Games closed and left the stadium to the strains of the Greek national anthem.

At Antwerp 1920 the Olympic flag had made its appearance at the opening ceremony, so symmetry dictated that the Games ended with its lowering. This ritual, which would become the central feature of the closing ceremony, was given suitable grandeur by a booming fusillade from the Belgian army's artillery and a cantata sung by a massed choir. Next time around, at Paris 1924, they raised the flags and sung the anthems of France (as current hosts) and the Netherlands (the next hosts) and handed the Olympic flag over to the latter. The Greeks, who had wanted to be hosts every time, had to be satisfied with having their flag raised and anthem sung at this handover ceremony.

The big full stop to the Games, the extinguishing of the Olympic flame, was introduced in a low-key way in 1928 (when the flame first appeared). But it was at Berlin 1936 that lighting and extinguishing of the Olympic cauldron became fixed and dramatic features of the Games.

The immediate post-war Games were rather low-key affairs, closing, as our man T.S. Eliot might have put it, not with a bang but a whimper. LONDON 1948 featured music from the Band of the Guards and a column of boy scouts carrying wooden name placards. King George VI and Queen Elizabeth sent a representative as they had already left London for Balmoral to catch the start of the grouse-shooting season. Most of the athletes had also already gone home. At Melbourne 1956, there was a bit more spirit to the occasion, and the last key element – the athletes entering the stadium together without national groupings – was introduced. It came about as the result of an anonymous suggestion – by, it turned out, a seventeen-year-old Chinese-Australian, John Ian Wing.

The ceremony in ROME 1960 was illuminated by the crowd simultaneously lighting thousands of paper torches, not a trick likely to get past any fire safety committee today. The Games then concluded with a giant FIREWORK DISPLAY. Unfortunately, hot sparks descended from the sky and fell on the dry grass of the Monte Marino hill, where thousands of people had gathered to watch the displays. Ten people were injured in the ensuing fires and stampedes.

Controversies again dogged the next two closing ceremonies. At MUNICH 1972 a light-hearted concoction of Bavarian kitsch cast an odd note after the earlier assassinations of eleven Israeli athletes. Then at MONTREAL 1976 the organisers got in a dreadful pickle over how to represent Canada's First Nation peoples. The show included the creation of a tepee village in the centre of the stadium, from which Canadian Indians in traditional dress were meant to dispense necklaces and feathered headbands to the athletes and the crowd. Although the intention was to honour Canada's First Nation, the organisers bodged things by recruiting a Montreal troupe, made-up and dressed as native Canadians, to dance to *La Danse Sauvage*. The barefaced cheek of the display was best answered by Michael Leduc, who stripped off in the stands and headed into the arena to cavort among the performers. The Mounties let the world rediscover the ancient Olympic love of the naked male body for three minutes before moving in.

The Olympic dance routines had got going, predictably, at MEXICO '68, where a supersized mariachi band arrived in the midst of the athletes to whip up a frenzy. This was all a bit too undignified and spontaneous for the IOC and the organisers of Munich and

Montreal, who tried to keep athlete numbers and spirits down. But at least the Canadians' pseudo-Indian dances were recognition that the Games needed something more upbeat to go out on than sombre rituals, hymns and anthems.

In a clumsy, gargantuan way, MOSCOW 1980 was another step in the right direction. Once the flags and the speeches were done it was show time, albeit in a form calculated to float the boat of the octogenarian politburo of the Soviet Communist Party. The massed bands of various wings of the Soviet military were given a stomping outing, thousands of rhythmic gymnasts whirled their ribbons in formation and giant Russian dolls waddled their way around the field. Then a huge Misha – the Games' ursine mascot with its implausible fixed smile – came to say goodbye, clutching a bunch of balloons. A card stunt from the stands displayed Misha crying, then everyone cried as the balloons pulled the bear away from the sea of tearful Slavic schmaltz and up into the night sky.

The logic of the Cold War demanded that LOS ANGELES 1984 show the communist world how it should be done. Where Moscow had to make do with coloured cardboard squares, LA could hand out 100,000 electric torches for the crowd to light. Then in a live pastiche of every Hollywood alien UFO flick, a flying saucer came to hover above the stadium. At last, we had a proper Olympics party. Indeed a disco, spearheaded by the figure of LIONEL RICHIE.

PARTY, KARAMU, FIESTA, FOREVER ...

Since LA 1984, no Olympic closing ceremony can be complete without a performance from a leading figure or two from the world of popular music, and a playlist that people can dance to. What now seems obvious was once a mystery, and it fell to the king of Californian soul schmooze, Lionel Richie, to show us the way. From the moment he appeared in his blue sequinned tracksuit and tight white slacks, Lionel oozed class and confidence. As befits the man who brought us 'Easy Like Sunday Morning', Lionel brought laid-back charm and mellow grooves to an occasion previously notable for its tight-arsed aesthetic. A stadium-sized, neon-lit dance floor pulsated around him as he thanked the crowd and sang an

LIONEL RICHIE AT LA 1984 – THERE ARE SERIOUS OLYMPIC COMMENTATORS
WHO RANK HIM AMONG THE GREAT ALL-TIME OLYMPIAN FIGURES

Olympic length version of 'All Night Long' – the late-disco classic spiced with salsa rhythms and a horn section of gilded smoothness.

After working the crowd Lionel ascended onto a pulsating multi-coloured Olympic podium while more than 400 break dancers took to the floor. Mummified figures span round on their heads; ladies in red leather miniskirts struck a sequence of robotic poses. Lionel's injunction to the world? 'Party, Karamu, Fiesta, Forever'. The closing ceremony would never be the same again.

BARCELONA 1992 was big on pageantry, planetary balloons and fire dancing. Placido Domingo, Jose Carreras and that well-known Spaniard Sarah Brightman all sang beautifully, while FREDDIE MERCURY provided the Games' best-known theme tune. More hits followed at ATLANTA 1996, which shrugged off its critics (commercial crassness … and a bomb attack on the Centennial Olympic park that killed two people and injured over 100), as everyone took their cue from President BILL CLINTON. He was smiling like a Cheshire cat as

Boyz II Men did their a capella take on the 'Star-Spangled Banner', alongside an A-list that included Little Richard, Stevie Wonder, Gloria Estefan, Tito Puente and B.B. King. To top it all, REVEREND AL GREEN, pastor to the global soul, delivered an epic version of 'Take Me to the River' backed by The Pointer Sisters.

SYDNEY 2000 presented the nation's cultural crown jewels: supermodel Elle McPherson, comedian Paul Hogan (AKA Crocodile Dundee), golfer Greg Norman and, of course, Kylie Minogue. The set mixed up Kylie's super camp version of 'Dancing Queen' with thumping Oz rock from John Paul Young and INXS, before going out with a sentimental sing-song of 'Waltzing Matilda' by folk legend Slim Dusty.

It is just as well that the Greeks invented satire, for they can hardly blame the rest of us for retrospectively reading the closing ceremony of ATHENS 2004 as a biting commentary on the nation's tragic borrowing binge. The opening music, perhaps addressed to the gods of the derivative and bond markets, was entitled 'May the Dances Last for Ever'. How prescient that the Games were closed by young girl extinguishing the Olympic cauldron with a single breath. Job done, Greece got down to the party with an unrelentingly domestic line up of old chanteuses, melancholy crooners, pop playboys in testosterone overdrive and mass bouzouki madness.

BEIJING 2008 was acrobat-heavy but musically rather light and while no one could accuse the Chinese of skimping, there was no way they could top their opening ceremony. Still they threw in a gigantic orange human tower, representing the eternal Olympic flame, thousands of drummers, bell dancers and the best of East Asian pop. Beijing let us know in no uncertain terms that China is the rising power of this world, though the pop stars on offer may just have revealed its Achilles heel.

The organisers of London 2012 didn't have to bust a gut to top Beijing's finale on the music front. From The Who singing "My Generation" to a re-formed Spice Girls, and TaioCruz performing "Dynamite", the ceremony offered something for most folks. A pageant, pop concert and paean to British culture, the extravaganza somehow even found room for Timothy Spall to play Winston

Churchill and to celebrate – in scenes that must have baffled many foreign viewers – *Only Fools And Horses*. Foreign broadcasters (especially NBC) attracted some flak for not showing the whole thing but truth be told – at three hours and eleven minutes – it was a bit long.

THE 27 PREVIOUS OLYMPIC GAMES

THE SUMMER OLYMPICS HAVE COME A LONG WAY SINCE 241 amateur gentlemen sportsmen took to the field in Athens in 1896. Having not just survived but flourished in the face of two World Wars and a Cold one, they have grown into mighty big beasts ... so big (and corporate) that we're not even allowed to reproduce the Olympic rings, flame or – alas – the strange array of mascots.

ATHENS 1896

NATIONS 14 | COMPETITORS 241
SPORTS 9 | EVENTS 43

On a shoestring budget, BARON DE COUBERTIN mobilised enough goodwill to realise his dream of re-suscitating the ancient Olympics. The highlight, at least for the host nation, was local hero SPYRIDON LOUIS winning the marathon.

PARIS 1900

NATIONS 24 | COMPETITORS 997
SPORTS 18 | EVENTS 95

Effectively a sideshow to the simultaneous *Exposition Universelle*, the Paris Olympics was hideously disorganised. Tennis player CHARLOTTE COOPER became the first woman to win an Olympic title. ALVIN KRAENZLEIN (USA) was both hero and villain, winning four athletics events but duping a rival into giving him a clean run at the long jump.

ST LOUIS 1904

NATIONS 12 | COMPETITORS 651
SPORTS 17 | EVENTS 91

The Games were this time tacked on to the World's Fair and, to test the hosts' bizarre racial ideas, featured 'anthropology days' in which ethnic groups working at the Fair competed both in Olympic sports and in disciplines deemed 'primitive' like mud throwing and tree climbing. Ray Ewry (USA) won all the standing jump events (as he had in 1900 and would do again in 1908).

LONDON 1908

NATIONS 22 | COMPETITORS 2008
SPORTS 22 | EVENTS 110

The London Games were originally destined for Rome but the Italians spent the money on a relief fund following an eruption of Mount Vesuvius. Britain rode to the rescue, put on a splendid show – although the Games were spread over six months and four days – and won more golds than the rest of the world put together, a feat it has not come close to approaching since. Italian waiter DORANDO PIETRI, the plucky but disqualified winner of the marathon, became the darling of the home nation.

·········· STOCKHOLM 1912 ·········

NATIONS 28 | COMPETITORS 2407
SPORTS 14 | EVENTS 102

The Swedes finally produced a modern Olympics that wasn't a poor relation to a bigger show. Baron de Coubertin also insisted on introducing ARTISTIC COMPETITIONS, which would remain as incongruous counterparts to the sports up until 1952. The good Baron awarded himself a literature gold medal for a poem entitled 'Ode to Sport'. JIM THORPE (USA) was the star of the sporting show, winning the pentathlon and decathlon – medals cruelly stripped form him by the IOC after it was revealed he had been paid a penance to play baseball in North Carolina one summer.

·········· ANTWERP 1920 ·········

NATIONS 29 | COMPETITORS 2627
SPORTS 22 | EVENTS 154

Belgium's pay-off for becoming one of the First World War's principal battlefields was the 1920 Games. The IOC left it to the hosts to send out invites and, not surprisingly, Germany, Austria, Hungary and Turkey were not on the guest list. The OLYMPIC RINGS, FLAG and ATHLETE'S OATH got their first outings and Oscar Swahn won a shooting gold medal for Sweden at the age of 72.

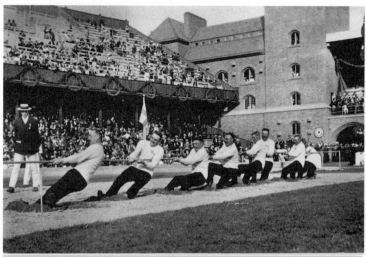

THE LATE, LAMENTED TUG OF WAR, STOCKHOLM 1912 – UNCONTESTED SINCE 1920

PARIS 1924

NATIONS 44 | COMPETITORS 3089
SPORTS 17 | EVENTS 126

The *Chariots of Fire* Games was an altogether better effort from the French than 1904. Paris 1924 was the first Games to boast a purpose-built Olympic village, the first broadcast live on radio and the first to feature the Olympic motto. On the sporting front, it belonged to 'Flying Finn' PAAVO NURMI (Finland), who won five middle and long-distance running titles.

AMSTERDAM 1928

NATIONS 46 | COMPETITORS 2883
SPORTS 14 | EVENTS 109

The 1928 Games – opposed by militant Dutch Protestants who saw the Games as the work of the devil – saw the arrival of the first Olympic FLAME, the Greeks leading the parade of nations and WOMEN finally allowed to compete in the athletics. A quarter of a million people applied for just 40,000 tickets to see URUGUAY beat Argentina in the football final, and the INDIAN MEN'S HOCKEY TEAM began a winning streak that wouldn't end until 1960.

LOS ANGELES 1932

NATIONS 37 | COMPETITORS 1332
SPORTS 14 | EVENTS 117

It wasn't easy to get folk to come to LA in the midst of the Great Depression. The number of competitors plummeted but they should have made the trip – the stadiums were beautiful and the weather fabulous.

The MEDAL CEREMONY as we know it made its debut and everything was condensed into just over two weeks. LA 1932 was a glimpse of the future. BABE DIDRIKSON (USA) was the belle of the ball – she qualified for all five women's athletic events, winning two golds and a silver.

BERLIN 1936

NATIONS 49 | COMPETITORS 3963
SPORTS 19 | EVENTS 129

When the IOC awarded the 1936 Games to Berlin, they had no idea that they were handing them to the Nazi party. Hitler was luke-warm about hosting the event until Olympic administrator Carl Diem convinced him otherwise. Then his regime pulled out all the stops, treating the Games as a powerful propaganda exercise. JESSE OWENS (USA) hadn't read the script. He won the 100m, 200m, long jump and 4 × 100m relay.

LONDON 1948

NATIONS 59 | COMPETITORS 4104
SPORTS 17 | EVENTS 136

The world was in ruins, but the show had to go on. There was no Olympic village but plenty of room in converted schoolrooms and Nissan huts. Athletes were provided with soap but had to bring their own towels. FANNY BLANKERS-KOEN (Netherlands) won golds in the women's 100m, 200m, 80m hurdles and 4 × 100m and was rewarded with the nickname 'The Flying Housewife'.

············ **HELSINKI 1952** ············

NATIONS 69 | COMPETITORS 4955
SPORTS 17 | EVENTS 149

The Cold War had turned hot, but Helsinki was open to all. The SOVIET UNION made its Olympic debut, the GERMANS and JAPANESE returned to the international fold, and the planet seemed to have recovered its sporting poise – more world records were broken at these Games than at any other. The greatest performer was EMIL ZÁTOPEK (Czechoslovakia), who won the 5000m, 10,000m and the marathon at his first attempt at the distance.

········ **MELBOURNE 1956** ········

NATIONS 72 | COMPETITORS 3314
SPORTS 17 | EVENTS 145

At one stage the Australians were so behind schedule that the IOC considered moving the Games, but they got their act together in the end. Referred to as the Friendly Games, Melbourne was nonetheless notable for fierce battles between SOVIET and HUNGARIAN athletes, who were competing against the backdrop of the Hungarian uprising. The Magyars prevailed in the men's water polo and LÁSZLÓ PAPP won a third straight boxing gold.

··············· **ROME 1960** ···············

NATIONS 83 | COMPETITORS 5338
SPORTS 17 | EVENTS 150

Utterly amateur and commercially unadorned, Rome represented a last blast for De Coubertin's vision.

Yet change was in the air, with the first major Olympic doping scandal, and a squabble between Adidas and Puma over whose shoes would be worn by 100m gold medallist ARMIN HARY. The Games introduced two superstars: light heavyweight CASSIUS CLAY (USA), and barefooted marathon runner ABEBE BIKILA (Ethiopia), who became the first black African to win a gold medal.

··············· **TOKYO 1964** ···············

NATIONS 93 | COMPETITORS 5151
SPORTS 19 | EVENTS 163

Asia's first Olympic Games heralded Japan's post-war economic miracle and its return to the centre of the international community. These were the most expensive Games since Berlin, with the Japanese taking the opportunity to build highways, subways, a trans-Pacific telecom cable and new port facilities. To the delight of the home fans, 'The Witches of the East' won the women's volleyball, while LARISA LATYNINA (USSR) collected her eighteenth Olympic gymnastics medal.

······ **MEXICO CITY 1968** ······

NATIONS 112 | COMPETITORS 5516
SPORTS 18 | EVENTS 172

Mexico '68 was intended to showcase the modernisation of the country. It didn't look that way a few weeks before the opening ceremony, when protests were repressed in the city streets and dozens of civilians killed. IOC president Avery Brundage saw no reason to delay so the Games went ahead. Dozens of world records were broken in the thin air of the capital – BOB BEAMON (USA) smashed the long jump record by more than half a metre. The popular hero was VERA ČÁSLAVSKÁ (Czechoslovakia), who won the women's all-round gymnastics and, in a protest against the Warsaw Pact's repression of the Prague Spring, snubbed the Soviet anthem.

MUNICH 1972

NATIONS 121 | COMPETITORS 7134
SPORTS 21 | EVENTS 195
MASCOT: WALDI THE DACHSHUND

West Germany went out of its way to ensure the Games were everything Berlin 1936 was not – transparent modern architecture was preferred to imperial bombast and officials were dressed in nursery colours. Tragically, the sport was overshadowed by the murder of eleven ISRAELI ATHLETES by the Palestinian Black September group. MARK SPITZ (USA) swam his way to seven gold medals and OLGA KORBUT (USSR) enchanted the planet in the women's gymnastics.

MONTREAL 1976

NATIONS 92 | COMPETITORS 6084
SPORTS 21 | EVENTS 198
MASCOT: AMIK THE BEAVER

Responding to fears over the costs of staging the Games, Montreal's Mayor Jean Drapeau claimed that 'the Olympics can no more have a deficit than a man can have a baby'. The city didn't clear its Olympic debts until 2006. The headlines belonged to NADIA COMANECI (Romania), who scored the first

perfect 10 in Olympic gymnastics, then repeated the feat six times.

MOSCOW 1980

NATIONS 80 | COMPETITORS 5179
SPORTS 21 | EVENTS 203
MASCOT: MISHA THE BEAR CUB

The Cold War had lingered over every Games since the Soviet Union joined the party in 1952. Here it took centre stage. Moscow put on an extravaganza to demonstrate the sporting and economic power of communism but the intended audience didn't show up, as the USA decided to boycott the event following the Soviet invasion of Afghanistan. 'COVETT' (Sebastian Coe and Steve Ovett) won the men's middle distance titles for Great Britain and TEÓFILO STEVENSON (Cuba) became heavyweight boxing champion for the third time.

LOS ANGELES 1984

NATIONS 140 | COMPETITORS 6829
SPORTS 21 | EVENTS 221
MASCOT: SAM THE BALD EAGLE

'Anything you can do, I can do better' should have been the theme tune of LA '84. While many communist nations staged a tit-for-tat boycott, La-La land mobilised its corporations and the magic of the movies. This was the first Olympic Games to make a profit, amid a riot of sponsorship and Hollywood glamour. CARL LEWIS (USA) secured immortality by repeating Jesse Owens' feat of forty-eight years earlier.

⋯⋯⋯⋯ SEOUL 1988 ⋯⋯⋯⋯

NATIONS 160 | COMPETITORS 8391

Sports 23 | Events 237

MASCOTS: HODORI AND HOSUNI

(TIGER CUBS)

Perhaps the only Games that has fundamentally changed the course of the host nation's history, Seoul '88 was intended to glorify South Korea's economic miracle and authoritarian government. When massive pro-democracy protests broke out in 1987, the rulers decided that political reform was better than a blood-stained Olympics. South Korea got the Games and a constitution. GREG LOUGANIS (USA) was one of the heroes, winning two golds after knocking himself out on a diving board. BEN JOHNSON (Canada) was the zero; he won the 100m in world record time, then failed a dope test.

⋯⋯⋯ BARCELONA 1992 ⋯⋯⋯

NATIONS 169 | COMPETITORS 9356

SPORTS 25 | EVENTS 257

MASCOT: KOBI THE SHEEPDOG

Barcelona's brilliant mix of operatic staging and urban rebranding convinced a hundred city mayors that hosting the Olympics was the way to get their cities redeveloped. The first post-Cold War Games saw a reunited GERMAN team, the return of SOUTH AFRICA, and the arrival of a raft of nations that had left the Soviet Union. VITALY SCHERBO, of new entrants Belarus, won six out of eight men's gymnastics golds. JAN-OVE WALDNER (Sweden) broke Asia's table tennis monopoly.

⋯⋯⋯⋯ ATLANTA 1996 ⋯⋯⋯⋯

NATIONS 197 | COMPETITORS 10,320

SPORTS 26 | EVENTS 271

MASCOT: IZZY, A BLUE THING

The centenary Games – held in America rather than Greece, as had been anticipated – were brash, commercial and not to everyone's taste. The sport was overshadowed by the bombing of the Centennial Olympic Park, which killed two people and injured more than a hundred. IOC president Juan Antonio Samaranch famously declared every Games to have been 'the best ever' but was unable to roll out the cliché to describe Atlanta. The abiding sporting image was MICHAEL JOHNSON (USA) knocking a third of a second off the world 200m record and winning the 400m in his gold Nikes.

⋯⋯⋯⋯ SYDNEY 2000 ⋯⋯⋯⋯

NATIONS 199 | COMPETITORS 10,651

SPORTS 28 | EVENTS 300

MASCOTS: OLLY (KOOKABURRA),

SYD (PLATYPUS), MILLIE (ECHIDNA)

Melbourne 1956 had been a modest hurrah for Anglo-Australianism. Sydney 2000 belonged to the new nation, multicultural and super-charged with enthusiasm. The sporting and social legacies fell a long way short of the organisers' claims, but the Aussies sure knew how to party. Their pin-up girl was CATHY FREEMAN, who lit the Olympic flame then powered to victory in the women's 400m. STEVE REDGRAVE (Great Britain) won a rowing gold for the fifth consecutive Games.

ATHENS 2004

NATIONS 201 | COMPETITORS 10,625
SPORTS 28 | EVENTS 301
MASCOTS: ATHENA AND PHEVOS,
PECULIARLY PHALLIC GREEK DOLLS

These were the Games that broke the bank. Greece spent more per person than any nation before – about US$1500 per head. They threw a great party, but many of the magnificent buildings constructed for the occasion are now rotting. The biggest surprise of the Games was the ARGENTINIAN MEN'S BASKETBALL TEAM, which beat the supposedly unassailable USA in the semis en route to gold.

BEIJING 2008

NATIONS 204 | COMPETITORS 10,942
SPORTS 28 | EVENTS 302
MASCOTS: A FISH, GIANT PANDA,
OLYMPIC FLAME, TIBETAN ANTELOPE
AND SWALLOW

What do you get for forty billon dollars? Answer: the biggest coming out party ever. On the back of the fastest industrial revolution in history, the hosts rebuilt Beijing and put on a gargantuan show that left no one in any doubt that China was back at the centre of world affairs. USAIN BOLT (Jamaica) broke the men's 100m and 200m records, seemingly without breaking sweat, and MICHAEL PHELPS (USA) went one better than Mark Spitz, winning eight golds in the pool.

LONDON 2012

NATIONS 204 | COMPETITORS 10,768
SPORTS 26 | EVENTS 302
MASCOT: WENLOCK, A METALLIC
CYCLOPS WITH A TAXI HEADLIGHT

Blessed by surprisingly blue skies, hosted by a nation that revelled in the Games, London's Olympics inspired Great Britain's athletes to secure 29 gold medals, the country's best haul since 1908. Yet the sporting limelight was stolen by two stars of 2008: Phelps, who secured four golds and two silvers to become the most decorated Olympian ever, and Bolt, who broke his own record in the 100m. The Games captured the world's imagination too with Italian writer Beppe Severgnini summing it up: 'Bolt, Boyle, Bond, Brenda and Mr Bean: all the champions took to the field, no-one disappointed.'